District Gazetteers of India Series 222

UNITED PROVINCES OF AGRA AND OUDH DISTRICT

GORAKHPUR

District Gazetteers of India Series 222

UNITED PROVINCES OF AGRA AND OUDH DISTRICT

GORAKHPUR

H. R. NEVILL

49 VOLUMES

(VOL. XXVI)

GYAN

Published by

GYAN

Gyan Publishing House
5, Ansari Road
Daryaganj, New Delhi-110002
Phone: 011-47034999, 9811692060
E-mail: books@gyanbooks.com

Distribution Network
gyanbooks.com
India, USA, Canada, UK, Australia, France

ISBN: 978-93-6208-218-3 (Set) 49 Volumes
978-93-6208-027-1 (PB)

First Published, 1909

2nd Impression 2024

Printed at: Gyan Press, Delhi.

UNITED PROVINCES OF AGRA AND OUDH DISTRICT GAZETTEERS (Vol. XXVI)
Author: H. R. NEVILL

LIST OF VOLUMES

S. NO.	ISBN NO.	VOLUME	TITLE	AUTHOR	PRICE	PAGES
			ASSAM DISTRICT GAZETTEERS			
1	9788121285926	1st	Cachar	B. C. Allen	600	300
2	9788121285919	2nd	Sylhet	B. C. Allen	750	378
3	9788121285902	3rd	Goalpara	B. C. Allen	400	203
4	9788121285896	4th	Kamrup	B. C. Allen	675	344
5	9788121285889	5th	Darrang	B. C. Allen	725	364
6	9788121285872	6th	Nowgong	B. C. Allen	560	280
7	9788121285865	7th	Sibsagar	B. C. Allen	675	343
8	9788121285858	8th	Lakhimpur	B. C. Allen	690	347
9	9788121285841	9th	Naga Hills and Manipur	B. C. Allen	580	294
10	9788121285834	10th	The Khasi And Jaintia Hills, The Garo Hills And The Lushai Hills	B. C. Allen	675	363
11	9788121285827	11th	The Sadiya and Balipara Frontier Tract	B. C. Allen	375	190
			BENGAL DISTRICT GAZETTEERS			
12	9788121218672	1st	Angul	L. S. S. O'Malley	340	168
13	9788121259637	2nd	Bakarganj	J. C. JACK	970	194
14	9788121218696	3rd	Balasore	L. S. S. O'Malley	450	228
15	9788121259590	4th	Bankura	L. S. S. O'Malley	1000	199
16	9788121218375	5th	Bhagalpur	J. Byrne	390	194
17	9788121218290	6th	Birbhum	L. S. S. O'Malley	300	150
18	9788121259651	7th	Eastern Bengal and Assam - Bogra	J. N. Gupta	940	188
19	9788121218351	8th	Burdwan	J. C. K. Peterson	450	227
20	9788121259538	9th	Calcutta District Gazetteer - Statistics, 1901 - 02		340	68
21	9788121218313	10th	Champaran	L. S. S. O'Malley	410	205
22	9788121259613	11th	Eastern Bengal District Gazetters - Chittagong	L. S. S. O'Malley	1080	216
23	9788121259552	12th	Chota Nagpur Tributary		130	26
24	9788121259415	13th	The Cooch Behar Gazette: Statistics		1460	292
25	9788121218412	14th	Cuttack	L. S. S. O'Malley	490	248
26	9788121261357	15th	Eastern Bengal District Gazetteers Dacca	B. C. Allen	400	207
27	9788121218436	16th	Darbhanga	L. S. S. O'Malley	360	180
28	9789362089335	17th	Darjeeling	L. S. S. O'Malley	500	248
29	9788121259453	18th	Eastern Bengal District Gazetteers - Dinajpur	F. W. Strong	890	178
30	9788121259392	19th	Faridpur	L. S. S. O'Malley	700	140
31	9788121218474	20th	Gaya	L. S. S. O'Malley	540	270
32	9788121214032	21st	Bihar and Orissa District Gazetteer: Hazaribagh	E. Lister	715	234
33	9788121218337	22nd	Hooghly	L. S. S. O'Malley	680	340
34	9788121218191	23rd	Bengal District Gazetteer Howrah	L. S. S. O'Malley	390	199
35	9788121259293	24th	Eastern Bengal and Assam - Jalpaiguri	John F. Gruning	890	178
36	9788121259279	25th	Jessore	L. S. S. O'Malley	960	192
37	9788121259231	26th	Khulna	L. S. S. O'Malley	1100	220
38	9788121259217	27th	Malda	G. E. Lambourn	670	134
39	9788121267854	28th	Manbhum	H. Coupland	600	313
40	9788121218498	29th	Midnapore	L. S. S. O'Malley	500	252
41	9788121218597	30th	Monghyr	L. S. S. O'Malley	560	280
42	9788121259156	31st	Murshidabad	L. S. S. O'Malley	1250	250
43	9788121259576	32nd	Bengal District Gazetteers - Muzaffarpur	L. S. S. O'Malley	940	188
44	9788121259132	33rd	Mymensingh	F. A. Sachse	960	192
45	9788121259118	34th	Nadia	J. H. E. Garrett	1070	214
46	9788121259095	35th	Eastern Bengal and Assam - Noakhali	J. E. Webster	580	115
47	9788121218450	36th	Feudatory States of Orissa	L. E. B. Cobdenramsay	790	395
48	9788121259071	37th	Pabna	L. S. S. O'Malley	710	142
49	9788121218511	38th	Palamau	L. S. S. O'Malley	380	190
50	9788121218634	39th	Patna	L. S. S. O'Malley	500	250
51	9788121218535	40th	Puri	L. S. S. O'Malley	650	328
52	9788121218757	41st	Purnea	L. S. S. O'Malley	440	220
53	9788121258937	42nd	Rajshahi	L. S. S. O'Malley	1080	216
54	9788121256681	43rd	Bihar and Orissa District Gazetteers: Ranchi	M. G. Hallett	1350	278
55	9788121258913	44th	Eastern Bengal and assam - Rangpur	J. A. Vas	890	178
56	9788121218559	45th	Sambalpur	L. S. S. O'Malley	480	242
57	9788121214056	46th	Santal Parganas	L. S. S. O'Malley	940	308
58	9788121218610	47th	Saran	L. S. S. O'Malley	380	190
59	9788121218658	48th	Shahabad	L. S. S. O'Malley	380	190
60	9788121256704	49th	The Gazetteer of Sikhim	H. H. Risley	960	481
61	9788121218573	50th	Singhbhum, Saraikela And Kharsawan	L. S. S. O'Malley	560	280
62	9788121259439	51st	Eastern Bengal District Gazetteers - Tippera	J. E. Webster	730	146
63	9788121259033	52nd	24 Parganas	L. S. S. O'Malley	1420	284

S. NO.	ISBN NO.	VOLUME	TITLE	AUTHOR	PRICE	PAGES

CENTRAL PROVINCES DISTRICT GAZETTEERS

S. NO.	ISBN NO.	VOLUME	TITLE	AUTHOR	PRICE	PAGES
64	9789362081728	1st, Vol. A	Akola (Descriptive)	A. E. Nelson, C. Brown	870	436
65	9789362085481	2nd, Vol. A	Amraoti (Descriptive)	S. V. Fitzgerald, A. E. Nelson	1050	524
66	9789362089267	3rd,Vol. A	Balaghat (Descriptive)	R. V. RUSSELL	430	216
67	9789362083494	4th, Vol. A	Betul (Descriptive)	R. V. RUSSELL	610	306
68	9789362085146	5th, Vol. A	Bhandara (Descriptive)	R. V. RUSSELL	580	292
69	9789362088390	6th, Vol. A	Bilaspur (Descriptive)	R. V. RUSSELL	870	434
70	9789362086044	7th, Vol. A	Buldana (Descriptive)	A. E. Nelson	1090	543
71	9789362089014	8th, Vol. B	Chanda (Descriptive)	R. V. RUSSELL	470	234
72	9789362086938	9th	Chhattisgarch Feudatory State	E. A. De Brett	880	440
73	9789362082961	10th	Chhindwara (Descriptive)	R. V. RUSSELL	550	274
74	9789362089342	11th, Vol. A & B	Damoh (Descriptive and Statistical Tables 1891-1901)	R. V. RUSSELL	830	414
75	9789362081230	12th, Vol. A	Durg (Descriptive)	A. E. Nelson	460	232
76	9789362086037	13th, Vol. A	Hoshangabad (Descriptive)	R. V. RUSSELL	860	430
77	9789362086792	14th, Vol. A	Jubbulpore (Descriptive)	A. E. Nelson	950	474
78	9789362089663	15th, Vol. A & B	Mandla (Descriptive and Statistical Tables 1891-1901)	R. V. RUSSELL	370	186
79	9789362086419	16th, Vol. A	Nagpur (Descriptive)	R. V. RUSSELL	790	394
80	9789362080646	17th, Vol. A	Narsinghpur (Descriptive)	R. V. RUSSELL	510	257
81	9789362084835	18th, Vol. A	Nimar (Descriptive)	R. V. RUSSELL	600	299
82	9789362087737	19th, Vol. A	Raipur (Descriptive)	A. E. Nelson	790	396
83	9789362080264	20th, Vol. A	Saugor (Descriptive)	R. V. RUSSELL	570	285
84	9789362081117	21st, Vol. A	Seoni (Descriptive)	R. V. RUSSELL	460	232
85	9789362084965	22nd, Vol. A	Wardha (Descriptive)	R. V. RUSSELL	600	302
86	9789362083401	23rd, Vol. A	Yeotmal (Descriptive)	R. V. RUSSELL	550	277
87	9789362080325	24th, Vol. I, Pt. I	Gwalior (Text and Tables)	R. V. RUSSELL	980	489
88	9789362087133	24th, Vol. I, Pt. II	Gwalior (Maps)	R. V. RUSSELL	400	198
89	9789362086341	24th, Vol. I, Pt. III	Gwalior (Village List)	R. V. RUSSELL	810	406
90	9789362085467	24th, Vol. I, Pt. IV	Gwalior (Photos)	R. V. RUSSELL	1400	698
91	9789362087393	25th, Vol. II	Indore (Text and Tables)	C. E. Luard	1050	524
92	9789362084422	26th, Vol. III	Bhopal (Text and Tables)	C. E. Luard	540	272
93	9789362086815	27th, Vol. IV	Rewah (Text and Tables)	C. E. Luard	500	250
94	9789362087584	28th, Vol. V, Pt. A	Western States - Malwa (Text)	C. E. Luard	1520	762
95	9789362087300	29th, Vol. VI, Pt. A	Eastern States - Bundelkhand (Text)	C. E. Luard	930	463
96	9789362082169	30th, Vol. VI, Pt. B	Eastern States - Bundelkhand (Tables)	C. E. Luard	830	417

GAZETTEER OF THE BOMBAY PRESIDENCY:

S. NO.	ISBN NO.	VOLUME	TITLE	AUTHOR	PRICE	PAGES
97	9788121283441	1st, Part I	History of Gujarat	Ed.: James M. Campbell	3220	644
98	9788121285582	1st, Part II	History of the Konkan Dakhan and Southern Maratha Country	Ed.: James M. Campbell	4200	840
99	9788121285568	2nd	Gujarat, Surat and Broach	Ed.: James M. Campbell	2990	598
100	9788121285544	3rd	Kaira and Panch Mahals	Ed.: James M. Campbell	1690	339
101	9788121285520	4th	Ahmedabad	Ed.: James M. Campbell	1860	372
102	9788121285506	5th	Cutch, Palanpur, and Mahi Kantha	Ed.: James M. Campbell	2390	478
103	9788121285483	6th	Rewa Kantha, Narukot, Cambay, and Surat States	Ed.: James M. Campbell	1450	290
104	9788121285469	7th	Baroda	Ed.: James M. Campbell	3260	652
105	9788121285445	8th	Kathiawar	Ed.: James M. Campbell	3790	758
106	9788121285421	9th, Part I	Gujarat Population - Hindus	Ed.: James M. Campbell	3170	636
107	9788121285407	9th, Part II	Gujarat Population - Musalmans and Parsis	Ed.: James M. Campbell	1520	304
108	9788121285384	10th	Ratnagiri and Savantvadi	Ed.: James M. Campbell	2500	501
109	9788121285360	11th	Kolaba and Janjira	Ed.: James M. Campbell	2550	513
110	9788121285346	12th	Khandesh	Ed.: James M. Campbell	3190	638
111	9788121285322	13th Part I	Thana	Ed.: James M. Campbell	2050	413
112	9788121285308	13th Part II	Thana	Ed.: James M. Campbell	1770	357
113	9788121285285	14th	Thana - Places of Interest	Ed.: James M. Campbell	3290	659
114	9788121285261	15th Part I	Kanara	Ed.: James M. Campbell	2340	348
115	9788121285247	15th Part II	Kanara	Ed.: James M. Campbell	1740	348
116	9788121285223	16th	Nasik	Ed.: James M. Campbell	3490	698
117	9788121285209	17th	Ahmadnagar	Ed.: James M. Campbell	3860	772
118	9788121285186	18th Part I	Poona	Ed.: James M. Campbell	2930	586
119	9788121285162	18th Part II	Poona	Ed.: James M. Campbell	2680	537
120	9788121285148	18th Part III	Poona	Ed.: James M. Campbell	2500	503
121	9788121285124	19th	Satara	Ed.: James M. Campbell	3450	692
122	9788121285100	20th	Sholapur	Ed.: James M. Campbell	2730	547
123	9788121285087	21st	Gazetteer of the Bomaby Presidency: Belgaum	Ed.: James M. Campbell	2570	514
124	9788121285063	22nd	Dharwar	Ed.: James M. Campbell	4200	841
125	9788121285049	23rd	Gazetteer of the Bombay Presidency:Bijapur	Ed.: James M. Campbell	3550	712
126	9788121285025	24th	Kolhapur	Ed.: James M. Campbell	2250	450

S. NO.	ISBN NO.	VOLUME	TITLE	AUTHOR	PRICE	PAGES
127	9788121285001	25th	Botany	Ed.: James M. Campbell	2040	408
128	9788121284981	26th, Part I	Materials Towards a Statistical Account of the Town and Island of Bombay - History	Ed.: James M. Campbell	2500	504
129	9788121284967	26th, Part II	Materials Towards a Statistical Account of the Town and Island of Bombay - Trade and Fortifications	Ed.: James M. Campbell	2690	538
130	9788121284943	26th, Part III	Materials Towards a Statistical Account of the Town And Island of Bombay - Administration	Ed.: James M. Campbell	2450	702
131	9788121284929	27th	General Index	Ed.:R. E. Enthoven	2190	428
			MADRAS DISTRICT GAZETTEERS			
132	9788121258814	1st	Anantapur	W. Francis	1140	227
133	9788121258555	2nd	Malabar	C. A Innes & F. B Evans	3010	602
134	9788121258791	3rd	Bellary	W. Francis	1890	377
135	9788121258777	4th	Statistical Appendix For Chingleput		280	56
136	9788121258753	5th	Coimbatore	K. N. Krishnaswami Ayyar	3420	628
137	9788121232814	6th	Madras District Gazetteers District Gazetteer Cuddapah	C. F. Brackenbury	1120	285
138	9788121258715	7th	Statistical Appendix For Ganjam		370	73
139	9788121256766	8th, Vol. 1st	Godavari District Gazetteer	F. R. Hemingway	650	320
140	9788121256803	8th, Vol. 2nd	Godavari District Gazetteer	F. R. Hemingway	160	83
141	9788121258678	9th	Statistical Appendix For Kistna		640	127
142	9788121258654	10th	Statistical Appendix For Kurnool		270	54
143	9788121258616	11th	Madura	W. Francis	1900	379
144	9788121258579	12th	Statistical Appendix For Madura		740	148
145	9788121258630	13th	The Nilgiris	W. Francis	2190	437
146	9788121234276	14th	Madras District Gazetteers Gazetteer Of The Nellore District Brought Upto 1938		1150	386
147	9788121258517	15th	North Arcot		590	118
148	9788121258494	16th, Vol. 1, Part I	Salem	F. J. Richards	1710	343
149	9788121258593	16th, Vol. 1, Part II	Salem	F. J. Richards	1800	360
150	9788121258456	17th	South Arcot	W. Francis	2400	480
151	9788121258470	18th	Statistical Appendix For South Canara		400	80
152	9788121258432	19th, Vol. 1st & 2nd	Tanjore: Main Volume and Statistical Appendix		2070	401
153	9788121258395	20th	Tinnevelly	H. R. Pate	2740	547
154	9788121258418	21st	Statistical Appendix For Tinnevelly		320	64
155	9788121258371	22nd, 1st & 2nd	Trichinopoly: Main Volume and Statistical Appendix	F. R. Hemingway	2440	487
156	9788121241953	23rd	Vizagapatam District Gazetteer	W. Francis	760	385
			PUNJAB DISTRICT GAZETTEERS			
157	9788121255943	1st	Ambala District 1883-84		620	124
158	9788121255967	2nd	Amritsar		1180	236
159	9788121255981	3rd	Delhi		1300	260
160	9788121256001	4th	Ferozepore		950	188
161	9788121256025	5th	Faridkot		350	70
162	9788121256049	6th	Gujranwala 1893-94		1270	254
163	9788121256063	7th	Gujrat	C. E. Luard	1140	228
164	9788121256087	8th	Gurdaspur 1891-92		1260	252
165	9788121256100	9th	Gurgaon 1883-4		1020	203
166	9788121256124	10th	Hazara	H. D. Watson	2290	458
167	9788121256148	11th	Hissar district and Lohar State		1840	367
168	9788121256162	12th	Hoshiarpur		1420	283
169	9788121256186	13th	Jhang		1070	213
170	9788121256209	14th	Jhelam		1010	202
171	9788121256223	15th	Jalandhar District 1883-84		540	108
172	9788121256247	16th, Vol. XIV-A	Jullundur District, with maps and Kapurthala		1990	398
173	9788121256261	17th, Pt. I	Kangra (Proper)		1450	290
174	9788121256285	17th, Pt. II	Kangra (Kulu, Lahual, Spiti)		1800	357
175	9788121256308	18th	Karnal		1930	386
176	9788121256322	19th	Kohat		1540	307
177	9788121256346	20th	The Lahore District 1883-84		1220	244
178	9788121256384	21st	Ludhiana and Maler Kotla		1680	335
179	9788121256407	22nd	Lyallpur		735	147
180	9788121256421	23rd	Mianwali		1170	234
181	9788121256445	24th	Montgomery	P. J. Fagan	1590	318
182	9788121258364	25th	Multan (1901-02)	E. D. Maclagan	2400	480
183	9788121258708	26th	The Rohtak District 1883-84		980	196
184	9788121258746	27th, Vol. III A	Dujana State 1904		500	16
185	9788121256483	28th	Shahpur District		1780	356
186	9788121256506	29th	Simla District		800	159

S. NO.	ISBN NO.	VOLUME	TITLE	AUTHOR	PRICE	PAGES
187	9788121256520	30th	The Chamba State		2040	408
188	9788121256544	31st	The Chenab Colony 1904		1550	310
189	9788121256568	32nd	Kalsia State		270	53
190	9788121256582	33rd	Suket and Mandi		770	154
191	9788121256605	34th	Phulkian States, Patiala Jind And Nabha 1904		2070	414
192	9788121256643	35th	Simla Hill States		2220	443
193	9788121256667	36th	Sirmur		920	183

RAJPUTANA DISTRICT GAZETTEERS

S. NO.	ISBN NO.	VOLUME	TITLE	AUTHOR	PRICE	PAGES
194	9789362088994	1st, Vol. I-A & B	Ajmer-merwara (Text and Statistics Tables)	C. C. Watson	1230	246
195	9789362080882	2nd. Vol. II-A & B	Mewar Residency (Text and Statistics Tables)	K.D. Erskine	1700	339
196	9789362088444	3rd, Vol. III-A & B	The Western Rajputana States Residency And The Bikaner Agency	K.D. Erskine	3590	718

UNITED PROVINCES OF AGRA AND OUDH DISTRICT GAZETTEERS

S. NO.	ISBN NO.	VOLUME	TITLE	AUTHOR	PRICE	PAGES
197	9789362087560	Vol. I	Agra	H. R. Nevill	2260	452
198	9789362082466	Vol. II	Aligarh	H. R. Nevill	1300	260
199	9789362089779	Vol. III	Allahabad	H. R. Nevill	2050	409
200	9789362081346	Vol. IV	Almora	H. G. Walton	1670	333
201	9789362085658	Vol. V	Azamgarh	D. L. Drake Brockman	1750	349
202	9789362080547	Vol. VI	Bahraich	H. R. Nevill	1410	281
203	9789362085214	Vol. VII	Ballia	H. R. Nevill	1750	350
204	9789362084668	Vol. VIII	Banda	D. L. Drake Brockman	1750	349
205	9789362086518	Vol. IX	Bara Banki	H. R. Nevill	1720	344
206	9789362084101	Vol. X	Bareilly	H. R. Nevill	1640	327
207	9789362086631	Vol. XI	Basti	H. R. Nevill	1610	321
208	9789362083814	Vol. XII	Benares	H. R. Nevill	2290	458
209	9789362086105	Vol. XIII	Bijnor	H. R. Nevill	1820	363
210	9789362081674	Vol. XIV	Budaun	H. R. Nevill	1890	378
211	9789362086891	Vol. XV	Bulandshahr	H. R. Nevill	2100	419
212	9789362081520	Vol. XVI	Cawnpore	H. R. Nevill	2210	442
213	9789362088031	Vol. XVII	Dehra Dun	H. G. Walton	1710	342
214	9789362088710	Vol. XVIII	Etah	E. R. Neave	1600	320
215	9789362082992	Vol. XIX	Etawah	D. L. Drake Brockman	1390	277
216	9789362082220	Vol. XX	Farrukhabad	E. R. Neave	1620	324
217	9789362083869	Vol. XXI	Fatehpur	H. R. Nevill	1890	377
218	9789362085962	Vol. XXII	Fyzabad	H. R. Nevill	1700	339
219	9789362087997	Vol. XXIII	Garhwal	H. G. Walton	1270	254
220	9789362089892	Vol. XXIV	Ghazipur	H. R. Nevill	1600	320
221	9789362085436	Vol. XXV	Gonda	H. R. Nevill	1650	330
222	9789362080271	Vol. XXVI	Gorakhpur	H. R. Nevill	1890	378
223	9789362086129	Vol. XXVII	Hamirpur	D. L. Drake Brockman	1390	277
224	9789362087638	Vol. XXVIII	Hardoi	H. R. Nevill	1680	336
225	9789362081636	Vol. XXIX	Jalaun	D. L. Drake Brockman	1180	236
226	9789362084309	Vol. XXX	Jaunpur	H. R. Nevill	1750	350
227	9789362084187	Vol. XXXI	Jhansi	D. L. Drake Brockman	1960	391
228	9789362089168	Vol. XXXII	Kheri	H. R. Nevill	1650	330
229	9789362086778	Vol. XXXIII	Lucknow	H. R. Nevill	1760	352
230	9789362088635	Vol. XXXIV	Mainpuri	H. R. Nevill	1740	348
231	9789362080424	Vol. XXXV	Meerut	H. R. Nevill	2170	434
232	9789362081087	Vol. XXXVI	Mirzapur	D. L. Drake Brockman	2430	486
233	9789362085443	Vol. XXXVII	Moradabad	H. R. Nevill	1900	380
234	9789362082763	Vol. XXXVIII	Muttra	D. L. Drake Brockman	2140	428
235	9789362089915	Vol. XXXIX	Muzaffarnagar	H. R. Nevill	2260	451
236	9789362086143	Vol. XL	Naini Tal	H. R. Nevill	1890	377
237	9789362086761	Vol. XLI	Partabgarh	H. R. Nevill	1560	312
238	9789362081124	Vol. XLII	Pilibhit	H. R. Nevill	1570	314
239	9789362084453	Vol. XLIII	Rai Bareli	H. R. Nevill	1610	322
240	9789362088284	Vol. XLIV	Rampur	H. R. Nevill	1170	234
241	9789362083654	Vol. XLV	Saharanpur	H. R. Nevill	2190	438
242	9789362083142	Vol. XLVI	Shahjahanpur	H. R. Nevill	1510	302
243	9789362083623	Vol. XLVII	Sitapur	H. R. Nevill	1590	317
244	9789362089939	Vol. XLVIII	Sultanpur	H. R. Nevill	1330	266
245	9789362080851	Vol. XLIX	Unnao	H. R. Nevill	1530	305

GORAKHPUR:

A GAZETTEER,

BEING

VOLUME XXXI

OF THE

DISTRICT GAZETTEERS OF THE UNITED PROVINCES OF AGRA AND OUDH.

BY

H. R. NEVILL, I.C.S., F.R.G.S., F.S.S., M.R.A.S.

ALLAHABAD:

Printed by F. Luker, Superintendent, Government Press, United Provinces.

1909.

GAZETTEER OF GORAKHPUR.

REFERENCES.

Description Historique et Geographique de l'Inde, by Joseph Tieffenthaler, 1787.

The Kingdom of Nepaul, by W. Kirkpatrick; London, 1811.

Political and Military Transactions in India, 1813—23, by H. T. Prinsep; London, 1825.

The History, Antiquities, Topography and Statistics of Eastern India, by R. Montgomery Martin; London, 1838.

An Account of the Kingdom of Nepal, by O. Cavanagh; Calcutta, 1851.

Narrative of five years' residence at Nepaul, by Captain Thomas Smith; London, 1852.

Mutiny Narratives, N.-W. P.; Allahabad, 1859.

Manual of the Statistics of the District of Goruckpoor, by A. Swinton; Allahabad, 1861.

Report on the Settlement of the Goruckpore-Bustee District, by H. LeP. Wynne; Allahabad, 1871.

Sketch of the portion of the Country of Nepal open to Europeans, by D. Wright; Calcutta, 1872.

History of Nepal, by D. Wright; Cambridge, 1877.

History of the Indian Mutiny, by Sir John Kaye and Colonel Malleson; London, 1888.

Buddhist Records of the Western World, by S. Beal; London, 1890.

The Gorakhpur Tarai in days gone by, by W. F. Gibbon; Birmingham, 1890.

Final Report on the Settlement of the Gorakhpur District, by A. W. Cruickshank; Allahabad, 1891.

Treaties, Engagements and Sanads, by C. U. Aitchison; Calcutta, 1892.

The Remains near Kasia, by V. A. Smith; Allahabad, 1896.

Selections from State Papers preserved in the Military Department, 1857-58, by G. W. Forrest; Calcutta, 1902.

ABBREVIATIONS.

J. R. A. S.—Journal of the Royal Asiatic Society.
J. A. S. B.—Journal of the Bengal Asiatic Society.
C. R. A. S.—Cunningham's Archæological Survey Reports.
E. H. I.—The History of India as told by its own Historians, by Sir H. M. Elliot.

PREFACE.

THE original Gazetteer of Gorakhpur was compiled by Mr. E. B. Alexander, assisted by Mr. H. C. Conybeare and Mr. W. Crooke. The volume, though containing much valuable material, was not published till 1881, and in a few years became almost obsolete owing to the revision of settlement and the immense mass of fresh statistics collected by Mr. A. W. Cruickshank, whose monumental report is a veritable mine of information. In preparing the present volume I have been most generously assisted by Mr. E. A. Molony and Mr. J. M. Clay, to the latter of whom I am particularly indebted for his laborious collection of material, while the former has rendered me valuable assistance in the revision of the proofs. The district is one of unusual size, necessitating much compression in order to confine the book within the prescribed limits.

ALLAHABAD :
January, 1909.

H. R. N.

GAZETTEER OF GORAKHPUR.

CONTENTS.

CHAPTER I.

General Features.

The district of Gorakhpur occupies the extreme north-east corner of the United Provinces, and comprises a huge stretch of country lying to the north of the river Ghagra, the deep stream of which forms the boundary of Azamgarh and Ballia to the south. On the west the border marches with Basti, and on the east with the districts of Champaran and Saran in Bengal, the dividing line being partly artificial and in part supplied by the Great and Little Gandak rivers. To the north lies the territory of Nepal, separated from Gorakhpur by a conventional boundary line marked by masonry pillars running down the centre of a narrow strip of neutral ground. The geographical limits of the district are determined by the parallels of 26° 5′ and 27°29′ north latitude and of 83°4′ and 84°26′ east longitude. The total area is apt to vary from year to year owing to the erratic action of the Ghagra. In 1889 it was 2,931,921 acres, but this was materially reduced in 1904 by the transfer to Azamgarh of a considerable tract of 122 villages, some 67 square miles in extent, consequent on the resumption by the main stream of a more northerly channel which had long been abandoned. This transfer left an area of 2,889,043 acres or 4,514·13 square miles, while the average for the five years ending with 1907-08 was 2,899,712 acres. The district is thus far larger than any other in the plains of the United Provinces, far too large, in fact, for a single administrative unit; and though attempts have been made to remedy this defect by the creation of subdivisions in the charge of resident magistrates, such measures can only be regarded as palliatives, and the re-formation of the Gorakhpur division into a larger number of districts of more manageable size is merely a question of time. **Boundaries and area.**

A general topographical account of so vast a territory must necessarily, owing to considerations of space, be confined within **Topography.**

narrow limits; but a more detailed description of the various component tracts will be given in the separate articles on the several parganas and tahsils. Taken as a whole, the country presents very different characteristics from those which prevail in Oudh and the western districts. This difference is due primarily to the relative proximity of the Himalayas. The outermost foot-hills are but a few miles distant from the northern borders, while the great peaks of the snowy range, culminating in the huge mass of Dhaulagiri, some 27,000 feet above the level of the sea, are clearly visible under favourable atmospheric conditions, especially during the rains and the cold weather, as far south as Gorakhpur itself. Below the outer hills is a dry, boulder-strewn tract, corresponding to the Bhabar of Kumaun and lying for the most part in Nepal, and here the bulk of the moisture contributed by the rainfall and the small hill streams is absorbed by the soil, to reappear by syphonic influence in the moist and unhealthy tract known as the Tarai. The latter comprises a belt, some ten miles in width, running along the northern borders of the Maharajganj tahsil. It is extensively cultivated, but the climate is poisoned by malarial fever, and in most places the tillage is poor and precarious. South of the Tarai, in the same tahsil, comes a stretch of forest land, for the most part Government reserves, and this forest extends southwards in patches as far as the very centre of the district. Its presence is in a large measure responsible for the abundance of the rainfall, which, in combination with the effect of numerous rivers and a remarkably high water level, renders the soil damp and the climate moist, so that the luxuriant vegetation and the general greenness of the landscape cannot fail to arrest the attention of those accustomed to the dry districts of the south.

The open plains.

The open plains country forms an apparently level tract, which in reality slopes gently from north-west to south-east; the height above sea level averaging some 316 feet and ranging from 350 feet in the north-west to 305 feet in the south-eastern extremity. Higher elevations occur in places where the general flat surface is broken by irregular ranges of sandhills. The most clearly defined ridge of this nature starts near Harpur in the Maharajganj tahsil and runs in a winding course almost to

Deoria, presumably marking the long abandoned channel of the Gandak or some great rivers; since throughout its length it is bordered by a chain of depressions and *jhils*, while in several places pebbles and boulders have been encountered in sinking shafts for wells. Another range of sandhills of a like nature crosses the road between Padrauna and Kasia, and has the distinction of being the highest portion of the district, although the maximum elevation is only 386 feet above the sea. In contradistinction to the high ridges of the water-partings are the low and often broad valleys of the rivers, known generically as *kachhar*, as opposed to the *bangar* or uplands. The transition from one to the other is in most cases clearly marked, and the valleys of the larger rivers are not only depressed well below the general level of the country, but are of considerable breadth. There is thus a wide area of lowland which is apt to be inundated in years of heavy rainfall—a factor of high importance in the economic conditions of the district.

The *Bhat*.

Before dealing with the river valleys and their floods, however, it is necessary to refer to the conditions of the eastern portion of the district, which forms a tract of a quite unique character. It is known as the *bhat* and consists of the alluvium brought down by the Great Gandak, the distinguishing feature being its remarkable whiteness, which is due apparently to the unusual proportion of lime in the soil. The peculiarities of the *bhat* are great, and in a large measure determine the special characteristics of the topography and the agriculture in this tract. The soil is extremely retentive of moisture, so that artificial irrigation is practically unknown; though, on the other hand, the friable nature of the *bhat* renders the construction of unprotected wells extremely difficult, if not impossible. Another result is that walls built of mud will not stand the effects of the climate, and consequently the houses are mostly built of wattle with thatched roofs, giving the villages an appearance of squalor and poverty unequalled in the south and west of the district. It is owing to this fact that the word *chhapra* occurs so frequently in the names of villages in these parts. Roughly speaking, the *bhat* is cut off from the rest of the district by a line drawn from Thuthibari on the Nepal frontier to Bhatpar railway station, although there are several detached blocks of *bangar* east of this line. The whole of the south of the district, including the tahsils of Deoria and Bansgaon, as well as a part of Hata, approximates far more closely than the rest to the country south of the Ghagra and offers few peculiarities. A noteworthy feature throughout the whole of Gorakhpur is the almost entire absence of sterile *usar* plains, so common in Oudh and in the Benares division to the south.

Drainage system.

The drainage of the entire district ultimately discharges itself into the Ghagra, excepting that carried off by the Great Gandak, which falls into the Ganges a considerable distance below the confluence with the former river. The whole takes a south-easterly direction, following the general slope of the country; but there are two main internal subdivisions, comprising the Rapti system in the west and those of the Great and Little Gandak on the east. In many places the drainage is imperfect, especially in the basins of the Rapti and its affluents. The valleys of the Ghagra, the Rapti, the Rohin and the Ami, at any rate in its lower reaches, are broad and sufficiently depressed below the ordinary level of the country to confine their floods within the limits of the high banks on either side. Extensive inundations occur annually in these valleys, and in years of heavy rainfall the entire area is submerged. This constantly occurs in a very large tract to the south and west of Gorakhpur, where the swollen volume of the Rapti holds up the waters of the Rohin and Ami at the respective points of junction, resulting in the formation of two huge sheets of water in the Domingarh lake and the Amiar Tal. When the floods are severe almost the entire tract between the Rapti and the Ami is inundated, and only the village sites appear amid a sea of water. Similar floods occur from time to time in the south-west corner of the Bansgaon tahsil along the course of the Kuwana, which, though a small stream, is capable of doing an immense amount of damage. Both the Rapti and the Rohin carry down enormous quantities of silt, and when the stream overtops its banks most of this silt is deposited within a short distance of the river bed; so that in the course of time raised *levées* or banks are formed, with the result that the highest part of the valley is that immediately adjoining the channel, while the lowest portion lies close to the old high banks on the outermost extremities. These raised embankments are seldom continuous, for breaks occur at the junctions of tributary streams and also where erosion sets in at the angles of bends in the river's course. But for this the valleys would be submerged only in abnormally wet seasons, and in order to prevent inundation of the lowlands artificial embankments have in many instances been erected by the *zamindars*. In few cases, however, can these *bandhs* withstand the force of heavy floods, owing to the lack of co-operation between neighbouring villages, the want of engineering skill and a general unwillingness to expend sufficient money on such works.

Floods.

The earliest great flood of which any record is extant occurred in 1823, when a sudden rise in the Ghagra caused extensive inundations over the parganas of Dhuriapar and Chillupar. The waters of the Rapti were held up, and this river reacted in a similar manner on the Ami, so that the city of Gorakhpur became an island in a waste of waters; at the same time much damage being done, while at the same time communication with Azamgarh was suspended for several days. In 1839 a flood of great magnitude was experienced in the Rapti valley, and this was followed by a similar inundation in the succeeding year, though neither was so serious as that first mentioned. No further flood is chronicled till 1871, in which year, as again in 1873, extensive damage was done to fields and buildings. From the latter year more precise records are available. In 1889 the whole district suffered greatly. The Rapti rose on the 4th of August to a height of 253·25 feet above the sea at the railway bridge near Sahjanwa, while the Rohin at the Chilwa Tal bridge was even higher. The height registered on the gauge at the Ilahi Bagh sluice-gates in Gorakhpur city was 16½ feet—a figure which has never since been exceeded. Three years later in 1892 the Rapti flooded the city and endangered the pontoon bridge at Bhauapar, while in the same year the Ghagra ran very high, and for some time the town of Barhaj was surrounded with water. Another sudden flood of unusual magnitude occurred in 1903, when the water rose at the Rapti and Rohin bridges to 252·41 and 251·66 feet respectively. A still more destructive inundation was that of 1906, when the water rose to within three inches of the maximum recorded in 1889. Generally speaking, it may be assumed that a flood of ten feet at the Ilahi Bagh sluice-gates will cause little or no damage to the crops, but that anything above this height is serious, every additional foot involving progressive loss.

Great Gandak.

Beginning from the north-east the first important river of the district is the Great Gandak. This takes its rise in the snowy range of Nepal and leaves the hills by the gorge near Tirbeni, about ten miles north from the boundary of this district. The river, which is also known as the Narayani and, in Nepal, as the Saligrami, flows in a south-easterly direction and for a short distance forms the boundary between this district and Champaran, while a few forest villages of tahsil Padrauna are situated on the left bank of the stream. Thereafter its course lies wholly through Bengal as far as its confluence with the Ganges at Patna; though it again skirts this district in tappa Bank Jogni, while in the intervening space the boundary for several miles is formed by a branch channel or backwater known as the Sota. The Great Gandak is a stream of the first magnitude, and even in the hot weather its volume is immense, the minimum discharge being at least double that of the Ganges at Hardwar. On its first entry into British territory the bed is stony and the water is cold and clear, with a very rapid current. It is navigable by boats of considerable onnage, though progress is rendered difficult and sometimes dangerous by reason of eddies or whirlpools and numerous snags; small boats too can ascend the river for 15 or 20 miles above the Tirbeni gorge. The Gandak is subject to violent and sudden floods, which cause extensive inundations of the forest tract in Nepal and on the frontier, reaching the Chandan, and thus pouring its waters into the Rohin, so that the latter is directly affected by the rise of the Gandak. A similar spill into the Little Gandak occurs at Domakhand, causing that river to overflow its banks, notably in two places. At the first the flood water spills into the Banri, which near Padrauna unites with the Bansi, an affluent of the Great Gandak, so that it eventually finds its way back to the river whence it came. The second place is where the overflow is taken by the Khanua, which flows through the Ramabhar Tal, and in a swollen condition causes extensive inundations in the neighbourhood of Kasia. Further south the Khanua floods some 15 villages to the north and east of Bhatpar station, but these floods, both here and elsewhere, last only a short time and ordinarily subside before the rice has been destroyed. Little damage is done unless the deposit of mud and silt be excessive or the inundation prove of unusual duration; for generally the early *kharif* crops have been reaped wholly or in part before the country is submerged. It will be seen, however, that the Great Gandak exercises a very decided influence on the eastern half of the district, and it has recently been suggested that the erection of an embankment and regulator across the river at Domakhand would entirely prevent the recurrence of these disastrous and extensive overflows. A railway bridge over the river is now under construction at Bagaha, but elsewhere the passage has to be effected by ferries, of which there is a fair number, the most frequented being those at Gola Pipra-ghat and Sahibganj, the two principal places on the river in this district.

Gandak affluents.

The affluents of the Great Gandak are inconsiderable. The Bansi, already mentioned, is in reality a mere backwater, and for a long distance forms the boundary of the district, ultimately discharging into the Sota near Sahibganj. The Jharai, though now a tributary of the Ghagra, similarly represents an old channel of the Gandak, at all events for some distance below Gagalwa. It rises in the north of tahsil Padrauna and takes a southerly if winding course, passing out of this district into Saran a few miles below Tamkuhi. Near the latter place a large waterworn boulder was discovered in digging the foundations for a bridge, and higher up excavations exposed numerous stumps of old trees, indicating the great accumulation of silt which had taken place. These excavations were made some years ago, when an intake was made from the Bansi into the Jharai near Gagalwa, and an earthen dam was erected over the former river so as to force its waters into the Jharai for the use of the indigo plantations on the Babhnauli and Tamkuhi estates. Ordinarily the Jharai is a very small stream, running almost dry in the hot weather, while all the country along its course bears an evil reputation for malarial fever. The channel in question was deepened and widened in 1908 so as to admit a larger volume of water, and it is hoped that this measure will tend to reduce the unhealthiness of the tract.

Little Gandak.

The Little Gandak again represents an old channel of the Great Gandak. Starting in the Baghban forest in Nepal, it flows southwards in a channel called the Purnahwa and thence into British territory at the village of Sitlapur. About a mile below this point the channel divides, one branch running in a north-westerly direction into the Chandan, while the other continues on a southerly course as the Little Gandak, much reinforced by spill water from the Great Gandak. It forms the western boundary of the Padrauna tahsil as far as Hetimpur, and thence flows through the parganas of Shahjahanpur and Salempur to join the Ghagra near Simaria in the extreme south-east corner of the district. Save during the rains the Little Gandak is quite dry to the north of a *man* or old river bed in the Domakhand forest, which always holds water. Below this point too, it is much reduced after the close of the rains, and for the greater part of the year is an insignificant stream, seldom exceeding 60 feet in breadth. It is crossed by ferries at Captainganj, Hetimpur and one or two other places, but in the dry season the river is generally fordable. A proposal was mooted in 1859 to make the river into a navigable channel, but nothing was done in this direction, and under existing circumstances boats can ascend the stream as far as Ragarganj only during the rains. There are several unimportant affluents of the Little Gandak, apart from the Banri and Khanua, which are outflows rather than tributaries. The latter rejoins the Little Gandak near Salempur station, and in its turn receives on its left bank a number of insignificant watercourses, such as the Sundra, Ghaghi, Ghaghar and Sonda, the last for some miles forming the district boundary. The tributary streams which fall into the Little Gandak on its right bank are the Khekra, Hirni, Ghatni, Maun, Duhari, Kanchi and Koilar, of which the largest is the Maun, falling into the river just above Hetimpur. All these, however, carry water only during the rains, forming drainage channels from the high ground of the central watershed.

The remaining rivers in the north of the district discharge themselves into the Rapti, which is in every way the most important of all the streams of Gorakhpur. The Rapti, originally Iravati and then corrupted into Ravati, has its source in the outer ranges of Nepal, and after traversing Bahraich, Gonda and Basti enters this district at Magalaha in pargana Haveli. Thence, after forming the boundary for a few miles, it resumes its old channel, now known as the Dhamela, just above Rigauli, and flows in a south-easterly direction, but with an extremely tortuous course, past the town of Gorakhpur to its junction with the Ghagra near Barhaj in pargana Salempur. The river, which has a high temperature and bears in solution a large quantity of mud, is constantly carving out new channels for itself, and occasionally transfers whole villages from one bank to another. The annual floods leave behind them extensive deposits of silt and sand, which are generally beneficial, since the silt is of an exceedingly fertile description; while even the sand after two or three years' exposure weathers into a loam capable of bearing good crops. In former days the river was extensively utilized for the transport of timber and grain, and a brisk trade was carried on in boats running to 100 tons burthen; but the superior facilities afforded by the railway have caused the traffic to shrink to modest dimensions, though even now, especially during the rains, a number of local craft may be seen. Statistics of the trade are not available, owing to the absence of any system of registration. The Rapti is spanned by a pontoon bridge at Bhauapar-ghat and by a bridge of boats at Bird-ghat, where the Azamgarh and Basti roads respectively cross the river. The latter is replaced during the rains by a ferry, while elsewhere many ferries are maintained, both by the district board and by private agency. **Rapti.**

The tributaries of the Rapti are numerous and important. The first to join the river on its left bank is the Ghunghi, which has its rise in the outer range of hills above the Nepalese Tarai. Flowing in a south-westerly direction, it forms for several miles the boundary between this district and Nepal, and in this part of its course it receives on its left bank two small Tarai streams called the Danda and the Dunri. Then it turns south **Ghunghi.**

and for some distance forms the Basti boundary, flowing past Bridgmanganj. Subsequently it separates into two channels, both of which unite with the Dhamela at Sikri and Girui near Rigauli respectively. It is fed by one or two insignificant streams from the forest country to the east, such as the Poh and the Kalan. The river is known as the Tinan in Nepal, and there is dammed for irrigation purposes after the rains; it has a deep and well defined channel with a sandy bed and the water is clear. Though usually much swollen during the rains, it shrinks rapidly and soon becomes fordable. The Dhamela is merely an old channel of the Rapti, which receives the waters of the Kunhra and other rivers of the Basti Tarai, and after a course of some ten miles through this district rejoins the original bed of the Rapti just above Karmaini-ghat. It is a fine navigable river with steep and high banks, and rises some twenty feet in the rains, frequently causing considerable damage by its inundations of the surrounding country. The Dhamela once bore a large traffic from the town of Uska and the important grain market of Dhani, which lies at a short distance from the left bank; but conditions have been materially changed by the construction of the railway, and the grain is now conveyed by cart to Bridgmanganj.

Rohin. The next affluent of the Rapti is the Rohin, a stream of some magnitude which enters pargana Binayakpur from Nepal and, after traversing pargana Haveli in a southerly direction, falls into the Rapti between Domingarh and the western extremity of Gorakhpur city. At first its banks are steep and the bed is formed of sand and small pebbles, but on its entry into pargana Haveli it loses these characteristics and approximates more closely to the ordinary type of river in the plains. It is navigable for some distance above the confluence, but is very little used for traffic. The river is spanned by a railway bridge at Domingarh and near Maniram on the line to Uska. Close to the latter there was formerly an iron bridge on the unmetalled road, but this was washed away in 1903 and its place has since been taken by a pontoon bridge. The Rohin receives near Sakhui on its left bank the Baghela, a river of Nepal, which is in turn fed by the Madrahi and other streams; the Piyas or Jharai, which enters this district at Thuthibari and is joined by the Malaun, rising near Madhaulia, and the Nadani and other small watercourses, before falling into the Rohin just above the crossing on the road from Pharenda to Maharajganj ; the Balia, which rises near the latter place and falls into the river near Jarlahia ; and the Chillua, which rises in tappa Katahra of pargana Haveli and is fed by the Temar and some minor streams before passing into the Chillua Tal and thence into the Rohin near Maniram. On the right bank the only affluent is a watercourse called the Kalan, which rises near Lehra and flows southwards to effect its junction with the larger river to the north-east of Peppeganj. The Rohin, as well as the Baghela and Piyas, is dammed for irrigation purposes in Nepal, and proposals have recently been made to put its waters to similar use in the north of this district.

The Tura is a small stream which rises in tappa Unti of pargana Haveli and flows southwards through the Ramgarh forest to the east of Gorakhpur till at the village of Jhangha it joins the Gurra or Gaura. The latter carries off the overflow from the Ramgarh and Narhai Tals, and the combined stream continues for a considerable distance parallel to the Rapti. It is connected with that river at Kuin by the Simrauna *nala*, a broad channel half a mile in length, by means of which the Gurra is filled with flood water from the Rapti during the rains, to the great detriment of the surrounding country. Further south the Gurra is joined by the Pharend, a stream of considerable length, which rises near Pipraich and flows southwards, fed by the Bharhan and Kapuri on the right and subsequently by the Patraina and Bhainsahi on the left bank. The name Pharend is derived from the thick growth of *pharend* or wild *jamun* trees along its course. The combined stream continues southwards, but with a very tortuous course, to its junction with the Rapti at Samogar, the river in its lower reaches being frequently called the Katna. At Madanpur, just above Samogar, it is joined by the Majhna, an affluent of some importance, which rises near Mansurganj and flows in a southerly course parallel to the Pharend. The Majhna in its turn receives several small tributaries. The first is the Bari, falling into the river on its right

Tura.

Gurra.

Pharend.

Majhna.

bank near Dumri, from which point the Majhna forms the boundary between the Haveli and Silhat parganas as far as Khandauli. The next is the Barhari on the left bank, but this is quite unimportant. A larger stream is the Karna, which rises near Balkuan, and forms the dividing line between Silhat and Salempur almost as far as its junction with the Majhna at Rudarpur. The Karna in turn is fed by the Nakta, which rises near Kataura in pargana Silhat and flows southwards to its junction some four miles west of Deoria.

Ami. The tributaries of the Rapti on its right bank are of no importance, with the exception of the Ami and the Taraina. The former rises in pargana Rasulpur in Basti, and after a course of some 44 miles enters this district near Rampur in pargana Maghar. Thence it follows the usual south-easterly direction, falling into the Rapti near Sohgaura in pargana Bhauapar. It is a narrow and sluggish stream save in the rains, when its swollen waters develop into the Amiar Tal, of which mention will be made later; while it receives the drainage brought down by several minor watercourses at other seasons dry, such as the Saraia, Sunwan and Harsandi on the north or left and the Dhadhi on the right bank. The river is bridged by the Tucker *bandh*, across the eastern portion of the Amiar Tal, and also at Chatai, where is a modern iron structure on the road from Gorakhpur to Rudrapur and Bansgaon. It is not improbable that at some distant period the course of the Ami was taken by the Rapti, and the lower portion of the Ami *kachhar*, from Bharsand to Kauriram, is practically a part of the *kachhar* of the Rapti. The spill from the latter during heavy floods enters the Ami valley, submerging the whole country as far west as the high right bank, save for two islands of *bangar* which always remain above the flood level. One stretches from Kalesar to Newas along the south side of the Basti road, and the other lies on either side of the Azamgarh road from Hardia almost to Malaun. The lower part of the Rapti *kachhar* must inevitably be submerged in wet years, but the upper portion might possibly be protected by embankments. Under existing circumstances the landholders usually construct a *bandh* from the *bangar* ridge at Kalesar to the railway embankment protecting the Rapti bridge, but this generally gives way under the pressure of heavy floods. Formerly too the embankment of the Basti road protected the country between Kalesar and the Bird-ghat bridge of boats, but a southerly set of the river has recently carried away a considerable length of this embankment, which will probably necessitate a realignment of the road between Hardia and Bird-ghat. It is doubtful whether it would be possible or advisable to close up all the channels by which flood water can escape. The largest work of the kind hitherto attempted is the embankment, 16 miles in length, from the pontoon bridge to Kuin Bazar on the east bank of the Rapti, constructed as a famine relief work during the cold weather of 1906-07, and designed to protect the whole of this section of the *kachhar* from the floods which have so often devastated it. The embankment varies from three to twelve feet in height, with a minimum uniform breadth of four feet at the summit, save where it crosses the Lahsari *nala*, the channel excavated in a misguided attempt to drain the Ramgarh Tal. At this point it rises to a height of 30 feet and is some twelve feet wide on the crest. There appears to be some danger of the Rapti opening a large channel into the valley of the Ami, and this would entail serious consequences ; for if the larger river once adopted the course of the Ami the bridges on the Tucker *bandh* would be swept away, destroying the main road to Azamgarh and devastating a rich tract of country.

The Taraina takes its rise in the south of pargana Unaula and flows in a south-easterly direction through Dhuriapar till it reaches the Bhenri Tal. Emerging from the eastern extremity of that lake, it finds its way into the Rapti by an almost direct route due east. During the hot weather the stream runs very low, but in the rains it assumes considerable dimensions, and in 1871 it swept away the bridge on the Azamgarh road. The bridge was rebuilt, but that on the road from Kauriram to Gola was broken by floods some years since and has never been repaired. The river is not navigable, but its waters are extensively requisitioned for irrigation purposes. Taraina.

The Ghagra, known variously as the Sarju and Dehwa, contains the combined waters of the Chauka or Sarda and the Kauriala, which unite near Bahramghat in the Bara Banki Ghagra.

district. Both rivers have their source in the snowy heights of the Himalayas, the former rising in the Almora district and the latter in Nepal. The Ghagra is a mighty river, flowing in a wide and sandy bed, within the limits of which the channel shifts at pleasure to an astonishing extent. The deep-stream forms the boundary between this district on the north and Azamgarh and Ballia on the south. In the case of the latter district the channel is confined within comparatively narrow limits, owing to the existence of a hard ridge of *kankar* and stiff soil near Turtipar on the southern bank, but along the Azamgarh border the variations are almost unlimited, resulting in constant changes in the areas of both districts. The river first touches Gorakhpur at Majhdip in pargana Dhuriapar, and thence flows nearly due east past the market towns of Gola, Barhalganj, Rajpur and Bhagalpur to the borders of the Saran district in Bengal. All these places have declined in importance since the diversion of the river-borne trade to the railways, but Barhaj, which stands a short distance inland, close to Rajpur, is one of the chief marts of the district, having risen to eminence through the possession of a railway station. The bed of the river as a rule is flanked by steep and well defined banks, but occasionally the waters rise in heavy floods, inundating the low country in the neighbourhood with disastrous results, since the deposit left behind is invariably sandy. When the river subsides after the rains numerous sandbanks and islands appear in the channel, which becomes tortuous and in some places shallow. None the less, country boats of the largest size can at all times navigate the river, and the steamers of the India General Steam Navigation Company maintain a regular service up and down the stream, calling at Bhagalpur, Paina, Barhaj, Barhalganj and Gola. The only bridge over the river during its course along the borders of this district is that carrying the railway at Turtipar near Bhagalpur, but there are numerous ferries, of which the chief is at Dohri-ghat on the provincial road to Azamgarh, leading from the town of Barhalganj.

Kuwana.

Besides the Rapti and Little Gandak, the only direct affluent of the Ghagra in this district is the Kuwana, or Kuano as it is generally pronounced. This river has its source in the east of

Bahraich, whence it flows through Gonda and Basti. For a few miles it separates the latter from this district, and then passes through the west of pargana Dhuriapar to join the Ghagra near Shahpur. In this portion of its course it has a sandy bed with fairly steep and high banks; the stream is of considerable depth, and has been reinforced from time to time by the spill from the Ghagra through the Malda and other channels in the Basti district. Such additions to its volume occurred frequently between 1855 and 1872, with the result that the Kuwana became a deep, navigable stream, and was sometimes adopted as an alternative channel by boats descending the Ghagra during the rains, when snags rendered the main stream dangerous for navigation. Of late years, however, its volume has diminished, and, except in the rains, navigation is now impossible above Dhakwa Bazar. During the monsoon a small trade in grain is carried on, but the carrying business has shrunk to insignificant dimensions under competition on the part of the railways.

Lakes and *jhils*. Gorakhpur is remarkable for the number of its large perennial lakes, formed in most cases in the abandoned channels of rivers, which have become blocked by the accumulation of silt, or else merely consisting in deep natural depressions in which the surface drainage collects without finding an adequate outlet. Besides these the district possesses a vast number of temporary swamps and *jhils*, varying in appearance from a broad sheet of water during the rains to a shallow marsh or even arable land in the dry seasons. It would be impossible to give even a mere enumeration of these lakes and *jhils*, and it will be sufficient to mention the most important.

Ramgarh Tal. Close to Gorakhpur, on the south side of the metalled road to Kasia, is the Ramgarh Tal, extending from the European cemetery to the iron bridge which carries the road over a creek at the eastern extremity. It was formerly covered, save during the rains, with a dense growth of reeds, and as these were considered a menace to the health of the town, the municipality took a lease of the lake, cut down the reeds and attempted to drain off the water by a channel from the southern end into the Rapti. This measure proved ineffective, while the absence of sluice-gates afforded an easy passage into the lake of flood water from the river, with the result that for many years extensive damage was caused by inundations. The villagers endeavoured to block the channel, but the earthen dam gave way in the great flood of 1906, the water in the lake rising as high as the Daudpur *muhalla*, close to the civil courts. The next year the mouth of the channel was very solidly blocked at Lahsari by a broad embankment forming part of the larger work in connection with the Rapti bank, and by this means it is hoped that the spill into the lake will be effectually prevented. It has been calculated that under such conditions the rise in the level during the rains will not exceed four or five feet, and a proposal has recently been made to utilize this fact by carrying into the lake the drainage from the lower portions of the city. The Ramgarh Tal contains great numbers of fish, and the fisheries afford a means of support to several villages of Mallahs on its banks.

Narhai Tal.

A few miles to the south-east of this lake is the Narhai Tal, a much smaller sheet of water lying in the *kachhar* of the Rapti. It is connected with the Ramgarh Tal by the Gurra river, which carries off the surplus water of the two lakes into the Rapti. The Tals doubtless represent a former channel of the latter river, which in all probability once traversed the site of Gorakhpur city. During the hot weather the Narhai Tal becomes almost dry, and is then of great value as a grazing ground for buffaloes, since it contains immense quantities of weeds and grass suitable for fodder.

Domingarh Tal.

The Domingarh and Karmaini lakes to the west of Gorakhpur are formed by the overflow of the Rohin just before its confluence with the Rapti. The two Tals are separated by some rising ground, but as this is completely surrounded by water when the floods are at their height, they may for all practical purposes be considered as one. From the railway embankment at Domingarh the water extends northwards in a continuous stretch for some seven miles, and in former days the European residents used frequently to indulge in yachting on the lake during the rains; but the practice was abandoned on account of several fatal accidents. After the end of the rains the water rapidly drains off into the Rapti and the lakes shrink to comparatively small dimensions or wholly disappear.

There are many lakes of a similar nature on the right bank of the Rapti. About six miles south from Gorakhpur, lying close to the east of the Azamgarh road, is the Nandaur Tal, a great sheet of water about two and a half miles long and half a mile in breadth. This is of a perennial character and its size is little affected by the rains. The water is remarkably clear, and the lake yields an inexhaustible supply of excellent fish. **Nandaur Tal.**

A few miles further south is the Amiar Tal, formed by the flood waters of the Ami, which fill the whole of the valley between Belipar on the north and Bansgaon on the south, both these places standing on ridges of high ground. The intervening depression thus becomes a lake several miles in length, terminating at the Tucker *bandh*, to the east of which is a second lake known as the Bijra Tal. The water level drops quickly after the rains, and the land thus exposed yields abundant *rabi* crops. **Amiar Tal.**

In pargana Chillupar, between the Rapti and the Ghagra, lies the Bhenri Tal, formed by the swollen waters of the Taraina, which passes through the lake. In the dry weather it contracts to relatively small dimensions, but in the rains it becomes an expanse of water some five miles in length. It would appear, however, that the lake is shrinking permanently, owing to the continuous accumulation of silt. A channel from the eastern extremity carries off the surplus water into the Rapti, but occasionally in times of abnormal flood the lake overflows its banks, submerging all the country to the south as far as the Ghagra. There is good fishing in the Bhenri Tal, and large quantities of shells are gathered on its shores for conversion into lime. **Bhenri Tal.**

The Chillua Tal is formed by the expansion of the Chillua river in pargana Haveli, some seven miles north from Gorakhpur. It is a long and somewhat narrow stretch of water, which again contracts into a river near Maniram and soon afterwards joins the Rohin. The unmetalled road to Maniram and Campierganj formerly crossed this lake at a narrow spot near the village of Siktaur by means of an embankment and two large brick bridges; but the latter were undermined and carried away by floods, leaving only a series of ruined arches, and the road now crosses the Tal by the same bridge which carries the railway line. **Chillua Tal.**

West of the bridge the lake usually goes by the name of the Maheshra Tal, and in this stands a small island, which tradition alleges to be the site of the fortified palace of some raja, though nothing remains to prove or disprove the legend. The lake is a noted fishery, and numerous Mallahs reside on its banks. To the west of the Rohin, in the *duab* between that river and the Rapti, there is an extensive series of lakes stretching from Maniram to Rigauli. The chief are known as the Jamuar, Likhia, Koela, Komar, Taru and Sarwa Tals, and every year in the cold weather they are the haunt of innumerable water-fowl.

Ramabhar Tal. There are but few lakes of any magnitude in the eastern half of the district. The most important is the Ramabhar Tal, lying a short distance to the west of the metalled road from Kasia to Deoria, about half a mile south from the former. During the hot weather it is not more than half a mile in length and 200 yards broad, but in the rains the area is doubled, while abnormal floods on the Khanua cause the lake to rise and spread over all the surrounding country, so that Kasia becomes an island in a wide sea of waters. The lake is of some value as a fishery and is extensively utilized for irrigation purposes. Other lakes of which mention may be made include the Kuseshar Tal near Dhara on the road to Kasia, the Chakahwa Tal and its connections in the south-east of pargana Shahjahanpur, the Dumrani Tal to the east of Tarkulwa, several sheets of water in the vicinity of Qazipur, and the numerous *mans* or abandoned river channels along the course of the Great and Little Gandak, many of which are of very large dimensions.

Waste land. Taking the average of the returns for the five years ending with 1906-07, the total area of waste and uncultivated land amounts to 829,536 acres or 25·8 per cent. of the entire district, excluding the reserved forests. From this figure certain deductions must be made, since 127,153 acres are covered with water and 85,458 acres are permanently occupied by railways, roads, sites, buildings and the like. Of the rest only 29,419 acres are shown as actually barren and unfit for cultivation, and the bulk of this consists of sterile sand along the course of the Ghagra in the parganas of Dhuriapar, Chillupar and Salempur. The balance is nominally culturable, though from this again must be deducted 64,687 acres of groves and 100,539 acres of new fallow, left temporarily untilled under the ordinary system of rotation. This leaves 235,256 acres of unbroken waste and 187,024 of old fallow, the distinction being generally arbitrary and of little moment. The former lies mainly in the forest tracts, since the Maharajganj, Padrauna and Gorakhpur tahsils alone contain 209,000 acres of land coming under this description; while apart from the forests there is a residue of nearly 100,000 acres occupied for the most part by scrub jungle and grass pasture. Still the area of old fallow is very considerable, even in the southern tahsils, and in spite of the density of the population there can be no doubt that the district has by no means reached the limit of cultivation, and that there is yet room under favourable circumstances for a very marked expansion of tillage, particularly in the northern tahsils.

Forests.

The forests in this district are of great economic value, although they are far less extensive than was formerly the case. They are generally of old standing, but it would appear that during historical times large areas have periodically been reclaimed and again suffered to lapse into jungle. At the time of the cession the extent of forest was very great, and a map of 1835 shows that not only was the whole of the north of the district up to the Nepal frontier covered with an unbroken expanse of forest, but there was also a belt of varying width stretching from the north-west corner along the northern bank of the Rapti and on both sides of the Rohin as far as Gorakhpur and thence onwards in an almost unbroken line to Deoria. These forests were at first held as waste lands under the collector, but about 1830 jungle grants were for the first time assigned to applicants on a progressive demand which culminated in the tenth year. The large number of such applications and the unprofitable nature of the bargain led to the abandonment of this system about 1840, and thenceforward leases were issued for terms sufficiently long to enable the grantee to clear and cultivate the land with a fair expectation of profit. It was stipulated that on the expiry of the lease the grant should be liable to re-settlement like an ordinary estate, and further that failure to comply with the conditions of the lease, the chief being the reclamation of a prescribed minimum of the area, should entail the resumption and confiscation of the grant. The result of this policy was that by 1850 so large an extent of forest land was held by grantees and so much timber had been felled that considerable anxiety was felt on the subject. Accordingly no further grants were made, and the forest still remaining was declared to be Government reserve, in which all felling was prohibited. To these reserves were added grants confiscated from time to time for breach of agreement, such grants being known as *zabti*, a term which has since been applied indiscriminately to all Government forests in the district. It is to this haphazard method of selection that the existence of so many scattered blocks and their most irregular outline may be traced. The policy of resumption and confiscation was definitely dropped when the rules regarding forest grants were revised in 1874. It had then come to be recognized that the preservation of the remaining forests was at least as important as any further extension of cultivation; and consequently all penalties were withdrawn in the event of any grantee preferring to keep his lands under forest. The reserved area remained under the management of the collector till 1868, when a large proportion of the *sal*-bearing land was handed over to the Forest department. This continued under the charge of the conservator, N.-W. P., till 1877, when on the amalgamation of Oudh with the rest of the province the Gorakhpur forests were made over to the charge of the Oudh conservator. They now form one of the seven divisions of the eastern circle of the United Provinces, and are in the charge of a deputy conservator stationed at Gorakhpur. The area was declared Government forest under G. O. no. 418 F.C., dated the 12th of September 1877, and was subsequently constituted reserved forest under section 34 of Act VII of 1878, further additions being made in 1883 and 1891.*

Character. The aggregate area of these forests is 110,926 acres or about 173 square miles, split up into fourteen detached blocks ranging from 55 to 26,500 acres in extent, and demarcated by means of

* Notifications no. 93, dated the 26th October 1883, and no. $\frac{321F.}{981-16}$, dated the 24th April 1891.

serially numbered stone monoliths. The soil is the usual sandy loam topped with a light layer of vegetable mould of varying thickness. In the more swampy portions clay predominates, while in places the subsoil is of *kankar*, or else of pure sand, as in the north-east. The Domakhand forest is drained by the Great Gandak, the northern and central ranges by the Rohin and Piyas, which unite at the southern extremity of the Dudhai block, and the southern portion by several small affluents of the Rapti. Along the drainage lines the land is swampy and liable to be submerged during rains. Such areas consist mainly of grass lands, and the only trees are *jamun (Eugenia jambolana)*, the *paniari (Berringtonia acutangula)* and the *paniar (Randia uliginosa)*. Here and there patches of miscellaneous forest are to be found in grass lands, but only on slightly higher levels. Domakhand, owing to its situation on the new alluvium of the Gandak, is full of swamps and depressions, but elsewhere the only open areas of any extent and importance occur in the northern and central ranges along the Rohin, Piyas and Malaun. The most valuable crop is the *sal (Shorea robusta)*, which grows on land raised from ten to forty feet above the surface depressions and covers in all 103·5 square miles. It is found in an almost pure state, with only a light admixture of its usual companions. Big trees are scarce, except perhaps in the north, and in most cases they are unsound, knotty and crooked, while in nearly every case they have been tapped for resin. The bulk of the crop consists of poles and saplings, which are generally straight and sound, the best specimens occurring in the Sonari forests, though in many other parts the *sal* is of very fair quality. Reproduction is irregular, but in most places patches of seedling growth of sufficiently large size and regular type are to be found; but elsewhere the forests suffer from the effects of heavy grazing, from overcrowding by inferior stems, many of which are crooked and hollow, and from the presence of grass and rank undergrowth of inferior species. The *sal* forest disappears wherever the drainage is defective or the soil stiffens into heavy clay, even trivial depressions in the midst of the *sal* area forming blanks devoid of seedlings. There is one enormous blank to the east of the Nagwa forest, but this appears to owe its origin to the reclamation of the land for cultivation at a recent date. In the grass lands on the edges of the *sal* blocks there is a somewhat abundant growth of *asaina* (*Terminalia tomentosa*), but all the larger trees are unsound, most of them having been lopped for fodder, so that the growth is chiefly in the form of pollards. Miscellaneous forest is confined to the intermediate levels, and its extent is nowhere great save in Domakhand, Nagwa and Sonari. The *jamun* grows freely along the banks of watercourses, but seldom attains any size, and the only other serviceable trees are *khair* (*Acacia catechu*) and *haldu* (*Adina cordifolia*). There are of course many more species in these areas, such as the *semal, jhigna, mahua* and *aonla*, but they are of no particular value, while the undergrowth of shrubs and small trees is wholly worthless. On the far side of the Gandak in Domakhand there are some 600 acres of pure *khair*, and in the same direction is a good deal of *shisham* (*Dalbergia sissoo*) of recent growth. In several other localities plantations of *shisham* have been started with success, the largest being known as the Sakhwi plantation, with an area of 2,356 acres, which was laid out in 1881-82 on grass and fallow lands in the south-west of Nagwa.

Management.

Subordinate to the deputy conservator are two rangers, one deputy ranger, one forester and 36 forest guards, while during the working season an additional temporary staff of export *muharrirs* and *chaprasis* is entertained, and from March to June five watchers are employed. Fire conservancy was first attempted in 1875, and has been fairly successful : fires are easily controlled, for the *sal* forest is quite separate from the grass areas, and even in the most unfavourable season fires make very little progress. A complete system of fire-lines was introduced in 1892, and there is now a regular network of lines, 134 miles in length, which are cleared every year before the forest and the grass lands are dry. Further protection is afforded by the numerous roads, aggregating 171 miles in length, which have been constructed by the department. There are rest-houses at Ramgarh, Campierganj, Pharenda, Sarbar, Bhilampur and Banki in the south, at Lachhmipur, Tehri-ghat, Jagpur and Pakri in the centre and at Chauk Daibhar, Madhaulia and Nichlaul in the north. The exploitation of the forests is conducted on a working plan drawn up in 1893. The first plan was compiled in 1874, but this proved impracticable and was cancelled in 1876, from which year to 1887 work was conducted on the lines of notes drawn up by Mr. Greig. In 1887 a rough plan was submitted but was not sanctioned, and the same fate attended the plans of 1889 and 1891, after which Mr. Eardley Wilmot was deputed to compile the present plan. This was introduced simultaneously with a rearrangement of the forest administration. The two ranges were divided into three, of which the southern range has a total area of 23,954 acres, divided into twelve beats, and comprises the forests of Ramgarh, Tilkonia, Bhilampur, Banki, Bhari Babban, Bhari Baisi, Chhitahi and West Lehra; the central range of eight beats, 24,168 acres in extent, includes Manjhar Dudhai, Dudhai and East Lehra; and the northern range, with an area of 57,854 acres, forming 16 beats, consists of Sonari, Madhaulia and Nágwa, the last including Domakhand. Till about 1883 the permit system for the extraction of produce was in force, permits being issued by the forest guards and *muharrirs*, while the permit-holders were at liberty to cut whatever and wherever they liked, so that the disappearance of the better trees was hardly surprising. Orders were consequently given that only unsound and tapped trees should be felled; but these directions were more honoured in the breach than in the observance, and it often happened that good and sound timber was removed and paid for as unsound. Departmental fellings, though started as early as 1875, were confined at first to the Ramgarh forest; but when in 1885 the opening of the railway created a large demand for sleepers, regular coppice fellings and sleeper operations were started everywhere. There was little scientific selection, and in many cases large quantities of sound material were removed while much unhealthy growth remained; but it is probable that these fellings proved generally beneficial to reproduction in spite of the clumsy manner in which they were effected. Subsequently the southern range was worked for the supply of fuel and timber to the railway and the general public, while annual leases of fuel and dry timber were given in the northern forests. The working plan of 1893 divided the area into six working circles, and prescribed coppice fellings with standards in the two circles of the southern range on a rotation of twenty years. In the *sal* areas of the central and northern ranges improvement fellings are carried on with the intention of creating a regular growth of high forest, and elsewhere, as in Domakhand and the *manjhar* tract, the existing forest is merely protected and the rest used as a grazing ground. There are no rights of any kind in the forest, but grazing is permitted on payment in an area of 32,685 acres, the total number of cattle in 1906-07 being 59,736.

Revenue. The chief produce of the forests is *sal* in the shape of both timber and fuel. It is a heavy wood, able to resist the ravages of white ants, and is used for piles, beams, planking and sleepers. Its export is effected partly by road and partly by rail: in water it will not float by itself but requires the assistance of bamboos and other light-wood floats. The neighbouring villages take but a small proportion of the forest produce, and the chief markets for timber are Gorakhpur, Barhaj, Basti, Dinapur, Patna and Benares. Besides timber the forests yield large quantities of fuel, bamboos, thatching grass and *mahua* flowers, the first being greatly in demand for brick kilns and sugar refineries. Grass too is an important source of revenue, and in several areas its sale constitutes the entire receipts. Financially the Gorakhpur forests have yielded very satisfactory results, in large measure owing to the facilities for cheap carriage afforded by the railways. From 1879 to 1888 the surplus revenue averaged Rs. 35,042 annually, while from 1889 to 1897 it was Rs. 33,825. Since that time a marked improvement has taken place, and between 1898 and 1907 the net annual receipts averaged Rs. 56,193, the highest surplus being Rs. 86,328 in the last year. The working expenses for the same period amounted on an average to Rs. 49,974 per annum.

Private forests. Apart from the Government reserves, there are 78,596 acres of forest and jungle in the possession of private owners. The bulk of such land lies in the Maharajganj and Padrauna tahsils and a large proportion consists of scrub jungle, no less than 25,000 acres in Padrauna alone coming under this category. The area also includes much grass land, which in many places adjoins the jungle and is of great value for grazing, supporting immense numbers of cattle. The actual extent of tree forest cannot be ascertained, but it is relatively small: the stock is principally *sal*, but for many years the private forests have been ruthlessly felled to meet the growing demand for timber created by the advent of the railway. The only large area of *sal* remaining intact is that owned by the Mian Sahib at Kusmahi, some nine miles east from Gorakhpur. This is preserved as a sacred grove to provide fuel for a perpetual fire at the Imambara in Gorakhpur, and it serves to illustrate the possibilities of a *sal* forest under mere protection without any scientific treatment.

Groves.

While it is but natural that in the forest tracts of the north, where timber is abundant and cultivation backward, the number of artificial groves should be relatively small, the rest of the district is remarkably well provided in this respect. At the time of the last settlement the total grove area was 68,121 acres or 2·32 per cent. of the entire district, the proportion ranging from 1·4 per cent. in Maharajganj to 3·4 in Deoria and 3·8 in Bansgaon, figures which compare not unfavourably with those of the well wooded districts of Oudh. Since the settlement there has been some decrease, owing partly to the destruction of old groves and the conversion of the land to agricultural purposes, and partly to the incentive to sell the trees provided by the enhanced cost of wood for fuel, especially on the south-east, where there is a growing demand on the part of the sugar refiners. The average for the past five years is 64,687 acres or 2·23 per cent. of the whole area, Bansgaon as before taking the foremost place with a proportion of 3·7 per cent. It is probable that no further decrease will take place, since new plantations are in evidence everywhere, particularly in the *kachhar* tract, in which groves do exceedingly well and form an asset of much importance. The groves consist in most cases of mango trees, though occasionally other species are to be seen, such as guavas, which are extensively planted in the neighbourhood of Gorakhpur. The district abounds also in *mahua* trees, but these are for the most part of spontaneous growth, and are to be seen principally on land recently reclaimed from the forest or not yet brought under cultivation. The area covered by these trees must be very considerable, though it is all included in culturable waste, and the crop is of great value. Some of the most extensive groves in the district are to be found immediately to the north of old Gorakhpur, while of single isolated groves perhaps the largest and finest is that belonging to the Bhuinhars of Dihghat, tappa Rajdhani, in the *kachhar* of the Rapti.

Mineral products.

As the geology of the district exposes nothing beyond ordinary river-borne alluvium, the mineral products are necessarily few and unimportant. Those of commercial value include the nodular limestone conglomerate known as *kankar*, brick earth and saltpetre. The last occurs principally in the south and south-east, and is manufactured in the crude state in considerable quantities, most of it being exported by river to the markets of Bengal. In the southern tahsils *kankar* is most abundant, and quarries are to be seen in many places, generally within a short distance of the metalled roads, carriage being the most important item in the cost. At the quarry *kankar* fetches as a rule Rs. 2 per 100 cubic feet, while the usual rate for transport is eight annas per mile; the average cost at Gorakhpur, inclusive of all charges, being Rs. 7 per 100 cubic feet. Lime is obtained by burning *kankar*, and ordinarily costs Rs. 20 for the same quantity; but more is paid for a superior kind of lime produced from shells, which are collected from several of the larger lakes, such as the Bhenri and Chillua Tals. Brick earth is everywhere abundant, and bricks are made all over the district. Those of the English pattern, employed by the Public Works department, are manufactured in three qualities, costing respectively Rs. 8-8-0, Rs. 7 and Rs. 5 per thousand, while the small *lakhauri* bricks of the native type fetch from Re. 1-12-0 to Rs. 5 for the same number.

Building materials.

Of the other building materials country tiles for the ordinary dwellings in the towns are made everywhere at the rate of Rs. 2 per thousand. Tiles of the Allahabad pattern are burnt at Gorakhpur and occasionally in other places. The current rates are Rs. 50 for flat, Rs. 30 for half-round tiles, Rs. 40 for semi-hexagonal, Rs. 100 for ventilating ridge tiles and Rs. 75 for half-round ridge tiles. As might be expected, timber for building is plentiful and cheap. For houses of the better class *sal* beams are generally employed, while in poorer dwellings recourse is had to *shisham, mahua, tun, jamun* and mango, all of which are readily procurable in the local markets. The cost of *sal* poles is about four annas per cubic foot at Gorakhpur, but sawn timber for door and window frames is considerably dearer. Bamboos of all sizes are abundant in the district, the larger kinds being sold for Rs. 20 and the smaller for Rs. 12 or Rs. 15 per hundred. The only other items of any importance in the houses of the poor are thatching grass and string, both of which can be obtained everywhere, the requisite amount being usually supplied by the landlord.

Fauna.

The proximity of Nepal and the wide extent of forest are responsible for the presence of an unusually large number of wild animals and a considerable diversity of species. There has, however, been a great reduction in the case of the larger animals during the past fifty years, and Gorakhpur no longer presents the same attractions to the sportsman which it offered in early days. It is related that in 1856 the mails to Padrauna were stopped by the tigers which then infested the roads, and as late as 1873 a tiger was shot by the magistrate in Gorakhpur itself. Nowadays they are confined to Domakhand and the adjoining forests near the Gandak, but even there they are becoming more rare year by year. The wild buffalo has disappeared, the last specimen having been obtained in 1896, and the rhinoceros has long ceased to be a resident of this district, though isolated instances are on record of such animals being carried down the Gandak from Nepal by floods. Of the larger carnivora the leopard is still fairly common, but the wolf is almost unknown. Bears are met with occasionally, and the wild pig is common, especially in the lowlands of the Ghagra. Several varieties of deer inhabit the forests, but the *chital* or spotted deer alone occurs in any numbers. Antelope are somewhat abundant in the shape of the black-buck and the *nilgai*, the latter resorting to the jungles and also to the Ghagra *diwara* lands. Other animals include jackals, foxes, hares, porcupines and monkeys, while in the rivers the alligator, *garial* and porpoise are frequently to be seen. Snakes are common, especially the cobra and *karait*, which are most often seen during the rains, and the python is occasionally found in the north. During the five years ending with 1907 the average number of reported deaths from snake-bite was 563 annually, while during the same period the rewards paid for the destruction of wild beasts averaged Rs. 139.

Birds.

The bird life of the district is remarkably varied, since, in addition to the ordinary species found throughout the plains, many others occur in the forest tracts of the north. Peafowl, black and grey partridges, quail and an occasional florican may be included among the game birds, while during the cold weather the numerous lakes and marshes are the haunt of almost every variety of waterfowl in great abundance. The district is celebrated for its small game shooting, but only the ordinary species are to be met with as a rule, and little further comment is necessary, though perhaps mention should be made of the remarkable numbers of the great crested grebe among the migrants.

Fish.

The fisheries of the district are of much importance; both the rivers, the lakes and the larger tanks containing vast numbers of fish in great variety. More than thirty different species have been recorded, the chief being the *rohu*, which is found everywhere, and the *mahsir*, which is confined to the Gandak and the big rivers. Fish are caught with the rod and line, with bamboo spears, and with nets of varying size and pattern. One kind is funnel shaped and is pushed in front of the fisherman's boat. Another, resembling an English shrimping net, is frequently employed in shallow water, the fisherman wading for the purpose. The *maha jal* or seine is sometimes used in the rivers and necessitates the employment of two or three boats; by this means a sweep of 200 yards or more is obtained, and often the results are most destructive, as much as 600 or 700 lbs. of fish of all sizes being taken in a single haul. It is perhaps fortunate that this method is seldom adopted; though an even more deadly device, causing far greater destruction of young fry, is very frequently resorted to at the close of the rains, its extreme simplicity and the absence of any exertion in its execution rendering it especially popular. A narrow place in a small stream or tank is selected, and the neck is almost closed by means of an earthen dam or a wicker fence, leaving only a small channel in the centre. Just below this dam at the extremity of the channel a trap is fixed, and the fisherman has merely to collect the fish which have swum down-stream into the basket. Under favourable circumstances, as for example where a lake discharges itself into a river, a trap of this nature will yield two or three boatloads of small fish daily for several weeks in the year. The consequent destruction of fry is immense, especially as no close season is observed, and it is indeed a matter for surprise that no apparent diminution in the stock has been observed. Fishing is carried on by Mallahs, Kahars, Pasis, Musalmans and many others, though few of these depend on fishing as their sole means of support. At the last census the number of professional fishermen and fish dealers was 9,916, including 4,141 dependants, but this by no means represents the entire fishing population. Fish find a ready sale at all times, and are much esteemed as an article of diet by almost all classes, the chief exceptions being Brahmans and Banias. In Gorakhpur the price of good fish is ordinarily four annas a *ser* in the cold season and half that amount during the hot weather, whereas in the district the price is somewhat lower. People of the poorest classes do not abstain from eating turtles, which are very common, and are caught by means of barbed spears, with which the fishermen probe the bottom of the river as the boat moves slowly down stream.

The ordinary cattle of the district are small and decidedly inferior in strength to those of the west, though they are reputed to be endowed with great powers of endurance, and are certainly able to do their work on very little food and that of a miserable quality. The *pual* or rice straw on which the vast majority of animals are fed during several months of the year is probably one of the poorest kinds of fodder on which plough cattle are enabled to subsist anywhere. Animals of the better class are few, and are invariably imported, in most cases from Kheri and Bahraich ; and no attempts at improving the local breed have been made on a large scale with any success, being reproduction left to the agency of the ownerless and half-wild bull. Locally bred animals are very cheap, fetching from Rs. 18 to Rs. 20 per pair, though of course the price depends on the size and strength of the bullocks ; while those imported from other districts cost from Rs. 50 to Rs. 100 Cattle.

a yoke. Owing to the abundance of pasture, especially in the northern tahsils, Gorakhpur ranks among the chief breeding districts and consequently possesses a considerable surplus of cattle beyond those required for agricultural purposes. The first regular cattle census was taken in 1899, and this showed a total of 602,778 bulls and bullocks and 8,899 male buffaloes, giving an average of 2·31 animals per plough. The surplus was of course much greater in the north than in the southern parganas, and in the latter the rate was below the general average for the province. Five years later in 1904 a second census showed a general increase, the number of plough cattle rising to 666,827, of which only 5,633 were male buffaloes; but at the same time there was a corresponding increase in the number of ploughs, the average being but 2·25 animals to each plough. Young stock had remained almost stationary, rising from 505,293 to 516,679; but, on the other hand, there had been a material improvement in the number of cows, which had risen from 411,012 to 457,031, while cow-buffaloes showed a total of 126,170 as compared with 117,155 at the former enumeration. At the last census in 1909 a further increase was observed. Bulls and bullocks aggregated 688,321 or 2·23 per plough, and male buffaloes 4,044; the proportion being much the same as before. There were 422,693 cows and 111,883 cow buffaloes, while the total of young stock was no less than 612,865. These figures are very high and point to the importance of the *ghi* trade, particularly in the north; for it is noteworthy that the majority of the cows and the cow-buffaloes belong to the Maharajganj and Padrauna tahsils. The chief resorts of the graziers are the open grass wastes of Domakhand and the low *manjhar* between the Rohin and Piyas, whither great herds are driven up annually from the south, occasionally from considerable distances, to pick up a living on the pastures from October to June, the return journey taking place just before the commencement of the rains. As already mentioned, some 60,000 head of cattle are regularly grazed in the Government reserves, and the private forests and pastures support much larger numbers. Their utility in this respect is incalculable, and it is of high importance that these grazing grounds should be preserved for the purpose. The conversion of such areas into arable land would remove one of the principal safeguards for the cattle of this and several of the neighbouring districts, especially in seasons of scarcity and drought.

The last census showed a total of 13,209 horses and ponies, but with few exceptions these are of an even more inferior type than the horned cattle. The bulk of them consist of wretched little ponies, undersized and underfed, which are employed for transport purposes. No attempts have been made to improve the breed, and, in fact, such an undertaking could hardly be said to offer the slightest prospect of success, nor are any stallions maintained either by Government or on the part of the district board. Small as is the present figure, there appears to have been a decided decline in the total within recent years, and this is probably connected with the extended use of bullocks as pack animals and the great increase in the number of carts, the last census showing a total of 32,996. This substitution represents an immense gain in efficiency, for given good roads carts are in every way superior to pack ponies, even though the latter be habitually overloaded. There were 11,276 donkeys in 1904, but these again are of a very poor type and their use is practically confined to washermen and potters. They are quite valueless for mule-breeding, and no experiments have been attempted in this direction. Camels are unsuited to the climate, and only 92 were registered at the last enumeration. On the other hand, the number of elephants is unusually large, the district containing several hundreds of these beasts, which are kept by all the more prosperous landowners. There remain sheep and goats, the former being of little importance. The total was 58,678 at the time of the census, and these are mainly to be found in the south, where they are kept for their flesh and their wool, which is woven by the Gadariyas into rough blankets; while they are also of value for their manure, tenants readily paying a small sum to the shepherds for the privilege of penning them on the fields. Goats are extremely numerous, aggregating 612,865 in 1909. This represents an immense increase on the figure of the previous census, though probably the rise was more apparent than real. They are of a small and inferior type, yielding little

Other animals.

milk, but they require scanty attention, picking up food in the most unpromising places, and are amazingly prolific.

Cattle disease.

The district is never free from cattle disease in some form or other, the most prevalent types being foot and mouth disease, which is at the same time the least deadly, rinderpest and anthrax, while in the low lying areas haemorrhagic septicaemia or malignant sore throat is far from uncommon. Occasionally rinderpest assumes an epidemic form during or immediately after the rains, particularly in the Maharajganj and Gorakhpur tahsils, but the returns are wholly unreliable. There are now three veterinary assistants attached to the district, with headquarters at Gorakhpur, Kasia and Deoria, and at the first of these is a cattle hospital. The latter is not under the immediate control of the district board, but is supported by fees and contributions. A proposal has recently been made for a system of free treatment in return for a grant from Government, but at present there are fixed fees for every kind of animal. The institution is in the charge of a veterinary expert. During recent years useful results have been obtained by inoculation of cattle against rinderpest and anthrax, and in the past three years 1,238 operations have been performed, though only one of the veterinary assistants has been trained in inoculation work. The district is reputed to be unhealthy for horses, and in certain localities tetanus is prevalent, while glanders and worm in the eye occur with considerable frequency.

Climate.

The climate of the district is far more equable that in the western tracts in that great extremes of heat and cold are rarely experienced. The proximity of the hills and the comparatively heavy rainfall combine to avert the great heat prevalent in the districts of the Benares division to the south, the maximum temperature in the shade during May and June rarely rising above 105° and scarcely ever reaching 110°, while it not unfrequently remains below 100°. In the early summer months the air is often refreshed by storms from the hills, and the burning west winds, so marked a feature of the Doab, seldom persist for more than a few days together, at most prevailing for two or three weeks in the year. Dust storms are consequently of rare occurrence, for at almost all seasons the wind blows from the east, and if not so invigorating is at least cooler than the fiery blasts of the western districts. In former days Gorakhpur had an evil reputation for fever, but matters have greatly improved with the reclamation of large areas of forest and the extension of cultivation; and though the southern half of the district is now generally admitted to be as healthy as the country lying on the other side of the Ghagra, Gorakhpur bears a no better reputation than Gonda and Bahraich among the natives of these provinces whose homes lie further to the west and south. The two northern tahsils of Maharajganj and Padrauna must still be considered unhealthy, especially those parts which border on the Tarai, since fever is there very prevalent during and immediately after the rains. It cannot be denied that the climate is in some degree enervating, for, while avoiding the extremes of heat, the district seldom enjoys any cold or bracing weather during the winter months, and the average minimum temperature for December and January falls little short of 50°.

Rainfall.

Records of rainfall appear to have been maintained at certain stations from very early times, the figures in some cases going back to 1844, though these are of little value and almost invariably understate the actual amount. No reliable returns for the outlying tahsils exist for years prior to 1870, but Gorakhpur itself has long been an observing station from which daily returns are supplied to the meteorological authorities. Taken as a whole, the district enjoys a heavier rainfall than any other part of these provinces, excepting the hilly tracts, the annual average being no less than 52·01 inches per annum. Owing to the great difference in the climatic conditions of the several parts, the local variations are very marked. The large expanse of forest and the proximity of the hills in the north secure a much more abundant precipitation than in the south, where conditions approximate to those prevailing in the neighbouring districts beyond the Ghagra. Between 1891 and 1906 the general average was 50·68 inches, while during the same period 60·03 inches were registered annually at Maharajganj, though the total for Deoria was no more than 46·38. In abnormally wet years the amount of rain received is surprising. The average fall for the entire district was no less than 72·79 inches in 1899, when 81·76 inches were recorded at Maharajganj. Another wet year was 1903, when large areas were flooded for the space of nearly two months, Maharajganj then receiving 80·92 and the district as a whole 63·75. On the other hand, there have been few occasions on which any marked deficiency has been observed, and in only two within the last sixteen years has the total been less than 40 inches. One of these was 1896, when the district average was 26·7 and Hata received only 18·6 inches, but in spite of this extraordinary defect no public relief operations had to be undertaken in the ensuing year. The other season of abnormal drought was 1907, when the district average was no more than 28·69 inches, and on this occasion again, although acute distress was felt in several parts, it was not found necessary to include Gorakhpur in the famine area.

Health. It is not possible to demonstrate by means of statistics to what extent the healthiness of the district has improved as the result of extended cultivation and the reclamation of large areas of forest, for the reason that the returns of mortality do not go back for a sufficiently long period, and also because the earliest figures extant are unreliable on account of defective methods of record. The registration of deaths seems first to have been attempted about 1865, but the figures at first were hopelessly inadequate, and, though an improved system was adopted in 1872, it was not till the famine of 1877-78 that the matter received much official attention. For the four years ending with 1880, a period marred by excessive mortality from fever and other epidemics, the annual average death-rate was 34·72 per mille. That this figure was above the normal is shown by those of subsequent years, for in the next decade the average was but 27·47 as compared with a mean annual birth-rate of 41·93 per mille. The following ten years were less healthy, for while the death-rate from 1891 to 1900 averaged only 28·08, that of births fell to 32·19, and on more than one occasion the former exceeded the latter. Such was the case in 1894, when fever was abnormally prevalent and great havoc was wrought by cholera, the death-rate being 43·78 or higher than in any previous or subsequent year, and also in 1897, a season of general famine, when fever again caused widespread mortality and the rate rose to 35·92 per mille. Subsequent years have shown an improvement, for from 1901 to 1907 inclusive the average death-rate was 27·57 and that of births 36·88 per mille. In the appendix will be found details for each year since 1891: the subsequent period has by no means been abnormally healthy, but the returns compare favourably with those of the other districts north of the Ghagra, as well as the country lying immediately to the south of that river.*

A second table shows the number of deaths attributed in each year to the principal forms of disease. Among the latter fever takes its customary place of preeminence, being undoubtedly the most common of all ailments. At the same time it is a very elastic and comprehensive term, embracing many deaths resulting from diseases in which fever is a symptom and also from those which do not obviously come under any other category. On the other hand, there can be no question as to the general prevalence of malarial fever, which has at all times had a firm hold of the district, while the high water level and the defective drainage provide innumerable breeding places for the anopheles mosquito. From 1877 to 1880 the deaths from fever averaged 51,218 annually or 73·04 per cent. of the total recorded mortality, and this high figure was mainly due to the appalling ravages of the disease in 1878, when 72,740 persons were carried off, the height of the death-rate being due in large measure to the low state of vitality to which the people had been reduced by famine. From 1881 to 1890 there were no exceptional epidemics, save in the first year, and the deaths from fever averaged only 40,254, or 55·99 per cent. of the total, the low proportion being attributable to the unusual amount of cholera and other diseases. The following decade showed an annual average of 46,748 deaths from fever, while the proportion to the recorded total was 55·6 per cent. or much the same as before; but there were two very bad years, 1894 and 1897, with 62,144 and 69,770 deaths respectively, in both of which the conditions were abnormal. The succeeding period, from 1901 to 1907 inclusive, has been characterized by many violent epidemics

Fever.

*Appendix, tables III and IV.

of fever, which has accounted on an average for 57,628 deaths yearly, or 70·68 per cent. of the total mortality. The rate has been high throughout, and it is difficult to understand the increasing virulence of the disease in a period of general prosperity and favourable seasons.*

Cholera.

The district is never free from cholera, which frequently assumes an epidemic form and owes its rapid dissemination to the absence of precautionary measures on the part of the people, and also to the ease with which the wells, with their generally high water level, become infected. From 1877 to 1907 there was only one year in which the reported deaths from cholera numbered less than a hundred, and in all but six years they exceeded a thousand. For the first four years the average was 3,217 or 4·59 per cent. of the total mortality. In the ensuing decade the figure rose to 4,419 or 9·77 per cent., the increase arising mainly from the epidemic of 1887, which accounted for 15,135 deaths. Matters were still worse from 1891 to 1900, when the disease carried off 6,313 persons annually or 7·51 per cent. of the total number reported. Serious epidemics were frequent, but all were eclipsed by that of 1894, which resulted in 26,081 deaths. Since 1901 matters have improved a little, the average for seven years being 4,157 deaths, but this would have been far lower save for the widespread outbreak introduced from Nepal in 1906.

Small-pox.

With regard to small-pox the returns are far more encouraging. In early days the ravages of the disease were very extensive and direct inoculation was the sole preventive measure. Vaccination was performed at the Government dispensaries on those who desired it, but it was not till 1865 that any active measures were taken in this direction and a regular vaccination staff was organized. It failed at first to attain general popularity, and, though its advantages have been brought out on many occasions and the number of persons vaccinated annually has gone up by leaps and bounds, it is far from being universally adopted in the district and small-pox has by no means been eradicated. From 1877 to 1880 the disease was responsible for 2,385 deaths annually, and a bad outbreak in 1879 lasted for a long time. Small-pox

* Appendix, table IV.

appeared with renewed intensity in 1881, and three years later occurred the worst epidemic on record, no fewer than 17,469 deaths being reported. The annual average for the ten years ending with 1890 was 3,344, and this was enhanced by a recurrence of the disease in the last year, followed in 1891 by a great visitation which was responsible for 11,117 deaths. This and an isolated outbreak in 1897 brought the average for the next decade up to 1851, though apart from the two years in question the period was relatively free. The figures of succeeding years have shown a great improvement save in 1907, when small-pox raged throughout the United Provinces and the deaths in this district numbered 3,166.* The decline in the mortality from the disease is closely connected with the advance of vaccination. For the first four years of the period under discussion the average number of primary operations was 26,627, and this rose to 38,080 and to 62,109 in the two following decades, while for the last seven years the average has been 89,900. Taking seven years as the period of immunity conferred by vaccination, it follows that nearly 630,000 persons or 21·3 per cent. of the total population have been protected, though this figure must to some extent be discounted owing to the high rate of mortality among infants. The figure is low as compared with the results obtained in many districts, but the improvement is beyond dispute. Vaccination is in the general charge of the civil surgeon, subordinate to whom are two assistant superintendents and 47 vaccinators: of the latter two are paid by the municipality and one by the Majhauli estate, while the rest are supported by the district board. Vaccination has been compulsory since 1893 in the Gorakhpur municipality, which for this purpose includes the present notified area.

Plague first made its appearance in 1902, when 3,677 persons were carried off by the disease. Since that time it has raged with varying intensity, especially in the south of the district, for so far it has not penetrated the Maharajganj tahsil or the north of Padrauna. The city has suffered severely, and is now almost deserted when plague attacks any of the *muhallas*. At the same time few effective measures have been taken to eradicate the disease, for evacuation has seldom been complete and Plague.

* Appendix, table IV.

disinfection has never been popular. Towards the end of 1907 inoculation was started, but up to the present time has made little headway.

Other diseases.

Among other diseases the most fatal are bowel complaints and dysentery, which frequently follow on malarial fever, while pneumonia and influenza are responsible for many deaths, especially in the cold weather. A noticeable feature in the medical aspects of the district is the prevalence of hydrocele, elephantiasis and goitre, the first two being common everywhere and contracted not only by natives of the district but also by those whose business or occupation has necessitated residence here. On the other hand, goitre is mainly confined to the northern tracts, and particularly to the Padrauna tahsil. The fact is interesting, for while it is by some attributed to the peculiar nature and composition of the soil, the prevalence of the disease along the Gandak lends colour to the old theory that goitre results from drinking the water of snow-fed rivers.

Infirmities.

Statistics of infirmities have been compiled at each successive census since 1881, but comparison is of little value owing to the different systems of definition adopted on various occasions. It is clear, however, that blindness has decreased in common with small-pox, and the total of 1,065 blind persons in 1901 is remarkably low. Lepers numbered 585—a fairly high figure, which has been adduced in testimony of the theory that this affliction is caused by an unwholesome fish diet. There were 482 insane persons and no fewer than 1,150 deaf-mutes, the proportion in either case being most common in the Padrauna tahsil. This is but natural, since the connection between cretinism and goitre has been firmly established, both the infirmity and the disease arising from affections of the same organs.

CHAPTER II.

AGRICULTURE AND COMMERCE.

While the natural conditions are eminently favourable for agriculture, the district may still be described as backward and there can be no comparison between the standard of husbandry in Gorakhpur and the careful and intense cultivation seen in Oudh and other parts of the United Provinces. The soil is generally fertile and little land can be described as wholly sterile; and though irrigation is not carried on to the same extent as in other parts, it is generally sufficient for the needs of a district possessing a moist climate and an abundant rainfall which very rarely fails. In spite of these advantages, large areas still depend almost wholly on a single harvest in the year, and while such a condition of affairs is inevitable in the low *kachhar*, where the *kharif* is necessarily precarious on account of the constant risk of floods, there is still an immense amount of land in the north and east, in which, till recently, no attempt was made to raise anything beyond an autumn crop. The reason lay in the abundance of land at the disposal of the cultivator, who was in consequence relieved of any inducement to exert himself, and partly in the enervating character of the climate, which rendered exertion unpalatable. In the fertile *bhat* tract there is still but a small amount of *rabi* cultivation, and in places nothing is grown for the spring harvest save the most inferior grains. This state of affairs is to some extent the result of the political history of the district. The indescribable confusion and misgovernment which prevailed before the cession of Gorakhpur to the Company had resulted in the abandonment of much arable land and the consequent spread of the jungle and forest area. From the dawn of the historical era the inhabitants had been mainly Bhars, Pasis and others of low caste, in a state of hopeless subjection to the local Rajput chieftains, and under

Cultivation.

such circumstances progress was not to be expected in a remote tract, devoid of all means of communication with the outer world and cursed with a bad climate. The elimination of the idle and inefficient cultivators was an extremely slow process, and as late as 1869 it was stated that the Bhars and Pasis were still gradually leaving the Bansgaon tahsil, now perhaps the most highly developed portion of the district, to make way for Koeris, Kewats and other capable agriculturists. These emigrants for the most part made their way to the deserted lands of the north, where their descendants are still to be found, though even there the pressure of an increasing population is already having its effect, both in an improved standard of husbandry and in the growing proportion of the superior cultivating castes.

Cultivated area. Though progress has necessarily been retarded by local conditions, the expansion since the first advent of British rule has been none the less remarkable. The substitution of relative security for chaos and tyranny caused cultivation to advance by leaps and bounds, and though no accurate figures are available, the fact is amply demonstrated by the increase in the revenue demand from less than five lakhs in 1802 to more than three times that figure in 1840. By the time of the seventh settlement, carried out between 1856 and 1871, the total area under tillage was 1,524,422 acres or 62·9 per cent. of the entire district, excluding the large extent of forest. The proportion ranged from 68 in the Deoria tahsil to 37 in Maharajganj, and taken all round the figure was surprisingly high. Subsequent years showed further rapid progress, for during the currency of the settlement 150,000 acres were reclaimed in the Maharajganj tahsil and 100,000 in Gorakhpur, the total average for the four years ending with 1887-88 being 1,821,996 acres. The stimulus afforded by the last settlement had a marked effect, for the average rose in the following decade to 1,966,026 acres, and this would have been even higher but for the temporary decline due to bad seasons in the second half of the period. The recovery was, however, rapid and from 1898-99 to 1907-08 cultivation reached a higher figure than even before, the average for the ten years being 2,042,445 acres, while in the last five years it was 2,064,058 or 71·17 per cent. of the entire district, or 76·16 per cent. if the forest area be excluded. This is a remarkable proportion, particularly in view of recent bad seasons, while the constant expansion of tillage is shown by the fact that the greatest cultivated area on record was 2,086,805 acres in 1907-08. As shown in the preceding chapter, there yet remains a considerable area to be brought under the plough. Apart from the forests, which are of more value as timber and fuel reserves than as arable land, and the large extent of culturable waste which is required for pasturage, there are more than 200,000 acres of old fallow; and although much of this is doubtless of inferior quality, it is practically certain that the increasing pressure of the population on the soil will render it necessary to bring such lands under regular tillage within the near future.

Soils.

The character of the agriculture depends mainly on the nature of the soils in the different tracts, and some description of these must necessarily find a place in an account of the economic condition of the district. The main division is that which has already been sketched out in the foregoing chapter. The whole eastern side of the district, comprising the Padrauna tahsil and an extensive block in the eastern extremity of Deoria, is *bhat,* which stretches inland to the Little Gandak and is varied only by two large wedges of *bangar,* which run up northwards from the Saran district, terminating respectively near Padrauna and Kasia. The whole of the remaining area is upland *bangar,* with the exception of the broad belt of *kachhar* along the course of the Rapti and two similar blocks, one of which occurs in the extreme north-east near the Great Gandak, while the other is formed by the new alluvium of the Ghagra in the south-western corner. This *kachhar* varies in quality, for that along the Gandak and Ghagra contains an undue proportion of sand and is consequently endowed with inferior fertility; but that of the Rapti and its affluents, the Rohin and Ami, is either rich silt or sand which weathers rapidly into culturable and productive soil. In the *bangar* the variations in the soil are of the usual type, depending primarily on the proportion of sand present. Where this proportion is high, the soil is known as *balua,* corresponding to the *bhur* of other parts, while at the opposite end of the scale comes *matiar* or clay; though in the *bangar* even this contains a considerable amount of sand and is by no means so stiff or heavy as the *matiar* of the Benares division. The intermediate soil, comprising the bulk of the area, is loam of varying consistency, going by the generic name of *doras*, which is equivalent to the *dumat* of the west. There is a similar classification in the *bhat* tract, where the lightest soil is the *dhusi bhat*, and the loam has its counterpart in the *chauriar bhat*, while the heaviest kind is the *chaur bhat* in the east, though in each case the proportion of fine sand is higher than in the corresponding soils of the *bangar*. Reference has already been made to the chief characteristics of the *bhat*, but it has further certain chemical peculiarities. It sometimes contains as much as 25 per cent. of carbonate of lime, and the amount of iron oxide is only ·25 per cent., whereas the former in the *bangar* occasionally amounts to no more than 2 per cent. and the latter rises in places to 3 per cent.

Tarai. These three main classes form three clearly defined agricultural tracts, to which must be added the *tarai* belt on the Nepal border. This *tarai* is properly a subdivision of the *bangar*, though it differs from the centre and south of the district in the large extent of heavy clay soil found there. The belt has an average breadth of about ten miles, and in the western half, between the Piyas and Ghunghi, conditions are favourable to irrigation from small canals called *kulas*, which are taken out of the numerous streams by means of earthen embankments constructed by the Tharu cultivators. The water supply is abundant and rarely fails, and consequently the main staple is late rice, for which pargana Binayakpur is famous. Canals are not found east of the Piyas, and there the late rice is comparatively scarce, its place being taken by the early variety sown broadcast. The *rabi* area throughout the *tarai* is small, and the main product is linseed. It may be expected, however, that the near future will witness an expansion of *rabi* cultivation, for the conditions are gradually changing with the increase of population, the advent of cultivators possessing greater agricultural skill and the slow but certain reclamation of the large culturable area; though at the same time the enervating and unhealthy climate of the tract constitutes a perpetual obstacle.

In the *bangar* the nature of the crops depends on the composition of the soil. In the north, where the rainfall is abundant, and throughout the clay areas rice is the chief staple, the early variety being grown on the higher levels and the late in depressions which may be expected to hold sufficient water. There is no clear line of demarcation between the *tarai* and the northern *bangar*, but further south the *rabi* harvest becomes of increasing importance, till in the lighter soils it includes the main rent-paying crops of the year, such as barley, wheat, gram, oilseeds and poppy. Where *balua* is prevalent, as is the case for some miles on either side of the Rapti and Rohin and in tracts reclaimed from *sal* forest, rice is less common and its place in the *kharif* is taken by maize, *arhar*, sugarcane and the small millets. Bangar.

The *kachhar* produces little but maize and the millets in the *kharif*, for though *arhar* is widely sown in certain parts, the harvest is necessarily of a speculative character, since it is of the highest importance that the crops should be of the early ripening kinds capable of being reaped before the advent of the floods. The *kharif* is in fact of relatively small importance and the cultivators devote all their energy to the *rabi*, which is normally of a high quality and is composed of the principal grain crops and oilseeds. Kachhar

Rice is again the staple crop in the northern portions of the *bhat* and in lowlying areas elsewhere. In the tract of light *dhusi* on the eastern border, between Kindarpatti on the north, Padrauna on the west and Tamkuhi on the south, the chief products are maize and the millets; while further west is the *chauriar*, in which early rice and sugarcane preponderate. The low alluvium of the Great Gandak is locally called *dhab*. This tract suffers much less from floods than the *kachhar*, in spite of the sudden and extensive inundations caused by the river, for the reason that in the *bhat* the autumn crops mature fully a month earlier than in the rest of the district, while at the same time the floods are seldom of long duration, often subsiding before they have caused any appreciable damage. In the *dhab* it is a frequent practice to sow *chena*, early rice and late rice broadcast in the same field, each being cut in succession as it attains maturity. There is also much sugarcane cultivation, the cane being of a Bhat.

species, *sawara*, which is not damaged by submersion. Throughout the *bhat* area the spring harvest is of secondary importance, the yield being inferior to that in the *bangar*, and the crops take from a fortnight to a month more before they ripen. In the *dhab* the presence of *latri* or *kesari* in large quantities indicates a very low standard of cultivation, but elsewhere the products are much the same as in the uplands.

Precarious tracts.

Each of these tracts has peculiar requirements in the matter of rainfall, so that similar meteorological conditions produce by no means similar results throughout the district. The rice lands of the north need good rain for transplanting in July and August, as well as a copious *hathiya* in September and October to bring the crop to perfection. The early rice demands good rain in August, when the crop is coming into ear, whereas the light soil requires moderate rain early in the season. While the later rice tract is independent of the winter rains, the rest of the district is greatly benefited not only by the *hathiya*, which facilitates the *rabi* sowings, but also by the so-called Christmas rains, which are required to mature the crop. Then again the *kachhar* can always get on very well without any rain till Christmas, and frequently prospers without any supplementary precipitation. Unseasonable weather in the early months of the year will often do far more damage in the *kachhar* than imposing floods in the rains, the latter being disastrous only when they follow on a failure of the spring crop. In the *bhat* area the early rice is fairly secure and even the late rice fails only in seasons of exceptional drought, owing to the remarkable capacity of the soil for retaining moisture. For the same reason a heavy rainfall is far more likely to cause damage in the parts where maize and millets are the chief staples than any deficiency in the monsoon, and similarly in the *rabi* wet weather is to be feared as likely to cause rust. Throughout the district the most dangerous period for the spring crops is when the grain is in the ear during February and March, since rain, hail or frost at such a season is certain to result in extensive injury to the harvest.

Harvests.

Of the two main harvests the *kharif* has always been the most important. In 1869-70 the area under autumn crops was 1,175,548 acres as compared with 911,273 sown for the *rabi*, and a similar relation was observed in later years, the averages between 1877-78 and 1888-89 being respectively 1,200,994 and 1,042,861 acres. In the year of settlement the *rabi* area was abnormally large, but even so it failed to equal the *kharif*, and the subsequent extension of tillage has only served to increase the difference, the average for the five years ending with 1907-08 being 1,540,046 acres under autumn and 1,216,087 under spring crops. The relative position, however, varies greatly in different parts of the district. In Maharajganj the *kharif* area is nearly double that of the *rabi*, and an almost equally marked preponderance is to be found in Padrauna. In the Hata tahsil too the *kharif* covers decidedly the larger area; but in Deoria the difference is very slight, while in Gorakhpur and Bansgaon, and especially the latter, owing to the wide expanse of *kachhar*, the *rabi* takes the leading place in all but most exceptional seasons. The total area of each harvest, as well as that occupied by each of the more important crops, in the various tahsils will be found in the appendix, where figures are given for every year from 1897-98*.

Double-cropping.

The area bearing two crops in the year has always been large, and its increase has been even more rapid than that of the total cultivation. The practice of double-cropping extended to 361,404 acres in 1869-70, whereas from 1884-85 to 1887-88 it averaged 463,054, and for the two following decades 606,502 and 677,980 acres. In the last five years the average was no less than 705,662 acres, or 34·2 per cent. of the net area under the plough. This is an unusually high proportion, but it requires some qualification. The figure is highest in the tahsils of Padrauna and Maharajganj, where the standard of husbandry is lowest, and the reason lies in the widespread practice of sowing linseed and other crops broadcast in the wet rice stubble without any further preparation of the tilth. Fully half the *dofasli* area in Maharajganj is under linseed, but elsewhere the place of this staple is commonly taken by the mixture of peas and barley or oilseeds called *kirao*, which flourishes greatly in the rich clay soils. In like manner the *bhat* is well adapted to a second crop, owing to the small amount of labour involved. In

* Appendix, table VI.

the rest of the district the *dofasli* area has expanded far more rapidly than in the north, where double-cropping has always been prevalent, and at the present time the lowest proportion for any single tahsil is some 24 per cent. of the net cultivation in Bansgaon. In Deoria the area has increased by more than 100 per cent. since the last settlement: and there too the quality of such cultivation is very remarkable, since that subdivision contains more irrigated *dofasli* than all the rest of the district. This is due partly to the superior skill and energy of the cultivators in that tract, and partly to the higher efficiency of the spring wells there found, in comparison with the percolation wells of other parts.

Rice. By far the most important of the *kharif* products is rice, for which the district has at all times been celebrated, and on which the prosperity of a large area depends. In both 1878 and 1881 the crop covered some 700,000 acres; but since the latter year a remarkable expansion has occurred, and for the five years ending with 1906-07 the average area under rice was no less than 932,315 acres or 60·5 per cent. of the entire *kharif*. On the other hand the distribution is very uneven, since the proportion is only 27·9 in Deoria as compared with 66·5 per cent. in the Hata tahsil and the surprising figure of 85·9 per cent. in Maharajganj, the last containing nearly one-fourth of the entire rice-land in the district. Though the different species of rice are almost innumerable, there are two well recognised divisions of the crop, comprising the *bhadain* or early rice sown broadcast in the fields and usually cut in the month of Bhadon, and the late *aghani* or transplanted rice ordinarily reaped in the month of Aghan. The latter is by far the more valuable, though at the same time it requires more labour and is also more precarious inasmuch as it occupies the ground for a longer period. The cultivation of late rice postulates an abundance of water, and the area devoted to it is consequently much smaller than that covered by the early variety, amounting in fact to little more than one-third of that sown with the latter, and the bulk of it is confined to the Binayakpur pargana in the extreme north. The rice harvest is always a great event in the agricultural year, and numbers of labourers annually migrate northwards to take part in the reaping; especially in a season of floods, when the loss of the crop in the *kachhar* induces the cultivators of that tract to resort to the northern parganas so as to earn a livelihood till their fields are ready for the *rabi* sowings.

Kodon.

Next in order comes the small millet known as *kodon*, which is extensively grown throughout the district and forms an important item in the food supply of the poorer classes. The present average area is 157,851 acres or 10·2 per cent. of the *kharif*, exclusive of 55,649 acres sown with *kodon* in combination with *arhar*. There has been little change in the area since the last settlement, and the distribution remains the same as before, the crop being most popular in the Padrauna and Gorakhpur tahsils, in which the proportion amounts respectively to 15·4 and 18·4 per cent. of the total *kharif*. A peculiarity of the grain is that when new it often has the effect of a powerful intoxicant, and for this reason it is kept as long as possible: occasionally *kodon* is eaten by landholders and others of the well-to-do classes, who are accustomed to keep the grain stored for ten years or more, the process being considered to improve its flavour.

Maize.

Maize is now a very important staple, at least in some parts of the district, and its cultivation has rapidly increased of late years, the present average of 114,044 acres or 7·4 per cent. of the *kharif* being nearly double the figure recorded in 1888. More than half of this amount comes from the Padrauna tahsil, where maize occupies 18·6 per cent. of the area under autumn crops. It is also popular in Deoria and Gorakhpur, but it flourishes most abundantly in the higher *bhat* lands of the east. The crop is generally sown on a good soil, in which there is a plentiful supply of manure, and its presence, even in relatively small areas, generally betokens stability of cultivation and agricultural prosperity. At the same time it has the great advantage of reaching maturity at an early date, so that it is less affected than other staples by a premature cessation of the rains.

Sugarcane.

A still more valuable product is sugarcane, which covers on an average 97,203 acres or 6·3 per cent. of the *kharif*, and like maize gives excellent results in the *bhat* soil. This fact accounts for its predominance in the Padrauna tahsil, where nearly 40,000 acres are sown annually, while the bulk of the remainder is to be found in Hata and Deoria. Of late years the cultivation of sugarcane has been slowly spreading northwards into Maharajganj, and a large extension in that direction may be confidently predicted within the near future. The crop is one that generally gives a better result than others in a dry year, and it is to this fact that the recent expansion of the cane area may in a large measure be attributed, while its relative absence in the west is due partly to the lighter nature of the soil and partly to the fact that wells are more difficult to construct than in the east and south-east of the upland area.

Arhar. Another important *kharif* staple is *arhar*, which, though sown with the other autumn crops, remains on the ground till the gathering of the spring harvest. By itself it averages no more than 25,958 acres, but far more frequently it is found in combination with *kodon* and less commonly with *juar*, rice and *til*, the mixture of rice and *arhar* being peculiar to this district. In this manner it acts as a kind of insurance against the failure of the rains, for if the rice or *kodon* come to nothing the cultivator at least can count on his *arhar*, since this crop flourishes with very little moisture. The average area under mixed *arhar* crops is shown as 56,871 acres, though this excludes the combination of *arhar* and rice, which is invariably entered as rice only. These mixtures are found almost entirely in the Hata and Deoria tahsils, whereas nearly half the pure *arhar* comes from Maharajganj; the rest being grown principally in Gorakhpur and Bansgaon. The crop attains it greatest luxuriance in the *kachhar*, where frequently it grows to a height of eight or nine feet: but at the same time it is there liable to destruction in years of heavy rainfall, when the same fate attends much of that sown in the *bhat*. It is almost impossible to compare present figures with past, owing to the fact that heavy inundations cause extraordinary variations in the area recorded as sown, since usually young *arhar* submerged or destroyed by floods is not entered in the village papers, and also because different methods of abstracting mixed *arhar* have been in vogue at different periods. On the whole, however, it may safely be asserted that at all events there has been no diminution in the area under this crop.

Indigo.

In the early years of the last century the cultivation of indigo seems to have been quite unimportant, and it was not till 1838 that the crop attracted much attention. The settlement report of that year refers to its successful introduction in the forest grant of Mr. Sym and its cultivation at Babhnauli in pargana Sidhua Jobna. From that time forward the area under indigo showed a rapid and constant increase, and by the time of the seventh settlement amounted to 33,000 acres, in spite of the set-back caused by the Mutiny. Nevertheless the crop even at that time was unpopular with the cultivators, who showed a decided preference for sugarcane and opium, and towards the end of the settlement the area showed a marked decrease, the total in 1888 being only 18,907 acres. The crop was then grown all over the district, save in the parganas of Binayakpur and Hasanpur Maghar. Since the settlement, and especially during the last ten years, the area has decreased with greater rapidity, and in the five years ending with 1906-07, the average was but 8,670 acres, almost entirely grown in the *bhat* tract of Sidhua Jobna and Salempur. The bulk of the indigo is cultivated on behalf of the Babhnauli factory, which is now the only concern of importance. The dye is manufactured both at Babhnauli and at three outworks located at Domath, Baikunthpur and Sapaha. With so variable a product as indigo it would be misleading to give the average outturn of the dye for a term of years, but it may be stated that in a good season the amount of indigo manufactured varies from 2,000 to 2,500 maunds, the whole of which is exported to Calcutta. The decline in cultivation is of course due to the competition of the synthetic dye. The planters have already done much to improve the process of manufacture and further experiments are now being undertaken, while the outturn has been materially increased by the introduction of the Java-Natal variety of indigo, though it yet remains to be seen whether the industry will regain its lost position.

Other crops.

The remaining *kharif* crops are of little importance, the largest area being taken up by *mandua,* one of the small millets, which on an average covers 35,271 acres, principally in the Deoria and Padrauna tahsils. Mention may also be made of *juar,* which is here invariably called *bajra,* grown chiefly in

Padrauna and Hata; the well known *bajra* of other districts, which requires a light soil and little moisture, being seldom seen in these parts. The remaining crops include the pulses called *urd* and *mung*, in Bansgaon and Gorakhpur; garden and miscellaneous produce in Deoria and Padrauna; *juar* grown for fodder in Bansgaon, and the oilseed known as *til* in Maharajganj. There are barely 1,000 acres under hemp, and more than half of this is in Padrauna, while that tahsil and pargana Tilpur grow considerable quantities of turmeric, the garden crops also including cardamums, red pepper, ginger and *pan*. In the immediate neighbourhood of Gorakhpur are fairly extensive market gardens which supply the bazars of the city, while the pineapples of the same neighbourhood have attained some celebrity.

Wheat. Among the *rabi* crops the foremost place is taken by the cereals, and of these the most valuable is wheat. Owing to the confusion introduced by the extensive practice of growing mixed *rabi* crops, it is difficult to establish an exact comparison between former and present figures. In 1878 the recorded area under wheat was 135,574 acres, and by the time of the last settlement this had risen to 215,873, whereas the present average is 153,793 acres or 12·15 per cent. of the entire harvest. It is possible that the cause of the decrease may lie in the growing popularity of *gujai*, a name given to the mixture of wheat and barley, though at the same time it is at least doubtful whether the old returns can be taken as accurate. The portion of wheat is highest in pargana Haveli, where it amounts to 16·17 per cent., and next come the Padrauna and Bansgaon tahsils with 11·12 and 10·9 per cent. respectively; but the crop is to be found all over the district, the wheat of pargana Hasanpur Maghar and of Unaula being especially celebrated. The hard white wheats do not flourish in this district, the best results being obtained with the soft red varieties, for which there is no great demand in the export trade; so that probably the cultivator has found it more profitable to devote his attention to crops more adapted to the climate and subject to a brisk external demand. The *gujai* area is very much greater than that under pure wheat, and at present averages 309,600 acres or 23·3 per cent. of the harvest. The latter figure is largely exceeded in the Deoria tahsil and also in Bansgaon, while pargana Haveli shows no less than 73,000 acres under this combination, although this only represents 20·3 per cent. owing to the enormous extent of *rabi* cultivation in that part of the district. If the old returns can be accepted, there would appear to have been an immense increase in the *gujai* area during recent years, for at the last settlement the total was only 211,875 acres.

Barley by itself occupies 179,229 acres or 14·16 per cent. of the entire *rabi* area, and here again pargana Haveli takes the lead with over 46,000 acres. This gives a proportion of 14·5 per cent.: but higher figures occur in Padrauna and Deoria. Of recent years the decrease in pure barley has been even greater than is the case with wheat, for the returns of the last settlement showed 246,795 acres under the former crop. With regard to the cereals generally it may be noted that at the seventh settlement, about 1865, the total area of wheat and barley, both alone and in combination, was 546,227 acres; the figure rising to 578,008 acres in 1891 and to 674,544 at the last settlement, the increase being attributed mainly to the reclamation of the land from forests. The last year, however, would seem to have been an exceptionally favourable *rabi* season, for between 1878 and 1889 the average area devoted to cereals was only 552,725 acres; so that the subsequent decrease is more apparent than real, while the contraction of the area sown owing to the early cesssation of the rains on more than one occasion during the past five years has also to be taken into account. **Barley.**

Next in order come peas, but these are seldom grown alone, the usual practice being to sow peas in combination with linseed, mustard and occasionally barley, gram or vetches, the mixed crop being called *kirao* or else *jau kirai* when there is a considerable admixture of barley. Altogether it averages 213,588 acres or 18·3 per cent. of the harvest, the highest proportion being 26·7 per cent. in pargana Salempur, while the Bansgaon tahsil shows almost as high a figure. The crop has grown rapidly in popularity, for if the area of 18,826 acres in 1865 was below the mark, the total was at all events no less than 134,004 acres in 1878, whereas ten years later it had risen to 173,472 acres. **Peas.**

Gram.

Another crop of considerable importance is gram, which by itself or mixed with barley occupies a very large area. Sown alone it averages 104,544 acres or 8·2 per cent. of the *rabi* and nearly half of this is to be found in pargana Haveli, where gram is generally grown in the clay soils after the rice harvest. The crop is rarely to be seen in pargana Sidhua Jobna, but elsewhere it is fairly popular, particularly in the Bansgaon tahsil. The mixture of gram and barley called *bijra* averages 73,427 acres or 5·8 per cent. of the total *rabi* area, and its distribution is exactly similar to that of gram sown alone.

Oilseeds.

In the north of the district much land is devoted to the cultivation of oilseeds in the shape of linseed, *tora,* rape and mustard. Of these the first is commonly sown as a second crop after rice, while the others are almost invariably grown with various *rabi* crops, especially cereals. Consequently it is impossible to ascertain the exact area, and the present average of 89,985 acres or 7·1 of the spring harvest refers mainly to linseed, the rest not appearing in the returns. This is further proved by the fact that as much as 43,000 acres was recorded in the Maharajganj tahsil alone, where linseed is a particularly important staple, whereas the oilseeds of the mustard type are to be seen in abundance throughout the district. The total in 1865 was 90,361 acres, and from 1877 to 1889 the average was 107,831, so that it is difficult to account for the sudden rise to 182,245 acres recorded at the last settlement, or to believe that subsequent years have witnessed a great decline in oilseed cultivation.

Poppy.

The cultivation of the poppy for the production of opium seems to have been introduced early in the last century, and it does not appear that this valuable product was of much importance in Buchanan's time. The records of the Salempur and Sidhua Jobna parganas show that from 1827 onwards there was a steady increase in the area under poppy, and though the collector in 1840 expressed a fear that this staple would be ousted by indigo and sugarcane, it continued to maintain its position and from 1860 to 1865 the average area was 15,601 acres, the figure rising to 22,724 in the following five years, while by 1878 it was no less than 27,381 acres. At that time the crop was mainly confined to the holdings of prosperous cultivators in the Padrauna tahsil, but subsequent years have witnessed a radical change. The area dropped to 19,481 acres in 1888 and to 15,877 in 1899, but the average of the last five years has been but 14,050 acres, of which less than 3,000 are in Padrauna; whereas Deoria with over 5,000 acres is the only part of the district in which poppy cultivation can be described as even moderately extensive. It would appear that the best lands are no longer devoted to this crop, possibly owing to the high prices realised for cereals and the absence of any rise in the selling value of opium. It is now grown for the most part by low caste tenants of small means, and this again may account for the diminished outurn; for it is at least significant that the average yield per *bigha* dropped from over six *sers* between 1860 and 1870 to somewhat more than five during the ensuing decade and to less than 3½ *sers* from 1890 to 1900.

Other crops.

Little need be said of the remaining products of the *rabi* harvest. The largest area, some 45,000 acres, is taken up by *masur* or lentils, confined almost wholly to the Maharajganj and Padrauna tahsils. Garden crops, for the most part vegetables, and the miscellaneous food crops, consisting of *latri* and other vetches, oats and *boro* or winter rice, are extensively grown in Padrauna but are comparatively scarce elsewhere; and the same tahsil has a practical monopoly of the spices and condiments, mainly turmeric and chillies, grown during this season. There are some 3,000 acres under tobacco in the Maharajganj, Deoria and Gorakhpur tahsils, while in Deoria and Bansgaon tobacco is produced in insignificant quantities. The tobacco for which the city of Gorakhpur has attained a wide reputation is not a product of this district, but is imported from Tirhut, as much as 35,000 maunds being received in a single year. It is here made up into a smoking mixture called *khamira*, containing various drugs and flavourings, among which the juices of the Gorakhpur pineapple and the Butwal orange are said to be prominent. This *khamira* is well known throughout the United Provinces, and is sometimes exported to places situated far beyond their limits.

Zaid crops.

The *zaid* or intermediate harvest of hot weather crops is of relatively little importance. Of late it would appear to have increased very rapidly, and for the five years ending with 1906-07 it averaged 17,800 acres, the area in the last year rising to 26,714. This increase, however, is probably a sign of unfavourable seasons and is not likely to be permanent; for cultivators will not go to the labour and expense of irrigating a hot weather crop if their stores of grain are sufficient. Rather more than one-third of the area is occupied by the early millet called *chena*, which is grown mainly in the *bhat* soils of Salempur and Sidhua Jobna. Another third is composed of miscellaneous food crops, such as hot weather rice and *sanwan*, principally in the tahsils of Gorakhpur and Bansgaon; and the balance consists for the most part of melons, which are cultivated extensively in the beds of the Rapti and other rivers, particularly in the neighbourhood of the city.

Irrigation. While irrigation in various forms is extensively practised, it must be remembered that in large areas it is either unnecessary or not feasible. Mention has been made of the difficulties attending irrigation in the *bhat* tract, where the soil is too friable for the construction of any but masonry wells. The same quality accounts for the rapid absorption of water in large quantities, resulting in much waste of labour and excessive loss of water in the channels from the well to the field. Moreover irrigation is rather dangerous owing to the prevalence of rust, so that in this part of the district artificial watering is practically limited to the poppy lands and garden crops in the immediate vicinity of the village site. Similarly there is very little irrigation in the *kachhar* save in very abnormal seasons, for the natural moisture in the soil is ordinarily sufficient for the needs of the *rabi* crop. If water be required, it is obtained in some places from lakes and tanks, while in parts earthen wells are practicable; though as a rule the sandy nature of the subsoil forbids their construction, and masonry wells are seldom sunk save for domestic purposes, their cost being altogether out of proportion to the advantages derived on the rare occasions on which they might be utilised for irrigating the crops. Again in the great rice tract of the north, where little attention is paid to the scanty *rabi*, irrigation is unneeded except for the late rice, and this is watered by means of channels from the *tarai* streams. The returns of the last settlement show that of the entire clay area some 83 per cent. was never irrigated, so that it is obvious that the great bulk of the irrigated area is confined to the *doras* and *balua* lands. Of these the latter are relatively unimportant, for not only is the area small, but its sandy character renders irrigation unprofitable owing to the frequent and copious waterings required. The actual extent of irrigation in former days cannot be determined, owing to the usual practice of classifying irrigable land as irrigated. It was on this account that the returns of 1869-70 show an irrigated area of 907,432 acres or 59·5 per cent. of the net cultivation, a proportion which could not be attained under any conceivable circumstances. Further, it is useless to rely on the figures of any single year, owing to the variation in the requirements of different seasons, and consequently a fair idea of the irrigated area can be derived only from the averages of a more or less prolonged period. Thus for the four years ending with 1887-88 the actually irrigated area averaged 517,887 acres or 28·42 per cent. of the total cultivation, and the corresponding figures for the ensuing decade were 510,166 acres and 29·51 per cent. From 1898-99 to 1907-08 the average was 656,477 acres or 32·14 per cent. of the area under the plough, the maximum being 736,534 acres or 37·24 per cent. in 1900-01. From these figures it is clear that irrigation has made a rapid advance of late, and has more than kept pace with the extension of tillage. Since the last settlement the improvement has been most marked in the northern tahsils. In the last five years the general average for the district was 660,221 acres or 32 per cent. of the cultivated area, the Deoria and Hata tahsils coming first with 50·8 and 50·7 per cent. respectively, while Bansgaon and Gorakhpur follow close behind. The lowest figure is 12·1 per cent. in Padrauna, as is only to be expected. Among individual parganas Silhat takes the lead with the remarkably high percentage of 62·06, and at the other end of the scale come Tilpur with 6·6 and Binayakpur with only 3·2 per cent.

Sources of supply.

Irrigation is derived from wells, rivers, tanks, lakes and other natural reservoirs. The most noticeable feature in the extension of irrigation is the increase in the area watered from wells, which are in every respect preferable to other sources, inasmuch as the latter are apt to fail in seasons when they are most in request. From 1884-85 to 1887-88 the average area supplied by wells was 223,864 acres, rising to 228,216 and to 312,939 in the two succeeding decades, whereas for the last five years ending with 1907-08 the figure was 348,438 acres or 52·6 per cent. of the total irrigation, the largest amount in any one year being 497,290 acres or 81 per cent. in 1906-07, which illustrates the capabilities of the district in a time of stress. Well irrigation is, however, confined for the most part to the south of the district, especially pargana Salempur. The returns do not differentiate other sources, but the bulk of the irrigation coming under this head is derived from tanks, which are extremely numerous.

Wells. Throughout the district the water level is high, averaging about 15 feet from the surface in the *bangar* and very much less in the eastern tracts. For this reason the only difficulty to be encountered in sinking wells lies in the nature of the subsoil, and where circumstances are favourable immense numbers of earthen wells are excavated for temporary use in dry years with little labour or expense. These shallow wells are worked in almost all cases by means of the *dhenkli* or lever, the *mot* or leathern bucket being practically unknown, so that bullocks are not required for irrigation purposes. In ordinary years masonry wells preponderate, and these in most cases are filled by percolation, the sandy subsoil extending to a great depth. Such wells yield but a limited supply, and this accounts for the use of the *dhenkli*; since with bullocks at work the well would be emptied rapidly at considerable risk to the cylinder. Spring wells are confined to a few localities, such as the greater part of the Deoria tahsil, the tract south of Hata and a narrow strip between Gola and Barhalganj; and it is noteworthy that the parganas of Salempur, Silhat and Dhuriapar, which comprise these areas, possess half the total number of masonry wells in the whole district. Such spring wells are rare in the north and west, though possibly the development of the more backward parganas may lead to the discovery of fresh localities in which they can be constructed. The usual form of masonry well is a plain cylinder of burned bricks put together without mortar, and such wells, when of narrow diameter, cost from Rs. 70 to Rs. 80 and are fairly durable. The *indara* or large well necessitates the use of mortar and is mainly confined to the village site, its cost amounting to several hundred rupees. The *kachcha* or earthen well is merely a shallow pit, lasting only for a single season and is filled up before the *kharif* is sown. It goes by the name of *chaunrs* and is generally lined with a *dol* or cylinder of bamboo wicker-work to protect the sides. In 1869 there were 18,114 masonry wells used for irrigation, and twenty years later the total was 24,000, but in 1907-08 the figure stood at 40,344, of which 32,147 were put to actual use during the year.

Tanks and jhils.

Tanks for irrigation are as common here as in any other part of the eastern districts. They are the usual square or rectangular excavations dug down to water level, the spoil earth forming high banks which in many cases are planted with trees. These tanks are often of considerable size, and they supply a very large area, averaging some 273,000 acres, though this figure must be accepted with some qualification owing to the confusion that often arises between artificial tanks and natural pools. Lakes and *jhils* are extensively utilised in certain parts of the district, particularly the parganas of Haveli, Silhat, Unaula and Dhuriapar. As is the case with tanks, the water is conducted along narrow channels, and from these raised to the level of the fields by *beris* or swing-baskets of wicker-work in the manner well known throughout the United Provinces.

Rivers.

The larger rivers flow at too great a depth below the surface of the surrounding country to be of any use for irrigation, but in places the subsidiary channels and backwaters, called *sotas* and *dohars*, can be utilised when the floods subside; and for this purpose the water is sometimes held up by means of earthen dams and raised to the required level by lifts worked with *beris*. In the extreme north of the district the Tharus have elaborated a small system of canals from the *tarai* streams of the Binayakpur and Tilpur parganas, the water being collected by means of earthen embankments and conducted to the fields along shallow channels called *kulas*. Of late years, however, the extent of this form of irrigation has been much reduced, owing to objections raised by the Nepalese authorities to the building of the dams, while the supply of water has diminished with the construction of similar embankments by the cultivators in Nepal. Of more importance is the canal system on the Lehra estate, now held by Mr. J. J. Holdsworth. There a substantial dam provided with sluice-gates has been built over the Poh in its upper reaches, so as to form the large Srinagar reservoir, from which a series of irrigation channels carry the water to various parts of the estate. Besides this main work there are several smaller enbankments, intended to hold up water in depressions, and these canals are of the greatest value for the transplanted rice and the *rabi* sowings. It has recently been proposed to take a large canal out of the Great Gandak at Arjunahi in the extreme north-east of the district, the contemplated line running as nearly direct as possible to Nichlaul and thence along the watershed between the Rohin and the Little Gandak. By this means it would provide water, should the project prove feasible, to all the *bangar* between the Piyas and Rohin on the west, the Rapti on the south and the Little Gandak on the east, while at the same time it might afford a perennial supply to the canals in the Saran district.

Early famines. Gorakhpur has generally been fortunate in playing a very inconspicuous part in the history of the famines which from time to time have devastated northern India. On few occasions has the failure of the rainfall been so complete as to put a stop to agricultural operations, while often acute famine elsewhere has been reflected in this district only in high prices and distress among certain classes. Of late years the effects of drought in other parts of Inda have been felt more severely here than was formerly the case, owing to the general equalisation of prices as the result of railway construction and the development of means of communication; but this was not unknown before the days of railways, for in 1873 the famine in Bengal and the high rates there prevailing induced a too extensive export of grain from Gorakhpur with disastrous results to all but the dealers. Regarding the early famines mentioned by the Musalman historians we have hardly a single reference to this district, either because it escaped such calamities or for the reason that it was too remote to be taken into account. Vague tradition tells of a terrible famine in the days of Aurangzeb, when no rain fell for two years and the Rapti ran almost dry. This may be identical with the general famine of 1661, though on that occasion grain was imported to Dehli from Bengal, and it might therefore be presumed that Gorakhpur was untouched. Another famine undoubtedly occurred in 1769-70, when even the wild beasts were affected, and it is said that the depredations of the famished tigers in the vicinity of Bhauapar caused the terror-stricken inhabitants to evacuate that village. The partial failure of the autumn crop of 1768 and of the succeeding *rabi* caused prices to rise to unprecedented heights, and distress was worst in Bihar and the northern districts of Bengal, in which province more than one-third of the population was computed to have perished. It is impossible to say in what degree Gorakhpur suffered during the great famine of 1783, but in all probability the district was not unscathed, since the distress was general and acute throughout the province of Benares.

The record of famines during the first half-century of British rule is happily meagre, and on no occasion was anything worse than scarcity experienced. The first drought was that of 1803, when the rains ceased in the middle of August, destroying the late rice and injuring the other crops, while fears were entertained for the *rabi* sowings. Matters improved with a fall of rain at the end of September, and the situation was saved: the district was then sparsely populated, and the absence of actual want is shown by the fact that large quantities of grain were exported into Oudh. The revenue was collected with little difficulty and no remissions were found necessary. Of still less importance was the scarcity of 1809, and in 1814 the district seems to have been untouched. Such too was the case in 1819 and in 1825, when scarcity was felt in the west of the province. The general famine of 1837-38 made itself felt to some extent in the high prices which then prevailed, gram rising from 60 to 15 *sers*, and wheat from 33 to 14 *sers* for the rupee; but no relief measures were undertaken, and the remissions of revenue amounted only to Rs. 208 for this district and Basti. The rainfall was

1801 to 1870.

very short in several parts of the district in 1860, but the tract was quite unaffected by the famine which raged in the western divisions, nor did the drought of 1864-65 have any more serious consequences than a rise in prices. and an increased volume of emigration eastwards. In 1868-69 Gorakhpur and Basti escaped almost entirely and were beyond the scope of relief operations: the early rice failed, but the late rice was saved by the exertions of the cultivators in digging wells and utilizing the resources afforded by the lakes and *jhils*, and a very fair *rabi* was harvested. Prices were remarkably high, and this must have affected certain classes of the population: and some difficulty was experienced in collecting the revenue, though no remissions were ultimately found necessary.

1873-74. The first real famine which visited the district was that of 1873-74. On this occasion an unusual shortage of the rainfall followed on a series of indifferent seasons, which had left little grain in store. The difference between this year and 1868-69 was that the rice crop failed far more extensively, since September was almost rainless, and a similar failure occurred in Nepal and Bihar, while the same causes involved a very serious contraction of the *rabi* area, more than a third of the land lying fallow. The rains of 1873 commenced a fortnight later than usual and stopped prematurely, the average fall for the entire district being 32 inches. Sowings were delayed and eventually the crops withered, less than one-third of the early rice being harvested; whereas the late rice was wholly destroyed, for the tracts which suffered most from drought were the northern and eastern parganas. The cultivators displayed the greatest energy in preparing and irrigating the land for the *rabi* sowings, but no rain fell till the beginning of February; even then, however, it was of immense value, and fields which had been partially irrigated yielded a bumper harvest. The total outturn was about half the normal, for little gram, linseed and *masur* were sown, while peas and *arhar* suffered from frost in January and from hailstorms in March. The produce in the Maharajganj tahsil was extremely scanty, many localities obtaining no more than one-eighth of the usual amount. Such conditions inevitably mean distress, and the pressure of high prices was greatly enhanced by the exportation of grain to Bengal, which continued till the rapid rise of prices in January 1874 caused a cessation, the end of that month witnessing the first importations from Oudh and the west. The constant rise in prices led to increased emigration towards the end of 1873; but no relief measures were considered necessary till in the middle of January a poorhouse was opened in the city, where distress was most prevalent and visible. Later in the month relief works were started in the north on the Lotan and Nichlaul roads, while in the vicinity of Gorakhpur there was a work on the Fyzabad road, and in the city itself the improvement of the Bagladah tank was commenced. At the same time the planters and *zamindars* opened numerous private works, and the increasing distress which accompanied the upward movement of prices led to the starting of fresh works in the Bansgaon tahsil on the Tucker *bandh* and the Taraina bridge, followed in March by similar works on the Gola road and on the tank near the jail. In April the discovery that labourers were migrating from the Deoria tahsil to Bansgaon induced the authorities to open a small work on the Kurma embankment near Deoria. Simultaneously a hospital was started for the sick and debilitated at Kauriram, and poorhouses were established at the various tahsil headquarters and at Gola and Mithaura. The advent of harvest led to a slight fall in prices; but there was little mitigation of distress, and in April the attendance at the works actually increased. It appeared that in the Bansgaon and Maharajganj tahsils many persons resorted to the works after harvest as a means of earning money during the slack season, and in consequence the rates of wages were reduced. None the less the numbers continued to increase, though the newcomers were unmistakably better off than those who had come at an earlier period. The inrush was checked to some extent by closing the work on the Gola road in the second week of May, but no marked reduction occurred till rain fell on the 30th of that month. Soon afterwards the rains set in vigorously, and all the works were closed by the 10th of June, a few indigent persons being maintained in workhouses at Gorakhpur, Kasia and Mithaura, of which that at Kasia was the last to close on the 22nd of September. The total expenditure on relief works was Rs. 3,20,445 and the aggregate attendance was 5,667,145, counted by daily units: the highest daily attendance for any month being 78,054 in May, though for one week in April the figure exceeded 100,000. The chief works were those on the Lotan and Nichlaul roads and the Tucker *bandh*. In the north distress was caused by the failure of the rice, the only staple of importance. In Gorakhpur the preponderance of artizans and day-labourers among the city and suburban population accounted for the necessity for relief; and in Bansgaon the reason seems to have been the lack of employment for field-labourers, since in that part of the district most of the land is cultivated by coparcenary communities of proprietors. The poorhouses supported 141,981 persons, of whom a third were children, at a cost of Rs. 5,865, raised principally by subscriptions. In the workhouses 103,015 persons, chiefly women and children, were fed at a cost of Rs. 7,353 and were employed in various occupations such as weaving, rope-making, spinning and basket-work. In addition outdoor relief was given to a small number of poor but respectable women in Gorakhpur, chiefly of Musalman families. For the agriculturists an arrangement was made with the Nepalese authorities by which *jarhan* rice seed could be imported under a system of passes, and advances to the extent of Rs. 91,471 were given for seed. Further advances were made to certain grain merchants and contractors, free of interest, on condition of their storing grain at fixed centres. In this manner Rs. 2,30,348 were advanced and 100,000 maunds of grain were collected, especially in Maharajganj; but none of the grain was purchased, and the dealers were released from their contracts, though several suffered considerable loss owing to the fall of prices when the *kharif* of 1874 was assured. Half the revenue for the year was remitted in the Maharajganj tahsil, but elsewhere the demand was eventually collected in full, the total loss on this account being Rs. 66,111.

1877-78. The famine of 1877-78 was less serious and extensive. The late rice was saved in the north, but the early rice was an almost entire failure in the south and west, the tracts most affected being the Bansgaon and Hata tahsils, excepting pargana Shahjahanpur. The classes which suffered most were the artizans, weavers and day-labourers, and in the cold weather much distress was felt, necessitating relief measures. On the 1st of January 1878 a work was opened on the Lotan road, but the daily average attendance for that month was only 338. In the beginning of February a poorhouse was opened, as well as certain municipal works, while on the road the figure rose to 2,347 daily for that month, dropping to 1,957 in March. The decline was caused by the approach of harvest, which caused a great improvement, though the crop was indifferent, wheat being fair, while barley was very small in grain and the gram did badly. The Lotan road work was closed at the end of March, but the municipal works remained open for some time; the daily attendance averaging 628 in April, 404 in May and 529 in June, after which it again rose to 1,307 in July, though the demand for labour in the fields was fairly general. As field work decreased in August numbers came forward for employment on relief works, the average for the month being 804 daily; but in September the works were closed, though poorhouse relief, given at Gorakhpur and nine other places in the district, was continued till the beginning of November. The total number of persons employed on relief works was 160,739, of whom more than half were women, and the cost was Rs. 10,708. The famine on this occasion was of a strictly local character, though the failure of the crops was almost general, the northern parganas alone escaping. The revenue was collected in full, and the distress was limited to a few classes who suffered much from the extraordinarily high prices then prevailing.

Scarcity was not again experienced till the failure of the rains in 1896, which caused much anxiety in August, though a subsequent fall saved a portion of the *kharif*, at least in parts of the district, for the rain was unevenly distributed and certain tracts suffered greatly. To meet the needs of the situation advances to the amount of Rs. 1,92,214 were given for the excavation of wells and the purchase of seed, and thanks to this timely aid an excellent *rabi* harvest was secured. The high range of prices, however, rendered necessary gratuitous relief and the establishment of poorhouses in the distressed tracts, comprising the tahsils of Gorakhpur, Bansgaon and Hata, as well as part of Maharajganj. Five test works opened between the 20th of De- **1896-97.**

cember and the 6th of January failed to attract many workers, but on the 6th of January famine was declared and a week later the first regular relief work was started. Four more were added by the end of the month, and by May the number had risen to 23. At the end of March all works were converted from the Famine Code system to the new intermediate or piece-work system, which at once caused a reduction in the attendance. In May and June, when the closure of the works was imminent, Rs. 80,000 were distributed for the purchase of seed and cattle, while the advent of the monsoon of 1897 removed all further anxiety, the ensuing harvest being one of the best ever garnered. The works consisted principally in raising roads and embankments and in deepening existing tanks: they afforded employment to 3,042,945 persons counted by daily units, the highest daily attendance being 31,183 in the last week of February. Poorhouses were maintained at Gorakhpur, Gola, Barhaj, Maharajganj, Kauriram, Bridgmanganj and Kasia. These remained open till the 15th of September 1897, and the total amount expended on these poorhouses and on other gratuitous relief was Rs. 1,40,000. In addition a large amount was provided from private sources, by which the Gorakhpur and Barhaj poorhouses were at first maintained, and the local committee expended Rs. 3,720 on these objects and subsequently distributed blankets to the value of Rs. 1,156 and Rs. 1,138 for seed.

1905-07. Heavy floods in 1906, following on a series of indifferent harvests, caused much distress in the *kachhar* tracts. The *rabi* of 1905 was severely damaged by frost, and in the next year the crop was injured by excessive rain as it was reaching maturity, while the *kharif* in 1903 and 1905 had suffered much from floods. Prices were already very high, when incessant rain for 25 days in 1906 ruined the *kharif* in the *kachhar* and the *dhab*, the area affected being some 800 square miles in extent, and the distress was greatest in the valleys of the Rapti and great Gandak. At the same time the heavy and continuous rain did much harm in the light *bhat* tract in the south-east of the Padrauna tahsil, where maize, the principal crop of those parts, yielded little or no grain. The first measure of relief was the distribution of advances to the amount of Rs. 3,22,293 before the beginning of November, and this was followed by the establishment of poorhouses at Tamkuhi, Kindarpatti and Gorakhpur. The only work undertaken was the construction of the long embankment from the pontoon bridge to Kuin on the east bank of the Rapti, for elsewhere there was a large demand for labour in the fields. When the heavy rain ceased little more fell till February 1907, but the *rabi* area was greater than usual and an immense amount of irrigation was carried out. Relief ceased with the arrival of the *rabi* harvest and the consequent fall in prices. The works had been undertaken through the agency of contractors and consequently no statistics are available to show the numbers employed; but it is noteworthy that the distress was much less than in 1897, although the limit of prices then reached was far surpassed. The revenue demand was suspended to the amount of Rs. 1,91,220, but the whole of this was eventually realised.

Prices.

Unfortunately there are no extant records of prices in this district prior to the Mutiny, with the exception of a few scattered references. It is certain that in years of normal plenty the rates in the beginning of the nineteenth century were very low when judged by modern standards, though the early development of water-borne traffic with the eastern markets tended to steady prices, which do not appear at any time to have reached the extraordinarily low levels recorded in Gonda and other more remote districts. In the ten years prior to 1860 the cheapest rates were those of 1854, when wheat sold at 28 *sers* to the rupee, rice at 26·6, barley at 43·9 and gram at 40·7 *sers*. From 1861 onwards official returns are available, and from these some idea may be obtained of the general tendency of prices, the better by taking averages of decennial periods, so as to eliminate as far as possible the effects of abnormal seasons and unusual influences. From 1861 to 1865 prices remained lower than at any subsequent period, the averages in the case of the principal food grains being 26·19 *sers* of common rice, 25·93 of wheat, 37·29 of barley, 23·95 of *arhar* and 28·61 of gram. The following decade showed a great rise, though famines in 1868-69 and 1873-74 had a very marked effect on the averages, which were 18·93 *sers* for rice, 17·89 for wheat, 25·85 for barley, 18·55 for *arhar* and 22·28 for gram. Rates became much easier in 1875 and the following year, but the prolonged scarcity which ensued sent prices once more up to famine levels, much higher indeed than was the case during the worst months of 1874. By 1880, however, the market recovered, and two or three years of unusual plenty ensued, prices being lower that at any time since 1865. The averages for the decade ending with 1885 were consequently somewhat lower than in the preceding period, rice selling for 17·5, wheat for 18·18, barley for 29·6, *arhar* for 19·15 and gram for 24·52 *sers* to the rupee. In 1886 prices rose everywhere, and the year marks an epoch in their history; for though the reason has never been satisfactorily explained, it seems that various causes produced a simultaneous effect, such as the extension of communications, the consequent development of the export trade, and the fall in the price of silver. In any case the result was that rates took a decided step upwards, from which they have never descended in subsequent years. The practical effect of this change was the raising of the normal level, and in later years the only variations were those due to famine and the state of the external markets; for with the development of the railway system the Gorakhpur rates became practically identical with those prevailing throughout the United Provinces, the cost of railway freight alone differentiating various localities. From 1886 to 1895 the only change occurred with the bad seasons in the second half of the decade, the averages being 14·67 *sers* for rice, 13·92 for wheat, 20·75 for barley, 19·7 for *arhar* and 20·43 for gram. The next ten years opened with a famine, during which the rates rose to an unprecedented height. They remained high till 1900, owing to scarcity elsewhere, but the next four years witnessed a great improvement as the result of the magnificent harvests that were reaped throughout the country, though at the same time they never fell to the rates prevailing before 1886 and in 1905 an extensive failure of the *rabi* caused a stringency in the market; the average for the ten years being 13·02 *sers* of rice, 13·93 of wheat, 19·58 of barley, 18·37 of *arhar* and 16·9 of gram to the rupee. Subsequent seasons have been so unfavourable that the rise in prices may be regarded as abnormal, and it is but reasonable to suppose that a return to fair conditions will entail a fall in prices, though it is a generally accepted rule that after a rise due to scarcity the recovery is never complete, but that the normal standard remains permanently heightened. In 1907-08 the rates were far higher than ever known before, in spite of the relative immunity of the district from famine, and the permanent effect on the market yet remains to be seen. As it is, the rise in the past 45 years has been sufficiently remarkable, amounting on the whole to 18 per cent. from 1861 to 1885 and to 46 per cent. from the former year to 1905, an enhancement which has had an immense effect on the economic condition of the district, especially in the case of the landowners and tenants, who have derived incalculable benefit from the increased value of their produce.

Throughout the district wages rule much lower than those prevailing in the western parts of the United Provinces, the scale resembling that of the eastern districts generally. Early records of wages are not available, but it would appear that from 1858 to 1868 the remuneration of field-labourers remained at the same level, varying from six to eight pice daily, although cash wages were relatively rare. In 1878 the higher rate generally prevailed, though more usually labourers were paid partly in cash and partly in grain. At the present time the general average for the district is from six to eight pice, though in rare instances more is given, while payment in grain is of approximately the same value, varying from two to three *sers*. In practice cash remuneration takes the form of the so-called Gorakhpuri pice, and amounts from 5 to 10 of these coins daily, the equivalents in Government currency being one and two annas. The rate depends on the locality and the nature of the work performed, wages being generally higher in the north, where labour is less abundant, while digging and irrigation with the large wooden shovel used for distributing the water are paid more highly than weeding and water-drawing. The lowest wage of one anna is probably paid only to regular retainers of the *zamindar*, who gives them constant employment throughout the year, and supplements the cash remuneration with various extras, such as a daily dole of grain, a blanket in the cold weather, or a few maunds of grain at harvest. The heavy work entailed no Wages.

the latter occasion receives specially liberal pay, but this is usually in kind, at any rate in part. When paid wholly in kind, the reaper ordinarily receives every sixteenth sheaf. The rates in the case of skilled labourers appear to have undergone no change of late, varying from Rs. 6 to Rs. 9 per mensem; but such rates apply only to the rural tracts. In the city the personal element usually determines the wage and the rates are much higher, a really skilled artizan earning from Rs. 15 to Rs. 20 in the workshops of the railway company.

Weights and measures.

The local standards of weights and measures are extremely complicated, to a greater extent perhaps than in any other district of the United Provinces. This result is due to several causes, of which the foremost is the introduction of an unusual element in the currency in the shape of the so-called Gorakhpuri pice, which is still current here and in other tracts adjoining the Nepal boundary. These pice, which are tokens rather than coins, consisting of small billets, roughly square in shape, cut from a narrow flat bar of copper and innocent of any inscription or device, are minted at Butwal in Nepal, and for a long time, even subsequent to the introduction of the Company's pice, were the only small coins current outside Gorakhpur city. This state of things continued till some twenty years ago, and even to-day they are still the most popular form of currency outside the larger towns. In 1875, during the famine, it was actually found necessary to import a supply from Butwal for local needs, while it is narrated of a certain district officer, desirous of popularising the orthodox Government coin and redeeming it from the slight cast upon it by the shapeless lumps brought from Nepal, that he passed an order to the effect that all officials should in future draw a certain proportion of their pay in copper. Unfortunately no conclusive result was obtained from this interesting, though undoubtedly unpopular, experiment in forcing a particular currency into circulation; for no long time expired before the matter came to the ears of the Local Government and the order was promptly rescinded. The Gorakhpuri pice varies in weight and value. It would appear that at one time it was worth half the Company's pice, since the latter invariably goes by the name of *dabal paisa*; but if 128 of the Butwal coins ever went to a rupee, the value has certainly gone up of late, for the common ratio is 80 pice to a rupee at the present time, though occasionally, and more often in the outlying tracts, exchange drops to 100 or more. In the rural area wages are almost universally calculated in *kachcha* pice, and these fluctuations in their value cause much inconvenience to planters and other employers of labour. The variation in the weight too has similarly confusing results. Throughout the district local standards of weight are in general use, and the Government *ser* is seldom adopted save at railway stations, the octroi posts and the jail. Now the ultimate unit of weight is the *ganda* or handful, and this is here a group of four; but the group may consist of four Gorakhpuri pice or else of four rupees. In the latter case we obtain an exact standard of weight, but in the former there is no uniformity, although generally 100 pice are equivalent to 92 rupee. The local *ser* consists of a varying number of *gandas*, which varies from village to village, and even in the same bazar there may be one standard for sugar and onions, a second for salt and oil, a third for spices and brassware, and so forth. Matters are further complicated by the presence of other standards besides the *ser*, in the shape of the *sei* and the *raziya*. The *sei* is a real measure of weight, but the *raziya* is properly speaking a measure of capacity and is used only for grain. The various *raziyas* in use are, however, commonly expressed in their equivalent weight of pice, though strictly a *raziya* of wheat would not weigh exactly the same as one of rice: but the measure is common only in the north of the district, and in all probability it was at first employed solely in the case of rice, the great staple of that tract. At the last settlement it was ascertained by enquiry that altogether 46 different *sers, seis* and *raziyas* were in existence, apart from the *lambari* or Government standard. They varied from a *ser* of $8\frac{1}{2}$ *gandas* of pice, whose equivalent is but $6\frac{2}{11}$ *chhataks* in standard measure, to a *raziya* of 44 *gandas* of pice, which weighs two Government *sers*; but these two extremes occur only in the Padrauna tahsil, and the latter is restricted to a single bazar. Between the two limits is to be found an ascending scale of varying standards, differing from one another perhaps by a mere quarter of a *ganda* or in the fact that the *ganda* of one bazar is reckoned in pice and that of another in rupees. The *ser* of Gorakhpur city is a definite measure, consisting of 36 *gandas* of rupees or 144 *tolas.* As usual 40 *sers* go to the maund, whatever their weight, but in the case of the *sei* the scale is different, 16 *seis* making one *mani,* while 16 *manis* make a *gon.*

Measures of area are perhaps more simple, since the variations in the local *bigha* are generally restricted to particular parganas, while the two northern parganas of Binayakpur and Tilpur have a single measure in common, and the same may be said of the three parganas of Unaula, Chillupar and Bhauapar. As the remaining eight have each their own standards, there are ten local *bighas* in use in various parts of the district. The difference in the several cases is immense, the *bigha* ranging from 1,883 square yards in Unaula and its neighbours to 4,400 square yards in Binayakpur and Tilpur. The size of the *bigha* depends on the length of the *jarib* or chain which forms the side. This generally consists of 20 *lathas,* and the length of the *latha* is five *haths* or cubits. Reckoning the cubit at its accepted length of 18 inches, the *bigha* would be of 2,500 square yards, which is roughly the mean between the various standards, though no single local *bigha* approaches this area very closely. In simple measures of length the villagers usually give the term *bigha* to the *jarib,* and this is from 40 to 50 yards. One-fourth of this amount is called a *manda,* and one-twentieth is the *biswa,* in lineal measure generally termed a *khatta.* The local *kos* is of two miles, and half this distance is a *dhab* or mile, while the half mile is styled *pao bhar* or a quarter *kos.*

Interest. The prevailing rates of interest are much the same as those ruling in all the rural tracts of the United Provinces. In the city the rate depends largely on the nature of the transaction. Petty cash loans for short periods ordinarily carry interest at one anna in the rupee per mensem, which works out at the extortionate rate of 75 per cent. per annum, though such loans are rarely of long duration and considerable risk is involved, since personal credit is the only security. When larger amounts are advanced under the same conditions the rate falls to 24 per cent., whereas if jewellery or valuables are given in pledge the prevalent interest is Re. 1-9-0 per cent. monthly or 18¾ per cent. for the year. The interest on a simple mortgage given by a moneylender ranges from 16 to 24 per cent., according to the circumstances of the borrower. In the villages the great bulk of transactions consists in advances of grain for seed, and these are repaid at the common rate of *sawai* or 25 per cent., though sometimes the old *deorhi* rate of 50 per cent. is still exacted when the risk is unusually heavy.

Village banks.

With the object of securing easier rates to agriculturists and others, and to free them from the trammels of indebtedness in which they are so frequently involved, attempts have recently been made to introduce banks on the co-operative credit system. The District Bank, Ld., at Gorakhpur was started in August 1906 and is registered under Act X of 1904. During the first nine months of its existence 75 village societies were affiliated and 348 individual shareholders were gained, the former receiving loans at 12½ and the latter at 15 per cent., while the amounts advanced were Rs. 30,575 and Rs. 15,825 respectively. The working expenses were only Rs. 464, and though the season was far from favourable, the bank experienced no difficulty in recovering the loans and the interest accruing thereon. Primarily the bank is agricultural in character, but money is advanced for other purposes. The profit for the year was Rs. 743, enabling a dividend of 5 per cent. to be distributed, and so far as it is possible to judge from the short period of its existence, the prospects are very satisfactory. It has been noted as a promising sign that the village moneylenders regard the work of the bank with disfavour, and in some cases have refused to have any dealings with borrowers from the institution. The Kasia Central Bank, Ld., is somewhat older, having been started as the Kasia Agricultural Bank in 1902, when working capital was raised by the sale of 6 per cent. debentures. Loans were given to cultivators at the rate of one pice per rupee per mensem or 18¾ per cent. per annum, and in the first year Rs. 1,043 were advanced to 120 persons, whereas in the second the figures rose to Rs. 2,261 and 262 persons, and in the third year 377 persons borrowed Rs. 2,900. In 1906 the bank was converted into a limited liability concern under Act X of 1904 and capital was raised by the issue of Rs. 10 shares, of which 7,478 were issued before the list was closed. Of this sum, however, only one-fifth was paid up, but between the 1st of April 1906 and the 30th of June 1907 a further sum of Rs. 37,000 was raised for use as working capital by means of debentures, and loans were obtained from Government and various banks. The system adopted in this concern is that of lending money only to members of affiliated village societies, the latter consisting of not less than ten persons in each case, who hold themselves jointly and severally responsible for all loans contracted by members of the society. From the 1st of July 1907 the rate of interest was reduced to 2½ pies per rupee monthly, and this resulted in a greatly enhanced demand for money, exceeding the capacity of the supply. There are at present about 150 affiliated socities, and the work done by the bank may be estimated from the fact that between March 1906 and July 1907 the sum of Rs. 64,713 was advanced to 3,081 persons. The working expenses for the year were Rs. 1,430, and a dividend of 10 per cent. was declared. In addition to the co-operative credit institutions, there are two ordinary joint-stock banks at headquarters. One is the Gorakhpur Bank, Ld., started in 1895 with a capital of three lakhs and the other is the Kayasth Trading and Banking Company of more recent date. Both are in a flourishing condition, but in neither case has it been found necessary to increase the initial capital.

Manufactures.

With few exceptions the manufactures of the district are limited to the production of the simple necessities of rural life, and in these industries there is little or nothing which calls for mention. There is no fine weaving as in Azamgarh and Fyzabad, and the Julahas produce merely coarse *garha* and *tat* for local consumption, while at Gorakhpur *dhusa*, a mixed fabric of cotton and wool, is woven to a small extent. The pottery too is perfectly plain and decoration is unknown, and glass is not manufactured here. Metal vessels are for the most part imported, though there are a few brass-workers at Gorakhpur, while Padrauna has a local celebrity for its vessels of the alloy known as *phul*. The principal maker has a large establishment and sends his goods as far afield as Ballia, but the material is a good deal more expensive than ordinary brass and its sale is consequently restricted. As in the other districts north of the Ghagra, wicker and basket-work are turned out in considerable quantities, but there is no export trade in these articles. A small but almost unique industry is carried on at Gorakhpur in embroidering *sabar* leather. There are but two or three families employed in this manner, and the demand for the products is merely local, though the industry may be described as flourishing. The skins of various deer, *sambhar, chital, parha* and *nilgai*, are tanned a rich reddish brown with *sal* bark, the outer surface being soft like velvet. The leather is then embroidered with coloured silks and sometimes finished off with a gilt edge. The commonest articles made from it are small round pillow-cases, 12 or 15 inches long, embroidered with appropriate mottoes in Persian, and these cost from eight annas to a rupee; while table-cloths, chair-covers and praying-carpets, called *asani* and *jainamaz*, for Hindu and Musalman use are also made, the last costing from Rs. 6 to Rs. 10. In every case the colours are somewhat gaudy and the design conventional, but the result is not ineffective. Mention has been made of the tobacco industry of Gorakhpur and also of indigo. Another speciality of the district is the manufacture of soap, which has long been established at Lar in tahsil Deoria. This soap is made principally from a grey earth called *khari mitti*, which is imported, the amount delivered at Lar Road station in 1906-07 being 2,369 maunds, while in the same year 2,150 maunds of soap were despatched from that place. There is but little sale locally, the bulk of the soap going to Nepal, where it is said that the Dhobi is non-existent and that the inhabitants are consequently glad of any expedient to assist them in the labour of washing their clothes. The connection with Nepal is doubtless due to the fact that several wealthy Muhammadan hide merchants dealing with that country reside at Lar.

Sugar-refining.

Undoubtedly the chief industry of the district, however, is the manufacture of sugar, for this alone is not confined to any one town or tract. At the present time there are 339 sugar factories in the district, the majority being in the Hata and Deoria tahsils, though there are also 48 in Padrauna, 24 in Gorakhpur and ten in Maharajganj. Some years ago the industry was located principally in pargana Sidhua Jobna, the chief sugarcane tract of the district; but it has now concentrated in the south-eastern tahsils, which contain the towns of Bạrhaj, probably the busiest mart in the district, and Rampur, generally called Rampur Karkhana from the number of its factories. Among other centres may be mentioned Pipraich and Chauri Chaura, the latter being the headquarters of the Dumri estate, in whose factory steam power and centrifugal refining machinery have recently been instituted on a small scale. There are no peculiarities in the manufacture of sugar, the method resembling that adopted in all the eastern districts. It may be noted, however, that the old wooden *kolhus* or crushing mills still survive to some extent, though their replacement by the iron roller mill is a mere matter of time. The yield of juice varies with the nature of the cane, the best variety being the *mango*, a straight tapering cane of a whitish green colour. Another good variety is the *reora*, a thick yellowish green cane, its sub-species, the *hemja*, being grown in lower levels. Many other kinds are cultivated, such as the *harwa*, the *muncha*, the red *baraukha*, the thin but valuable *dasli*, called *sarauti* in other parts, the *katara* and the *punsahi*, the two last being grown chiefly for chewing. The juice is boiled into *gur*, which is turned out in small round *bhelis*, each a quarter of a *ser* in weight, or into the thinner *rab* when required for the manufacture of *pakki chini* or white refined sugar, in contradistinction to the *kachchi chini* used for local consumption and seldom exported.* The average yield of *gur* per acre has been estimated 37 maunds, a very high figure, though lower than that obtained in Azamgarh, Partabgarh and Ghazipur. Reckoning that of the total output about one-half is refined locally, and taking the average sugarcane area at 97,000 acres, we get a total yield of 1,794,500 maunds of *gur* brought to the factories, giving an outturn of 598,000 maunds of *chini*, on the supposition that three maunds of the former yield one of the latter. It is impossible to state the exact amount of sugar exported, but it has been calculated recently that 300,000 maunds of *chini* and 275,000 of *gur*

* The process of manufacture is fully described in S. M. Hadi's "Sugar Industry of the United Provinces;" Allahabad, 1902.

were sent out in a year, exclusive of the *gur* exported by river, which alone constitutes a very considerable proportion of the whole, though the refined sugar is forwarded almost exclusively by rail.

Whatever trade the district may have possessed in former days seems to have disappeared wholly under the malign influence of Oudh rule. In 1802 the collector, Mr. Routledge, reported that the *amil* had wrung the last remnant of wealth from the desolated province, that in spite of the fertile soil nothing was grown beyond the bare necessaries of life, and that the produce was barely sufficient for local consumption. Nevertheless the officers of the Company were so jealous of the trade monopoly that from the first they endeavoured to restrain private enterprise, and they actually expelled from the district a Mr. McCleish who asked permission to build a bungalow. At first the export trade was limited to timber, which any one was allowed to cut on payment of a duty, the latter being farmed for Rs. 11,500 in 1803. There was also some traffic in cattle and coarse cloth from Nepal, and in salt and sugar from other parts; but everywhere trade was hampered by crushing imposts, including a tax on all goods crossing the Nepal frontier, the Ghagra and the Gandak, and *rahdari* or transit dues exacted at each pargana boundary passed, so that it is surprising to read that the collector hoped to establish a flourishing trade between Butwal, then included in the Company's territories, and Bhutan and Tibet. In 1806 another application made by a Mr. Yeld to build a bungalow and cultivate indigo, though strongly supported by the collector, was vetoed by the Governor-General; and it was not till 1830 or thereabouts that this policy was abandoned, since as late as 1827 the Supreme Government expressed fears that English and other European interlopers, "often men who have accumulated money by embezzlement," were attempting to take the whole trade of the country into their hands. By 1816 a considerable traffic in cloth, sugar and saltpetre had grown up with Benares, and in 1820 it appears that an *ad valorem* duty of 5 per cent., a precursor of the modern octroi, was levied on all goods coming into Gorakhpur, while in 1824 the collector suggested the imposition of a tax on the large lac trade in Bansi, requesting Trade.

a percentage for himself as a reward for his acumen. Mention is made in 1830 for the first time of the existence of a considerable export trade in grain, the collector in that year stating that large quantities of corn were despatched by road to the western markets, and this fact is confirmed by Buchanan, who referred to the export of grain and sugar, stating that commodities other than timber were sent by land carriage and not by river. He further estimated the rice trade in the north at 18 lakhs of rupees; and although this must be a gross exaggeration, it is clear that the traffic in rice, both from this district and from Nepal, was already of high importance. The same author states that the timber trade was of great extent, and mentions a large importation of copper, copper vessels and coin, all of which came from Nepal. A great impulse was given to commerce by the reorganisation of the police in 1835, followed five years later by the clearance of the forests effected under the system of grants to Europeans of capital and enterprise. Since that time trade has developed steadily by both road and river, the cheapness of the latter form of transport turning the rivers into trade routes of such importance that the general trend of commerce assumed an easterly direction, and it was not till the advent of the railways that grain began to find its way in any considerable quantities from Gorakhpur to the west. One of the principal articles of import is cloth, and the trade returns under this head bear witness to the rapid development of commerce. The value rose from half a lakh in 1860 to two lakhs in 1862-63, while 10 years later Gorakhpur city alone received cloth to the value of 3½ lakhs, the figure rising to five lakhs in 1876-77. Simultaneously the sugar trade was advancing with rapid strides till it became the chief article of commerce in the district. A still greater impetus was afforded by the opening of the railway in 1885, from which year Gorakhpur has enjoyed means of rapid communication with all parts of India.

Trade routes.

The great revolution effected by the railway has been accompanied the practical abandonment of the rivers. Formerly the rice from the *tarai* of Nepal and Binayakpur was carried to Dhani Bazar on the Dhamela, and thence consigned by boat along the Rapti and Ghagra to the markets of Bengal, while a certain proportion went through Nichlaul to Captainganj on the Little Gandak. The surplus rice and spices from pargana Sidhua Jobna were taken either to Ragarganj on the latter river or to Tiwaripatti and Sahibganj for shipment on the Great Gandak. In the south the grain of Bansgaon was sent either to the Rapti or the Kuwana and thus carried down to Gola, Barhaj and the lower marts. Timber was conveyed in great rafts from the northern forests down the Dhamela, the Rohin and the Great Gandak, and this practice still survives to some extent. The roads were of less importance. The produce of Nepal, brought into the district along numerous rough tracks, was collected at Dhani and Nichlaul, and in the latter case the bulk of it was carried by road to Gorakhpur. Thence it was carted into Bengal by two main roads leading to Chapra, one going through Kasia and Qazipur, and the other through Deoria and Salempur. Other trade routes led from Gorakhpur to Dohri-ghat and Azamgarh on the south, to Basti and Fyzabad on the west and to Pharenda and Lotan on the north. Recently, however, all these routes have in large measure been superseded by the railway, which extends from Gorakhpur in every direction, so that now the trade of the district is mainly rail-borne, though the rivers still play a certain part in the business of distribution.

Exports and imports.

Apart from timber the exports consist for the most part in agricultural produce, the chief items being rice, wheat, gram, pulses, linseed, sugar, both refined and unrefined, turmeric and hides. The principal imports are piecegoods, salt, iron and other metals, kerosene oil and tobacco. Much of the rice comes from Nepal for re-export, that of the higher grades, produced in relatively small quantities, generally going westwards, while the coarser kinds are distributed in the districts of Ballia and Azamgarh. Wheat normally is sent to Bengal, though the influence of high prices may at times divert it to the west. Sugar is exported to Cawnpore, Central India and Rajputana, but also finds its way in increasing quantities to Eastern Bengal. Of the other commodities linseed and other oilseeds go principally to Calcutta, peas, gram and *arhar* to Chapra, and turmeric to the Punjab, while timber is sent to Benares, Cawnpore and many other places. Calcutta supplies the district with kerosene oil, and a large proportion of the salt, piecegoods and metals; but much of the salt is obtained from Kharaghoda on the gulf of Cutch. Cawnpore supplies considerable quantities of cotton goods and metals. The bulk of the tobacco is imported from Tirhut. Since so much of the trade is unregistered, it is impossible to calculate its volume with any accuracy. No account is taken of the river-borne traffic or of that carried by road, save in the case of the Nepal frontier and the commerce with Bengal by way of Pipra-ghat, Makrauna and Bhingari. In the matter of rail-borne trade too it is difficult to distinguish local from foreign traffic. For example, the returns show as local very large amounts of rice and wood despatched by rail to Barhaj and Turtipar, whence they are exported by river and are consequently lost to sight. Recently an attempt was made to estimate the volume of the rail-borne trade after making due allowance as far as possible for these disturbing factors. According to this calculation the annual export of rice, husked and unhusked, is some 300,000 maunds; that of wheat 50,000, of gram and pulses 100,000, and of other food-grains about 160,000 maunds. The leading place is taken by sugar, the refined sorts aggregating 300,000 and the unrefined 275,000 maunds, though this is far from representing the total output of unrefined sugar from the district. Oilseeds amount to 180,000, firewood to 160,000, and timber in the shape of poles and logs to 130,000 maunds, while among other articles appear 45,000 maunds of hides and no less than 21,000 of turmeric. Of the imports on the other hand, cotton piecegoods come first with 51,000, while cotton twist, both Indian and European, contributes 9,000, and gunny bags 23,000 maunds. For the rest, the most important are iron goods with 41,000, tobacco with 35,000, salt with 32,000, kerosene oil with 28,000, and brass and other metals with 13,500 maunds.

Trade with Nepal.

Reference has already been made to the trade with Nepal, which has existed from the earliest times and is still in a flourishing condition. Throughout the predominant article of import has been rice, of which sometimes 200,000 maunds and upwards enter the district in a single year. The balance consists principally of other grains, oilseeds, spices, large quantities of *ghi* and hides. The last are a very valuable item, the estimated value being about a lakh of rupees per annum and are transported by rail to the tanneries direct under the agency of a single contractor, who for some years past has been a resident of this district. No record of any traffic in copper is now traceable, for the reason that the Nepalese authorities have prohibited the exportation of copper save in the form of Butwal pice. In return this district sends into Nepal large quantities of English and country cloth and thread, and smaller amounts of grain, salt, sugar and dried fish. In addition a certain number of goats and sheep are sent over the border, while a few ponies are imported : but the trade in animals is of little moment.

Many of the principal markets have already been mentioned in the foregoing account. Such are Dhani and Nichlaul in the north, which from the first have been the chief collecting stations for the Nepal trade, though of these Dhani has of late years been supplanted by Bridgmanganj owing to the advent of the railway. For the same reason Captainganj and Ragarganj on the Little Gandak, which received much of the trade from Nichlaul, were to a large extent deserted in favour of Mundera and the adjoining bazar of Chaura on the railway, though a further change has been effected by the construction of the branch line to Captainganj and Bagaha, resulting in the revival of the former place and the rapid growth of the market at Siswa. In like manner the railway has had a great influence on the timber trade, which is no longer carried by water, but is now concentrated at the stations of Maniram, Pharenda and Bridgmanganj on the Uska branch. The market of Pipraich has long been of importance as centre of the sugar industry, and its prosperity is assured by its position on the railway to Bagaha. In the east the chief centres of commerce are Padrauna, Tiwaripatti and Sahibganj. In the centre of the district the city of Gorakhpur is by far the largest market and still monopolises the tobacco business, though of late years the cloth trade has exhibited a tendency to remove itself eastwards to Deoria so as to avoid the heavy octroi duties. On the main line Sahjanwa is the collecting station for the produce of pargana Hasanpur Maghar, and boasts a thriving export trade in grain. Chauri Chaura possesses several sugar factories and is the centre of the hide business, while it also contains a

Markets.

number of oilseed crushing mills belonging to the Dumri estate. Close by is Keotali, the great cattle-market of central Gorakhpur. In the south the chief market towns are situated on the banks of the Ghagra and other rivers, and in most cases their importance has declined greatly of late years. Such are Gajpur, Dhakwa and Gola in the Bansgaon tahsil, which formerly enjoyed an extensive trade in grain on the Rapti, the Kuwana and the Ghagra, but no longer possess much importance excepting perhaps Gola, though even this is rapidly declining. Further east come Barhalganj, Barhaj and Gaura, all of which are still flourishing, the first by reason of its position on the main road to the south, and the others on account of their thriving sugar industry and the construction of the branch line of railway. In the south-east of the district is the riverside market of Bhagalpur, but this is of less importance than the others. Mention may also be made of Deoria and Rampur, especially the latter, whose sugar business rivals that of Barhaj, while the former has grown considerably in recent years, owing to the diversion of the cloth trade from Gorakhpur and its selection as the headquarters of a subdivision. There are, of course, numerous other markets and petty bazars in the district, and a list of these will be found in the appendix. With few exceptions they are mere local gatherings frequented only by the residents of the neighbouring villages.

Fairs.

Another list given in the appendix shows the numerous fairs held at different places in the district. These gatherings are seldom large, the majority being of a religious character and possessing no commercial significance. The best attended is the Dhanusjag festival at Baikunthpur in pargana Salempur, held to commemorate the contest for the hand of Sita; it takes place in Aghan and lasts for a fortnight, about 40,000 persons congregating there and utilising the opportunity for trade. Another popular assemblage is the fair held at Singaha near Bansi-ghat, where some 25,000 persons gather together for the purpose of bathing in the Great Gandak when the moon is full in Kartik. Of much the same size is the Akshai Tritia fair at Sohnag, whither crowds of pilgrims resort in Baisakh to worship at the shrine of Parasram. Some 10,000 persons attend the Sheoratri festival at Barpar and Rudarpur in the Hata tahsil and the Kubernath fair at Kahraulia in pargana Sidhua Jobna. Mention may also be made of the numerous bathing fairs at various places along the Ghagra, notably Barhalganj, the scene of large gatherings in Kartik and Magh. At Gorakhpur itself a considerable fair is held on the first Sunday in Jeth, the feast of Saiyid Salar Masaud, in the great mango groves to the north of the city. One of the most popular fairs at the present time is that of Tarkulha Debi, held at the small hamlet at Tarkulha on the Pharend river, some three miles west of Chaura. As many as 20,000 people assemble there, bringing offerings of goats, buffaloes, sweetmeats and *kauris* to the shrine of the goddess, while a brisk trade is carried on, chiefly in eatables and household utensils. The great day of the festival is the Ramnaumi in Chait, but the shopkeepers make it last for about eight or ten days, and special police arrangements are always necessary.

Communications.

In old days there was no recognised highway through the district, unless we go back to the times of Asoka and the Buddhists. None of the imperial routes from Dehli or Oudh to the east lay to the north of the Ghagra, and roads were practically non-existent till, at the end of the 17th century, Qazi Khalil-ur-Rahman constructed a road from Ajodhya to Gorakhpur through Khalilabad, the line closely following that of the present metalled road. No further progress was made during the ensuing century, and on the transfer of the district to the Company in 1801 communications were as backward as in any part of the ceded territories. At an early date the attention of the civil officers was drawn to the necessity of improving the roads, and the growth of trade led to rapid improvement, so that Buchanan was able to state that by 1815 or thereabouts most commodities were transported by road, while in 1830 Mr. Reade with fine optimism declared the routes to Nepal, Oudh, Saran, Ghazipur and Tirhut to be in excellent order. The necessity for qualifying this statement is proved not only by the complaint of a writer in 1837 that some of the roads seemed to have been constructed "merely for the convenience of gentlemen going on shooting parties," but also by the fact that communications for long remained in a deplorably backward state, from which they have not yet fully emerged. In the north the absence of bridges over the numerous streams causes a virtual suspension of traffic during the rains; and there has been little change since 1865, when the settlement officer remarked of tahsil Padrauna that for four months in the year wheeled traffic was impracticable, and that in the beginning of November almost every road was covered with green turf. In the south of the district the Bansgaon tahsil even to-day is dependent during the rains on the Tucker *bandh* for its connection with Gorakhpur, while of the six tahsil headquarters four are at a considerable distance from any metalled road. Indeed the growing work of the administration would be seriously hampered by the impossibility of rapid transit, but for the railway, though progress is slowly being achieved and special grants have been made with the object of improving the existing condition of affairs.

Railways. Gorakhpur is the headquarters of the Bengal and North-Western Railway, and contains not only the residences of the agent and the principal officials connected with the line, but also extensive constructing and repairing workshops. The main line traverses the southern half of the district for a distance of about 78 miles, entering pargana Salempur near Bankata station and thence running in a north-westerly direction through the stations of Bhatpar, Bhatni, Nunkhar, Deoria, Gauri Bazar, Chauri Chaura and Kusmahi to Gorakhpur, whence its course is almost due west through Domingarh, Jagatbela and Sahjanwa into the Basti district. The line was sanctioned in May 1882 and was opened for traffic on the 15th of January 1885. Near Jagatbela the line crosses the Rapti by a bridge of nine spans with a total length of 1,445 feet; it was completed in June 1886, the aggregate cost, including that of protective works, being Rs. 14,58,143. From this main line several branches diverge, the first to be constructed being that from Gorakhpur to Uska Bazar, opened on the 15th of December 1886, and recently extended from Uska to Tulsipur in Gonda. This runs northwards from the district headquarters through the stations of Maniram, Peppeganj, Rawatganj, Campierganj, Pharenda, Lehra and Bridgmanganj, where it turns west towards Uska entering Basti after a course of 37 miles through this district. The next branch to be completed was one of

17 miles from Bhatni to the bridge over the Ghagra at Turtipar, with stations at Salempur, Lar Road and Turtipar, the last being named after a town on the Ballia side of the river. This branch connects with that from Mau in Azamgarh and so gives access to Benares; it crosses the Ghagra by a magnificent bridge 3,911 feet in length, with 18 spans of 200 feet, finished in January 1903 at a cost of Rs. 20,72,495. From Salempur an offshoot of this branch, some 13 miles in length, runs westwards to Satraon and Barhaj on the Ghagra; it was opened to traffic on the 1st of December 1897. In 1903 sanction was accorded to the construction of a branch from Gorakhpur to Bagaha in Bengal, and this was completed in 1907. The line runs north-east through Pipraich and Badarwar to Captainganj, where it bends northwards, keeping to the west of the Little Gandak through Ghughli to Siswa. At a short distance beyond the latter it turns to the east, crosses the river and goes past Khada and Chhitauni flag-station to Chhitauni-ghat and the Great Gandak, the total length in this district being some 49 miles. It is now contemplated to construct a branch from Captainganj on this line to Padrauna and thence to Thawe in the Saran district; the course has been surveyed and the line will probably be built in the near future. In addition to the above, mention should be made of the line from Dohri-ghat to Kopaganj in Azamgarh, which was completed in 1904 and has brought Barhalganj within easy reach of the railway. The natural continuation of this line to Gorakhpur would be a very costly undertaking, necessitating bridges over the Ghagra and Rapti, while an obstacle of equal difficulty is presented by the Rapti *kachhar*. The effect of this extensive network of railways can hardly be over-estimated, owing to the enormous impetus thus given to trade and general development. Much, however, yet remains to be done, especially in the matter of linking up the road system with the railways, for at present only four out of 32 stations in the district possess metalled feeder roads.

Roads.

For many years the only metalled roads outside the civil station were the provincial highways from Gorakhpur to Azam garh and Benares on the south and to Basti and Fyzabad on the west; the former being metalled in 1865 as far as Barhalganj, a distance of 35 miles, while the 16 miles of the latter within the limits of this district were metalled between 1870 and 1880. In the last year there were also 15 miles of metalled road in the civil station, kept up by the municipality, which now is responsible for 18½ miles of such roads. From 1880 to the present time 74 miles of road have been metalled by the district board, the chief addition being that from Kasia to Deoria and Barhaj. Progress has also been made with the roads from Gorakhpur to Kasia and to Nichlaul, and though the lack of funds has caused much delay, the aggregate length of metalled road has increased from 66 miles in 1880 to nearly 140 miles in 1908. The unmetalled roads are 888 miles in length as compared with the former total of 912, and to this must be added the extensive network of departmental roads in the reserved forests. A list given in the appendix shows all the roads at present in existence with their length and official classification. The provincial roads represent the old imperial roads and are kept up by the Public Works department at an average cost of Rs. 16,900 per annum. The local roads are those entrusted to the care of the district board, which is the lineal descendant of the road and ferry fund committee, started at the time of the first regular settlement to administer the road cess then imposed, under whose auspices many of the unmetalled roads came into existence. The main lines of road in the north comprise that from Gorakhpur to Lotan, following the railway to Uska, and from Gorakhpur to Nichlaul and Thuthibari, giving off a branch to Maharajganj at Shikarpur. The road to Kasia has already been mentioned. At Kasia it bifurcates, one branch running eastwards to Babhnauli and Sahibganj and the other south-east to Qazipur and Chapra. Between the Kasia and Nichlaul roads is that to Captainganj, Padrauna, Bansi-ghat and Bettiah. The principal roads in the south comprise that from Chapra to Salempur, Deoria, Chaura and Gorakhpur, closely following the main line of railway, and a branch of the former from Lar in the south-east corner of the district along the bank of the Ghagra, through Barhaj, Barhalganj and Gola to Sikriganj, whence it turns northwards to Rudrapur and Gorakhpur. The remaining roads are extremely numerous: they are all shown in the appendix and their course can be seen by a reference to the map.

The district is fairly well provided with rest-houses and inspection bungalows. In addition to those already noted in the previous chapter as maintained by the forest department there are provincial bungalows at Sahjanwa, Gorakhpur, Kauriram and at the bridge over the Taraina. Inspection houses under the control of the district board are at Kasia, Deoria, Maharajganj, Gola, Barhaj, Nandapar and Bargadahi, the last being on the road to Nichlaul. There is only one dâk-bungalow, at Gorakhpur itself, and this is kept up from provincial funds. On the provincial roads military encamping-grounds are to be found at Sahjanwa, Gorakhpur, Belipar, Gagaha and Barhalganj. Those on local roads are at Adda Motiram, Gauri Bazar, Deorias Khukhundu and Salempur on the road to Chapra; at Jagdispur, Bhagnath, Kasia, Qazipur and Tamkuhi on the eastern road from Gorakhpur; and at Pipraich, Captainganj, Ramkola and Padrauna on the route to Bettiah. The district board maintains *sarais* for native travellers at Kauriram and Gola, while numerous others on the various roads are under private management. Bungalows.

The problem of providing an adequate number of bridges on the roads crossing the numerous streams is as acute in this district as in any other part of the submontane belt. Not only are many of the rivers of a torrential nature, but from their very number the provision of a complete system of communications would be exceedingly costly and it is doubtful whether the benefits thus secured would justify the expense. At the present time, however, it is beyond dispute that the existing number of bridges is insufficient for the obvious needs of the district, and much remains to be done before the limit of profitable expenditure is reached. The only bridge over the Ghagra is that at Turtipar, while on the Rapti also there is but one permanent bridge, and this is not open to road traffic. The bridge of boats at Bird-ghat, by which the Basti road enters the city, is converted into a ferry during the rains, and on more than one occasion the pontoon the bridge on the route to Azamgarh has been seriously threatened. The most imposing bridge in the district is the celebrated Tucker *bandh* on the same road Bridges.

the over Ami and the low stretch of *kachhar* between Belipar and Kauriram, which in the rains becomes a great lake. The embankment, begun by Mr. Tucker when collector in 1845 and completed five years later, is three miles long, and within this length are two large and two smaller bridges, while the western side is revetted with masonry so as to enable it to withstand the scour of the floods. It was built by means of convict labour, but even so the cost, apart from the maintenance of the workers, amounted to Rs. 70,000. There are other bridges over the Ami, one an old masonry structure on the Basti road near the district boundary, and the other a new girder bridge erected by the district board at Chatai on the road to Sikriganj. A similar bridge carries the Azamgarh road over the Taraina, in place of the masonry structure destroyed by the flood of 1871; that on the road from Kauriram to Gola was badly damaged in the same way, and has never been repaired. The road to Deoria is furnished with old masonry bridges over the Tura, the Pharend and the Majhna. The Lotan road now crosses the Chillua by the railway bridge, in place of the partially destroyed embankment and bridges on the original alignment; but there is only a pontoon bridge over the Rohin, which has been used since the destruction of the old permanent bridge in 1903. On the Kasia road a costly brick bridge has just been completed over the Pharend, replacing the former erection of wooden piles, and on the road from Deoria to Kasia and Padrauna a fine bridge, costing Rs. 1,25,000, has recently been built over the Little Gandak, while a second carries the road over the Duranchi at Rampur, and a third modern bridge of considerable size crosses the Bansi. Besides these there are some small wooden bridges in the north of the district over the minor streams, kept in repair by the district board.

Ferries. A list of all the ferries under local management will be found in the appendix. The chief crossing over the Ghagra, between Barhalganj and Dohri-ghat, is a provincial ferry, controlled by the Public Works department, but there are twelve other ferries over the same river, of which eight are managed by the district board and the rest by the corresponding authority in Azamgarh. The district board is likewise responsible for thirteen ferries over the Rapti, two over the Dhamela, two over the Rohin and three over the Little Gandak. These ferries bring in a considerable income, the average receipts by the board for the five years ending with 1906-07 being Rs. 18,590 annually.* In addition there are numerous private ferries for the convenience of local traffic on almost all the rivers, but an enumeration would be unprofitable, and many of them ply only during the rains. The most important of these ferries is at Ghutni-ghat on the Little Gandak.

Navigation. Little remains to be said on the subject of navigation, to which reference has been made in dealing with rivers, trade and the history of communications. The waterways are now of relatively slight importance, and on the Ghagra alone is there any semblance of activity, while it must be remembered that the traffic represents that of many districts. It was observed, during the building of the Turtipar bridge, that the average number of boats passing up and down was 448 monthly; and it is certain that a considerable quantity of rice and other grains is still exported by water, while the volume of trade is largely swelled by the operations of the India General Steam Navigation Company. Elsewhere the waterborne commerce is steadily decreasing. That on the Rapti is but a shadow of its former self, though during the rains a fair number of boats may be seen on the stream, and quantities of fuel are floated down for the sugar-refiners at Barhaj. The other rivers are now almost deserted, and their value as highways is negligible.

* Appendix, table XVI.

CHAPTER III.

THE PEOPLE.

Early enumerations.

As Gorakhpur and Basti formed a single district up to 1865, when the division was made without reference to the boundaries of the existing parganas, at any rate so far as Binayakpur and Maghar were concerned, it is not possible to ascertain with extreme accuracy the population of the present district according to the earlier enumerations; for although the figures for the separate parganas have been preserved, an adjustment can be obtained only by the rough method of including in this district one-third of the inhabitants of Maghar. About 1813 Buchanan endeavoured to estimate the population, calculating it from the number of families and ploughs in each police circle; and on this rough and untrustworthy basis he obtained an aggregate of some 1,226,110 persons in the present district, giving an average density of 271 to the square mile. As is but natural, the rate was lowest in the north, then exposed to the incursions of the Nepalese; but the estimate is mainly of interest as the first attempt at a census in the United Provinces. A regular census was undertaken in 1847, but this again was a crude affair, based on an assumed number of persons to each house, and the estimated population of the district on this occasion was 1,438,762. The only distinctions observed were those between Hindus and Musalmans and between agriculturists and others. A rather more elaborate census was that of 1853, based on an actual enumeration of persons, and on this occasion the approximate total was 1,852,154, of whom 882,182 were females. The density had risen to 410 to the square mile, and ranged from 669 in Dhuriapar and 616 in Bhauapar to 128 in Tilpur and only 88 in Binayakpur. Besides the city of Gorakhpur, the places with more than 5,000 inhabitants were Barhalganj, Gola and Amwa in pargana Sidhua Jobna. A third regular census was taken in 1865, but the district was still undivided and the total can be regarded as but approximate. The population then numbered 2,019,671, including 949,789 females, while the average density was 447 to the square mile, ranging from 592 in the Sadr tahsil to 571 in Bansgaon, to 562 in Deoria and Hata, to 435 in Padrauna and to 265 in Maharajganj. The chief towns, in addition to Gorakhpur city, were Rudarpur, Amwa and Barhaj, no other place possessing as many as 5,000 inhabitants.

Henceforward it is possible to give the actual figures of the existing area, save for the modification caused by the transfer of the villages south of the Ghagra to Azamgarh in 1904; and even this may be disregarded, as it occurred subsequently to the last census. The enumeration of 1872 showed that as the result of famine and pestilence the population had remained stationary, the total being 2,019,361, of whom 941,279 were females. It is generally supposed, however, that the concealment of females, often suspected in the past, was very prevalent in this census, so that possibly the decrease in the total number of inhabitants was more apparent than real. The density was the same as before, and there was little change in the relative position of the various parganas. The only place of any size was Gorakhpur itself, but Rudarpur, Amwa, Gaura, Paina, Gola and Padrauna contained over 5,000 persons apiece. Census of 1872.

During the next nine years the district was visited by two famines of some intensity and by several serious epidemics, but none the less the population increased at an incredible rate, for by 1881 the total was 2,617,120, of whom 1,310,997 were females, this sex for the first time exhibiting a preponderance. The average density was now 579 to the square mile, the highest figure for any single tahsil being 825 in Deoria, followed by Bansgaon with 689, Hata with 650, Gorakhpur with 638 and Padrauna with 603, the last subdivision having made immense strides during the two preceding decades. Maharajganj came last, as usual, with 295 to the square mile, but here too the improvement was very noticeable. Out of 7,238 towns and villages 7,155 contained less than 1,000 inhabitants and eleven more than 5,000, these including Gorakhpur, Barhaj, Rudarpur, Gaura, Lar, Salempur-Majhauli, Bansgaon, Gola, Madanpur, Barhalganj and Paina. Census of 1881.

Census of 1891.

The process of expansion went on steadily during the next ten years, the growth of the population being checked only by occasional epidemics of no great importance and by emigration. In 1891 the total number of inhabitants was 2,994,057, including 1,496,773 females. This great increase brought the average density up to 663 to the square mile, an extraordinarily high figure for a district containing so much unreclaimed land. The rate reached its maximum in the Deoria tahsil with 888, and this was followed by Hata with 753, Bansgaon with 736, Gorakhpur with 732 and Padrauna with 652, while even in Maharajganj it was 413, the increase being common to all parts of the area. There were then 7,574 towns and villages as before, and of these 7,487 contained less than 2,000 inhabitants, and 14 over 5,000. The latter included all those in the list of 1881 as well as Padrauna, Amwa and Bansgaon.

Census of 1901.

The next ten years were of a less favourable character, as for a considerable period the seasons were far from satisfactory and in one year actual famine occurred, while sickness was generally prevalent and a high death-rate synchronised with a reduction in the number of births. Bad agricultural conditions caused extensive emigration, and it was no matter for surprise that the census of 1901 showed an appreciable decline in the number of inhabitants. The total was 2,957,074, involving a decrease of 36,983, which brought the average density down to 655 per square mile of the present area. Every tahsil lost ground except Gorakhpur, where an increase of 18,423 was recorded; and the highest figure was 847 in Deoria, next in order being Gorakhpur with 761, Hata with 75, Bansgaon with 714, Padrauna with 642 and Maharajganj with 407 persons to the square mile.

Towns and villages.

The number of inhabited towns and villages was 7,562, of which 7,473 contained less than 2,000 inhabitants, 77 between two and five thousand, and twelve had larger populations. The last comprised Gorakhpur, Barhaj, Amwa, Rudarpur, Gaura, Lar, Padrauna, Salempur-Majhauli, Barhalganj, Bansgaon, Paina and Bansgawan. The urban population, including that of these towns, and also of Gola, Rampur Karkhana, Gajpur, Pipraich, and Deoria Bazar amounted to 5·4 per cent. of the whole: a very low proportion, though considerably higher than that of Basti and the other districts north of the Ghagra. The towns, though fairly numerous, are in most cases small, being as a rule local centres of commerce which are likely to grow in the near future. The villages also are small, as is the case throughout the eastern districts, and the average population is but 370 as compared with a provincial average of over 400. As many as 43·4 per cent. of the inhabitants reside in villages of less than 500 persons, and the figure would be greater but for the fact that in the north the area of the *mauzas* is often extremely large, such villages containing within their limits great numbers of petty hamlets, each of which represents a separate clearing and settlement in the forest.

Of the whole population 1,470,469 were males and 1,486,605 females, the latter comprising 50·3 per cent. of the total number of inhabitants. The preponderance of females was first observed in 1881, when the proportion was 50·09 per cent., though it dropped to 49·98 at the following census. Formerly there would appear to have been a marked defect, possibly due in part to concealment, since the proportion was 47·6 in 1853 and 47·03 in 1865, while in 1872 it was only 46·6 per cent. The excess of females is not general, since in the Sadr and Maharajganj tahsils it disappears, males there outnumbering females in a very noticeable degree, as is also the case throughout the other districts north of the Ghagra, though in Azamgarh and the Benares division to the south there is an equally decided preponderance of females. The same thing occurs in the adjacent districts of Bihar, and it has been suggested that the reason lies in the large aboriginal element in the tract; for by a well-known natural law the higher types reproduce themselves at a slower rate than those lower in the scale of evolution, a relative paucity of females being the outward and visible sign of such conditions. According to this argument one would expect to find a difference in this respect between the lower castes and those of Aryan descent; and this actually is the case, both Brahmans and Rajputs exhibiting a majority of males, while the same thing occurs among the Saiyids, Mughals and higher races of Musalmans. There is no question of female infanticide, which has never been prevalent in Gorakhpur. It is said that the practice was discountenanced Sex.

by the Brahman advisers of the Satasi Rajas, and that the Bisens abandoned it when their chieftain became a Musalman.

Migration. On the other hand, it is probable that the disproportion between the sexes in the eastern districts is largely due to the temporary migration of large bodies of labourers. It is difficult to determine in what degree this affects the population of Gorakhpur. The volume of emigration beyond India is relatively small, for during the ten years preceding the census only 7,568 persons were registered as coolies proceeding under the usual contract to work for five years in the West Indies, Fiji and Natal. The number increases in bad seasons, for some 4,200 persons were registered in 1905 and the two following years, though even so the effect is hardly appreciable on a total population of three millions. Of much more importance is internal emigration to Bengal, whither numbers of labourers betake themselves for several months every year, earning high wages from October to the beginning of the rains. During this period natives of Gorakhpur are to be found in Eastern Bengal and Assam, Calcutta, Howrah and even distant Rangoon. The volume of such migration is, however, small in comparison with that from all parts of the Benares division, in which labour is more abundant and the pressure of the population on the land is far more severe. These emigrants go by river as well as by rail, and for this reason exact figures are unobtainable, but in an ordinary year the number is about 10,000, though in seasons of high prices and agricultural distress it may rise to three times that figure. It is certain that between 1891 and 1901 the district gained nothing by immigration, since in the former year 8 per cent. of the inhabitants were born elsewhere, whereas at the last census the proportion was only 4·15 per cent., and the number of natives was relatively greater than in almost any other part of the United Provinces. On the other hand, it is unfortunately impossible to discover how far the decrease in 1901 was due to loss by emigration, for while of all the persons enumerated in India who gave Gorakhpur as their birthplace 4·46 per cent. were found elsewhere, there are no means of ascertaining the period within which such emigration took place. Undoubtedly the district lost on the exchange, but it cannot be said whether the loss was extensive or almost insignificant.

Religions.

Of the whole population as enumerated at the last census 2,658,074 or 89·89 per cent. were Hindus, 297,019 or 10·04 per cent. Musalmans and 1,981 of other religions. The proportion of Hindus to the total is large, much higher in fact than in other districts north of the Ghagra, but at the same time it has shown a considerable decline during the past forty years, dropping from 90·1 in 1872 to 90·02 in 1881 and to 89·88 in 1891, since which year it has remained stationary. The reason lies partly in the spread of Christianity and the Arya Samaj, though in either case the total is insignificant; but mainly in the fact that Musalmans tend to increase more rapidly than their Hindu neighbours, being longer lived by reason of their more liberal diet and perhaps more prolific owing to the later age held customary for marriage. The present proportion of Musalmans to the whole population is about normal for this part of the country. It varies, however, in different tahsils to a considerable extent, being as much as 14·7 per cent. in Padrauna and 11·7 in Maharajganj, while elsewhere it is below the average, being 9·3 in Gorakhpur, 8·4 in Hata, 8·1 in Deoria and 6·1 in Bansgaon, in the two last of which the Rajput chieftains always remained in undisputed possession.

Hindus.

Hinduism as a creed presents no peculiar features in this district. The attempt made at the last census to distinguish between the various sects and forms of worship proved a signal failure, for less than 4 per cent. of the population professed attachment to any particular denomination, and more than half of these worshipped the Panchon Pir, a cult which is mainly confined to the lower castes in this and the Benares division. The only important classification of the Hindu community is that according to castes, and it is but natural that in so large a district an immense number of castes should be found, and that among them should be enumerated nearly all the castes occurring in other parts of the United Provinces, owing to the fact that immigration during the last century has been responsible in large measure for the development of the country. It naturally follows too that with a population of nearly three millions the actual numbers in the case of many castes should be considerably greater than those recorded in other districts; but at the same time there are several which occur in unusual strength, relatively to the number of inhabitants, and some which are seldom met with elsewhere. Altogether, exclusive of 154 persons in whose case no caste was specified, representatives of 85 different castes were found, apart from subdivisions. Many of these, however, are quite unimportant, since in 31 instances the number of persons was less than 1,000, and in 19 others it was less than 5,000. There were seven castes with more than 100,000 persons apiece, and these constituted 59·13 per cent. of the total population, while a further 33·03 per cent. was contributed by 17 castes with numbers ranging from 100,000 to 25,000 in each case. It should be added that most castes are too well known throughout the provinces to merit detailed attention, and therefore separate mention will be made only of those which are numerically preponderant or which present features of ethnographical or other importance.

Chamars. The foremost place is occupied by the Chamars, who take the lead in every tahsil except Deoria and Padrauna, aggregating 353,101 persons or 13·28 per cent. of the Hindu community. Curriers and tanners by tradition, they are mainly engaged in general and agricultural labour, and are frequently employed in field work by Brahmans and other high caste tenants. They are probably not of aboriginal descent, and indeed, there seems nothing incredible in the assertion that 400 years ago there were no Chamars in the district, for their numbers have increased of late with amazing rapidity, since in 1872 the total was but 210,000. They have many subdivisions, the majority styling themselves Kanaujias, while others worthy of note are the Jaiswar, Dakhinha, Utarha and Desi, names which indicate the country of their origin.

Ahirs. Almost as numerous are the Ahirs, who are strongest in Padrauna and Deoria, but are fairly evenly distributed throughout the district, with 342,210 representatives or 12·87 per cent. of the total Hindu population. Their existence is doubtless due to the presence of extensive grazing grounds, and in early days they seem to have adhered to their traditional calling; but now the majority are engaged in agriculture, and as a caste they form the backbone of the cultivating community. They are said to have accompanied the Rajputs as herdsmen, and in many instances their women were employed as wet nurses, several families, now known by the distinguishing title of Bargaha, having been raised to wealth by the favour of a Rajput foster-brother. Similarly the Rawats of Maghar and elsewhere are said to be of partly Rajput descent, and consider themselves superior to the rest of their caste-fellows. The vast majority of the Ahirs belong to the great Gwalbans subdivision, found throughout the eastern districts and Oudh, the remainder being principally of the Dhindhor clan.

Brahmans. Next come Brahmans with a total of 262,987 or 9·89 per cent. of the Hindu population. They occur everywhere in strength, though their numbers are relatively small in the Bansgaon tahsil, in which the predominance of the Chamars and Ahirs is more than usually marked. The bulk of the Brahmans, though the Sakaldipi, Kanaujia and other subdivisions are somewhat sparsely represented, are described as Sarwarias, a contraction of Sarjuparis or inhabitants of the country north of the Ghagra. They rank low among their caste-fellows, and it has been suggested that they are the descendants of the earliest Aryan invaders, who were cut off in the days of aboriginal supremacy and perhaps retired to the hills of Nepal. The Sarwaria is less restricted by the rules of caste than other Brahmans, and is not always averse from handling the plough and working in the fields. They hold a large area as tenants and are foremost among the landowning castes of the district, but their skill and industry in agriculture are by no means conspicuous. According to their traditions the most ancient settlements are those of the Tiwaris in Gorakhpur itself and in Pidi of pargana Salempur; the Shukuls in Dhedi of pargana Silhat; the Dubes of Sarar in pargana Haveli; the Misras of Beri in the same pargana, and the Bhargiwas of Bhagalpur on the Ghagra. There are many Brahmans called Sawalakhis, who are said to be of low origin, the story going that a king of Benares gave a feast to 125,000 Brahmans, but that as the requisite number was not forthcoming, he made requisitions on other tribes and gave them Brahmanical rank. The tale is not peculiar to this district, but it serves as an illustration of the theory that in ancient days the caste system was in a comparatively fluid state: a conclusion which is almost unavoidable in the case of many Rajput clans.

Kurmis. The Kurmis are similarly ubiquitous, but are strongest in the east, where they claim descent from Mayur, the founder of the great Bisen clan of Rajputs. The total at the last census was 198,289 or 7·46 per cent. of the Hindus, this figure including the Sainthwars, of whom there were 63,388, found in all tahsils but notably in Hata and Gorakhpur, as well as considerable numbers passing under other names, which really represent subdivisions rather than castes. Such are the Patanwars of Maharajganj, the Dhelphors or clod-breakers of Hata, the Chanaus of Padrauna and many others. The Sainthwars claim precedence as being of the purest descent, and are endogamous; for which reason they are often considered as a separate caste. Of the endless subdivisions of Kurmis the chief, after the Sainthwar, are the Jaiswar, Dhelphor, Patariha, Utarha and Naipali, the two last obviously coming from the hills. All the Kurmis are excellent and hardworking cultivators, and in general farming have few equals. They are largely aided by their womenfolk, who almost invariably work in the fields, though of late the custom has been dropped by some who assert their claim to a higher social status.

Koeris. The Koeris possess the greatest skill of all the cultivating castes, but devote their attention mainly to market gardening and the production of opium, sugarcane and other valuable crops. They correspond to the Kachhis and Muraos of the west, castes which are hardly represented in this district, and in all numbered 152,283 persons or 5·73 per cent. of the Hindus. They are strongest in the Deoria tahsil, where their presence accounts in great measure for the superior cultivation and development of that subdivision; but in all parts of the district they are fairly numerous, no tahsil containing fewer than 16,000 of these invaluable husbandmen. Their sub-castes are unimportant: the majority are styled Kanaujias, while the rest call themselves Bhagatiyas, Katiyas, Jurihars and so forth.

Rajputs. The Rajputs numbered 140,520 in all, or 5·29 per cent. of the Hindu population, but this proportion bears no relation to their influence and importance. They are most numerous in the Hata and Bansgaon tahsils and fewest in Maharajganj, though in all parts they occur in considerable strength. By occupation they are generally agriculturists, but their skill in cultivation is indifferent. In former days many entered the army, and large numbers still emigrate in search of service. The Rajputs of this district belong to an endless variety of clans, the census of 1901 showing representatives of 38 different subdivisions, and this excludes a number of well-known clans which are more or less confined to the eastern parts of the United Provinces, no fewer than 62,361 persons coming under this category. Not many of these, however, are of much local importance. The foremost place is taken by the Bisens, of whom there were 16,388, distributed all over the district, though the largest number is naturally to be found in the Deoria tahsil, in which is situated Majhauli, the headquarters of this ancient clan. The Panwars, 10,912, are strongest in Hata and Deoria, but they never seem to have attained a position of much prominence, but apparently came to the district in small detachments, gaining a footing gradually by marriage with the daughters of the Majhauli house. The Bais, 7,546, belong mainly to the Bansgaon tahsil. Though they claim connection with the celebrated families of Unao and Rai Bareli, their high rank is not generally admitted, and they are in all probability of mixed descent, as are the Bais of Fyzabad and the eastern districts as a whole. They style themselves by several names, and this seemingly accounts for the great reduction in their number, since in 1872 and in 1891 there were more than 12,000 persons of this clan. The Sarnets were not separately enumerated at the last census, but in 1891 they numbered 11,810, chiefly in the Gorakhpur, Hata and Bansgaon tahsils. They are said to be identical with the Nikumbhs, and their history will be given later. Similarly the Kausiks numbered 7,215 in 1891, residing mainly in Bansgaon, and some account of this clan will be found in the article on the Dhuriapar families. There were 6,444 Surajbansis in 1901, the largest number belonging to the Maharajganj tahsil: the name is often adopted by so-called Rajput immigrants from the hills, while in other cases the Surajbansis represent offshoots of the ancient house of Amorha in Basti. The other clans, though in many cases well represented, are of singularly little importance; generally because their settlement in this district is of recent date, their ancestors coming rather as agricultural colonists than as conquerors. The strongest are the Chandels, 5,330, chiefly in Deoria and Padrauna; the Palwars, some 3,500 in number, who spread over the Ghagra into Dhuriapar from Birhar in Fyzabad; the Amethias, 3,138, who reside for the most part in Deoria and came from the south of Bara Banki; the Dikhits, 2,953, from Ghazipur and elsewhere; and the Chauhans, 2,878, who are found everywhere, those in the north claiming connection with the Butwal house and often calling themselves Chitorias, in support of the story that their ancestors fled hither from Chitor on its capture by the Musalmans. Others include the Sikarwars, the Bandhalgotis from the Sultanpur district, the Sengars from Ballia, Sombansis from Partabgarh, the Rathors, who are said to have settled at a very early date in Hata and Gorakhpur, the Raghubansis from Ajodhya, the Raikwars from Gonda and Bahraich, the Bachhils from Kher and the Bachgotis from Sultanpur. All these occur in numbers exceeding 1,000 apiece, as do several other clans less generally known. Such are the Donwars or Domwars, who are sometimes supposed to be the descendants of the old Domkatar rulers of Gorakhpur, and the numerous local clans of low social status and probably mixed descent.

Kewats and Mallahs.

After the Rajputs come the Kewats, with a total of 122,654 or 4·61 per cent. of the Hindu population, the majority residing in the Gorakhpur and Maharajganj tahsils. By occupation they are cultivators, fishermen and boatmen; many of them call themselves a subdivision of Mallahs, with whom they are closely connected. Others are styled Kharbinds or pure Binds, so that they seem to be midway between these two castes, of which the Mallahs had 46,826 representatives and the Binds 11,771. To the same class belong the Goriyas, 4,359; the Beldars or navvies, 16,552, who also call themselves Kharbinds, and are more nearly allied to the Binds than to the Mallahs; the Sorahiyas, who numbered 3,488, almost all in Maharajganj, and are practically a subdivision of the latter caste; and the Chais, numbering 825 persons, who are in almost all respects identical with Mallahs, but are notorious for their thieving propensities.

There were 89,335 Kahars, evenly distributed over the district, and this total includes the Gonds, a subdivision which has no connection with the Gonds of Central India. They are water drawers, palanquin bearers, servants and cultivators by occupation, and are well known everywhere. The difference between the Kahars and the Mallahs is very slight, and probably both have a common origin, the castes being separated solely on occupational grounds. Closely akin to them are the Kamkars, numbering 13,786, principally in the Padrauna tahsil. They are mainly domestic servants, as also are the Baris, 3,724, who draw water for all castes and make the leaf platters used at feasts. Kahars.

Banias numbered 85,674 in all or 3·22 per cent. of the Hindu community, and are strongest in the Deoria and Padrauna tahsils, though they take a prominent place throughout the district, monopolizing the greater part of the trade and the money-lending business. Among then are found representatives of all the principal subdivisions, but far outnumbering the rest come the Kandus, 41,532, and the Kasaundhans, 21,445. The former are often treated as a separate caste, and their social status is relatively low: they are sugar manufacturers and grain-parchers, little different from the Bharbhunjas, of whom only 3,432 were enumerated. The Kasaundhans are money-lenders and stand higher than the Kandus: they are found throughout the United Provinces, whereas the Kandus are mainly confined to the east. Other sections of the caste are formed by the Patanwars, Parwars, Rauniars and Unais, all of whom belong for the most part to the eastern districts. Mention may also be made of the Agraharis and Agarwalas, the last generally residing at Gorakhpur, where they include among their number many persons of wealth and a few large landowners. Banias.

The remaining castes call for little comment. Nothing need be said of the Telis, 73,259; Bhars, 69,686; Lunias, 66,492; Kumhars, 59,197; Lohars, 51,933, and Pasis, 48,886. These castes are common everywhere, and their numbers are unusually large only because of the unusual size of the district. The Mallahs have been mentioned already, and then follow Dhobis with 45,946, Kalwars with 43,712, Nais with 38,899 and Barhais Other castes.

with 35,562 persons. Of much more importance are the Bhuinhars with 32,037 representatives: they occur throughout the district, but are naturally strongest in Padrauna, in which the great Tamkuhi estate mainly lies. Their general characteristics are a matter of common knowledge, the caste holding a high position owing to its traditional connection with the Brahmans and Rajputs. They are mainly cultivators, but are hampered by similar disabilities, in that they will not handle the plough. Their subdivisions are as numerous as the Rajput clans and are often synonymous, the chief being the Kausik, Bagochhia, Baksaria, Sikarwar and Gautam. The Dusadhs, 31,603 in all, are strongest in the eastern tahsils, but they are found everywhere as *goraits* and village servants, while they are as notorious for their drunken habits and criminal instincts as in Ballia and other districts. The other castes with more than 10,000 representatives are Kayasths, 29,768; Barais or *pan*-growers, 29,305: Sonars, 23,971; Beldars, Kamkars and Binds, already mentioned; Gadariyas, 15,715; Atiths or priestly mendicants, 13,944, the caste being strongest in Padrauna and still more common in the adjoining district of Saran; Khatiks or greengrocers, 12,597 and Musahars, 12,597. The last again belong principally to the east, and are an aboriginal tribe resembling the Doms; as also do the Basors, 4,041, almost all in the Padrauna tahsil, the Dharkars, 2,937, and the Bansphors, 624. The Doms themselves numbered 7,959, nearly half belonging to tahsil Deoria. They are regular gypsies, seldom choosing for themselves a fixed habitation and exhibiting the true gypsy characteristic of basket-making.

Criminal tribes.

The Magahiya Doms of Gorakhpur are very different from the great majority of the caste, and have come in for special treatment. Their thieving habits and their inability to settle to any regular agricultural or industrial pursuit led eventually to the institution in 1884 of a special system of supervision. All Doms were registered and compelled to reside in quarters called *domrakhanas*, built in various parts of the district, but always close to a police station. Every night a roll-call is taken to prevent absconding, and a Dom caught at any distance from his *domrakhana* is prosecuted for bad livelihood. All attempts at inducing them to take up agricultural work have failed, and at present the only honest method of earning a livelihood open to the Dom is by working on the conservancy staffs of the municipality, the Act XX towns and the notified areas. Otherwise they eke out a precarious existence by begging and thieving, while their women are not seldom prostitutes. The system is far from satisfactory, and a fresh effort towards reclaiming the Magahiyas has recently been made. The old police lines at Gorakhpur have been made over to the Salvation Army, which will endeavour to train a number of the Doms to some industrial occupation, though the ultimate success of the experiment is highly problematical. In 1907 there were 34 Dom settlements in the district with 1,460 inmates, including 541 women and 457 children. Other criminal and wandering tribes comprise the Badhaks, who passed themselves off under other names at the census, and who in former days were the terror of the district; the Bahelias, 2,081, who in most cases are harmless; the Barwars, 917, all in the Maharajganj tahsil; the Nats, 819; the Kanjars, 798, and a few more of little note.

Tharus and others.

The Tharus, 2,747 persons in all, belong principally to the northern parganas of Binayakpur and Tilpur, but occur in small numbers everywhere. They resemble their namesakes of the Kumaun Tarai, and are generally supposed to be fever-proof, but the reason of their relative immunity lies mainly in their careful habits of living and their domestic arrangements, especially with regard to the water-supply. The Tharus are great rice cultivators and in the Tarai are the best of all husbandmen, but they are very shy, always preferring the neighbourhood of the jungles and invariably living near running water. The traditions of the district point strongly to a Tharu supremacy in former days, and they themselves assert a Rajput origin, still wearing the sacred thread, while it has been suggested that there is a connection between this race and the Sakyas of Buddhist times. Besides the Tharus this district contains small numbers of many aboriginal tribes, who are elsewhere found only in the wilds of Mirzapur and the adjacent parts of Bengal. Such are the Kuneras of Deoria and Maharajganj, who make pipe-stems of *khair* wood, and the Dhangars of

Deoria and Padrauna, who are generally employed as ploughmen. In the Maharajganj tahsil there were 1,359 Paharias or Thapas from Nepal, who usually go by the generic name of Gurkha.

Musalmans.

The Musalman element is strongest in the Padrauna and Maharajganj tahsils; but except in Gorakhpur and the immediate vicinity, there are no families of importance, and the great bulk of the Musalmans are in reality of Hindu descent, while in many respects the conversion has been but partial. Thus Musalmans often observe Hindu festivals and customs, worshipping at the shrines of Gorakhnath at Gorakhpur and of Kabir at Maghar, while those of the better class will in numerous cases eat nothing but food cooked by a Brahman. At the last census 97·8 per cent. of the Musalmans were Sunnis and only ·7 per cent. Shias, while the remainder belonged to minor sects, usually following the teaching of some particular saint. The list of Musalman tribes and castes is of considerable length, numbering 61 in all, apart from subdivisions; but few are of any importance, since in 22 cases less than 100 persons were enumerated, and in 12 more the total did not exceed 1,000, while at the same time the great majority have their Hindu counterparts and require no detailed mention. Only seven castes are over 10,000 strong, and these together constitute 74·5 per cent. of the whole Muhammadan population.

Julahas and Dhunias.

The most numerous are the Julahas or weavers, counting in all 73,408 or 24·71 per cent. of the Musalmans. They are mainly found in the Padrauna, Maharajganj and Sadr tahsils, but are fairly numerous elsewhere. While many still follow their traditional calling, in the north they are usually agriculturists and in this vocation they have achieved considerable success, especially in the undeveloped parts of Padrauna. There are no important subdivisions among the Julahas, but almost all of those in this district describe themselves as Momins. Closely akin to them are the Dhunias Dhunas or Behnas, cotton carders by profession, but often found in other occupations. They numbered 29,175 persons or 9·82 per cent. of the Musalmans and are more evenly distributed than the Julahas.

Sheikhs.

The second place is taken by Sheikhs with a total of 47,809 or 16·1 per cent. of the Muhammadan community. They are most numerous in the Hata tahsil, where they constitute the principal Musalman caste. Many of the Sheikhs are of Hindu extraction and owe their name either to pure invention or else to their adoption of the tribe to which the *qazi* or *mufti* belonged, through whose agency they were admitted into Islam. Of the many Sheikh subdivisions the chief, as usual, are the Qurreshis and Siddiqis, the former numbering 12,321, principally in Maharajganj, Padrauna and Deoria, while the latter included 11,215 persons and are found in all tahsils. Others are the Ansaris in Padrauna and Gorakhpur, the Abbasis in Bansgaon and Gorakhpur, the Faruqis in Bansgaon and the Usmanis of Gorakhpur, while the many unspecified Sheikhs of Hata are probably the descendants of converted Rajputs.

Pathans.

Next come Pathans with 38,695 or 13·03 per cent. of the total, more than one-third belonging to the Maharajganj tahsil and over 10,000 to Bansgaon, whereas elsewhere their numbers are comparatively small. The principal Pathan clans in this district include the Lodi, 5,347, mainly in Maharajganj; the Yusufzai, 4,999, in Bansgaon, Maharajganj and Padrauna; the Kakar, for the most part confined to the first two tahsils; the Ghori and Dilazak in Bansgaon, as well as the Rohilla and Bangash in various parts of the district. There are many others, but it often happened that no clan was specified, such Pathans being generally of Rajput extraction.

Rajputs.

The ordinary term for a Musalman Rajput is Khanzada, and this probably accounts for the confusion. Under the head of Rajputs were enumerated 11,484 persons, almost all of whom resided in the Padrauna, Gorakhpur and Deoria tahsils. The chief clans are the Bais, Panwar, Chauhan and Bisen, while Chandels, Dikhits, Raghubansis and Surajbansis also occur in some numbers. Though one of the Bisen Rajas of Majhauli adopted Islam few of his clansmen appear to have followed his example, and in many cases the Khanzadas are the descendants of fairly recent immigrants from Oudh.

Other Musalmans.

The remaining castes of importance are Darzis, 10,723; Faqirs of various denominations, 10,003; Nais or Hajjams, 9,632; Churihars and Manihars, makers of glass bangles, 8,831; and Saiyids, 5,780. The last are strongest in Bansgaon, Deoria and Gorakhpur, and are drawn principally from the Husaini, Rizwi and Zaidi subdivisions, but there are few families of any note. Then follow Bhats, Kunjras, the Gaddis or Musalman Ahirs of Padrauna, Dafalis, Dhobis, Nats, Qassabs and Mughals. None of the minor castes call for note, though it is curious to find 144 Musalman Banias in the Maharajganj tahsil.

Christianity. The number of Christians at the last census was 1,443 and of these 1,040 were natives, the latter figure having risen from 808 in 1881 and from 852 ten years later. Of the native Christian community 731 belonged to the Anglican communion, which also probably included some of the 300 persons in whose case no specific denomination was returned. The Gorakhpur Mission was founded by Mr. R. M. Bird, who in 1821 raised a sum of money from the residents of the station and applied to the Church Missionary Society for a missionary chaplain. Three years later the Rev. M. Wilkinson arrived to take up the work at Gorakhpur, and in 1831 he obtained from Lord William Bentinck the grant of 2,000 *bighas* of unreclaimed forest, to be brought under cultivation by the converts, and on this property stands the Christian village of Basharatpur. In 1854 the Rev. H. Stern came to the Gorakhpur mission, and during the forty years of his incumbency the work was greatly extended. The village of Sternpur was established in 1881 and the hamlet of Dharampur was added in 1884. The inhabitants of these villages are principally cultivators, but some are employed on the railway as guards, signallers and clerks. Much attention is paid to industrial training, and the women and girls are particularly expert in drawn-thread work, which commands a ready sale, while the boys are employed in the carpenters' shop and the Church Missionary Society Press, which does a good deal of job-work in the city. The educational work of the mission is of great importance but is undenominational. The chief institution is St. Andrew's College, which was raised to its present status in 1899. Attached to it is a high school, and in addition there is an anglo-vernacular middle school in Alinagar, the Swinton memorial vernacular middle school in Sahibganj and five primary schools. In connection with the Church Missionary Society is a branch of the Zanana Bible and Medical Mission, which has two ladies working in the city and managing primary schools for girls. Evangelistic work is carried on during the cold weather in the district, but nowadays conversions are not common and the numbers of the Christian community are increased mainly by the natural growth of the three villages and by the agency of the orphanages. There are two churches at Gorakhpur. Christ Church, the old station church, was built in 1829 by private subscription, and St. Andrew's owes its origin to the railway company, by whom it was built in 1898. The senior Church Missionary Society missionary acts as chaplain to the station.

Other religions.

Of those professing other religions 281 were members of the Arya Samaj, 116 were Sikhs, 105 Jains, 23 Buddhists, eight Jews and five Parsis. The Sikhs are for the most part in Government service, the only exceptions of importance being the owners of the Dumri estate; while the Jains are immigrant traders, in most cases Agarwals by caste. The Arya Samaj is of recent introduction and of little importance. There were no followers of this creed in 1891, and, though since the last census their number has somewhat increased, this may be attributed probably as much to the expansion of the city of Gorakhpur as to any enthusiasm for the new teaching. The bulk of the members are to be found in the Sadr tahsil, where they consist for the most part of persons employed by the railway, the rest being clerks or officials in Government service, or else members of the legal profession. The only lodge is at Gorakhpur, and there weekly meetings are held. No friction has arisen between the Aryas and other communities, whose general attitude is one of indifference.

Occupations.

Mention has already been made of the relatively small urban population, and from this and other characteristics it is abundantly clear that the district is essentially agricultural. The statistics of occupations compiled at the last census show that 72·39 per cent. of the people were directly dependent on agriculture and pasture, the latter being of negligible importance, while in addition a large number of persons were engaged in cultivation as a secondary means of subsistence. This proportion is much above the general average, as indeed is only to be expected; and for the same reason the industrial population, comprised under the category of the provision and supply of material substances, is relatively small, amounting to 13·62 per cent. Of the 402,841 persons coming under this head about 48 per cent. were engaged in the supply of articles of food and drink, including sugar, while 12·75 came under the category of textile fabrics, 10·38 under work in metals, 9·13 under work in wood, cane and forest produce, 8·14 under work in earthenware and 4·51 per cent. under leather. The next main class is general labour other than agricultural, which comprised 4·83 per cent. of the total population—a somewhat low figure, as is perhaps only natural in a district with so few important industries. Then follow personal and domestic service with 3·46 and commerce, transport and storage with 2·84 per cent., the actual commercial population being but 18,790 or ·6 per cent. For the rest 1·86 came under the head of administration, including Government, local and village service; ·69 under professions, a very wide term, which includes both lawyers and dancing girls; and the remaining ·81 per cent. under means of subsistence independent of any occupation; this again being a most comprehensive class, which ranges from persons of private means to beggars and prisoners in the jail.

Language. The common tongue of the people of Gorakhpur is practically a strange language to the new-comer from the western districts of the United Provinces. It is a form of Bihari, a language derived directly from the ancient Prakrit of Magadha, and the dialect is that known as northern standard Bhojpuri. This, in its turn, has two main divisions, the eastern or Gorakhpuri, spoken by about 1½ million persons in the Padrauna and Deoria tahsils as well as in part of Hata, and the western or Sarwaria, spoken by a somewhat larger population in the rest of this district, the same form prevailing in Basti. As Dr. Grierson has pointed out, there is no clear line of demarcation between the two forms of speech, the dialect in the south-west containing features common to both, while further there are some thousands in the south-east corner of Deoria whose language approximates to the northern standard Bhojpuri of the Saran district.* Some 6,000 Musalmans affect

* Linguistic Survey of India, volume V, part II, page 228.

the Urdu or Hindustani dialect of western Hindi, and the Tharus of the north speak another broken dialect of Bhojpuri. It is scarcely necessary to mention the secret language of the Doms and Nats, which is a mere thieves' Latin used only occasionally by a minute fraction of the population.

Literature.

There is no trace of any literature of an indigenous character, as is indeed only to be expected in a district so far removed from any centre of culture. Of late years one or two vernacular newspapers have come into existence at Gorakhpur. The first of these, the *Riaz-ul-Akhbar*, an Urdu publication appearing every fourth day, was started in 1881, but in 1907 was removed to Lucknow. The editor, Hakim Barham, started a newspaper called the *Mashriq* a month later, this being an Urdu weekly with a circulation of some 600 copies, devoted to local news and correspondence on social, religious and political matters. The same person owns a weekly comic paper, also in Urdu, entitled the *Itr-i-Fitna*, which contains contributions in verse and prose as well as illustrations; it was suspended in 1898, but was resuscitated in 1903. There are at present eight printing presses in the district, all at Gorakhpur excepting the *Masudi* press at Bharauli in the Deoria tahsil. The most important belongs to the Church Missionary Society, and contains a large Wharfedale printing machine and one press: it undertakes all kinds of printing in English and lithography. The *Dinapur* press is a hand press doing miscellaneous job work in English; the *Bharat Prakash* does similar work in English, Urdu and Hindi; while the other four are lithographic presses, including the *Barham* press, at which the two newspapers are printed. There are no literary or social institutions of any note. One was started at Gorakhpur in 1883 and still survives, but its membership is very small and its activity scarcely perceptible. A purely social open air club, called the Union Club, meets in the grounds of the Masonic Lodge, and books and newspapers are provided for the members, who for the most part belong to the legal profession.

Proprietary tenures.

With few exceptions, to be noted hereafter, the land tenures are the same as those found in the rest of the United Provinces. At the last settlement the district contained 8,647 *mauzas* or villages and 8,463 *mahals*, the excess of the former being due to the formation in the jungle grants of large *mahals*, containing in some cases as many as 30 *mauzas* apiece. Since the settlement the number of *mahals* has increased with rapidity owing to the frequency of partitions, and in 1908 the 8,520 *mauzas*, the number having decreased owing to transfers to Azamgarh, were divided into 14,586 *mahals*. Of the latter 2,963 were held in *zamindari* tenure, whether single or joint, 11,407 were *pattidari*, almost wholly of the imperfect variety, and 216 were *bhaiyachara*, this form being practically confined to the Padrauna tahsil. The coparcenary tenures are far more common than the *zamindari* in every part of the district; but while the majority of villages are held nominally in coparcenary tenure, there is an increasing tendency, especially in the south of the district, towards a condition of separate ownership among the shareholders. Partitions are constantly being effected and, as in parts of the Benares division, the *lambardari* system is rapidly falling into abeyance. Already it may be said to have broken down altogether in the Bausgaon tahsil, where there are now more than 90,000 *malguzars* and the number is still on the increase. Despite an abnormally large staff the work of the land records department has become extremely difficult and heavy, while the condition of the records leaves much to be desired.

Fractional shares.

Matters are rendered no more easy by the extraordinary variety and the complex nature of the methods of reckoning the fractional shares owned by the various co-proprietors and co-sharers. At the last settlement it was ascertained that no fewer than 227 systems of recording these shares were in vogue. Things were simple enough in the 1,071 *zamindari* and 34 *bhaiyachara* villages, and there were 3,993 in which the familiar notation of rupees, annas and pies was used, while in 41 the division was according to rupees, annas and *gandas*, at the rate of 20 *gandas* to the anna. This leaves 3,508 villages in which a more elaborate system exists owing to the need of expressing smaller fractions, and this is effected in 223 different ways. For this purpose 25 terms are employed, many of them with a diversity of meaning. The Arabic fractional terms, for example, are frequently made through ignorance to express more than one value.

Thus *khums*, a fifth, in some places denotes a third and in others an eighth, while *ushr*, a tenth, employed in a single village to express its proper value, masquerades in hundreds of cases with thirteen different values, ranging from one-fourth to one-hundredth. In some places the terms of the series are very numerous and the smallest fraction inconceivably minute: thus in 44 instances a series of nine terms is required, and in four no fewer than ten are in use, the extreme division being into microscopic shares, euphemistically styled *uns* or fractions, of which 1,105,920,000 go to the rupee.

Proprietary castes.

No statistics of the area held by the various castes comprising the proprietary body are available beyond those compiled at the last settlement; but, as little material change has occurred in subsequent years, they serve to give a fairly exact idea of the distribution of the land among the different sections of the community. More than half the district belongs to Hindus of the higher castes, and in 1889 Brahmans held the foremost place with 744,161 acres or 25·38 per cent. of the entire area. They are closely followed by Rajputs, with 653,370 acres or 22·28 per cent. and in either case their possessions are scattered all over the district, nor can any marked preponderance be observed in any particular tahsil. The Bhuinhars with 302,218 acres, or 10·33 per cent., take the third place, nearly two-thirds of this area lying in the Padrauna tahsil, in which the large property of the Tamkuhi Raja is mainly situated. The Hindu cultivating castes, Koeris, Kurmis, Kewats, Sainthwars, Malis and five others of less importance, held 308,384 acres or 10·52 per cent, but of this 271,169 acres or about nine-tenths were owned by the Kurmis, more than half their property being in the Padrauna tahsil, wherein lies the estate of the Padrauna Raja. Other Hindu castes, 23 in number, owned 274,719 acres between them, but the bulk of this, aggregating 184,509 acres, was the property of Kayasths, chiefly in the Sadr and Maharajganj tahsils. Musalman landholders of all denominations held 190,453 acres or 6·5 per cent. of the whole district, the greater part being situated in the same two tahsils, and there are very few Muhammadan estates of any size. For the rest 117,808 acres were shown as Government property, 72,272 were in the hands of Europeans and Eurasians, chiefly in the jungle grants of tahsil Maharajganj, and 17,902 acres, forming a single estate, were owned by Sikhs.

Leading families.

Though in former days this enormous district was parcelled out among a number of powerful chieftains, there are now few families of importance in Gorakhpur and still fewer of any great antiquity. The oldest is the Bisen house of Majhauli, which has maintained its position from remote ages and has again resumed its place after recovering from a recent period of depression. The ancient family of Satasi came to a disastrous end with the Mutiny, when the last Raja was deprived of his title and estates. The younger branch of Unaula survives, but this house has never figured prominently in history. The Dhuriapar family still lingers on in the houses of Barhiapar and Gopalpur, but its descendants have been reduced to insignificance by the reckless extravagance of successive Rajas. On the other hand two of the chief landowning families are of comparatively recent establishment in this district, the families of Tamkuhi and Padrauna dating their rise to prominence from the troublous days of the eighteenth century.

Majhauli.

The early history of the house of Majhauli is lost in the mists of antiquity. The founder is traditionally said to have been an ascetic bearing the name of Mayur or Mewar, and the story goes that he married three wives of different castes, a Brahmani, a Rajputni and a Bhuinharin, while a further legend states that he kept a Kurmin concubine. From their offspring sprang all the great families of eastern Gorakhpur and the neighbouring country, if the story may be believed; but it is at least curious that the houses of Majhauli, Tamkuhi and Padrauna should have had a common origin, and one is tempted to connect the name of Mayur with that of the mythical chieftain Mayura Dhvaja, of whom vague traditions exist throughout the submontane belt from the Ganges to the Gandak. Many accounts are given of the identity of this Mayur. Some state that he was descended from the Brahman Parasram, others that he was a Rajput, and others again allege that he was a Bhat: one story makes him come from Hastinapur, the home of his father Ashwa Thama, and another brings him from Maharashtra in the south,

The son of the Rajputni wife was Bissa Sen, from whom all the Bisen Rajputs claim descent. He came first from Benares to Kakradih in pargana Sikandarpur of the Azamgarh district, and thence he crossed the Ghagra, taking from the Bhars the fort of Surauli and building Kundilpur close to Majhauli; though another account states that his residence was at Nawapar, the modern Salempur. The traditional date of this settlement was about 1100 A.D., though the family chronicles show about 100 generations between Bissa Sen and Bhim Mal, who ruled from 1311 to 1366. At all events it is certain that Bisens were established in this part of the district at a very early date, and lived in peaceful isolation separated by a belt of dense forest from their only powerful neighbours, the Domwars or Domkatars of western Gorakhpur. The latter were expelled about the middle of the 14th century by Chandra Sen, the founder of the Satasi house, who at first, while his possession was still insecure, kept up amicable relations with the Raja of Majhauli. Two generations later war broke out between the adjoining principalities and is said to have lasted for a hundred years, the subject of dispute being a piece of land on the borders of the two territories near Rudarpur, which was eventually occupied by the Bisens, whose domains at this time must have extended over the whole of Silhat and Salempur. No further events of importance occurred till the rebellion in 1567 of Khan Zaman and Sikandar Khan. The latter fled across the Ghagra, pursued by a considerable force under Fidai Khan, and was assisted in his escape by Bodh Mal of Majhauli, who thus incurred the displeasure of the Musalmans and was soon brought into subjection. The story goes that he was summoned to Dehli and there became a Musalman under the name of Islam Khan, variously given as Muhammad Salim; and that on his return the Rani refused to receive him within the walls of the Majhauli fort, so that he was constrained to settle on the other side of the Little Gandak, where he founded the town of Salempur. Another account attributes the name to the celebrated Sheikh Salim Chishti, who is said to have accompanied the army of Fidai Khan and to have received a grant of land opposite Nawapar, whose name was changed to Salempur in his honour. It seems certain that one of the Rajas was actually converted to Islam; but very possibly this did not occur till some 200 years later, and in any case he was succeeded by his unconverted son. During the days of Akbar the Bisen territory was much enlarged towards the north by the addition of the lands held by the successors of Mardan or Madan Singh, who supported the Afghans of Bengal in their rebellion about 1590, from which date all the southern half of Sidhua Jobna was included in the Majhauli estate. In the 17th century Babu Bernath Singh of Semra, a kinsman of the Raja, crossed the Rapti and invaded Chillupar, taking advantage of the strife then raging between Todar and Pirthi, the rival claimants to the *raj* of Dhuriapar. He established himself at Narharpar near Barhalganj and his descendants for two centuries were known as the Rajas of Chillupar till the last was executed for rebellion in 1858. The Rajas of Majhauli, however, remained content with their possessions, and even during the second half of the 18th century, when the east was ravaged by Banjaras and the west plundered by the Oudh revenue officials, the Majhauli estate was the one place where some semblance of security for life and property was maintained. The Raja concentrated his available forces for the defence of his ancestral domains, and abandoned the more recent acquisitions of the family in Padrauna owing to the inroads of the Banjaras; though in order to form buffers for his territory he lent encouragement to the Rai of Padrauna and gave ready support to Raja Fateh Sahi when he left Bengal and settled at Tamkuhi. So successful was this policy that when the district was ceded to the Company the estate of Raja Ajit Mal, who had been in possession from 1753, was the only tract which could be described as fairly cultivated and inhabited. The Raja died in 1805 and for ten years the property was held by his widow, Rani Dilraj Kunwar, whose adopted son, Tej Mal, held Majhauli from 1815 to 1843; but the establishment of a settled and peaceful government, combined with an exact system of revenue collection, greatly diminished the importance of the Majhauli Raja, who made matters worse by reckless extravagance and bad management. Raja Udai Narayan Mal, who succeeded in 1843, was deeply involved in debt at the outbreak of the Mutiny. He was one of a committee of five Rajas to whom the care of the district was entrusted by Mr. Wynyard on its evacuation in August 1857: and though he abstained from attending their deliberations, he did not betray his trust. In return for this service he afterwards received great assistance from Government. In 1870 the estate was taken under the Court of Wards and was thus administered till July 1901, when possession was given to Raja Kausil Kishor Prasad Mal, who had succeeded his father in 1890. The estate is now in a flourishing condition, comprising 118 villages assessed at Rs. 52,502 in Gorakhpur, all of which lie in the Deoria tahsil except three in Hata and one in Maharajganj. The Raja also owns 32 villages in Saran and two in the Ballia district, with a combined revenue demand of Rs. 15,254.

Other Bisens.

A number of local families claim kinship with this famous house, such as the Bisens of Narharpur, who once held Chillupar but have now lost the whole of their remaining property, recently purchased for the Majhauli estate. Others are the Bisens of Baikunthpur, Mahend, Dharmua and Bhagalpur. In addition to these the Misra Brahmans of Piyasi, Dojari and Rewali claim to be connected with the Majhauli house by descent from the Brahmani wife of Mayur.

Dhuriapar.

Another ancient Rajput family is that of Dhuriapar, traditionally descended from one Dhur Chand of the Kausik clan, whose reputed ancestor was Raja Kausik, the uncle of Viswamitra, the teacher of Rama. According to the legend Rama granted Sarjupar, the country between the Ghagra and the mountains, to Viswamitra and his descendants for ever. More probably Dhur Chand was driven northwards by the Musalmans, and crossed the Ghagra about the middle of the 14th century He drove out the Bhars whom he found in possession, ejected from Harpur the Bhuinhars whose invasion had preceded his own, and established himself all along the northern bank of the river in the present parganas of Dhuriapar and Chillupar. He and his descendants distributed the conquered lands among their relations, and many of the local families trace their origin to younger members of the Dhuriapar house, such as the Babus of Belghat, Malanpar, Jaswantpur and of Hata in *tappa* Majuri. The headquarters of the family was at Dhuriapar, where the ruined remains of the great fort built by the Kausiks may be seen to this day. The Rajas appeared to have lived at peace with their neighbours, Satasi on the north and Majhauli on the east, while they are said to have received support from the Sultans of Jaunpur. It is related that in 1399 Raja Kukoh Chand sent an embassy to Timur during his invasion of Hindustan, and in the days of Babar the splendour of the court of Raja Suraj Pratab Chand was such that it has remained proverbial to this day. Not long after his death quarrels arose in the family. Raja Raghu Chand left five sons, of whom Pirthi Chand and Todar Chand simultaneously claimed the succession and took up arms in support of their pretensions, with the result that civil war ensued for more than a century. This led to encroachments by the neighbouring powers. The mention of Chillupar as a separate pargana in the days of Akbar probably shows that it was seized by Bernath Singh of Semra before 1596; while in the north ten *tappas* were seized by the Raja of Satasi, the estate being reduced from 40 to 24 *tappas*. In the beginning of the 18th century the *amil* intervened and the estate was divided into two equal parts containing 693 villages each, one-half being taken by the descendants of Pirthi Chand, who settled at Gopalpur near Gola, while the other went to the representative of Todar, who established himself at Barhiapar. Thus reduced and divided the Kausiks were unable to withstand the effects of Oudh administration, and the country was in a deplorable state at the time of the cession. The change of rule brought no improvement, for the mismanagement of the Barhiapar Raja caused a portion of his estates to be confiscated for arrears of revenue in 1818, the land being given to Karim Khan the Pindari. The Raja of Gopalpur plunged deeply into debt, and by 1836 his ruin was inevitable. On the outbreak of the Mutiny Raja Tej Partab Bahadur Chand of Barhiapar joined the rebels and in 1858 he absconded; his titles and estates were confiscated, and he remained a wandering exile for 14 years, at the end of which he was permitted to return to his home. Tej Partab had succeeded his brother, Raja Ram Bahadur Chand, and half the estate was recorded in the name of the latter's widow, Rani Sheo Nath Kuari. This portion escaped confiscation and was bequeathed by the Rani to Manik Raj Kuari, the widow of the rebel Raja's son, Lal Indar Partab Narayan Chand. She is still in possession and Lal Bajrang Bahadur Chand is the heir to the property, which now comprises only 15 villages in tahsil Bansgaon, with a revenue demand of Rs. 1,311.

Gopalpur.

At the time of the Mutiny Raja Kishan Kishor Chand of Gopalpur remained steadfast and during the course of the disturbances rendered loyal services to Government, being appointed a member of Sir Charles Wingfield's committee of administration. As a reward he subsequently obtained an estate assessed at Rs. 12,000 and the grant saved him from ruin, but much of his ancestral domains had to be sold in liquidation of debts. Part was purchased by Dulhin Harpal Kuari, wife of his nephew and heir, Lal Harihar Prasad Chand, who is now generally known as the Rani of Gopalpur. She is still alive and resides at the family seat at Gopalpur. She adopted as her heir Babu Kharag Bahadur Chand of the Hata branch of the family, whose son, Babu Dan Bahadur Chand, is now heir to the estate. The latter comprises 40 villages, paying a land revenue of Rs. 6,150, all in the Bansgaon tahsil.

Satasi.

About the 12th century a Sarnet Rajput named Chandra Sen is said to have come to this district from the neighbourhood of Lahore, and to have settled on the banks of the Kuwana. The story goes that he had offended the King of Dehli and was pardoned on the intercession of a Brahman of Majhauli, whom he accompanied eastwards. In his new home he soon came into conflict with the Domkatars, and was again rescued by his Brahman friend. On the advice of the latter he proposed to the Domkatar Raja to give his daughter in marriage to the chieftain's son on condition of being allowed to retain part of his newly acquired possessions. The flattering offer was readily accepted and great preparations were made for the ceremony; but when Chandra Sen with his followers were admitted into the fort of Domingarh, he treacherously murdered all the Domkatar leaders, while others of his retinue fell upon the Domkatars outside the fort. Thus Chandra Sen, following the example of many other Rajput colonists in other parts, became one of the most powerful chiefs in the district, and he secured his position by arranging a marriage between his house and that of Majhauli.

The story has several variants, one account attributing the original settlement to Rup Narayan, an ancestor of Chandra Sen, but it is agreed that the latter had three sons or grandsons between whom the property was divided. One brother founded the Bansi estate in the Basti district; from the youngest, Randhir Singh, is descended the Raja of Unaula, while the eldest, Jagdhar or Jai Singh, took the eastern portion and became Raja of Satasi, so called from the fact that his domain was 87 *kos* in circuit. The earliest residence of the Satasi Raja was a fort near the Ramgarh Tal, possibly identical with the old stronghold at Bhauapar. The first Raja, as already mentioned, entered into conflict with the Bisens of Majhauli, the latter being eventually victorious. In the beginning of the 15th century the Satasi Raja died childless, and Hoal or Mahawal Singh of Unaula was adopted in his place. Possibly on this account a quarrel arose in the family, and some members established themselves near the shrine of Gorakhnath, where they founded the town of Gorakhpur, the place becoming the headquarters of the Raja at a subsequent period. In 1567, when Fidai Khan entered the Satasi territory, the Raja refused to be converted and fled to Gajpur, while Fidai Khan occupied Gorakhpur. Soon after 1610 Raja Basant Singh attacked and expelled the Muhammadan garrison, and built a fort on the site of the old jail in the Basantpur *muhalla*. For 70 years the Satasi Rajas retained their hold on the place, but about 1680 the Sarnets were expelled by Qazi Khalil-ur-Rahman, created *chakladar* of Gorakhpur by Aurangzeb, and Rajá Rudar Singh retreated to the Silhat pargana, building a strong fort round which the town of Rudarpur sprang up. During the 18th century the Rajas resided mainly at Rudarpur, but their estates suffered both from the misgovernment of the *amils* and the inroads of the Banjaras, so that much land went out of cultivation and relapsed into jungle. Worse results attended a reckless expedition undertaken by the Raja of Satasi against the Raja of Butwal, which ended with the complete defeat of the former in 1788. After the cession extravagance and mismanagement brought Satasi to the brink of ruin, and the final act was the rebellion of the Raja, who had been appointed to the committee of administration in 1857. His title and remaining estates were confiscated, and he himself died in the Andaman islands, the present representative of the family being his son's widow, who still resides in the old fort at Gajpur. Connected with Satasi were the Babus of Dumri and Tighra, whose lands were confiscated in 1858, while other members of the same house are the Babus of Bishunpura, Kota, Pandepar and Paikauli.

Practically nothing is known of the chronicles of Unaula. The estate was small, being only 21 *kos* in circumference, and the Rajas do not figure in history, though on two occasions they provided adoptive heirs for the Bansi house and once gave a younger son to Satasi. At the time of the cession Unaula was held by Raja Harihar Sarfaraz Singh, and his son, Rudra Partab Singh, remained quiet during the Mutiny, continuing to hold his estate till his death at the age of 99 in 1890. He was succeeded by his son, Raja Mahesh Partab Singh, who was then over 65 years of age; the latter died in 1904, when the property and title passed to his son, Bhunesh Partab Narayan Singh. The Raja resides in the family house at Unaula, or Sangrampur as the town is sometimes called; he owns 68 villages, all of which are in Bansgaon with the exception of one in Maharajganj, and pays a revenue of Rs. 11,379. Unaula.

The house of Tamkuhi claims descent from the Bhuinharin wife of Mayur, the ancestor of the Bisens. The first to attain prominence was Raja Kalyan Sahi of Kalyanpur Kawari in the Saran district. His descendants remained at Husipur in pargana Kalyanpur Kawari till Raja Fateh Sahai joined in the league against the British, shared in the defeat at Buxar and was in consequence expelled from Saran. His successful resistance to the Company and his subsequent death as a *faqir* are told in the history of the Saran district; but the fact which is of most importance, so far as Gorakhpur is concerned, was his retreat to the *tappa* of Bank Jogni in pargana Sidhua Jobna and his establishment in the fort of Tamkuhi, where his arrival was welcomed by the Raja of Majhauli as promising a powerful bulwark against Banjara raids. Owing to the disturbed state of the country Fateh Sahai was soon enabled to extend his influence Tamkuhi.

and at his death held about 100 villages, though most of these were lost owing to the quarrels and mismanagement of his sons. One of them, Shamsher Sahi, eventually recovered some by purchase between 1830 and 1840 and settled at Salemgarh, where his descendants still reside. The eldest son, Amardhan Sahi, died without issue and was succeeded by his brother, Dalmardan Sahi, the father of Raja Dalip Sahi, whose widow transferred her rights to Kharag Bahadur Sahi, grandson of Raja Fateh Sahi's youngest son, Ran Bahadur Sahi. This man obtained the recognition of his title about 1840, and was succeeded by his son, Kishan Partab Bahadur Sahi, who died in 1892. During the Mutiny the Raja prudently kept in the background and remained loyal if inactive; in later years he made large additions to his estate, while much has since been contributed by gifts and bequests. Raja Satrujit Partab Bahadur Sahi died in 1898, and the estate has since been managed by the Court of Wards on behalf of his son, Raja Indarjit Partab Bahadur Sahi. The estate comprises 219 villages assessed at Rs. 81,073 in this district, of which five are in tahsil Hata, two in Gorakhpur, one in Deoria and the rest in Padrauna. Besides these there are 42 villages in Gaya, acquired partly by purchase and partly by a legacy to Raja Kharag Bahadur Sahi from his maternal grandfather, the Raja of Tikari; four villages in Chapra and the Sarsundia estate of 79 villages in Muzaffarpur, bequeathed to the present Raja's father by Raja Raghunandan Singh.

Salemgarh.

Various families claim connection with the Tamkuhi house, such as the Babus of Pakaha, Banbira, Pharenda, Badraon, Bandarhi, Akha and Tirwa Sohan, all in the Padrauna tahsil. The Babus of Salemgarh, however, are by far the most important of the collateral branches. Shamsher Sahi had two sons, but the elder died childless and the younger left a daughter, Babui Ram Charan Kuari, who was married to Babu Ambika Prasad Narayan Singh and had three sons. The eldest of these is Siddeshri Prasad Narayan Singh who, in recognition of his public services and liberality during the famine of 1896-97, received the title of Rai Bahadur, and in 1907 was awarded the personal title of Raja. His estates comprise 63 villages in the Padrauna tahsil, with a revenue demand of Rs. 22,000.

Padrauna.

The Kurmi family of Padrauna traces its descent from one Bhopal Rai, who is said to have come from Kara in the Allahabad district about 1650, and was employed by the Raja of Majhauli, from whom he obtained the grant of five villages in *tappa* Bansi Chirgora. These villages were brought under cultivation by Bhopal Rai and his descendants, who seized every opportunity of enlarging the estate, one of them named Nathu Rai taking many villages in *tappa* Batsara from the Chandels and others from the Raja of Butwal. The same man is said to have attended the court of Aurangzeb in 1681, and to have there received the grant of 33 villages in the Padrauna tahsil with a revenue demand of Rs. 5,500; but it is more probable that the real date of Nathu Rai's acquisition was in the 18th century, when the Banjaras were working great havoc in the district, especially as it is known that the Raja of Majhauli encouraged the Rais of Padrauna in the formation of a compact estate, and it was certainly at this time that the larger portion of the property was acquired. The descendants of Nathu Rai divided their possessions, but one-half was disastrously mismanaged and eventually was confiscated after the Mutiny for the rebellion of its owners, while the other half experienced many vicissitudes. About 1810 it was sold for arrears and fetched Rs. 8,000; but the sale was cancelled on the ground that the price was inadequate, and the Kurmis retained possession, though subsequently litigation with the Maharaja of Bettiah once more brought the estate to the verge of ruin. About the middle of the last century it recovered under the able management of Rai Isri Partab Rai, who purchased the valuable grant of Padrauna Jangal for the sum of Rs. 1,15,000, and derived such profits therefrom as to enable him to pay off his debts and even to regain some of the lost property. His son, Rai Madan Gopal, made further improvements and, on his death in 1890, left a rich estate to his cousin and adopted son, Rai Udit Narayan, who in 1897 received the personal title of Raja. He died in 1900, and was succeeded by his eldest son, Rai Brij Narayan, who was created Raja in 1906 in recognition of the distinguished position held by his family and of his public spirit and liberality. The Padrauna estate now comprises 364 villages in the Padrauna tahsil with a revenue demand of Rs.

86,365, in addition to a few villages situated in the districts of Ballia, Azamgarh and Champaran.

Dumri. The only estate held by Sikhs in the district is that of Dumri, which was confiscated for the rebellion of the Dumri Babus, descended from a younger branch of the Satasi family, and bestowed on Sardar Surat Singh, a relative of Ranjit Singh of Lahore, who had rendered loyal services during the Mutiny. On his death in 882 his sons, Sardars Amar Singh and Sundar Singh, were minors and the estate was administered by the Court of Wards till 1892. The property, which comprises 59 villages assessed at Rs. 15,429 in the Sadr tahsil, is in a flourishing condition and is managed by Sardar Harcharan Singh, a relative of the owner.

Mian Sahib The Musalman estates of importance are very few in number. The reputed head of the Musalman community is the Mian Sahib, an extensive proprietor belonging to a line of devotees who hand down the property and tradition from pupil to pupil. It originated with Saiyid Ghulam Ashraf, a native of Bukhara, who came to Dehli in the reign of Muhammad Shah, but fled from the city during one of the invasions by Ahmad Shah Abdali, and finally settled at Shahpur in pargana Dhuriapar. His son, Raushan Ali Shah, remained at Shahpur till middle life and then became a Shia devotee; he quitted his village, adopted a religious life and rapidly acquired a reputation for peculiar sanctity. He made it his object to build an *Imambara* at Gorakhpur, where he owned the *muhalla* of Haji Daud Chak, inherited from his maternal grandfather, and in his task he was assisted in 1790 by Asaf-ud-daula, the Nawab Wazir of Oudh, who also bestowed on him 15 villages in revenue-free tenure, the grant being recognised by the British Government in 1803 and subsequently confirmed by a new *sanad* in 1834. Raushan Ali Shah was succeeded in 1816 by his pupil Ahmad Ali Shah, who was the first to receive the name of Mian Sahib. He lived till the age of eighty, and for his loyal conduct during the Mutiny he was rewarded by a grant of money and several additional villages, to compensate for the damage done to the *Imambara* by the rebels. On his death in 1865 he was succeeded by his pupil Wajid Ali Shah, the present guardian of the *Imambara*. In addition to the 15 villages held revenue-free the property comprises 44 villages in the Padrauna tahsil and 17 in Gorakhpur, with an aggregate revenue demand of Rs. 8,889.

Sabzposh family.

Another family with considerable estates is that known by the peculiar title of Sabzposh. Tradition relates that in early days they migrated from Medina to Persia and thence came to India, Mir Saiyid Shah Ahmad settling at Ajodhya, where his son, Mir Saiyid Musa Sultan-ul-Ashiqin, was commissioned to build the mosque by Babar. His descendant, Mir Saiyid Shah Qayam-ud-din, left Ajodhya and came to pray in the solitudes of the Gorakhpur jungles, subsequently receiving grants of cash and revenue-free lands from the emperor. These grants were resumed by the Nawab Wazir, but in the days of Asaf-ud-daula, his grandson, Mir Saiyid Shah Abdullah, obtained a *sanad* for Bhathat and other villages to be held on a payment of Rs. 970 per annum. After the cession it was ordered that the grant and pension should be continued only for the lifetime of the three grandsons of Mir Saiyid Shah Ahmad-ullah, one of whom, Shah Ghulam, seems to have been given the surname of Sabzposh, when on a visit to the court of the Nawab Wazir. The title has since been held by the head of the family, which is at present represented by Mir Saiyid Shah Wilayat Ali. He owns 33 villages in the Sadr tahsil, 16 in Maharajganj and ten in Hata, the whole being assessed at Rs. 14,778.

Pindari jagir.

Shortly after the Pindari campaign of 1818 in Central India the Company endeavoured to avert the possibility of further disturbances in that quarter by settling some of the Pindari leaders in remote parts of the country. Among them were Qadir Bakhsh, who received the Ganeshpur property in the Basti district, and Karim Khan, who was given a large estate in the Bansgaon tahsil taken from the Raja of Barhiapar in satisfaction of arrears of revenue. At the first the grant was revenue-free; but after the death of Karim Khan it was assessed at Rs. 6,000 in perpetuity, a similar course being followed in the case of Ganeshpur. At the seventh settlement, however, engagements weretaken from the *birtias* and other occupants of the villages who held practically the whole of the grant, the Pindaris receiving 55 per cent. of the estimated rental. The present representatives of the family are Nur-ullah Khan, Abdur Rahim Khan, Abdul Majid Khan and Abdul Hamid Khan, who reside in an unpretentious brick house at Sikriganj on the banks of the Kuwana; their estate comprises no less than 145 villages, all in the Bansgaon tahsil, but the revenue assessment is only Rs. 7,105. The descendants of Karim Khan have arrogated to themselves the title of Nawab: but to this they have no sort of claim, and it is not recognised by Government.

Other landowners.

In Gorakhpur itself live a number of wealthy landowners possessing villages in various parts of the district. Such is Babu Bhagwati Prasad, an Agarwala banker, who holds 115 villages, assessed at Rs. 15,356, in the Hata, Bansgaon and Sadr tahsils. A family of Kayasths, represented by Rai Kishan Kishori Chand, has extensive possessions in the Sadr tahsil, paying Rs. 9,337 revenue on an estate of 21 villages. One of the largest single landowners in the north of the tahsil is the Goshain Mahant of Harpur, Ram Ratangir. The first Mahant came to this district from Benares about 150 years ago and received a grant of land from a family of Tiwaris in the neighbourhood, to which constant additions have been made, the property now comprising 36 villages with a revenue demand of Rs. 7,318. The Goshains are forbidden to marry, but are succeeded by their adopted *chelas* or pupils. In the Padrauna tahsil the Babus of Madhopur have a very considerable estate of 105 villages, with an annual revenue demand of Rs. 10,484; and the Babus of Paikauli in tahsil Hata own 26 villages assessed at Rs. 10,864. Maharani Janki Kunwar, widow of the late Maharaja of Bettiah in the Champaran district, may also be included among the landowners of this district: for the estate, now under the management of the Court of Wards, includes 23 villages in the Hata tahsil with an annual demand of Rs. 9,704. Among the coparcenary communities one of the largest and most wealthy is that of the Dube Brahmans, residing in the villages of Barhampur and Mithabel in *tappa* Rajdhani of the Gorakhpur tahsil: they own 29 villages with a revenue of Rs. 12,719. The Sainthwars of Pali in the Rapti *kachhar* hold 34 villages assessed at Rs. 11,197, and further south in the Bansgaon tahsil the Tiwaris of Rajgarh, half of whose estate is now under the Court of Wards, hold 127 villages on an annual revenue of Rs. 13,360, while in the north the Tiwaris of Balua in Maharajganj own 37 villages assessed at Rs. 8,957.

Other tenures.

Besides the ordinary forms of land tenure there are one or two others which deserve mention. In the Tilpur pargana 22 villages are held in fee simple, the proprietary rights having been purchased outright in 1858-59. This method of acquisition was adopted in the forest lands of several other districts for a time, but the permanent alienation of State rights in this way was definitely prohibited in 1860. In 31 villages of the Maharajganj tahsil there exists a special class of revenue-paying proprietors called jungle squatters, consisting originally of cultivators brought from other parts of the district, who were given unreclaimed land on lease on condition of bringing it under cultivation. In 1875 they and their representatives were recognised as proprietors by Mr. Lumsden in a conditional settlement, which stipulated that their sub-tenants should be regarded as tenants-at-will, and that they themselves should not allow their lands to relapse into a lower state of cultivation as regards the area under tillage and the number of inhabited houses. At the last settlement it was found that these conditions had been observed in five cases only, and though this entailed the forfeiture of the right to settlement in the others the Board declined to enforce the penalty.

Revenue-free holdings.

In the following chapter it will be seen how the fraudulent action of the subordinate revenue officials caused a large number of estates to be entered as revenue-free during the early years of British rule, in addition to the already considerable area so defined under the administration of the Nawab Wazirs of Oudh. Such procedure in the confused state of the revenue records was as easy as it was profitable, and it was not till 1823 that the practice came to light, while the first regular settlement in 1840 afforded the earliest opportunity for an exhaustive enquiry into the titles on which such lands were held. This brought about a great reduction in the area, which nevertheless amounted to 51,650 acres in 1845, affecting 83 villages and *mahals* held free of revenue in perpetuity and 48 in which the revenue was assigned for the lifetime of the possessor and one or more successors. During the currency of this and the next settlement further reductions were made, and in 1889, when the last revision was carried out there were but 27,230 acres of revenue-free land, comprising 87 villages or *mahals* held in perpetuity with a nominal demand of Rs. 28,227, assessed merely for the purpose of calculating cesses, and three villages with a nominal revenue of Rs. 574 held for a limited period.

Forest grants.

Some reference has been made in dealing with the forests of the district to the system of grants adopted by Government at the suggestion of Mr. Bird, with a view to bringing under cultivation the large tracts of waste land and jungle. In most cases the land was granted for fifty years on what were considered to be particularly favourable terms, subject to a progressive demand, reaching its maximum in the thirtieth year, and to the stipulation that the grantee should bring a specified amount of the area under tillage within a limited period under penalty of resumption. The experiment was attended with marked success, and very large grants were made to a number of well-to-do Europeans. The first grant was that of Basharatpur, 1,120 acres in extent, given to Mr. Wilkinson in 1830, and in the next ten years no less than 618,547 acres were distributed in this manner, 418,000 acres being in the hands of Europeans. Much of this lay in Basti, and in the present Gorakhpur district there were 22 grants with an area of 319,220 acres. The largest were the Lehra and Bargaona grants in the Haveli and Binayakpur parganas, with an area of 69.920 acres, given to Mr. Bridgman; the three grants of Sonari, in pargana Tilpur, Bhainsaha in Sidhua Jobna and Sumbhakhor in Haveli, aggregating 63,148 acres, given to Mr. Finch; the three grants of Bargaon Chaura in Sidhua Jobna, and Bhilaunji and Bhilampur in Haveli, 55,780 acres in all, held by Mr. Sym; the Banki, Rasulpur and Keotali grants of 35,372 acres in Haveli held by Mr. Fitzgerald; the two grants of Majhar and Lehra, 32,169 acres in all, given to Mr. Debnam; and Lady Malkin's grant of Nagwa, comprising 23,200 acres in Binayakpur. Others of considerable size were Mr. Campier's two grants of Bhari Baisi and Kauria in Haveli, covering 17,624 acres; the two grants of Bhawar in Tilpur with an area of 13,048 acres, given to Mr. Downes, and the Ramgarh grant of 11,198 acres in Haveli held by Mr. McCormish. Besides these, there were three small grants comprising Belwar in Haveli, 4,714 acres, owned by

Mr. Morais, Kahistan in Tilpur, 1,932 acres, held by Mr. Hastings and Mr. Wilkinson's grant of Basharatpur already mentioned. About 1840 the authorities became apprehensive that too large an area might be granted away for a long period on terms insufficiently profitable to Government, and the practice was consequently stopped, though other grants of a smaller kind continued to be made under somewhat more strict conditions till 1850, while very few new grants were assigned under the rules of 1852. In the meantime Mr. Tucker had conducted an investigation in 1846 into the conditions of the grants with the result that 280,179 acres, mainly in this district, were resumed and retained by Government as reserved forest or made over to the original settlers. In 1872 the existing grants covered an area of 362,035 acres, of which 194,414 were under cultivation. It was long before this date that the experience of the grantees had proved the groundless nature of the apprehension entertained by Government, since in most cases they found the task undertaken was beyond their capacity or their means. The unhealthiness of the climate made it very difficult to get settlers and to retain them on their lands; the proximity of the forest rendered cultivation precarious and the hostility of the local *zamindars* created constant trouble. In spite of the light revenue many grantees after a few years either resigned their estates or else sold them piecemeal to native *zamindars*, this practice being especially common in the eastern grants lying in this district, for in Basti the conditions were in every respect more favourable. Hence it has happened that, while six of the seven grants held in the latter district by Europeans in 1846 are still flourishing concerns, only four of the 22 in Gorakhpur have survived. The Sonari grant is now reserved forest; Ramgarh and Rasulpur were sold to various *zamindars*; Bargaon Chaura, also known as Jangal Padrauna, was bought intact on Mr. Sym's death by Rai Madan Gopal Rai, and now forms one of the most valuable parts of the estate held by his descendant, the present Raja of Padrauna; while the Sumbhakhor grant was resumed and given on fresh terms to other recipients. In the majority of cases the period for which the grant was made has terminated, and the land has been assessed to revenue in the ordinary way; but there are still 59 plots with an area of 81,877 acres, forming portions of 21 large grants, and at present paying a revenue of Rs. 26,932, whose terms have not yet expired. They are situated in the Sadr, Padrauna and Maharajganj tahsils, and the last will come under assessment in 1914.

Lehra.

Of the estates which have survived the largest and by far the most important is that of Lehra, situated in the Lehra *tappa* of pargana Haveli in the Maharajganj tahsil. It was granted originally in 1833 to Mr. J. H. Bridgman, and then consisted of 50,800 acres of forest and grass plains. By 1840 some 12,500 acres of the grass lands and 6,500 acres of forest had been cleared and brought under cultivation at great expense, when the outbreak of an epidemic caused the death or the dispersal of the tenants, with the result that much of the clearings relapsed into jungle and the rent was decreased by 25 per cent. in three years. Such vicissitudes were not the only difficulties to be faced. The neighbouring *zamindars*, who had been previously in the habit of levying a grazing fee on the great herds brought up annually to the Lehra pastures, made every effort to keep the land waste and to prevent the cultivation by systematic trespass and annoyance. A further great obstacle lay in the superstition of the tenantry, especially those who cultivated land reclaimed from forest, universally regarded as the special abode of demons and evil spirits. Even to-day the sawyers who work for the railway sleeper contractors in the forests of Nepal invariably commence operations by doing *puja* to the guardian spirits; and Mr. Bridgman tells of the desertion of a large body of labourers because one or two of their number were tripped up by concealed stumps when ploughing. Despite every effort it was found impossible to obtain tenants at remunerative rents, and in 1848 Mr. Bridgman resigned 25,000 acres of his grant. Subsequently cultivators were induced to take up holdings at lower rents, and the land was restored to cultivation when the drought of 1873-74 overtook the unfortunate estate, with the result that in 1880 about 125 villages had been completely deserted and much of the land was covered with young forest. A fresh start was again made with nominal rents at a small yearly increment, and in order to guard against another such calamity extensive irrigation works were constructed, to which reference has already been made in chapter II. By their means,* coupled with the indefatigable perseverance of the owner, success has been achieved and steady progress maintained. Mr. Bridgman died in 1892, and the estate passed to his former manager and son-in-law, Mr. J. J. Holdsworth, C. I. E., the present owner, on whose behalf it is managed, during his absence, by Mr. F. Howard. The present area is 36,399 acres and the revenue demand amounts to Rs. 16,039 annually.

South of Lehra, on the borders of the Sadr tahsil, lies Bhilaunji, representing part of the Bhilaunji and Bhilampur grants made originally to Mr. Sym. This property was split up and sold, some 1,700 acres, known as Agahi and Bahli, being bought by the Babus of Tighra. The lands of the latter were confiscated for rebellion, and the two plots, together with eleven *jagir* villages, were given to Mr. William Peppe in recognition of services rendered by him during the Mutiny. The Bhilaunji estate thus formed passed on the death of Mr. Peppe to his heirs, Messrs. W. C. and G. T. G. Peppe and their sister Mrs. Larpent, who are also part owners of Birdpur and Alidapur in Basti. They reside in England and the whole property is managed on their behalf by Mr. D. Ricketts. On this estate there are considerable protective works on the banks of the Rohin, consisting of a *bandh* more than three miles in length with masonry sluice-gates, and a second *bandh* over two miles long, which protects the lowlands in the vicinity of the Rapti. The present area is 5,456 acres and the revenue assessment Rs. 6,793.* Bhilaunji.

The Bhari Baisi grant between Lehra and Bhilaunji and the Kauria grant to the south of Bhilaunji were originally given to Mr. J. Campier. He left three sons, Messrs. J. C. Campier, E. Campier and A. Campier; but the second sold his share to the first and the third died without issue, so that the whole estate will once more be concentrated in the possession of a single party, Mr. A. Campier's widow having only a life interest in his share of the property. Mr. J. C. Campier died some years ago, leaving a daughter and a widow, of whom the former was subsequently married to Mr. Argles, now deceased, and her children are the heirs to the whole estate. It should be mentioned that Kauria Bhari Baisi and Kauria.

* Gazetteer of Basti, pp. 99 and 100.

belongs entirely to Mrs. Argles, and only Bhari-Baisi was divided between the three brothers. The former is 7,352 acres in extent and pays a revenue of Rs. 7,720, while the latter covers 2,776 acres assessed at Rs. 2,154.

Basharatpur. Mr. Wilkinson, the recipient of the first grant made to a European, was the C. M. S. missionary then stationed at Gorakhpur, as already mentioned on a previous page. The grant, known as Jangal Wilkinson, was 1,128 acres in extent, and was brought under cultivation by converts attached to the mission. A village sprang up on the spot and was appropriately named Basharatpur: it is still a flourishing Christian settlement, possessing a church and a school, and is under the care and superintendence of the representative of the C. M. S. at Gorakhpur. The present area is 967 acres and the revenue demand is Rs. 990.

Subordinate tenures. Subordinate tenures of an under-proprietary nature are extremely numerous. They are of diverse origin and varying value, the highest position being that of the *arazidars*, the owners of plots of land included within the area of a *mauza* but held on a distinct tenure from the rest. The origin of these *arazis*, which at the last settlement were 107,750 acres in extent and were held by 27,903 persons, seems to have been somewhat similar to that of the irregular *birts* of pargana Sidhua Jobna, hereafter described, and they are particularly common in that part of the district, the bulk of the remainder lying in the Deoria and Bansgaon tahsils. Their distinctive feature is that no *malikana* or seignorial fee is paid, the holders being entered along with the other proprietors, though on a separate engagement for the revenue.

Birts. The inferior proprietors proper are either *birtias* or *muqaddams*, the former occurring mainly in the parganas of Dhuriapar and Salempur, the two great Rajput principalities. For many centuries, owing to their isolated position, the local Rajas were practically the sole owners of the soil and not merely the representatives of a supreme authority, so that it was from this source that almost all the existing proprietary rights are ultimately derived. The *birtia* is an assignee of land granted by the Raja, and as such assignments were made for various reasons there are naturally several kinds of *birt* differing from one another in a somewhat marked degree. Thus the *jiwan birt* was an assignment in maintenance to cadet members of the ruling family; the *murchabandi birt* was a feudal tenure, the holder being bound to serve the Raja in war and attend him in peace, as occasion required; the *marwat birt,* also called *khumbaha,* was a grant made to the family or dependants of a man slain in battle; and the *shankalp* was a grant to a Brahman, made either as an act of piety or else in return for religious services rendered to the family. All such grants partook of the nature of a gift, but occasionally the *birt* involved the sale and purchase of land. Thus in 1817 the Rani of Satasi offered to sell outright 19,000 *bighas* at Rs. 2 per *bigha* or to give it in *birt* for Re. 1, subject to an annual payment of one-fourth of the produce. In any case the *birtia* had to clear and cultivate the land, paying an annual *malikana* to the overlord, though, subject to these and other well-defined conditions, his proprietary right was recognised, and there was no question of resumption on the part of the grantor. At the time of the cession there was an immense number of *birts,* comprising a large proportion of the cultivated area, but since that date they have been seldom created, owing to the change in the status of the Rajas. Altogether there were 78,434 inferior proprietors of all kinds at the last settlement, paying *malikana* to the amount of Rs. 55,014.

Other forms.

These figures include other forms than *birt,* but not the lands of the *arazidars.* The *muqaddam birt* is of a different description from the rest, being adopted generally in the reclamation of the waste and forest lands of the north, where the *birt* proper is unknown. The *muqaddam* was the headman of the settlement, acting as intermediary between the landlord and the tenants: he made and recovered advances, collected the rents and was generally responsible for the promotion of tillage. In recognition of his services he was allowed to hold at a nominal rate as much land as he could cultivate, and often received a percentage on the collections. This system was utilised by Government on occasions for the purpose of reclaiming waste, as for example in 1828, when a *muqaddam* was sent to settle the Tharus in Binayakpur; and it is clear that in its origin this tenure was wholly non-proprietary. Mention may also be made of an irregular form of *birt*, which seems to have taken its rise during the anarchy of the eighteenth century. Weak and impoverished *zamindars* at that time were often only too glad to surrender a large part of their lands to one of the powerful *taluqdars* in return for the protection he afforded them against the extortions of the *amil* and his subordinates or the depredations of the roving Banjaras. The *zamindar* would reserve a sufficient amount of land for the supply of his own needs and this he would hold rent-free or on *birt* tenure. In other cases the process was reversed, when the Raja forcibly usurped the *zamindar's* rights, permitting him a small share as a *birtia*. This happened most frequently in Sidhua Jobna, which was most exposed to attacks on the part of the Banjaras, and where the power of the great landlords was uncontrolled. In the early days of British rule these subordinate tenures formed the subject of long enquiries and anxious deliberation. The first settlements were made with the Rajas and *taluqdars*, and the *birtias* were not treated as proprietors or allowed to engage separately; but a change was made on the report of the collector, Mr. Armstrong, in 1835, when the tenure was held to be heritable and transferable, the rights of the *birtias* as under-proprietors, entitled as such to engage for the revenue direct with Government, being fully recognised. They had nevertheless to pay into the treasury the *malikana*, as a rule at the rate of 10 per cent. of the assessed demand; though in some cases it was a fixed sum, the amount being made over to the grantors of the *birt* or their representatives. The justice of this arrangement, while beyond question in *birt* and cognate holdings, is hardly clear in the case of *muqaddams*, since it certainly involves much loss to the *zamindars*; but the latter form of tenure is relatively uncommon in comparison with *birt*.

Cultivating castes. As with proprietors so in the case of the cultivating castes it is necessary to fall back on the returns of the last settlement for statistics of area. The subsequent lapse of time is a matter of little importance, for there has been no perceptible change in the distribution of the various classes of cultivators. Brahmans take the lead with 17·73 per cent. of the area included in holdings, the highest figure in any one pargana being 36·19 per cent.

in Bhauapar, while throughout the Sadr, Bansgaon and Deoria tahsils, excepting pargana Haveli, the proportion exceeds 20 per cent.; this tract being the special sphere of the great Rajput colonies, in whose train the Brahmans first came to settle in these parts. The Rajputs themselves cultivate 9·08 per cent. of the land and are strongest in the same tahsils, particularly Bansgaon. The Ahirs, who are unusually numerous in this district and have betaken themselves to agriculture in addition to their traditional occupation as graziers, hold 10·32 per cent. of the cultivation, the figure rising to 16·64 in pargana Chillupar. In the foremost rank of husbandmen stand the Kurmis, who occur in strength everywhere and are by no means confined to Padrauna: they hold 11·22 per cent. of the area, the highest proportion being 31·11 in pargana Haveli of the Hata tahsil, followed by 24·79 in Maghar. The Koeris, as a class the best of all cultivators, are in possession of 6·04 per cent., and are most common in Padrauna, while they also are found in large numbers in Shahjahanpur and Dhuriapar. The ubiquitous Chamars, though endowed with no great skill, have by sheer force of numbers acquired a considerable share, amounting to 5·95 per cent. of the cultivation, and the proportion is much the same in all parganas. Musalmans hold in all 6·09 per cent. and are strongest in Shahjahanpur, where the proportion rises to 10·61 per cent., while there is a large number of Julaha cultivators in Tilpur. No other castes are worthy of mention, save perhaps the Tharus, who cultivate 14·45 per cent. of the land in Binayakpur but are seldom found elsewhere. Christian agriculturists in 1889 occupied ·77 per cent. of the area, represented mainly by the home farms of the Padrauna planters and the mission settlements of Basharatpur and Stornpur near Gorakhpur.

The cultivating tenures are of the same form as those found everywhere, and the district presents no peculiarities in this respect. An exception may, however, be made in favour of a small class of tenants in pargana Bhauapar, where at the last settlement 370 holdings, with an aggregate area of 990 acres, were in the hands of *mandidars*. They have occupancy rights, which are not only heritable but transferable, and pay a fixed Cultivating tenures.

rent which is not subject to enhancement, the rate being sometimes the average revenue rate and sometimes four annas per *bigha* more than that amount. The privilege is said to have been granted originally by the Raja of Satasi and has always been recognised by the British Government. At the last settlement the total area included in holdings was 1,974,442 acres, and of this 427,403 acres or 21·64 per cent. were cultivated by proprietors and the remainder by tenants. The proportion of owners' cultivation was highest in the Bansgaon tahsil, reaching 45·58 in Bhauapar, and 40·08 in Dhuriapar, while in pargana Haveli it dropped to 15·23 per cent. On the other hand it was found that the average area of such holdings was far smaller in the south than in the north and centre of the district, being only 1·92 acres in Dhuriapar as compared with 30·88 in Binayakpur. This is due to the great area of the villages, especially in the jungle grants, and also to the fact that immense tracts in them are held as *sir* or *khudkasht* by one or two proprietors. In 1907-08 the total area included in holdings was 2,205,909 acres, and of this 555,015 acres were cultivated by owners, the proportion having risen to 25·16 per cent. It was no less than 43·62 in the whole Bansgaon tahsil and 34·95 in Deoria; but elsewhere the figure was not much below the district average save in Padrauna, where it amounted only to 16·21 per cent. Of the tenant-held area 9,041 acres, or ·41 per cent. of the whole, were in the hands of ex-proprietors. The area is everywhere small, but it has much increased since the settlement, when only 3,062 acres came under this head. Occupancy tenants held 686,739 acres or 31·13 per cent., and in this direction there has been a great decrease since the settlement, when the total was 834,020 acres. A similar decline has been observed in the Basti district, and it is due in large measure to the extended area of owners' cultivation, the proprietors doing all in their power to oust the occupancy tenant and, in the case of cultivating communities, to get as much land as possible into their own hands. At the same time the decrease is more apparent than real, for there is a very large area which has been held by tenants for the prescribed period, but which has not yet been recorded under occupancy holdings. The proportion is only 18·92 per cent. in the Maharajganj tahsil, where cultivation is still in a fluctuating condition, while the tract also contains a large amount of recent tillage. The highest figure for any tahsil is 40·71 in Hata, and next come Padrauna with 36·01, Deoria with 35·7, Gorakhpur with 34·11 and Bansgaon with 26·72 per cent. It is, however, remarkable that at settlement the proportion was as high as 31·56 in Maharajganj and 46·15 in Gorakhpur, showing that an immense number of old holdings have been resigned on account of famines and other causes. The recent decrease in the occupancy area is the more noteworthy because at the settlement of 1865 there were but 359,838 acres held by such privileged tenants, while during the currency of the settlement the figure was increased by 474,182 acres, the extension being most remarkable in the parganas of Shahjahanpur, Sidhua Jobna and Hasanpur Maghar.

Tenants-at-will. At the last settlement tenants-at-will held 672,622 acres or 34·26 per cent. of the total area in holdings, as compared with 807,411 so recorded in 1865. The decline of occupancy right, and the recent extension of the cultivation have led to a very great increase, for in 1907-08 the area in possession of ordinary tenants was 922,137 acres or 41·8 per cent. of the whole. The proportion varies widely in the different tahsils, being as much as 58·76 in Maharajganj and 45·89 in Padrauna, which contain the largest amount of new tillage. It drops to 40·8 in Gorakhpur, 35·73 in Hata, 26·76 in Deoria and 26·75 per cent. in Bansgaon, the last being the only tahsil in which privileged tenants are more numerous than others. As already mentioned, however, the area will probably be much reduced at the next settlement, since many of these tenants-at-will have been in possession of their holdings for a considerable period.

Rent-free holdings. There remains the rent-free area of 32,977 acres or 1·5 per cent. of the whole, the proportion varying from 2·36 in Bansgaon to ·95 per cent. in Maharajganj. The bulk of this represents the *jagirs* of the *goraits* or village watchmen, which are exempt from revenue. These *jagirs* aggregated 28,002 acres at the last settlement, the area of individual plots varying from an average of 4·48 acres in pargana Tilpur to 2·47 in Dhuriapar and depending on the amount considered necessary to support the *gorait* and his family. The other rent-free plots are not exempt from revenue, which is calculated on their potential rental. They are for the most part charitable grants and are usually very minute. Such plots are found mainly in the parganas which have been longest settled, about half the total area lying in the Bansgaon and Deoria tahsils.

Grain rents.

Throughout the district rents are almost universally paid in cash, and, whatever may have been the practice in former days, grain rents are now extremely rare, prevailing only in lands where the rice crop is particularly precarious owing to the risk of its being insufficiently watered or else ruined by floods. At the last settlement the total area thus held was but 5,540 acres, and the bulk of this lay in the parganas of Maghar and Sidhua Jobna, while elsewhere payment in kind is practically unknown. The share taken by the landlord ranges from one-third to one-half of the produce, the smaller amount being more usual; and the division is effected either by *kankut* or appraisement of the standing crop, or else by *batai* or actual weighment of the garnered grain on the threshing floor.

Cash rents.

Cash rents are of a simple nature and present few features of interest. In former days a peculiar form of rent was found in *tappa* Sirsia of pargana Binayakpur and still exists in parts of the Basti district. This was the *halbandi*, a fixed sum being paid per plough irrespective of the size of the holding; it continued in force till the last settlement, but was then commuted into a lump rent attested at the actual amount paid on the areas in the tenants' actual possession. In early days cash rents must have been very low, for between 1840 and 1865 the average rate per acre of cultivation rose by 36 per cent., and in the latter year the average in the settled tract was only Rs. 2·07 per acre, while at the last settlement the rate was Rs. 2·52, showing a further rise of 27·96 per cent. This rise was greatest in the Bansgaon tahsil, especially in the Unaula pargana and was lowest in Gorakhpur and Hata. In the expired jungle grants assessed for the first time at the last settlement the average was Rs. 2·13, and in the still unexpired grants it was only Re. 1·85. Naturally there was a great variation between the rates of different localities. Actually the lowest rent was Re. ·72 in the assessed grants of pargana Tilpur, which offers a remarkable contrast to the rate of Rs. 3·27 paid in the unassessed grants of Hata. In the settled tract rents were nowhere below Rs. 2·5 save in Padrauna and Maharajganj, the lowest rate being Re. 1·1 in pargana Binayakpur and the highest Rs. 3·07 in Hasanpur Maghar. The average for the Gorakhpur tahsil was Rs. 2·9, for Deoria Rs. 2·77 and for Bansgaon Rs. 2·71. The low average of the rates is very striking, and it is highly probable that the true rents were extensively concealed at the time of settlement. In 1907-08 the average for all tenant-held land was Rs. 3·16, but it is certain that this figure fails to represent the real rental of the district. Attestation has been in progress since 1907, and it appears that the recorded rents are at least 30 per cent. below the actual figure. The rents of occupancy tenants are almost always higher than those of tenants-at-will, for the reason that the land held by the former class is generally much superior in quality to that of the latter. Further the pressure on the land is not sufficient even yet to enable a landlord to effect much by threats of ejectment, and this was still more the case at the time of the settlement, when large areas in the north were untenanted. Then the occupancy rental in the settled tracts averaged Rs. 2·94 as compared with Rs. 2·55 paid by tenants-at-will. The recorded rate for occupancy holdings in 1907-08 was Rs. 3·32, and varied from Rs. 2·58 in Maharajganj to Rs. 3·76 in Deoria, the average for the other tahsils approximating closely to the district figure. The highest rate was Rs. 3·96 in pargana Hasanpur Maghar and the lowest Re. 1·59 in Binayakpur. The rate for tenants-at-will was Rs. 3·05, and ranged from Rs. 2·47 in the Maharajganj tahsil to Rs. 3·92 in Deoria, the relation to the occupancy rental being much the same everywhere. Higher rents are of course paid by *shikmis* or sub-tenants, who held as much as 274,795 acres on 12·46 per cent. of the area included in holdings ; but here again it is indubitable that much concealment has been practised. The general average was Rs. 3·85 per acre, the highest rate for any one tahsil being Rs. 4·15 in Deoria, followed by Rs. 4·11 in Padrauna and Rs. 3·91 in Bansgaon, while the lowest was Rs. 3·37 in Maharajganj. The area sublet is generally good land reserved by the proprietors for *khudkasht* and cannot therefore be taken as typical of the district as a whole.

Condition of the people.

When the district was first made over to the East India Company the cultivators of the soil were the mere serfs of the Rajas and their immediate dependants. They had no rights and no privileges, and their one duty was to obey the behests of the *zamindar*, from whose order there was no appeal and no redress. Since that time their condition has improved in an extraordinary degree. Occupancy rights were created in 1859 and ex-proprietary privileges came into being in 1873; regular procedure for the settlement, the realisation and the enhancement of rent has been established, and forcible ejectment, save by order of court, is becoming less frequent every year. But, while the tenant has been enabled to lift up his head and meet his landlord in open court, the change has been accomplished but slowly and is still incomplete. As late as 1869 it was reported that tenant right was non-existent, and the universal opinion prevailed that tenancy lasted only so long as the landlord pleased. The reason lay, naturally enough, in the ignorance of the peasantry and their inability to shake themselves free from the tradition of centuries. Improvement first became apparent in the south and thence gradually spread northwards with the immigation of cultivators of the better class; and it is now safe to say that, except in the northern half of the Maharajganj and Padrauna tahsils, the average rustic of this district is not appreciably inferior in capacity and intelligence to that of other parts of the United Provinces. In one respect he has a decided advantage, since in all differences with his landlord he has at his command the powerful argument that the culturable land is more than sufficient for the needs of the population. The improvement in his material prosperity is less obvious, for wages are very low in this part of the country and their rise has apparently not kept pace with the increased cost of living, although probably matters will be adjusted in the course of time. This affects the labourers rather than the tenantry, who benefit directly from the increased value of agricultural produce, while the advent of the railway has rendered the market very much more accessible than was formerly the case. The standard of comfort, itself a vague and elastic phrase, has generally risen, the improvement being visible in the clothing and household furniture of the people:

but besides cloth, salt, kerosene oil and metal vessels, there are few articles of commerce within the reach of the poorer classes. Indebtedness exists everywhere, as has always been the case, but the question is no more acute in Gorakhpur than in other districts; and it may be hoped that the continued success of the agricultural banks will render the tenantry less bound to the money-lender than has been customary in the past. The landowners are generally in good condition, save where the increase in the number of co-sharers has reduced the individual profits to an amount inadequate for their support in comfort. The great estates, such as Majhauli, Tamkuhi, Padrauna and Dumri, are at present singularly well managed, while the smaller *zamindars*, many of whom are none the less men of ample substance, are with a few salient exceptions prosperous and capable administrators of their possessions and affairs. In 1890 Mr. Cruickshank observed that the number of elephants kept by the *zamindars* of this district was a clear proof of their solid and solvent position; for, as he pertinently remarks, "few objects are less easily withdrawn from the sight of the revenue official in search of something to distrain."

CHAPTER IV.

ADMINISTRATION AND REVENUE.

District Staff.

Gorakhpur was in early days the headquarters of a division which included the modern districts of Gorakhpur, Basti, Azamgarh and part of Ballia; but after the Mutiny the whole was merged in the Benares division, the present commissionership of Gorakhpur, comprising this district, Basti and Azamgarh, dating from the 1st of April 1891. The district is in charge of a magistrate and collector, whose sanctioned staff consists of two covenanted assistants with full powers, six deputy collectors with full powers and one gazetted officer with less than full powers, in addition to six tahsildars. In practice, however, this allowance has been found insufficient for the needs of so large an area, and is always exceeded. In order to relieve the pressure caused by the constantly increasing volume of work the subdivision of Kasia, conterminous with the Sidhua Jobna pargana and the present Padrauna tahsil, was created in 1868. The assistant or joint magistrate, residing at Kasia, is invested with the powers of a collector throught out his subdivision, hearing appeals from all subordinate courts and performing the other duties of the office, the object being to mitigate the inconvenience of managing the eastern part of the district from headquarters so far distant as Gorakhpur. In 1905 another subdivision of a somewhat similar nature was formed out of the Deoria and Hata tahsils. It is administered in the same manner by an assistant or joint magistrate or deputy collector, assisted by a deputy collector in charge of tahsil Hata, both officers residing at Deoria. In addition to the regular magisterial courts there is at Gorakhpur a bench of six honorary magistrates, individually with third-class powers and sitting together as a bench of not less than two, for the trial of petty cases occurring within municipal limits. In the rest of the district the Raja of Padrauna has third-class powers in the Padrauna police circle, and Babu Dalip Narayan Singh of Kundwa, near Kasia, has similar powers within the police circles of Kasia, Qazipur and Tarkulwa; while others recently appointed include the Raja of Salemgarh for the Bishunpura and Taria Sujan and Pandit Harbans Prasad Tiwari of Rampur for Biraicha and Kothibhar. The district and sessions judge of Gorakhpur has both civil and criminal jurisdiction in this district and Basti; but in the latter all sessions cases are tried by the judge of Jaunpur as additional sessions judge, criminal appeals only from Basti coming before the sessions judge of Gorakhpur. The civil courts, in addition to that of the district judge, are those of the subordinate judge and of the munsifs of Gorakhpur, Bansgaon and Deoria, between whom the entire area is divided. The first sat formerly at Mansurganj, but when the headquarters of the tahsil were moved in 1862 to Maharajganj the munsif was transferred to Gorakhpur. At present there are two honorary munsifs, Sardar Sundar Singh of Dumri and Babu Tikori Singh of Siswa. In 1903 village munsifs were experimentally appointed in the Sadr tahsil, but at the present time there are only 24 such munsifs for the 90 circles into which the area has been divided, considerable difficulty being experienced in finding a sufficient number of qualified persons. The remaining executive staff of the district includes the assistant conservator of forests and his subordinates, the civil surgeon and two assistants, the executive engineer, the district surveyor, the superintendent of police and his assistants, the sub-deputy opium agent and his assistant, the superintendent of post-offices and the postmaster.

Garrison.

Till within comparatively recent times Gorakhpur was a cantonment for native troops, accommodating a regiment of infantry, and before the Mutiny artillery and cavalry also were quartered there. The cantonment has been abolished, and in 1904 it was given up by the military authorities, although the place still serves during the cold weather as a recruiting depôt for Gurkhas. Apart from this, the only military force is a squadron of the United Provinces Horse and the Bengal and North-Western Railway Volunteer Rifles, both with headquarters at Gorakhpur.

Formation of the district.

When first ceded to the Company by the Nawab Wazir of Oudh, the present district of Gorakhpur was but a part of a far larger area in the charge of a single collector. This tract comprised not only the whole of the modern districts of Gorakhpur and Basti, but also the seventeen parganas forming the *chaklas* of Azamgarh and Mahul, and the six parganas of *chakla* Nawabganj in Gonda, as well as the seven parganas of Khairagarh, lying far away to the north of Kheri and separated from the rest by a broad intervening stretch of Oudh territory. For obvious reasons Khairagarh was detached in 1802 and made over to a separate officer. In 1816, on the conclusion of the war with Nepal, the whole of the kingdom of Butwal, save the parganas of Binayakpur and Tilpur, was made over to the Nepalese, and about the same time Nawabganj was restored to Oudh, partly in extinction of a debt and partly in exchange for certain parganas in the Allahabad district. Further relief was afforded in 1820, when Azamgarh and the greater part of Mahul were transferred to Ghazipur and Jaunpur, and after the Mutiny a reduction was once more effected by awarding a strip of the Tarai in the north to Nepal. The district was still, however, far too large to be administered as a single unit, and in 1865 six parganas, together with the greater part of Maghar and a portion of Binayakpur, were formed into the new district of Basti. Finally in 1904 a small tract of 122 villages in pargana Dhuriapar was given to Azamgarh, owing to a change in the course of the Ghagra. It yet remains to be seen in what manner the dismemberment of the vast remaining area will be effected, for it is certain that the district is far too large as it stands, in spite of the failure of the many ingenious proposals made during the past thirty years.

Tahsils. In 1804 the greater part of the existing district, as well as a portion of Basti, was divided into five tahsils, one of which comprised the parganas of Salempur and Chillupar, a second those of Bhauapar, Unaula and Bakhira, a third those of Haveli, Silhat, Maghar and Rasulpur Ghaus, the fourth those of Dhuriapar and Mahuli, and the fifth was made up of Shahjahanpur and the present Padrauna tahsil. The remaining area in the north was wholly covered with forest, and little attempt was made to demarcate the boundaries of the Tilpur and Binayakpur parganas, wherein the Company's authority was little more than nominal. In 1810 the Unaula and Bhauapar parganas were added to the third or Sadr tahsil in exchange for Maghar and Rasulpur Ghaus, then given to the Bansi tahsil in Basti; and in 1818, after the fresh demarcation of the northern boundary, Tilpur and Binayakpur were formed into a new frontier tahsil. The next change occurred in 1840, when the parganas of Unaula, Bhauapar and Dhuriapar, to which Chillupar was subsequently added, were made into a tahsil with headquarters at Bansgaon. In 1845 the headquarters of the northern tahsil were moved south from Tilpur to Mansurganj, and a similar change from Salempur to Deoria took place in 1853. It was then found that Mansurganj was too far south for administrative convenience, and accordingly new buildings were erected in 1860 at Maharajganj, which thereafter gave its name to the tahsil. In 1871 a new tahsil was formed with headquarters at Hata, bringing the total up to six. This consists of pargana Silhat, taken from Deoria, pargana Shahjahanpur from Padrauna and a large part of Haveli. The remainder of Haveli is divided between Maharajganj and the Sadr or Gorakhpur tahsil, the latter comprising also a part of Bhauapar and the portion of Maghar not transferred to Basti. The Bansgaon tahsil includes the rest of Bhauapar, as well as Chillupar, Dhuriapar and Unaula; while the Deoria and Padrauna tahsils consist respectively of the single parganas of Salempur and Sidhua Jobna.

Tappas.

The parganas in this district are not only split up in a very confusing manner, but have ceased to be of anything more than historical interest. Of much more importance are the *tappas*, which are component parts of the parganas and of equally if not more ancient origin. In all cases they have been preserved intact, in spite of the mutilation of the parganas. It has been plausibly suggested that the *tappas* are the relics of a kind of feudal system among the Rajputs, each representing the feof of some vassal of the local Raja held in return for military service. There is not in this district that close connection between *tappas* and townships found in some parts of the country, so that there is no reason for supposing that the *tappa* was a mere arbitrary administrative division according to townships. The area varies greatly, and tends to increase in the undeveloped north, a fact which lends colour to an alternative suggestion that originally a *tappa* was a vague undefined tract representing the sphere of influence of each settlement or clearing in the forest. The largest is Lehra, no less than 152,181 acres in extent, while the smallest, *tappa* Qasba, near Barhalganj, covers but 663 acres. The average size of the 157 *tappas* into which the district is divided is 18,352 acres or 29 square miles. As these units are universally recognised to the present day a complete list is here given.

Pargana Bhauapar.
(Tahsil Bansgaon).
Pachisi.
Gurmhi.
Kotha Rampur.
Kuswasi.
Gagaha.

Pargana Unaula.
Haveli.
Bankata.
Mohsan.

Pargana Chillupar.
Majhaulia.
Semra.
Haveli.
Qasba.
Sikandarpur.

Pargana Dhuriapar.
Pali.
Tiar.
Gaur.
Dandi.
Narre.
Kohra.
Athaisi.
Majuri.
Khutahan.
Barhaj.
Chandpur.
Shahpur.
Bhadar.
Parsi.
Usri.
Thati.
Nakuri.
Haveli.
Bankat.
Ratanpur.

***Pargana Dhuriapar*-(cont.)**
Belghat.
Chaurar.
Bamhnauli
Kurmaut.

Pargana Haveli.
(Tahsil Maharajganj).
Lehra.
Katahra.
Mathkopa.
Rigauli.
Sikra.
Sumbhakhor.
Bhari Baisi.
Banki.
Unti.
Andhia.
Biraicha.
Lakhman.

Pargana Binayakpur.
Mirchwar.
Sirsia.
Nagwan.

Pargana Tilpur.
Khas.
Sonari.
Domakhand.
Bharatkhand.
Nai Karhi.
Purani Karhi.
Sukrahar.

Pargana Sidhua Jobna.
Khan.
Haveli.
Bank Jogni.
Batsara.
Naugawan.
Papaur.

***Pargana Sidhua Jobna*-(cont.).**
Dandupur.
Bansi Chirgora.
Bargaon Chaura.
Sandi.
Pakri Gangrani.
Parwarpar.
Mainpur.
Bhalwa.
Jhankaul.
Malsil Saraini.
Bhatahi Badraon.
Rampur Rogha.
Rampur Dhab.
Pirthipur.
Dhuria Bijaipur.
Sapahi Kuchia.

Pargana Haveli.
(Tahsil Hata).
Parkhauri.
Bharsand.
Parwarpar.
Agaya.
Dedupar.
Bindwar.

Pargana Silhat.
Banchara.
Singhpur.
Cheoraha.
Kataura.
Bakhra.
Binayak.
Chariaon.
Paharpur.
Adrakpur.
Donth.
Barnai.

Pargana Silhat—(cont.)
Gaura.
Dhatura.
Sirjam.
Indupur.
Nagwan Tikar.
Madanpur.

Pargana Shahjahanpur.
Majhwa.
Tarkulwa.
Bhainsa Dabar.
Patna.
Bhitni.
Bichhauli.
Chakdeia.
Nagwan.
Pariapar.

Pargana Salempur-Majhauli.
Salempur.
Haveli.
Ballia.
Baliwan.
Barsipar.

Pargana Salempur-Majhauli—(cont.).
Bairauna.
Bhatni.
Purainan.
Deoria.
Dondh.
Raipura.
Samogar.
Sohanpur.
Sathiaon.
Surauli.
Kaparwar.
Kachwar.
Khukhundu.
Gautaman.
Ghati.
Gobrain.
Mail.
Nai.

Pargana Haveli.
(Sadr Tahsil).
Qasba.
Haveli.

Pargana Haveli—(cont.).
Khutahan.
Patra.
Keotali.
Pachwara.
Marachhi Chandaur.
Gaura.
Rajdhani.
Rasulpur.

Pargana Bhauapar.
(Sadr Tahsil).
Haveli.
Ret.

Pargana Hasanpur-Maghar.
Bharsand.
Bhadesri.
Gahasand.
Khajuri.
Uttar Haveli.
Aurangabad.
Pachauri.
Satgawan.
Suras.

Fiscal history.

The fiscal history of the district begins with the cession of Gorakhpur to the Company in November 1801. The country was then in the most wretched condition owing to the effects of misrule, and the revenue had shrunk to insignificant proportions. At first it was only possible to attempt to collect the amount levied by the Oudh revenue-farmers; but these were found to be utterly untrustworthy, and Mr. Routledge, the first collector, appointed tahsildars for the purpose on a fixed salary together with a percentage of the collections should these amount to a reasonable proportion of the nominal demand. As was the case in after years, the enormous area of the district caused progress to be extremely slow, and much time was spent in ascertaining the condition of the country and its inhabitants, as also in enforcing the authority of the British Government. This proved a task of great difficulty, and it was found necessary to station a large body of troops in the district till a police force could be organised. The tahsildars found the Rajas and landholders strongly opposed to any form of police administration, and the Raja of Butwal not only refused to allow any police posts to be established within his domains, but absolutely declined to pay his arrears of revenue on the lands north of Tilpur, which the Oudh authorities had been unable to recover for many years. He was imprisoned in 1805, but an invasion of his territory by the Nepalese in the following year made it impossible to collect the balances. In other cases the *zamindars* offered armed resistance, and for the first four years the authorities were occupied in reducing them and destroying their forts. The cultivators too were equally suspicious, as the result of half a century of extortion, and attempts to induce them to reclaim the abandoned fields proved a failure. The Oudh *amils* had often made solemn engagements that the cultivators should hold at low fixed rates, and then had either seized the ripened crop or else extorted double or treble the amount agreed on; so that it was hardly surprising that the large advances made with the object of extending cultivation should have been appropriated and squandered, little being ultimately recovered.

First settlement.

On receiving the collector's report the Board of Commissioners at Farrukhabad ordered a settlement for three years at fair rates, with specially lenient terms for the cultivation of waste, the chief feature of the arrangement being the abolition of farming in favour of a settlement with the landholders themselves. Accordingly this measure was carried out in 1803-04, the old demand being considerably reduced. It had amounted to Rs. 6,27,570 gross and Rs. 5,49,855 net for Gorakhpur, Basti and Butwal; but this was now lowered to Rs. 5,44,555 gross and Rs. 4,78,382 net, of which Rs. 27,482 fell on Butwal, the demand for the present district being Rs. 3,46,705*. It was estimated that in the third year the revenue would increase by Rs. 1,70,000, but the collections fell far short of expectations, and in many cases the recusancy of the landholders rendered a return to farming leases unavoidable. In 1805 the allowance to the tahsildars was increased to 11½ per cent. on condition of their maintaining an efficient police force within their several jurisdictions.

* Appendix, table IX.

Second settlement.

As a matter of fact the reductions granted at the first settlement proved insufficient, since in several cases the *zamindars* were beginning to leave their villages for the forest, with threats of ejecting by force anyone who should presume to till the land in their absence. In the second triennial settlement, effected in 1805-06, a further reduction was made in the demand, while at the same time the internal transit dues were lowered and a tax on professions was abolished. Of the method of assessment nothing is known, save that some attempt was made to ascertain the value of estates from the village papers: and it is probable that the chief basis used here, as elsewhere, was the estimate furnished by the tahsildars. The existence of many large estates owned by Rajas rendered the task easier than in other districts, as each agreed upon a lump sum for the whole of his property. The revenue on this occasion amounted to Rs. 3,31,103 for the district as at present constituted; but in spite of the reduction the settlement did not work well, and frequent recourse was had to sales for arrears. In the task of collection the tahsildars were assisted by their police, who were little better than the underlings of the *amils* in former days, so that in 1808 the Board, as the result of a protracted enquiry into the state of the district, abolished the tahsildars altogether, substituting a system of direct payments to the collector. This experiment soon proved a failure and tahsildars were reappointed in 1810, but on a fixed salary and without control over the police. None the less the realisation of the revenue continued to be a task of the greatest difficulty in so large a district, and the defaulting landholders still persisted in retiring to the jungles when pressed, while the increasing frequency of sales was causing general dissatisfaction and serious disturbances, leading in more than one case to successful resistance of the authorities.

Third settlement.

Matters were mended somewhat by a fresh settlement in 1810-11, made with the Rajas direct on easier terms, and also by an order issued in 1812 to avoid sales as far as possible. The smaller landholders could cause little trouble without the aid of the Rajas, but the effect of the unrest was felt for years, since landholders were reluctant, for fear of sales, to settle on the vast areas of unreclaimed waste, especially in the northern tahsils.

This third settlement was originally made for two years, but was afterwards extended so as to terminate in 1814-15; the demand aggregating Rs. 3,49,866, an amount which was undoubtedly light in view of the spread of cultivation in the south.* It was collected without difficulty, the balances being small and eventually forgotten at the end of the period, when attention was diverted by the war with Nepal. In regard to this settlement it is noteworthy that a proposal, foreshadowed in 1803, was framed for making the demand permanent as in the Benares province, but was abandoned on the strong representations of the collector; while the latter's suggestion of settling villages with *birtias* and under-proprietors was sternly rebuked as a breach of faith with the Rajas.

Fourth settlement.

The war had a great effect on the district, once more reducing many of the cultivators in the north to destitution, while everywhere crime increased to an alarming extent and disorder became rampant. On the conclusion of the war a reconstitution of the boundaries took place, and Butwal ceased to form a part of this district, more than half of Binayakpur and a portion of Tilpur being given to the Gurkhas. In the meantime a new settlement had opened in 1814-15, but its introduction was postponed for a time, the assessment being ultimately sanctioned for five years terminating with 1819-20. Engagements were taken, as before, from the Rajas and *taluqdars,* Government receiving 75 per cent. of the estimated assets, while 10 per cent. represented the landlords' profits: a like amount was allowed for bad debts and failure of crops, and five per cent. was calculated to cover the cost of collection. The demand was raised to Rs. 3,87,770, though this was undoubtedly light even at the commencement. It was about this time that the development of the north made a start, largely as the result of a proclamation issued at the beginning of the war, calling on the Tharus and other cultivators residing north of Nichlaul to migrate southwards, with the object of inflicting loss on the Nepalese by stopping cultivation in the Tarai and of saving British subjects from falling into the enemy's hands. The result was most beneficial, for 55 villages in the north of Haveli, chiefly in the

* Appendix, table IX.

Lehra and Sumbhakhor *tappas*, were colonised, and this attracted immigrants from other parts. In 1818 the collector made a careful examination of the condition of the district, and reported that the south was well cultivated, order was fully maintained and fair roads existed in some places; but that the north was almost desolate, extremely unhealthy and devastated by elephants and other wild animals. Everywhere the cultivators were in miserable circumstances, without any attachment to their holdings and in almost all cases ill-treated by the landholders.

Fifth settlement.

The fifth settlement was merely nominal, for from 1820 to 1840 the fourth remained in force, revised from time to time in the various parganas for diverse periods, so that considerable augmentations were gradually effected, the Satasi estate alone giving an increase of Rs. 7,000 in 1828. The reason was that the settlement ordered for 1820 never came into being. It had been intended to make it permanent; but proceedings were arrested by the enactment of Regulation VII of 1822, which necessitated a professional survey and a thorough enquiry into the state of the several parganas. The survey was undertaken by Lieutenants Grant and Wroughton, who also were responsible for a classification of soils, the preparation of village papers and an examination of rights and tenures. This measure brought to light a large number of revenue-free holdings, in most cases innocent of title, many villages having been entered as revenue-free from the cession by collusion between the *zamindars* and the *patwaris*. The resumption of such fraudulent *muafis* led to a great increase in the total demand, while the information afforded by the survey enabled the revenue to be revised for the first time on a systematic basis. The process lasted from 1824 to 1830, pargana Shahjahanpur in the latter year yielding an increase of Rs. 26,600. In spite of its inherent defects the prolongation of the fourth settlement had the most beneficial results. The relief from uncertainty and suspense was the one thing needful for the development of the country, and it further gave the authorities time to organise the general administration of the district. The orders of 1812 prohibiting sales for arrears had been disregarded, and investigation proved that fraud and tyranny had been as rife in this as in other districts visited by the special commission. Many flagrant cases came up for revision and the sale was annulled, to the great content of the *zamindars*, who now for the first time began to pay revenue punctually. The judicial arrangements were overhauled, and in 1826 the tahsildars were invested with powers to settle land disputes decided hitherto by force or fraud. Crime decreased and dacoities, though still far from rare, became less frequent, while the police were enabled to turn to other duties than that of escorting Government treasure. This same security led to a rapid increase of commerce and the improvement of communications, and in 1830 the first jungle grant was given to Mr. Wilkinson, as the commencement of a policy which did, so much for the deserted tracts in the north of the district. On the other hand the administration was in many respects deplorably backward, especially in the matter of the subordinate officials. The revenue was collected quarterly, or even monthly in some cases, and the records were allowed to lapse into a state of hopeless confusion.

Sixth settlement.

The appointment in 1829 of Mr. R. M. Bird as the first commissioner of Gorakhpur led to further progress. This distinguished officer was the guiding spirit in the settlement operations conducted under Regulation IX of 1833, generally known as the first regular settlement. The system adopted was the same as elsewhere in its broad features, the assessment being based on carefully prepared statistics, accompanied by the compilation of a full record-of-rights. The fair rental of each village was determined by a classification and valuation of both soils and crops, the Government share being two-thirds of the assets. The work involved much time and labour, so that the settlement was not completed till 1841-42, the term being then fixed for twenty years. The demand was made progressive in many cases, owing to the immense increase realised, for the assessment of the present district was no less than Rs. 10,88,577. For this increase there were several reasons. In the first place the district had made very material progress during the two preceding decades, and cultivation had spread in every direction. Secondly, a large number of unassessed estates, which had survived the former investigation, now came under settlement, especially in the northern parganas, where their existence was due mainly to intrigues with the tahsil officials. But the chief difference between this and former settlements was that engagements were for the first time taken from sub-proprietors to the exclusion of the Rajas, whose rights were henceforward limited to a mere *malikana* allowance. Similarly the claims raised by some of the Rajas to the ownership of forests were disallowed, save in the case of areas specially granted to them. Naturally these measures aroused strong opposition, and the curtailment of their income led in many cases to the ruin of the great landholders. The Raja of Barhiapar was the first to mortgage his property; the Raja of Gopalpur became deeply involved; and the Majhauli and Satasi estates were brought to the verge of dissolution by the time of the Mutiny, while Padrauna was in little better plight and Tamkuhi alone appears to have made any headway. Nevertheless the settlement worked extremely well and little difficulty was experienced in collection. The clearance of forest and the extension of tillage went on rapidly, new roads were made, tahsil buildings and courts were erected in the outlying subdivisions, and between 1840 and 1850 treasuries were built at Captainganj, Paikauli and Pipraich. Progress was, however, checked by the Mutiny, which also effected a considerable change in the proprietary body, the estates of the Rajas of Satasi, Chillupar and Barhiapar being confiscated, as well as a part of Padrauna, while the stipend paid since 1845 to the descendant of the last Butwal Raja in compensation for his superior rights in Tilpur was abolished.

Seventh settlement.

Preparations for the next settlement were begun in 1856, but the work was interrupted by the disturbances of the succeeding year. It was resumed in 1859, but the last pargana was not assessed till 1867, and final sanction was not accorded before the end of 1873. From the first operations were entrusted to the collector, Mr. T. M. Bird, but owing to the immense amount of other business and the huge area of his district, which then included Basti, he was unable to do more than a fraction of the work himself, as a matter of fact assessing only the single pargana of Shahjahanpur, completed in 1861-62. The remainder of the settlement was entrusted to various assistants who were allowed their own discretion as to the methods to be adopted. Mr. J. J. F. Lumsden assessed Chillupar, Bhauapar, Dhuriapar, Unaula, Sidhua Jobna and south Haveli between 1859 and 1867; Mr. J. P. White assessed Tilpur and north Haveli in the cold weather of 1861-62; Salempur and Silhat were undertaken between 1859 and 1863 by Babu Piare Mohan; Maghar in 1860-61 and the following year by Mr. H. Wilson, and Binayakpur about the same time by Mr. H. le P. Wynne. The compilation of records and maps was conducted in four parganas by the *patwaris* alone, and elsewhere by survey *amins*. When these were completed the assessing officers proceeded to frame standard rates, and the methods adopted for this purpose differed very widely. Mr. Bird appears to have fixed three general rates for the three natural soils, though it is doubtful whether these were ever made to serve any practical purpose. Mr. Lumsden's method varied as his experience increased: in some parganas he adopted soil rates based on actual rents, while elsewhere he assumed an average rate for each tappa as a whole. Babu Piare Mohan used recorded rents, differentiating his rates according to the nature of the soil. Mr. White sometimes selected separate rates for different soils and sometimes took an all-round rate for an entire tract: but he gives no indication of the means whereby such rates were ascertained. Mr. Wilson admits that he used no soil rates at all, but depended mainly on the result of enquiry into the actual rental returns of each village; and lastly Mr. Wynne framed average rates for each *tappa*, based on returns of actual payments and checked by an examination of the average rental for each crop. It was but natural that under such circumstances the assessment should have been subjected to close scrutiny, causing much delay in the operations. The proposals of Messrs. Bird and Wilson were especially open to objection, but it was finally decided that the difference in the actual results to be obtained by a more scientific system would be insufficient to justify the labour and cost of revision. The Board, with much reason, pointed out that although each officer has showed the rent of land to be determined mainly by its position with regard to the village site, no one of them seemed to have adopted this arrangement as the basis of his calculations. As a matter of fact all except Mr. Lumsden had been largely influenced by an estimate of the probable revenue and rental prepared in

1860 by Mr. Reade who, when commissioner of Gorakhpur, had drawn up a careful statement showing the increase which might be expected from each pargana. The assessment was calculated at two-thirds of the gross assets, the total demand rising from Rs. 15,53,607 to Rs. 16,75,789 at the termination of the period of 30 years for which the settlement was sanctioned. As on the previous occasion, this involved an immense increase, amounting to more than 50 per cent.; but in spite of this little difficulty was experienced in the collection of the revenue. The accumulation of balances during the scarcity of 1865 caused some doubt as to the propriety of the enhancement; but these arrears were eventually collected, and balances did not again accrue till the famine of 1874, while even then the remissions were small and the district rapidly recovered its prosperity. It was significant that on no occasion was recourse had to sale of lands for arrears, and attachment was employed only in 1886-87.

Revision of settlement was ordered in 1883 and work was begun forthwith, operations lasting till 1890. The assessment of so large a district was naturally a long and costly affair, the total expenditure being nearly 19 lakhs or Rs. 410 per square mile, but of this more than 7½ lakhs represents the cost of the professional survey. The latter was entrusted to Major Sandeman, who was also responsible for the demarcation of soils and the preparation of the records. These papers were subsequently attested and corrected by the settlement officer, who then proceeded to revise the assessment after an inspection of each *mahal*. The work of settlement was first assigned to Mr. J. J. Digges La Touche, who assessed the Deoria and Bansgaon tahsils after inspection in 1884-85 and the following years. In 1886 he was succeeded by Mr. A. W. Cruickshank, who with the assistance of Mr. Vaughan inspected Hata in 1886-87 and Padrauna, Gorakhpur and Maharajganj in the three succeeding seasons. Instructions given to the settlement officer laid down that the revenue of each village should be based as far as possible on the actual rent-roll, corrected where necessary. He was not, however, allowed to revise the assessment of each individual *mahal* merely on the basis of the rental of tenants' land, but he was required to justify his judgment by reference to

Eighth settlement.

standard rents actually paid for each class of soil in the tahsil under assessment. These standard rates were not employed by Mr. La Touche, who relied solely on individual village rates for testing and correcting the rent-rolls; but the Board insisted on the preparation of standard rates for the remaining tahsils, although in actual practice they proved of very little use; the difference between the assets derived by their application and those obtained from the corrected rental being extremely small. This was largely due to the fact that extensive corrections had already been found necessary in attesting the papers, the rent-rolls in more than ten per cent. of the total number of villages being rejected on account of fraud, concealed cultivation or excessive rents. Further adjustments were made in the case of forest areas, while the improvements carried out by the European grantees were made the subject of an allowance of ten or twelve per cent. on the capital outlay thus expended.

The revenue.

The assessment was made on an area of 2,648,377 acres, the total assessable assets being Rs. 50,42,222, which included Rs. 62,336 on account of *sayar* income and an addition of Rs. 41,498 for concealed cultivation. The gross total of the final sanctioned demand amounted to Rs. 25,03,777; but from this must be deducted Rs. 36,104 on account of lands given in *jagir* to *goraits*, Rs. 760 assessed on lands belonging to Government and Rs. 28,801 as the nominal assessment of revenue-free areas. To the balance must be added Rs. 58,687, representing the demand on unexpired jungle grants in 1889, which raised the net realizable total to Rs. 24,96,799; representing 48·9 per cent. of the corrected rental and involving an increase of 57 per cent. on the demand of the former settlement.* Owing to the large enhancement the revenue was made progressive: rising from Rs. 23,13,405 in 1889-90 to Rs. 24,38,112 in 1899-1900. The settlement was sanctioned for a period of thirty years from 1889, and will expire in 1919. The revenue is payable in four *kists*, the *kharif* demand falling due on the 15th of November and the 15th of January, and the *rabi* on the 1st of May and the 1st of June.

Its results.

Notwithstanding this great increase, no difficulty has been experienced in realising the revenue. A considerable amount

*Appendix, table IX.

was suspended on account of famine in 1897; but the whole was subsequently recovered, and at no time has it been necessary to resort to any more severe process than distress and sale of moveable property. On a few occasions, it is true, recourse has been had to attachment, but in nearly every instance such attachments have been purely nominal. There can be no doubt that at the present time, considering the extension of cultivation and the general practice of concealing rents, the incidence of the Government demand is exceptionally light. In 1907-08, taking cesses into consideration as well, it averaged no more than Re. 1-5-11 per acre of cultivation, the highest rate for any tahsil being Re. 1-11-2 in Deoria and for any individual pargana Re. 1-11-10 in Chillupar, while in the Maharajganj tahsil it is only Re. 0-15-10, dropping to Re. 0-8-4 in pargana Binayakpur. *

Alluvial mahals.

The total demand is liable to vary from year to year owing to the large number of alluvial *mahals* affected by the Rapti, the Ghagra, the Great Gandak and the Kuwana. At the last settlement 555 such *mahals* were demarcated, consisting either of whole villages or portions, and the revenue assessed thereon was Rs. 1,01,879. The Bansgaon tahsil contained no fewer than 210, while there were 155 in Gorakhpur and only 25 in Hata. Since that date considerable changes have been effected and the number of *mahals* is now reduced to 481. Of this 391 are subject to the ordinary rules of quinquennial revision, 58 are held on conditional or unconditional long-term settlements of 30 years, while the remaining 32 are situated in jungle grants whose term has not yet expired. The total revenue now paid on the alluvial *mahals* amounts to Rs. 99,478 for the entire district.

Cesses.

The only cess now levied in addition to the ordinary revenue demand is the ten per cent. local rate, amounting in 1907-08 to Rs. 2,57,029. This came into existence in 1871, when several old cesses and rates were amalgamated and received the sanction of law. Such were the road cess introduced at the first regular settlement, the school cess for the maintenance of village schools, the district *dak* cess and the rural police rate. In 1878 an additional cess of two per cent. was introduced, but this was

* Appendix, table X.

abolished in 1905, and the four per cent. *patwari* rate of 1889 was withdrawn in 1906.

Police.

At the beginning of British rule the tahsildars, who were really revenue contractors, were supposed to maintain an adequate force of police; but they signally failed in this portion of their duties, and in 1809 a special force of *barkandaz* was organised to protect the treasuries and escort consignments of treasure. They were posted at the tahsils and a few places of importance along the high roads, while a strong body of mounted police patrolled the Oudh frontier. In 1818 the force was strengthened and the jurisdiction of the various police posts was defined, the number of *thanas*, which at first was quite inadequate, being largely increased. The present constabulary was formed in 1861, mainly from discharged soldiers. It was principally an armed force, under British officers from the Indian army; but in 1866 the armed and civil police were separated and the force in the reconstituted district was reduced to 625 officers and men of all grades. Subsequent years, however, have witnessed constant additions, the total rising to 994 in 1900. Three years later, on the reorganisation of the mounted police, Gorakhpur became a troop headquarters and the number of the civil police was slightly reduced; though an addition of 136 men resulted from the conversion of the municipal police at Gorakhpur into regular constabulary in 1907. The reallocation of the circles in the following year saw a reduction of 92 officers and men in the civil police of the district, the present (1909) total being four inspectors, 68 sub-inspectors, 71 head constables and 612 men. The armed police comprise a mounted force of 22 men of all ranks, two sub-inspectors, 23 head constables and 167 men, all under a European inspector.* The superior staff comprises a superintendent, two assistant superintendents and one or two deputy superintendents. Besides the above force there are the town police, 90 men of all grades, maintained in the notified areas and Act XX towns, 34 road patrols on the provincial highways, 2,329 village *chaukidars* paid in cash and 7,662 *goraits* or watchmen. The last are a survival of the old system whereby the village watchman was the servant of the landholder

* Appendix, table XVII.

and received a grant of land in lieu of wages. These *goraits* have been reduced in numbers from time to time, but they still are remunerated by means of rent-free *jagirs,* to which reference has been made in the preceding chapter.

Police stations.

After the separation of the Basti district there were 34 police stations and six outposts in Gorakhpur. Various changes have been made from time to time, and at present the district is divided for police administration into three divisions, containing in all 34 *thanas.* In the Bansgaon division are the stations of Gorakhpur, Sahjanwa, Bansgaon, Rudrapur or Khajni, Belghat, Gola, Barhalganj, Rudarpur, Barhi, Chauri Chaura and Pipraich. In the Deoria division there are also eleven stations, located at Deoria, Barhaj, Salempur, Khampar, Musela, Kasia, Hata, Qazipur, Bishunpura, Taria Sujan and Tarkulwa. The third is the Maharajganj division with twelve stations, situated at Maharajganj, Biraicha, Kothibhar, Nichlaul, Paisia, Pancra, Semra, Rigauli, Mansurganj, Ramkola, Padrauna and Thuthibari.

Crime.

The most prevalent forms of crime are illustrated by the statistics given in the appendix.* When first constituted the police had to deal with three factors peculiar to the Gorakhpur district, in the shape of the criminal tribes of Badhaks, the Doms and the armed gangs of dacoits from beyond the Nepal border. The Doms have been mentioned in the preceding chapter. They appear to be dying out, for while more than 3,000 were enumerated in 1874, the total in 1909 was 1,651, of whom 50 had absconded, 69 were in jail, 129 were in the Salvation Army settlement and the remainder in the various *domrakhanas.* They are still unregenerate robbers and thieves, and every year numerous crimes are traced to their agency. The Badhaks are no longer a source of anxiety, for they appear to have lost their old addiction to dacoity and robbery and to have taken to cultivation within the limits of their settlement. The history of the latter dates from 1843, when a jungle grant, resigned by one Salig Ram, was made over to a noted Badhak leader named Dalia, on the understanding that he was to locate Badhaks on the land and be responsible for the good behaviour of his tribe. After his death his widow was recognised as the grantee, but as she failed to

* Appendix, tables VII and VIII.

observe the conditions the land was farmed to a Kurmi in 1857. In 1861 the latter failed to pay his revenue and a settlement for five years was made with one Durga Prasad; but in 1864 this agreement was cancelled by the Board of Revenue and the grant was restored to the Badhaks. In 1868 a further allotment of forest, being half of the reserved plot of Tilkonia no. 2, was made over to the adult males of the Badhak community, the concession being placed under the control of the collector, while a lease was given for 30 years under certain conditions. The settlement at present contains 279 Badhaks, all of whom are peaceful agriculturists. The bad characters living just across the border in Nepal territory are still troublesome and organised dacoity is far from uncommon in the north of the district. Elsewhere crime is of the usual type common to rural tracts. The most prevalent forms are petty theft and burglary, criminal trespass and the resultant agrarian riots, cattle-theft and occasional murders. As a supplement to the tables given in the appendix it may be noted that from 1869 to 1878 there were on an average 4,759 cases of serious crime under the heads of murder, robbery, theft, burglary, cattle-theft and poisoning, including 9·6 dacoities annually. During the next decade the average was 5,423 with 2·1 dacoities; from 1889 to 1898 there were 7,914 cases and 15·6 dacoities per annum; and for the ten years ending with 1908 the annual average was 5,481, including 14 dacoities, the recrudescence of the latter being generally ascribed to the prevalence of scarcity.

Jail. There appears to have been a jail at Gorakhpur from the earliest days of British rule, but the site of the first building is no longer traceable. Between 1840 and 1845 a second jail was erected in *muhalla* Basantpur, on the site of Raja Basant Singh's fort, overlooking the Rapti. This building proved very unsatisfactory, and the health of the prisoners suffered to such an extent that in 1889 an enquiry was made, with the result that the jail was condemned. Accordingly a new first class jail, the most modern of its kind in the United Provinces, was built in 1894-95 to the south-east of the road to Pipraich and to the north of the railway settlement. The old buildings were demolished, save for a portion made over to the Opium department in 1903. The new jail is an extensive brick structure, covering an area of 19 acres; it has been in use since the beginning of 1897, and is under the superintendence of the civil surgeon. During the last five years the average daily number of inmates has been 492, and the full state of the prison necessitates frequent transfers to the central jail at Benares. The health of the prisoners is now satisfactory, the average death-rate being 25·5 per mille, and this would be much lower were it not for the fact that the most healthy prisoners are always selected for transfer, leaving an undue proportion of the old and infirm. The usual industries are carried on within the jail walls, such as the manufacture of matting, rope, sacking, coarse cloth, carpets and bricks. Besides this jail there is a small jail at Kasia, in which prisoners under trial and those sentenced for short terms were confined, but since 1906 it has ceased to be used as a jail, and now serves as the magistrate's lock-up.

Excise.

From a financial point of view the administration of excise revenue has always been of importance in Gorakhpur. In early days the usual farming system was employed, by which the right of manufacturing and selling liquor and drugs in each pargana, or often in groups of parganas, was leased only to a single contractor. The income thus derived was very considerable, amounting to Rs. 83,000 in 1810-11, and to Rs. 1,07,405 in the following year, while the subsequent development of the district caused a very material increase. The system was open to the objection that little or no control could be exercised over the production and sale of liquor; but it remained in force till 1863, when eight distilleries were set up by Government in various centres and the distillery system was introduced, the retail shops being licensed separately at rates varying from Rs. 8 to Rs. 15 monthly, while still-head duty was imposed on all liquor manufactured at the distilleries. Prior to this innovation there had been 649 shops for the sale of liquor, but the total was reduced to 171 in 1863. From time to time alterations were made in the rate of still-head duty and in the license fees, the latter being subsequently subjected to open competition. In 1874 the distilleries at Deoria and Maharajganj were closed as being unprofitable, and in 1878 a new policy was introduced in the shape of the modified distillery system, the licensees being given the monopoly for a pargana or other large area, while the only restriction was that they had to manufacture their liquor within the walls of a Government distillery. This experiment was of short duration and came to an end in 1880. At the time of its introduction the Bengal Government had started the outstill system in the bordering districts of Saran and Champaran, the immediate result of this measure being an enormous increase in smuggling into Gorakhpur. Indeed it is doubtful whether much legally manufactured liquor found its way into the distant tahsils of the district before this date, and it is certain that virtually none did after the Bengal outstills were established, the liquor supplied by the latter being more easily procured and far cheaper than that obtained from the distilleries. This necessarily had a marked effect on the receipts, and the only solution lay in the establishment of outstills on this side of the border—a measure which was carried into effect in 1879-80. In the first year it was applied to 44 *tappas*, but the number of outstills was afterwards increased till, in 1880-81, the whole district came under the system with the exception of tahsil Bansgaon and the Sadr tahsil west of the Ramgarh forest. In the latter areas the distillery system again came into force, and distilleries existed at Bansgaon and Gorakhpur, the others being closed as no longer necessary. In 1886 a new distillery was opened at Gorakhpur and that of Bansgaon was abolished. This system worked with success and no further change occurred till 1891, when the distillery system was extended to the whole of the Gorakhpur tahsil on the ground that such a step was justified by the improvement in communications. Lastly the same system was extended in 1906 to Hata and Deoria. There are at present 100 retail shops in the distillery area and 71 outstills in Padrauna and Maharajganj; but it is proposed shortly to reduce the outstill tract still further, and to leave only a narrow strip along the Nepal frontier under this system.

Revenue.

In 1862 the last year of farming, the revenue from country spirit amounted to Rs. 2,15,217, but a marked decrease ensued with the reduction in the number of shops, and for the next 15 years the average was little more than Rs. 65,000. It then rose with great rapidity, proving the success of the outstills, and from

1877-78 to 1886-87 it averaged Rs. 1,77,400 annually, including Rs. 1,00,767 from the outstills, Rs. 45,656 for still-head duty and Rs. 30,884 for licenses. The following decade witnessed a further improvement, although the revenue fell off towards the end of the period on account of bad seasons, the average being Rs. 2,04,062, of which Rs. 1,28,260 was derived from the outstills, Rs. 51,510 from duty and Rs. 24,204 from licenses. During the ten years ending with 1906-07 there has been a further increase, the total income rising to Rs. 2,56,442, to which outstills contributed Rs. 1,60,498, still head duty Rs. 71,113 and licenses Rs. 34,571. From the statement given in the appendix, showing the details of excise revenue from 1890-91 onwards, it will be seen that a great decline occurred in 1906-07 and the following year, owing mainly to the extension of the distillery system, coupled with very unfavourable seasons.* While the still-head duty had materially increased there appears to have been no rise in the consumption, which has varied from 40,000 to 50,000 gallons annually in the distillery tract during the past three decades. Owing to the outstills it is impossible to ascertain the total amount, and consequently to establish any comparison between Gorakhpur and other districts in the drinking capacity of their respective population. The figures given above do not include the receipts from foreign liquor. Until 1881 these appear to have been insignificant, but since that date they have steadily increased, the average for the last five years being Rs. 1,280. This sum is derived from license fees for retail sale by various hops in Gorakhpur, the only exceptions being the licenses for the refreshment room at Bhatni station and for the railway dining-car.

Tari.

A peculiar feature of the district is the large amount derived from licenses for the sale of *tari* and *sendhi*, made from the juice of the *tar* or toddy palm and the *khajur* or date palm. These trees are very common in all parts of the district, and the great majority are diligently tapped by Pasis and Bhars, who keep shops for selling the liquor during the season, which lasts roughly from May till August. The juice is drunk both fresh and fermented, and is said to be wholesome; in its fermented

* Appendix, table XI.

state it is intoxicating, but the potency of the liquor soon passes off and the after-effects are not serious. Owing to the temporary nature of the supply the shops in many cases are not permanent buildings, often consisting of a booth erected in a palm grove. Formerly their number was very great, the maximum being 1,123 ; but of late years a marked reduction has been effected, especially in the city, where at one time there were no less than 120 shops, and in 1908 the total for the whole district was reduced to 650. In 1899 the shops were leased individually as an experimental measure, but now the contracts are given to men of substance, who purchase the right of sale for a whole pargana or tahsil, subletting the shops in such an area to the Pasis who collect the liquor. In only one year since 1862 has the revenue derived from these licenses fallen below Rs. 10,000, and since 1880 it has always exceeded Rs. 20,000 save in 1897. Of late years the increase has been very remarkable, the average for the decade ending with 1907-08 being Rs. 33,592.

Hemp drugs.

Hemp drugs are an item of very small importance in this district, largely owing to the fact that the wild hemp is found almost everywhere and is cut and sold by the contractors without payment, although recently a small export duty has been imposed. Of the prepared drugs the most common is *ganja*, imported from Bengal, though a considerable amount is smuggled over the border from Nepal ; but the consumption is not large, averaging only 36 maunds annually. Of much less importance is *charas*, first introduced in 1879 ; the consumption averages but 13 maunds, and has never exceeded 19 maunds in a single year. The income from drug licenses remained below Rs. 10,000 till 1877-78, but has since increased gradually with changes in administration and enhanced duty, rising in the past three decades from Rs. 21,062 to Rs. 27,520 and to Rs. 39,777.* Formerly the lease for each pargana was given separately ; but subsequently the entire district was leased to a single contractor and in 1903 a system of triennial contracts was inaugurated with most beneficial results.

Opium.

As in all poppy-growing districts, the sale of poppy has constantly presented much difficulty on account of smuggling

* Appendix, table XI.

and the retention of small quantities of crude opium by the cultivators for their own consumption. Matters seem to have been worse, however, in Gorakhpur than elsewhere in the past, so that till 1872 the income derived from the sale of the excise opium was quite insignificant, and as late as 1884 free licenses had to be given to the drug contractors for the sale of opium, as no bids were made for shops in the district. For the ten years ending with 1886-87 the average consumption was 17·17 maunds and the income Rs. 6,692, but a large amount of the latter was derived from licenses for *madak* and *chandu*, the sale of which was finally abolished in 1888. In the next ten years the consumption rose to 29·5 maunds and the receipts to Rs. 11,455 annually ; while the corresponding figures for the ten years ending with 1906-07 were 41·6 maunds and Rs. 15,125. The system now in force is that of an annual contract for the whole district, the present number of shops being 40, of which five are in the city. Opium is also sold by the official vendor at each of the six tahsils. The recent increase in consumption may in part be attributed to the development of an illicit export trade with Calcutta, and an important case of smuggling came to light in 1906-07, explaining the unusual increase in the amount purchased in that year. The Gorakhpur opium division comprises the whole district with the exception of the Tilpur and Binayakpur parganas, where the cultivation of poppy is prohibited. It is split up into three subdivisions, known as Gorakhpur, Gola and Salempur, the two first being in the charge of the sub-deputy opium agent and the third in that of his assistant. There are opium bungalows and weighing godowns at Barhalganj, Bhatpar and Patherwa, while at Gorakhpur there are godowns only. The average weight of opium produced in the district is 2,451 maunds annually, calculated on the returns of the last ten years.

Stamps.

Under Regulation III of 1803, the collection of stamp duty on civil suits was first sanctioned in the ceded provinces, the income thus derived being enjoyed by the munsif in whose court the payment was made. The duty continued to be realised after the introduction of fixed salaries for munsifs in 1824, but from that date stamp receipts formed a part of general revenues. The amounts credited in this district, as assessed under the Court

Fees Act and the Indian Stamp Act, are very large, the annual figures from 1890 onwards being given in the appendix.* The average net receipts for the five years ending with 1878 were Rs. 1,63,100, while from 1894 to 1898 the figure was Rs. 2,93,300 annually, and from 1904 to 1908 the average was no less than Rs. 3,07,068, the maximum being Rs. 3,66,184 in the last year. Some 77 per cent. of this amount is derived from court-fee stamps, and the rapid increase during the last few years is due to the extraordinary activity of the *zamindars* in filing ejectment suits against their tenants, so as to prevent the accrual of occupancy rights, a tendency which had a great effect on the stamp revenue as soon as the existing tenancy legislation was promulgated.

Registration.

Under Oudh rule there was no registration, and the attestation of a document by the *qazi* or the *qanungo* was the sole presumptive evidence of genuineness. In 1803 a registrar was attached to the judge's court, but in 1832 the work was made over to the *sadr amin* and this arrangement lasted till 1864, when the district judge became the registrar and the tahsildars were declared to be deputy registrars for their several subdivisions. The only subsequent change was the appointment of departmental sub-registrars in place of the tahsildars. There are consequently six registration offices, in addition to that of the district judge, who is also registrar for Basti. By far the largest volume of work is done at the headquarters, while next in order come the Deoria and Bansgaon offices. The average receipts for the past ten years have been Rs. 21,265 annually, whereas thirty years ago the amount was little more than Rs. 13,000.

Income-tax.

Income-tax was first introduced in 1860, when it was levied on all incomes of Rs. 200 and upwards, though in the following year the rates were reduced and the minimum raised to Rs. 500. This tax in 1865 gave place to a license-tax on trades and professions, followed in 1868 by a certificate-tax on incomes of Rs. 500 and upwards, and a year later by a regular income-tax of six pies in the rupee. It was collected till the end of 1872-73, in which year it yielded Rs. 18,528 on 559 incomes of Rs. 1,000 and upwards. No further tax was levied till the

* Appendix, table XII.

license-tax of 1877, which in the first year brought in Rs. 43,214. Finally in 1886 the existing income-tax came into force, modified only by the exemption of incomes under Rs. 1,000 in 1903. Tables in the appendix show the gross receipts for each year since 1890-91, as well as the amount realised in the city and in each tahsil.* The total is large and is steadily on the increase, in spite of the recent reduction in the case of small incomes. From 1890-91 to 1899-1900 the annual average was Rs. 1,37,000 and in the following eight years it rose to Rs. 1,82,700, whereas in 1907-08 it exceeded two lakhs. More than half this amount is paid by companies, by far the largest contributor being the Bengal and North-Western Railway Company, while the Gorakhpur Bank, Ltd., and the Kayasth Trading and Banking Corporation pay considerable amounts. Of the tax on ordinary incomes the highest proportion is levied in the Deoria tahsil, owing mainly to the extensive and growing trade in cloth and grain which is carried on at Deoria and the sugar industry of Barhaj. Next comes Hata, which contains the thriving town of Rampur Karkhana, and then Padrauna, in which are many wealthy factory own ersand several European residents. At the bottom of the list stand the Sadr tahsil, excluding Gorakhpur city, and Maharajganj.

Post-office.

In the early years of British rule a postal line was maintained between Benares and Gorakhpur, and this formed the sole means of communication with the outer world. Within the district there was no public post of any kind, official correspondence being transmitted to and from the outlying police stations by the agency of the police. In 1833 the latter were replaced by a service of runners, maintained at the cost of the landholders, but it was not till 1846 that private letters were allowed to be carried along these mail lines and a fee of two pice was charged for each packet. After the Mutiny a considerable extension of the imperial post was effected, especially in the matter of a mail line from Gorakhpur to Basti and Fyzabad, while in 1863 the landholders were relieved from their personal obligation and a cess was instituted in its place. The most important postal reform was that effected under Act XIV of 1866, whereby the imperial

* Appendix, tables XIII and XIV.

post took over a number of district lines, the object being to acquire the whole gradually, save where offices required for administrative convenience were not considered sufficiently profitable to warrant their transfer. This process was continued steadily, the district *dak* being finally abolished in 1906. The work of the post-office has expanded enormously of late, not only in the actual carriage of the mails but also in the matter of money orders, a large amount of the revenue being now paid by this means, while very considerable sums are transmitted to the district by emigrants: the savings bank too is yearly increasing in importance. In 1878 the district contained 18 imperial and 18 local offices, and in the course of thirty years the latter have all been absorbed and the number of the former has risen to 72, including a head office at Gorakhpur, with sorting and cash offices in connection, 21 sub-offices, 45 branch offices, and five recently established experimental offices in different *muhallas* of the city. A list of all these offices, showing their distribution among the various tahsils, will be found in the appendix. A great change has been introduced by the railway, which is now utilised as far as possible, though there is still a distance of 314 miles served by runners, and a cart service is maintained on the 32 miles of road between Gorakhpur and Barhalganj. A divisional superintendent of post-offices, whose charge includes this and the other three districts north of the Ghagra, has his headquarters at Gorakhpur, where also the district postmaster and an inspector of post-offices are stationed.

Telegraphs. The lines of telegraph are carried along the railway, with the exception of that from Gorakhpur to Kasia, and its extensions to Padrauna and Tamkuhi, at each of which places are combined post and telegraph offices. The latter exist also at Deoria, Majhauli and Barhaj, while there are railway offices at the various stations on the main line and its several branches.

Municipalities. The only municipality is that of Gorakhpur. In early days there was the usual local agency, which was responsible for watch and ward, roads, conservancy and other matters, the cost of administration being met from a house-tax. This impost received the force of law under Act XX of 1856, and on the 7th of September 1869 the city was constituted a municipality. The elective principle was not introduced till 1873, when the boundaries were defined afresh. There is now, under Act I of 1900, a municipal board of 15 elected and five nominated members, exclusive of an elected chairman and a paid secretary. The income is derived mainly from an octroi-tax on imports, supplemented by a tax on horses and ponies, a wheel-tax, a tax on weighmen and a tax on burners of brick, lime and tiles. Other sources of income are rents of houses and lands, market and slaughter-house dues, pounds and the sale of manure. Details of the receipts and expenditure under the main heads for each year from 1890-91 onwards will be found in the appendix.* The cantonment of Gorakhpur was abolished in 1904 and became a notified area under Act I of 1900. This comprises not only the cantonment but also a considerable area to the south, taken up to form a sanitary buffer between the city and the civil station, while a portion of the latter, which formerly lay within municipal limits, was added to the notified area in 1907, and further extensions to the north are now contemplated. The affairs of the notified area are managed by a committee of four members, including the magistrate as chairman, the joint magistrate as secretary, the executive engineer and the civil surgeon. For the four years of its existence the average receipts, derived mainly from a house-tax and a conservancy-tax, have been just under Rs. 5,000, while the expenditure, devoted mainly to conservancy and lighting, has exceeded Rs. 5,500 annually. This deficit has been supported from the funds of the old cantonment committee, made over to the notified area on its constitution. It was due principally to the payment of compensation to the owners of insanitary houses destroyed by the committee, and the budget now shows a balance. On the 1st of April 1907 Deoria became a notified area instead of an Act XX town, and a year later a similar change was effected in Barhaj, including Gaura. In either case local affairs are managed by a committee of five members, with the subdivisional officer of Deoria as president and the tahsildar as secretary.

Act XX towns.

Act XX of 1856 was extended to Gajpur and Rudarpur in 1867, and in 1871 the towns of Pipraich, Lar, Gaura, Gola, Pad-

* Appendix, table XVI.

rauna, Siswa Bazar and Sahibganj were added to the list. These were followed by Rampur Karkhana in 1874, Barhalganj and the combined towns of Salempur and Majhauli in 1875, and Deoria in 1892, while in 1903 Barhaj was united with Gaura. In 1906 the operations of the Act were withdrawn from Salempur-Majhauli and Gajpur on the ground that they were not of sufficient importance, and two years later Deoria and Barhaj-Gaura were raised to the status of notified areas. The eight remaining towns are managed in the usual way, the income in every case being derived principally from a house-tax assessed by the local *panchayat* under the direction of the magistrate. Details of revenue and expenditure will be found in the several articles on the places in question.

District board.

The district board traces its origin to the various committees formed from time to time to administer the funds derived from cesses and local sources, such as the road and ferry fund introduced with the first regular settlement, the school cess, the district *dak* cess and others of a like nature. These were amalgamated in 1871, when the district committee came into existence; and this body was transformed into a partially elected district board, with members returned from the local or tahsil boards, under Act XIV of 1883. In 1906 the local boards were abolished, and the district board now consists of 18 members, six being elected annually for a term of three years, as well as the district magistrate and the six subdivisional officers. The board meets monthly for the transaction of business, which includes the management of the educational institutions, local roads and ferries, dispensaries and vaccination, cattle-pounds and the veterinary establishment. Statistics showing the income and expenditure of the board under the main heads for each year since 1890-91 will be found in the appendix.*

Education.

Till quite recently the district was extremely backward in the matter of education. In the early part of the nineteenth century Buchanan remarked that in many divisions of the district there was not a single school, and that none learned to read and write save children of the highest families or those born of literate parents. Things were no better in 1847, when the first

* Appendix, table XV.

reports on education were submitted. There were 243 Persian, 170 Sanskrit and 15 Hindi schools in this district and Basti, with an aggregate of 3,808 scholars, and the collector remarked that the whole of the vast population was in a state of utter ignorance save for some Brahman astrologers, a number of Kayasth officials and a few respectable Musalmans. A free school had been started at Gorakhpur in 1835, under the management of a local committee, but it failed to succeed and was broken up after an existence of nine years. The Church Missionary Society's school was started in 1844, and for a long time was the only educational institution of any importance in the district. Village schools on the *halqabandi* system were first opened in May 1856, and at the same time tahsil schools were established at Salempur, Pipraich and Sahibganj; but the work thus begun was interrupted by the Mutiny, and when the schools reopened in 1858 there were but 52 pupils in the tahsil and 108 in the eleven village schools. In addition there was the C. M. S. school with 180 scholars and 96 indigenous schools with an attendance of 793. Ten years later, in 1868, the numbers were much larger. Besides the C. M. S. high school and the orphanage, there were 176 *halqabandi* schools with 9,505 scholars, 11 girls' schools with 281 on the rolls, 185 indigenous schools with 2,243 pupils, and 14 middle schools with an attendance of 1,116. Of the last five were tahsili schools, located at Pipraich, Barhalganj, Piprauli, Bhingari and Ramkola, the first four dating from 1858 or 1860 and the fifth from 1868; and nine were anglo-vernacular "subscription" schools, started in 1867 or 1868 at Deoria, Gola, Rudarpur, Padrauna, Barhaj, Tamkuhi, Bhauapar, Rampur and Salempur. The following decade, however, witnessed no further improvement, for, though in 1878 the number of schools had risen to 407, the aggregate number of scholars was but 9,769. A *zila* or district school had been started at Gorakhpur, but it only taught up to the middle standard and even so was reported on unfavourably. There was one more tahsili school, but the anglo-vernacular schools had in most cases dropped out of existence, while of the former class Barhalganj alone was considered efficient. Matters remained in much the same state for another ten years, since by 1888 the *halqabandi* schools had diminished by 30, and the total number of scholars in all Government institutions was but 7,371. A similar absence of progress marked the ensuing decade and education remained stagnant till 1899, when the number of pupils rose at a bound to more than 20,000, and never since that date, save in 1903, has the total sunk below that figure. No doubt considerable benefit was derived by the transference of the schools to the district board: but considerable time elapsed before sufficient money was available for educational purposes, and it took long to awaken public interest. A great impetus was given to primary education in 1905 by the simultaneous opening of 100 new aided schools in all parts of the district, which caused an immediate increase of more than 6,000 pupils. A table in the appendix illustrates recent progress, showing the number of scholars and schools, both secondary and primary, in each year from 1896-97 onwards.*

Schools. Following this is given a list of all the schools in the district in 1908. These aggregated 527 institutions with the attendance of 34,335—by far the highest figure yet attained. Several of the more important schools are maintained by the C. M. S., including St. Andrew's College, teaching up to the first arts standard, a high school, an anglo-vernacular school, a vernacular middle school and five primary schools for boys, the number of pupils being 935 in all. The history of the mission and its development has been given elsewhere. The Jubilee high school was built originally as an oriental *zila* school in 1875, and was reconstituted in 1887 as a municipal high school. In 1907 it was handed over to the district board, and it is now intended to convert this most flourishing and popular institution into a provincial school under the immediate control of the department of Public Instruction. The other secondary schools comprise ten middle vernacular schools, two aided schools of a similar type, an anglo-vernacular school at Deoria and the model school at Gorakhpur. The last was opened in 1904 in a costly building, on which Rs. 1,58,632 were expended, in the magnificent grounds of Mr. Bridgman's bungalow in the Turkomanpur *muhalla*. It accommodates six teachers and 100 pupil teachers, drawn from the Gorakhpur and Benares divisions and from Gonda and

* Appendix, table XVIII.

Bahraich, 50 being passed out annually after a course of two years. Attached to this training school is a large middle vernacular school. Among the primary schools are 154 managed and 257 aided by the district board, and one private school kept up by the Tamkuhi estate. The girls' schools comprise two Government institutions, five under the district board, nine aided and one unaided school. The remainder are of a miscellaneous description, including the *patwari* school at Gorakhpur, three training schools attached to the middle schools at Bansgaon, Lar and Minwan, and 70 indigenous schools of an elementary type for teaching the Quran, Persian, Sanskrit and Hindi, with a total attendance of 1,330 pupils. Among the private schools mention should be made of a technical school at Gorakhpur, in the Khunipur *muhalla,* started in 1904 by M. Yusuf Ali. There are three assistant masters and over 100 pupils, who are taught drawing, mensuration, practical surveying, the use of the plane-table, the prismatic compass, the theodolite and the like, as well as printing. The success of the institution has been remarkable, and the proprietor is now about to remove his school to a better centre in Lucknow. From these figures it will be seen that the district is now well advanced: and though much remains to be done in the matter of extending and improving the school buildings, a great deal has been accomplished and Gorakhpur is free from the reproach under which it lay so long. A new inspector's circle with headquarters at Gorakhpur was created in 1908, and an assistant inspector has been here since 1904, his staff consisting of one deputy and six sub-deputy inspectors of schools.

Literacy.

Real progress has been so recent that it is of little use to discuss the educational statistics of the last census. In 1872 it was calculated that barely two persons in a thousand could read and write, but by 1881 the proportion had risen to 3·6 per cent. of the males and ·08 of the females. Ten years later the figures were respectively 4·4 and ·15 per cent., while in 1901 about 5·5 per cent. of the male and ·18 of the female population came under this category. The next census will doubtless show a great increase, but no exact estimate can yet be framed. The spread of education is still very uneven, for while in 1901 one-fourth of the Kayasth community was literate, only seven Koeris in a thousand and the same number of Chamars among ten thousand were able to read and write. Instruction is almost invariably given in the Nagri character in preference to the Persian, which is used only in the towns and is for the most part confined to the Musalman element. Of the whole literate population, excluding those who used English, 87·2 per cent. employed the Nagri script and 5·8 the Persian, while the remainder knew both, though better acquainted with the former.

Dispensaries.

The establishment of a Government dispensary at Gorakhpur dates from very early times, though the exact year cannot be determined. In spite of the unhealthiness of the climate and the crying need for medical assistance in the outlying tracts, no branch dispensaries were built till after the Mutiny, save that at Bansi, now in the Basti district. In 1868 the Rani of Satasi built, and for many years supported, the dispensary at Rudarpur and a year later that at Kasia was opened: the latter was enlarged in 1874, but the place was recently condemned, and a new building erected at the sole expense of the Raja of Salemgarh. The district committee started other dispensaries at Barhalganj in 1873 and at Maharajganj in 1876, while in the same year the Bela Haraiya dispensary was opened on the Lehra estate. These were followed by the establishment of dispensaries in 1887 at Tamkuhi by the Raja of that place, in 1888 at Deoria by the district board, in 1894 at Barhaj by the Majhauli estate, in 1904 at Dumri by the Dumri estate, and in 1907 at Bansgaon by the district board. This last authority exercises general control over these eleven institutions, and also over the Dufferin female hospital at Gorakhpur, dating from 1890; while the medical charge is vested in the civil surgeon, subordinate to whom are assistant surgeons at Gorakhpur and Kasia and hospital assistants in charge of the other dispensaries. The Sadr dispensary at Gorakhpur has been greatly enlarged and improved during the last five years, and now consists of a central block and four separate wards, the former containing offices, a dispensing hall, operating rooms and a room for outdoor surgical dressing. The medical ward contains eight, the eye ward twenty, the surgical ward twenty-four and the contagious ward eight beds; there are also quarters for the assistant surgeon and four compounders, while recently private wards for paying patients have been added. The Dufferin hospital has accommodation for 22 patients, and is supported partly by contributions from the municipal and district boards, partly by subscriptions and partly by the income from a small endowment, the whole amounting to Rs. 1,450 per annum. The average attendance at this and the district board dispensaries has been 155,000 annually during the last five years, fully one-fourth of this number being treated at Gorakhpur itself. Besides these hospitals there is a private charitable dispensary at Padrauna maintained entirely by the Raja of that place, as well as the usual police hospital at head-quarters and a railway dispensary for the servants of the Bengal and North-Western Railway Company.

Cattle-pounds.

A considerable income is obtained by the district board from the numerous cattle-pounds. These were originally under the direct management of the magistrate, and were made over to the board in 1891. The net receipts for the ten years ending with 1907-08 averaged Rs. 8,080 annually.* Apart from the two municipal pounds at Gorakhpur and the three managed by the notified areas, there are no fewer than 69 such institutions under the control of the district board, and these are located at all the places containing a police station and in most of the larger villages. The number has increased rapidly of late years, and it has been the practice on the part of the local *zamindars* who desire a pound in their neighbourhood to make a petition to this effect, the board supplying a *muharrir* if the landholders provide a suitable building. Such pounds are treated as experimental for a year or two, and if they are found to be profitable, they are taken over definitely by the board, those which fail to pay their way being closed. The reason for the large number of cattle-pounds lies not only in the abnormal size of the district but also in the fact that it is a great breeding centre, and that, save in the extreme north, legitimate grazing is scarce.

Nazul lands.

The amount of *nazul* land in the district is relativley small, the only extensive area being a block of 631·7 acres lying immediately to the east of the municipal boundary and constituting

* Appendix, table XV.

the old Gorakhpur cantonment. It is occupied principally by the bungalows of the residents in the civil station, though there are one or two large open spaces, such as the polo ground. The management of this land has been made over to the notified area committee, which derives a small income from the cultivated portion. The military encamping-grounds also come under this category, with an aggregate area of 370·2 acres, and these bring in an annual income of Rs. 154. Other *nazul* consists mainly in sites appropriated for Government buildings, police stations, schools and the like. In the Captainganj bazar there are 10·6 acres of *nazul*, yielding an annual sum of Rs. 285 in rents; and the only other extensive plot, 146·4 *bighas* in area, is at Barhalganj, the revenue of Rs. 55 being credited to the town fund.

CHAPTER V.

HISTORY.

Despite the presence of many ancient sites, some of which, like Kasia and Sohnag, are of extreme interest, very little definite information can be gathered as to the early history of Gorakhpur. The district was doubtless included in the ancient kingdom of Kosala. Ram Chandra of Ajodhya is said to have passed some time in practising austerities at the junction of the Rapti and Ghagra, and it was here that he received instruction from the sage Viswamitra, to whose Kausik descendants he in gratitude bequeathed all the land north of the latter river. After the destruction of Ajodhya tradition relates that the fugitive ruler endeavoured to found a new capital at Rudarpur, but that he or his successors were overthrown by the aborigines, Bhars, Cherus, Tharus and the like. At all events it would appear that an early Aryan civilisation gave way to aboriginal rule for a very long period till it was eventually replaced by an Aryan reconquest. **Ancient.**

Whether Kasia be the ancient Kusinagra or the less known Vethadvipa, it is certain that the place played some part in the life history of Gautama Buddha. We are not, however, told anything of value with regard to the temporal power in the days of the great teacher, and though Buddhism flourished in the district for several centuries we do not know whether its adherents were Rajputs or Bhars. In the 3rd century B. C. the country was under the direct rule of Asoka Maurya, who had his capital at Patna; but no records of that monarch's reign have yet come to light in this district. The kingdom of Patna was seized by the Sungas in 184 B. C., and on the fall of this dynasty a century later general confusion ensued till the advent of the Gupta empire. Bihar and Gorakhpur seem to have been ruled by the Lichchhavis, and from them to have passed into the hands of Chandra Gupta at the beginning of the 4th century **The Buddhists.**

A.D. From the Kahaon inscription we learn that the country was held in tranquillity by Skanda Gupta in 460.* It would seem however, from the accounts given by Fa Hien, who had visited Kasia some fifty years before, and from the clearer narrative of Hiuen Tsang in 635 that the country had for the most part relapsed into forests and that there were no towns of importance, while ruins of monasteries and stupas were to be seen in every direction.

Local dynasties.

With the decline of the Guptas the district appears to have passed into the hands of the aborigines: but contemporary records show that there were occasional colonies of Rajputs, whose leaders ascribed to themselves the dignity of sovereign rulers. The Bhagalpur pillar of the tenth or eleventh century refers to a Raja of the Surajbansi race, who claimed descent from the kings of Ajodhya. The Bisens of Majhauli, whatever may have been their origin, are among the oldest Rajput families of the United Provinces and were settled at Majhauli long before the Musalman conquest. A black stone discovered near Kasia in 1875 by Mr. A. C. Carleylle with an inscription in Sanskrit of the eleventh century refers to a line of Kulachuri princes who had been established in that neighbourhood for at least eight generations. The presence of the Kulachuris had already been determined by the Kahla plate.† They are said to be identical with the Hayobans Rajputs, who came from the homes of the Kulachuris at Chedi and Ratanpur in the Central Provinces; and it is known that the Hayobans, now represented by the Raja of Haldi in the Ballia district, first settled on the north bank of the Ghagra before moving to Shahabad and thence to Ballia. The Kulachuris of Sawaya near Kasia may therefore have been another branch of the Hayobans.

The Musalmans.

It is by no means clear whether in the early days of Musalman rule this district was included in the government of Oudh or in that of Bihar. The boundaries in all cases were very indeterminate and depended mainly on the personality of the governor; but in either case it is certain that the rule of the

*C. A. S. R., I, P. 92; Fleet, *Gupta Inscriptions*, no. 15.

†*Epigraphia Indica*, VII, p. 85; *Epigraphic Notes*, by F. Kielhorn: Gottingen, 1903.

Sultans of Dehli was more nominal than effective, since on very rare occasions did the Musalman armies penetrate beyond the Ghagra into the trackless forests of Gorakhpur. Thus when Qutb-ud-din Aibak conquered Oudh and Bihar in 1193 the effect on this district must have been of the slightest, and probably the occupation of Bihar in 1200 by Muhammad Bakhtiar Khilji, who is said to have subdued the Hindu chieftains of that country, was of little more importance.* Similarly Shams-ud-din Altamsh conquered the province of Bihar in 1225, and in the following year his son, Nasir-ud-din Mahmud the elder, effected a complete subjugation of the Bhars in Oudh; but these campaigns seem to have been limited to the more accessible parts and in the east the invaders seldom went far inland from the Ganges. In the course of time the kingdom of Bengal extended westwards as far as Oudh, but Gorakhpur would appear to have been a no-man's land, for no garrisons were established in the district and the growing power of the Rajput chieftains during this period in itself proves the absence of any controlling authority. When the Dehli Sultans made their expeditions into Bengal by the northern route they went from Ajodhya by boat, as was the case with Ghias-ud-din Tughlaq and Firoz. The latter in 1353 according to Ferishta, however, when engaged in a campaign against Haji Ilias Shah of Bengal, stopped in the neighbourhood of Gorakhpur, where the local chieftains assembled to pay their respects.† Udai Singh, styled the *muqaddam*, presented two elephants and other offerings, while the Rai of Gorakhpur, whether Sarnet or Bisen, paid up the arrears of tribute which had accumulated for several years, both afterwards accompanying the monarch on his march. This mention of tribute is significant, since it clearly indicates that the Rajputs had been in the habit of paying nothing at all. In like manner it is very doubtful whether the Sharqi kings of Jaunpur had any hold on the district. Their suzerainty was doubtless acknowledged, since they made it a leading feature of their policy to conciliate the Rajputs and to treat them as allies rather than as subjects, a fact to which express reference is made in the history of the Dhuriapar house. The overthrow of

* E. H. I., II. pp. 300. 305. | † *Ibid* VI. p. 224.

Jaunpur by Bahlol Lodi certainly did not affect the northern districts, and subsequently the Rajas became so powerful that they were left in peace by the Afghan nobles among whom the country was divided. Even Sher Shah, perhaps the strongest ruler of Hindustan, seems to have made no impression on this outlying tract, although doubtless he managed to extract tribute from the Rajput chiefs.

The Rajputs.

From the twelfth century to the days of Akbar the history of Gorakhpur is merely the record of the leading Rajput clans, the main features of which have already been given in Chapter III. The Bisens were the first to attain prominence, but it seems that at an early date a colony, said to be of Rathors, had settled near Gorakhpur, where the Mansarowar and Kaulada tanks are assigned to rulers of this clan. They were expelled by the Domkatars, a race of doubtful origin which seems to have possessed a large admixture of aboriginal or Tharu blood. These people held a wide tract of country, and appear to have brought the Bhars, Doms and other tribes under their control, while their principal seat was at Domingarh, on a small island formed by the river Rohin. To the same period may be assigned the advent of the Bhuinhars, another mixed race who came from the south and east, settling first at Harpur in pargana Dhuriapar. Then came the Kausiks and then the Sarnets, the latter driving out the Domkatars, of whom nothing further is heard save in the extreme north, whither the scattered remnants of the tribe fled for refuge. Lastly came Mukund Singh, a Chauhan of dubious origin, who in the fourteenth century founded the principality of Butwal. His descendants intermarried with the Tharus, and were people of some importance; but their influence on this district was small, for though they were constantly at war with the Sarnets of Bansi, they were separated from Satasi by a wide belt of forest. In Padrauna to the east there would appear to have been a Rajput principality, of which only vague traditions exist, though it seems to have endured till the close of the sixteenth century, when it was overthrown and absorbed by the Raja of Majhauli. Thus it came about that the whole area was occupied by a small number of Rajput principalities, in most cases separated from one another by rivers or forests, the Rajas living in a state of complete independence, wholly cut off by the absence of communications from the outer world.

With the accession of Akbar we reach firmer ground, though it was not till several years had passed that the country attracted the attentions of that monarch. Ali Quli Khan, Khan Zaman, reconquered Oudh and Jaunpur for the Mughal in 1559, but he seems to have devoted his attention mainly to the Afghan leaders, and to have done little more than conciliate the Rajas. The latter were encouraged to assist in his rebellion against Akbar owing to their unwillingness to admit the existence of a supreme authority. The history of this rebellion is somewhat confused, but it would appear that in 1565 Khan Zaman sent his brother, Bahadur Khan, and Sikandar Khan to raise the country north of the Ghagra, and that in consequence an expedition was despatched thither by Akbar in command of Mir Muiz-ul-Mulk, assisted by Todar Mal and others.* The imperial forces were defeated: but the battle appears to have taken place in Oudh, since the beaten army fell back upon Kanauj. A peace was then effected, but Khan Zaman almost immediately rose again in rebellion. On the approach of Akbar in person he fled northwards through the Azamgarh district across the Ghagra, taking refuge in the submontane forest. A detachment of the imperial army followed in pursuit but scoured the country in vain, returning to Akbar's camp at Jaunpur.† On their retirement Khan Zaman emerged from his retreat and joined his brother on the banks of the Ganges. Once more he was pardoned, but once more he rebelled in 1567, with the result that he was defeated and killed, along with his brother; but Sikandar Khan escaped to Ajodhya, whence he took boats and descended the Ghagra, landing and marching to Gorakhpur.‡ Thence he was pursued and fled into Bengal, where he remained till he was again pardoned and reinstated in the government of Lucknow. The pursuing force, however, did not confine its energies to Sikandar. Tradition states that it was led by Fidai Khan and Todar Mal, and that they first received the submission of the Dhuriapar Raja, who had always professed allegiance to the house of Timur. They then came into conflict with Majhauli, as

Akbar.

* E. H. I., V, pp. 301, 303. | † *Ibid*, p. 307. | ‡ *Ibid*, p. 324.

the Raja's servants had opposed the imperial patrols; but though the Bisens at first contemplated resistance they came to the conclusion that discretion was the better part of valour and submitted, though probably there is little truth in the legend that the Raja on this occasion became a Musalman. The imperial forces then marched up the Rapti to Gorakhpur, where they defeated the Raja of Satasi, who was compelled to fly. A Musalman garrison was then established at Gorakhpur, and for the first time the district became a corporate part of the empire. The result was the same, whether the story of Fidai Khan be true or not; for, while no such name occurs in the list of Akbar's grandees, we are told that in 1572 Payanda Khan was in charge of Gorakhpur as the deputy of Munim Khan, Khan-i-Khanan, the governor of Jaunpur. In that year the place was seized by Yusuf Muhammad, son of Suleman of Bengal, who had escaped from prison at Agra and had repaired to the nearest point in his father's dominions; for it is clear that in the early years of Akbar's reign this district was regarded as at least nominally a part of the Bengal kingdom.* The garrisons of Gorakhpur were unable to resist the invasion of the Afghans, supported in all probability by the Rajput chieftains, and Munim Khan himself had to proceed to the relief of the beleaguered town. The Afghans managed to escape and join Daud Khan and others, who were then raising a rebellion in Bengal; but in the next two years Munim Khan effected the complete conquest of Patna and Bihar. It seems clear that by this time the district was in a flourishing condition and no longer remained an unknown and inaccessible tract, for Gujar Khan, the minister of Suleman, offered to enter the imperial service on condition of receiving Gorakhpur in *jagir*. Certainly from the days of Munim Khan the town became a place of considerable importance, being the capital of a *sarkar* and possessing a mint for copper coin. In 1610 it was the residence of Afzal Khan, governor of Bihar, in preference to the official capital of Patna, when the insurrection of Qutb Khan and his Ujjain Rajput allies occurred at the latter place, and the district continued to be the *jagir* of Afzal Khan till his death at Agra in 1612.

* E. H. I., VI, p. 39.

Akbar's administration.

When the *Ain-i-Akbari* was compiled in 1596, Gorakhpur gave its name to one of the five *sarkars* comprising the province of Oudh. It contained 24 *mahals* or parganas, situated in this district, Basti, Gonda and Azamgarh. The identification of these *mahals* presents little difficulty, especially in the case of this district; but it is practically certain that the *sarkar* did not embrace the whole of the existing area, and that the parganas of Sidhua Jobna and Shahjahanpur formed one of the *mahals* of *sarkar* Saran. It was not till 1730 that the *mahal* was transferred to Gorakhpur, and the division of the two parganas did not take place till 1743. The double *mahal* of Gorakhpur, made up of the town and the suburban country, corresponded roughly with the present pargana Haveli, in addition to Silhat, from which it was separated on its reconquest by the Sarnets of Satasi about 1700. It had a cultivated area of 12,658 *bighas*, and was held by Surajbansi Rajputs, presumably the Sarnets, who paid a revenue of 571,304 *dams*, including 3,919 as *suyurghal* or assignments for troops and other purposes, and supplied a contingent of 40 horse and 200 foot. At that time the house of Majhauli seems to have been in the ascendant, for the Bisens are recorded as the *zamindars* of Dhuriapar, Chillupar, Unaula and Bhauapar, as well as of the twin *mahal* of Dewapara and Kotla, called by Elliot Dewapara Kuhana, which represented the country beyond the Dewa or Ghagra corresponding to the modern Salempur-Majhauli; the name being changed to Salempur after the conversion of Raja Bodh Mal and his adoption of Salempur as his capital. No mention is made of the Kausiks of Dhuriapar or of the Sarnets of Unaula, possibly for the reason that both were at that time in a state of obscurity, whereas Majhauli was undoubtedly the dominant power in the district. Dewapara and Kotla had a combined area of 16,195 *bighas* under tillage and were assessed at 717,840 *dams*, the local levies numbering 20 horse and 2,000 foot. Bhauapar had only 3,106 *bighas* of cultivated land, paying 155,900 *dams*, while the contingent was 200 infantry. In Unaula the cultivated area was 4,115 *bighas*, the revenue 203,290 *dams*, including 2,170 as *suyurghal*, while the military force was 400 infantry. Chillupar had 6,537 *bighas* under tillage, assessed at 289,302 *dams*, but the Raja was responsible for a force of 2,000 infantry. Dhuriapar furnished only 60 horse and 400 foot, but was in a far higher state of development, having 31,358 *bighas* under cultivation and paying 1,522,685 *dams*, inclusive of 5,607 as *suyurghal.* The greater part of Maghar lay in the Basti district and this *mahal* may be disregarded. There remain the two northern *mahals* of Binayakpur and Tilpur, at the headquarters of each of which was a brick fort, maintained doubtless for the security of the frontier. They were held by Surajbansi Rajputs, a term which probably refers to the Chauhans from the hills, and the most remarkable feature is the large military force there maintained, the former *mahal* supplying 400 horse and 3,000 foot, while the contingent from Tilpur was 100 horse and 2,000 infantry. The latter had 9,006 *bighas* under cultivation and paid 400,000 *dams*. In Binayakpur the area was 13,857 *bighas* and the assessment 600,000 *dams*, the round figures in either case suggesting the absence of any detailed assessment and the payment of a lump sum by the semi-independent chieftains.

The revenue.

These statistics are of considerable interest as throwing light on the economic condition of the district at that period. Exclusive of Maghar and Sidhua Jobna, the area under cultivation was only 84,727 acres, more than half of which belonged to the southern parganas along the Ghagra. The rest seems to have been very backward, although the population could not have been particularly sparse. The district was capable of raising nearly 11,000 armed men, although it is questionable whether much reliance can be placed on the returns of troops, which were always given in round numbers; and it is at least remarkable that in every pargana of the *sarkar* the column for elephants is blank. The revenue demand was Rs. 1,11,508, giving an incidence of Re. 1·31 per acre of cultivation, a remarkably high figure; not only is it almost as much as the present rate, but it must be remembered that the value of money in Akbar's day was at least four times as great as at present. Doubtless allowance was made for the difficulty of collection, at all times a formidable question under native rule: but there was very little difference between the rates in the various parts of the district: and even in the north, where the assessment can have been little more than nominal, the incidence was no greater than in the more accessible parganas of the south.

The later Mughals.

After the death of Afzal Khan scanty attention seems to have been paid to Gorakhpur. The garrison was small and its commandant incurred odium by some petty act of tyranny, with the result that in 1625 a simultaneous attack was made on Gorakhpur and Maghar by the Rajas of Satasi and Bansi. The attempt proved successful and the Musalmans were ejected; so that once again the Rajputs were left in independence and almost all the local chieftains withheld the payment of tribute. No steps appear to have been taken in order to avenge this insult to the paramount power, and it was not till the reign of Aurangzeb that measures were adopted for bringing this part of the country into subjection. About 1680 Qazi Khalil-ur-Rahman was appointed *chakladar* of Gorakhpur, and he forthwith proceeded to reduce the Rajas to submission, marching with a large force from Ajodhya. He drove the Raja of Bansi from Maghar, where he left a garrison, and then expelled Rudar Singh of Satasi from Gorakhpur, where he rebuilt the old fort of Basant Singh. The Sarnet chieftain retired to pargana Silhat and there founded the town of Rudarpur. The governor built Khalilabad in Basti near the right bank of the Rapti, and laid out a road from Gorakhpur to Ajodhya, while he succeeded in collecting the revenue with some regularity. From that time the Musalmans never relaxed their hold on Gorakhpur, the office of *faujdar* of the latter place being combined with that of the *subadar* of Oudh, as in the case of Chin Qulich Khan, Khan Dauran, who held the double appointment from 1707 till his resignation in 1711. A few years earlier Gorakhpur had received imperial recognition by a visit of Muazzam, afterwards known as Bahadur Shah, who had come for the purpose of hunting in the forests of the neighbourhood. He was the founder of the Jami Masjid, and in his honour the name of the town was changed to Muazzamabad, this appellation being given to a newly formed division which embraced the old *sarkars* of Gorakhpur and Saran. All the same, the real power remained vested in the Rajas, from whom the imperial officers were content to receive a merely nominal submission. Their independent position was perhaps more strongly marked here than in any other part of the United Provinces except the hill country and the north of Oudh. It was they who assigned lands and honours, the imperial sanction to such grants being seldom solicited, and they never seem to have dropped to the position of mere middlemen, or even to that of representatives of any central authority.

The Oudh Nawabs.

A considerable change was effected when in 1721 Saadat Khan obtained the province of Oudh, including Gorakhpur. He made it his special policy to reduce the power of the strongest Rajas; but while he succeeded fully in the southern parganas his authority was far less generally acknowledged or enforced in the north. About 1725, however, he was compelled to direct his attention more closely to affairs in that quarter. The younger branch of the house of Butwal had for some time held the pargana of Tilpur, and Tilak Sen, the head of that branch, had created much disturbance by his aggressive attitude, aided by swarms of Banjara mercenaries, with whose assistance he plundered and laid waste a large portion of the district. The Banjaras were responsible for the destruction and desertion of numberless villages, with the result that the jungle spread in every direction and much of the country was left desolate. A force was despatched northwards from Fyzabad; but the effect produced was small, since on its withdrawal Tilak Sen again made his appearance and resumed his guerilla warfare unchecked. The whole district was plunged into anarchy, and the Raja of Majhauli was the only chieftain strong enough to keep his territory in peace and security. At length intervention became imperative, matters being rendered more serious by a mutiny of the garrison at Gorakhpur, who reopened the old quarrel with the Raja of Satasi. About 1750 a large army was marched into the district under Ali Qasim Khan, who first reduced the Musalmans to order, destroying a fort which they had erected on the site of the old stronghold at Domingarh. He then proceeded northwards, defeated a force led by the son of Tilak Sen, who had followed in his father's footsteps, and continued his march into Butwal to recover arrears of tribute. A protracted struggle ensued, and it was not till twenty years had passed that the Raja made his submission, a compromise being effected whereby the country held by Tilak Sen was annexed to Butwal. No attempt was made to conduct the administration through Musalman officials, and the tribute can have been little more than nominal. Similarly while a strong force was cantoned at Gorakhpur the control exercised over the Rajas in the south was very slight. The *chakladars* were dependent for the collection of the revenue on the aid of the local chieftains and were powerless when such aid was withheld. The revenue moreover was a mere tribute, and there were no attempts at farming out large tracts or at dispossessing the Rajas, for the reason that such a step would have been impracticable.

Major Hannay.

Such at any rate was the case till Shuja-ud-daula, after his defeat at Buxar in 1764, devoted his attention to the consolidation of his power in Oudh. His agent in these parts was a Major Hannay, who was entrusted with the command of the troops and the collection of the revenue in Gorakhpur and Bahraich. This man seems to have exercised supreme power and to have enforced it by cruelty and oppression. He abolished, it appears, the office of *chakladar* and in its place created a number of *amils,* who were mere contractors for the revenue. At first these *amils* bargained with the local Rajas for a certain sum in return for absolute non-interference; in time the Rajas became *amils* themselves, if strong enough, their place being taken in the alternative case by some professional farmers from Oudh, who took a lease of a tract of country for a fixed period, ranging from one year to three or five. When a Raja was weakened by war with his neighbours, or from other causes, the farm of his domains would be bought by some noble or farmer, who seized the opportunity of collecting direct from the Raja's dependants or tenants; and when the Raja recovered his strength he would either take the farm himself or else buy out the farmer by guaranteeing the latter a certain profit on his engagement. Sometimes it happened that the farmer after taking compensation would abscond, and in such cases the revenue was seldom realised at all. As a matter of fact the demand was rarely paid in this district without resort to coercion, save in the south and in a few *tappas* along the Rapti held direct by Musalman delegates of the *chakladar* at Azamgarh. In this haphazard manner the administration of the country was conducted till the arrival of Major Hannay. He seems to have concerned himself but little with the ordinary work of government; but his troops enabled him to coerce the Rajas so effectually that a regular land tax was for the first time imposed and actually realised. The fault lay with the method rather than the system, for the demand exacted was so severe that many were compelled to abandon their villages, and his name was recalled with detestation for a long period. He was accused by Burke of having done incalculable mischief, and Mill states that he laid waste a vast tract of country which in former days was rich and flourishing. The fact was that the presence of his military force enabled the revenue officials to collect the sum due, and further to give full play to their extortionate instincts. They were mere contractors who had taken up leases for their own profit, and consequently had no interest whatever in the country beyond extorting iniquitous rents from an impoverished and helpless peasantry. The result was only to be expected. Most of the cultivators relinquished their holdings in despair, agriculture dwindled to a vanishing point, lawlessness and discontent were rife, and everywhere the prevailing feeling was one of general insecurity.

The Banjaras.

Matters were rendered worse by the inroads of the Banjaras, who in the course of time became a scourge to almost the entire district. Their activity was greatest in the east, where there was no one to withstand or repress them. With their increasing strength they began to take an active part in the politics of the district, fomenting quarrels between the Rajas, aiding whichever side offered the best prospect of advantage or revenge, and in many cases posing as the agents of the Nawab Wazir. To this end they usurped all manner of titles, such as *chakladar*, *nazim*, *naib-nazim*, *amil* and *taluqdar*; but in every case their sole object was plunder, to be achieved in the shortest time possible. The Rajas were helpless in the presence of these pests, though they might have rid themselves of them by combination. Instead they indulged in intestine war, the Raja of Satasi conducting a most foolish and disastrous campaign against Butwal in 1788, although in the Basti district his kinsman of Bansi managed two years later to inflict a serious defeat on the Banjaras and to drive them from his dominions. The Kausiks of Dhuriapar were in a miserable condition, owing to protracted family feuds and the treatment they had experienced at the hands of both Major Hannay and the Banjaras. Majhauli alone was flourishing, for the Raja reserved all his strength to keep his ancestral domains intact, abandoning Sidhua Jobna to the Banjaras, and subsequently aiding in the creation of the two great estates of Padrauna and Tamkuhi with the express intention of utilizing them a interposed defences against the raiders of the north. The experiment was most successful, for the new *taluqdars* rapidly gained the support of their weaker neighbours, to the advantage of both parties : and it was preferable for them to be the dependants of chieftains who were interested in the maintenance of security than to be the prey of lawless marauders. Recourse was doubtless had in many instances to force and fraud in the formation of these estates, but in those days might was the only law : one rapacious master was at least better than a host of petty tyrants, and the successful resistance eventually offered to the Banjaras afforded abundant justification for the action of the *taluqdars*, while it is beyond question that the security thus obtained was of the utmost value to the subordinate landholders whose estates were thus enclosed. Moreover they were free from the extortions of the *amils*, who dared not touch the great landowners of the east, with the result that in Padrauna and Deoria matters were infinitely better than in the sorely harassed country to the west.

By the treaty of the 10th of November 1801 Gorakhpur and other tracts were made over by the Nawab Wazir to the East India Company in liquidation of debts. The charge of this and the adjoining district was entrusted to Mr. Routledge, and probably no other officer among those who first undertook the management of the ceded districts had a more difficult task. He was appalled at the state of the country on his arrival ; he had no reliable subordinates, no police and no means of assessing or collecting the revenue ; and he was constantly harassed by the presence of the discharged officials and troops, who were still busily engaged in plundering the unfortunate inhabitants. In the previous chapter it has been shown how order was gradually The cession.

established, and how the obstinate resistance of the Rajas was by degrees overcome : the process was extremely slow and the results were often disappointing, but matters steadily mended till fresh trouble arose in a new direction.

The Nepalese.

Long before the cession the Nepalese had taken advantage of the prevailing anarchy to increase their possessions in the plains, first annexing the Tarai and then the parganas of Tilpur and Binayakpur. For these tracts they professed to pay tribute to Lucknow, but it is doubtful whether the Nawab Wazir ever received much on their account. In 1805 the Gurkhas claimed to hold Butwal by right of conquest and sent officials to collect the revenue. Certainly the Raja of Butwal, contumacious as he was from the first, was unable to meet the demands of the Company's servants, and had suffered imprisonment in consequence; while on his release he fell into the hands of the Nepalese, by whom he was murdered at Kathmandu. His family, in return for a pension, gave up their rights to the British, but by 1806 the Gurkhas had annexed two-thirds of the disputed territory. In the same year Sir George Barlow agreed to give up Sheoraj, a tract to the north of Basti, on condition that Butwal was evacuated : but they replied by retaining possession and offering to pay the revenue demand of the first settlement. Sir George was shortly afterwards superseded by Lord Minto, whose attention was directed elsewhere; and the matter dropped out of sight while the annexation of Butwal was completed. Thus emboldened, the Nepalese in 1810-11 crossed the Butwal boundary and seized some villages in Pali; and on a remonstrance from Lord Minto in 1812 they asserted their right to the occupied territory. Thereupon a boundary commission was appointed, Major P. Bradshaw being the British representative. His report, submitted in 1813, showed that the Gurkhas had no right to either Butwal or Sheoraj ; but on being ordered to withdraw, the Nepal *darbar* sent a respectful and even affectionate answer, in which they urged that the investigation had led them to a conclusion exactly the reverse of that formed by Major Bradshaw. The demand was reiterated in 1814 by Lord Moira, and military preparations were made. The collector of Gorakhpur, Sir Roger Martin, was ordered to march troops into the disputed tract if no answer should be received in 25 days; with the result that three companies occupied Sheoraj and Butwal without any opposition and police posts were established at Chitwa, Busauria and Saura in April.

War with Nepal.

Unfortunately the troops were allowed to return too soon, for in May the police posts were attacked and taken, the fugitives retiring on Bansi. War was now inevitable, but its declaration was postponed till the 1st November 1814. The operations in Kumaun and Bihar do not immediately concern this district, and attention need here be paid only to the doings of one out of the four invading columns. This was based on Gorakhpur and was commanded by General J. S. Wood, who was ordered to march through Butwal into Palpa, his force comprising 14 guns and some 4,000 infantry, including the 17th Foot. The story of his exploits is not inspiring. He reached Butwal without opposition on the 3rd of January 1815, to find the pass in which the town lies fortified and held by a force under Wazir Singh. Guided through the forest by a Brahman servant of the Butwal Raja, he reached the stockade which barred the way. The Nepalese opened fire, but the arrival of the main body enabled the position to be turned and the enemy fled up the hills. For some unaccountable reason, however, the general considered the place untenable, and forebore to press his advantage, sounding the retreat and leading back his grievously disappointed troops with a loss of 24 killed and wounded. Similar imbecility characterised his subsequent actions, for he seems to have greatly over-rated the strength of his opponents and to have remained content with a weakly defensive attitude. Instead of attempting to penetrate the hills, he threw up an entrenchment at Lotan to guard the main route to Gorakhpur, while he himself moved to Nichlaul in order to repel the incursions which were now events of almost daily occurrence. Reinforcements constantly arrived, but during January, February and March the general remained inactive while villages in the north of this district were being plundered and burned, and the only acts of retaliation consisted in meting out similar treatment to some deserted Nepalese villages. He always believed the enemy's force to be superior to his own, and in April he was ordered to justify this belief by actual contact with his opponents. He then marched to Butwal, which was subjected to an ineffective bombardment, and then after devastating the Nepalese Tarai he returned to Gorakhpur. In the meanwhile Ochterlony had conquered Dehra Dun and Kumaun, but the Gurkhas were unwilling to accede to the terms demanded and to relinquish the Tarai : so that preparations were made for a second campaign, and Colonel Nicholls was placed in command at Gorakhpur for the advance on Butwal and Palpa. The negotiations, however, lingered on till the end of October, with the result that a compromise was reached and a treaty was signed at Sigauli on the 28th of November. It soon transpired that this step was merely intended to deceive ; for the treaty was never ratified, and in February 1816 it became clear that the Nepalese intended to continue the war. On this occasion Sir David Ochterlony entered Nepal from Bihar, completing the campaign by the beginning of March. The treaty was then accepted, and all the Tarai between the Sarju and the Gandak excepting Butwal proper, was given up to the British ; although subsequently the Governor-General decided, as a politic act of conciliation, to restore to the Nepalese as much of the lowlands as might not be required to form a straight and even frontier. The boundary was demarcated in the same year ; it ran in a fairly direct line parallel to the trend of the hills, and did not approach their foot except just to the north of Pali and Sheopur.

The Mutiny. The effect of the war, enhanced by the inactivity of the troops, was little less than disastrous. Lawlessness became rampant, and it was not till the conclusion of hostilities that the numerous bands of dacoits and robbers were captured or dispersed. In this manner development was greatly retarded and much of the work accomplished during the past fourteen years was destroyed. Gradually, however, order was restored and the district continued to advance in prosperity till its peace was rudely shaken by the great rebellion of 1857. At that time the district was in the charge of Mr. W. Paterson as collector, with Mr. W. Wynyard as judge and Mr. F. Bird as joint magistrate. The military force comprised 2½ companies of the 7th N. I., whose headquarters were at Azamgarh, under Captain Steel, and a squadron of the 12th Irregular Cavalry from Sigauli. On the 25th of May Mr. Wynyard, who had practically assumed command under the authority of Mr. Tucker, the commissioner of Benares, and had countermanded Mr. Paterson's departure on furlough, heard from Azamgarh that the 17th were no longer to be trusted. He accordingly enlisted recruits for the jail and other local guards, and instructed the loyal *zamindars* and the European planters to take similar steps, while he despatched 125 men of the 17th and 34 of the cavalry with the surplus treasure to Azamgarh. By the end of May the district was showing signs of infection, crime was on the increase, the *zamindars* of Paina plundering boats on the Ghagra, while the Raja of Narharpur ejected the police from Barhalganj, liberated 50 convicts at work on the road and seized the ferry, thus cutting off communication with Azamgarh. On the 5th of June news arrived of the mutiny of the 17th at the latter place, whereupon Captain Steel paraded his men and addressed them, apparently with effect, since everyone professed his undying loyalty. The following day, however, they refused to obey when ordered to march for Azamgarh, asserting their intention of seizing the treasure. On the 7th a desperate attempt at escape on the part of the prisoners in the jail was frustrated by the guard under Mr. Bird, 20 convicts being shot; and the next day, when the sepoys endeavoured to seize the treasury, they were foiled by the firmness of Mr. Wynyard and the attitude of the cavalry. Matters looked brighter on the 9th, when news came from Major Ramsay, the Resident at Kathmandu, that he was sending 200 Gurkhas from Palpa, and in spite of the disturbing news from other districts Wynyard endeavoured to maintain order by sending out detachments of the cavalry to Basti and other parts of his district. Martial law was proclaimed with good effect, but the northern and western parganas were utterly disorganised, and the Rajas of Satasi and Narharpur were evidently conspiring with the rebels in other parts. On the 17th and 19th of June the fugitives from Gonda and elsewhere reached Gorakhpur, escorted by the Raja of Bansi, and the next day they were sent on with the ladies of the station to Azamgarh, whence they made good their escape to Ghazipur. The Gurkhas from Palpa arrived on the 30th of June, and for the next month Gorakhpur was secure and

Wynyard retained his hold on the district, though crime was rife and in the outlying tracts little or no attention was paid to the central authority. On the 26th of July news came of the Sigauli mutiny, and Wynyard at once wrote to Colonel Wroughton, who was marching on Gorakhpur with 3,000 Gurkhas from Kathmandu by way of Nichlaul, to hasten his advance. A regiment was sent on ahead and the remaining five reached Gorakhpur on the 29th. Their arrival enabled Wynyard to disarm the remnant of the 17th N. I., which was quietly effected on the 1st of August, though a disaffected body of the cavalry from Sigauli, who had joined Wroughton's column, rode off with their horses, the loyal remainder pursuing them into the jungles and killing several of their number. The mutineers at Sigauli had marched southwards to Salempur, where they destroyed the house of the opium agent, but were prevented from carrying off the treasure by a detachment of the 17th, who brought it safely into Gorakhpur.

Evacuation.

The Gurkha brigade was under orders to march by way of Azamgarh to Allahabad, and as the former place was again occupied by the rebels, Colonel Pahlwan Singh declined to leave a single man at Gorakhpur, though the place was now threatened by the mutinous troops from Sigauli. It is true that the Gurkha force had been much reduced by cholera and sickness, but few incidents have caused more discussion than the evacuation of Gorakhpur. Sir Charles Wingfield states that Colonel Wroughton offered to leave two regiments, but that the civil authorities would not be content with less than four, a statement which conflicts directly with other accounts. Certainly the condition of the district was by this time deplorable and the protection afforded by the Gurkhas was somewhat slight, as the people stood in no great awe of the hillmen, and the general anarchy was not in the least checked by their arrival. Moreover Mr. Tucker constantly recommended the abandonment of the station, and six weeks earlier Lord Canning himself had written to Mr. Wynyard, bidding him have no scruples in retiring in time. When therefore the Gurkhas were on the eve of departure Wynyard summoned all the European planters to Gorakhpur, and then made over the charge of the district to the Rajas of

Majhauli, Satasi, Bansi, Gopalpur and Tamkuhi, while Mr. Bird insisted on remaining behind to supervise their labours. The others accompanied the Gurkhas, taking the treasure with them, and marched out on the 13th of August, crossing the Ghagra into Azamgarh on the 22nd. They were followed by a body of mutineers under Muhammad Hasan, who had recently shown loyalty by protecting Colonel Lennox and other fugitives from Fyzabad, but had now openly joined the rebel cause and had been proclaimed *nazim* of Gorakhpur, and on the 18th a spirited attack was made at daybreak on the Gurkha camp at Gagaha, some ten miles north of the Ghagra on the Azamgarh road, but this was successfully repulsed, the insurgents losing about 200 killed, while their leader himself had a very narrow escape from capture. On the 27th the column reached Azamgarh, and Mr. Wynyard was appointed to the charge of that district.

Rebel rule.

In the meantime the uselessness of the committee of Rajas was fully proved. The only one to attend on Mr. Bird was Raja Kishan Kishor Chand of Gopalpur, and even he was helpless. The magistrate found that only 17 out of the 150 men of the jail guard would assist him to destroy the bridge of boats over the Rapti, while the Rajas of Satasi, Barhiapar, Chillupar and Nagar were now openly hostile. He refused an offer of the Gopalpur Raja to go with what remained in the treasury to Gopalpur, and then the Raja departed. Thereupon Muhammad Hasan returned, released the prisoners in the jail and compelled Mr. Bird, who for some days had been openly insulted, to fly for his life. A reward was set on his head and he was hotly pursued, but his intimate knowledge of the jungles served him in good stead and he eventually succeeded in reaching Bettiah after a difficult journey of 82 miles. At Gorakhpur the *nazim* proceeded to act as if in permanent possession. Most of the bungalows in the civil station were set on fire by the rebels, but Muhammad Hasan did all in his power to prevent the destruction of property, save with regard to Mr. Bird's house. He preserved the records, so as to ascertain the revenue demand; he ordered all Government servants to remain in their posts under his authority, and maintained the fiscal and criminal jurisdictions, in spite of the great objections on the part of the landholders to the police, whom they represented as an altogether foreign institution. Even the decrees of the civil courts were executed on payment of half the amount adjudged. None of the deputy collectors and only one tahsildar obeyed the summons, though several *thanadars* accepted service under the new ruler. The great proprietors who joined his cause received salutes and other honours, and in return for contingents furnished were given full civil and criminal authority within their estates; but the chief offices were awarded, naturally enough, to the leading Musalmans of the city. Nevertheless the general disorder was unbounded. In Gorakhpur large sums of money were extorted from the merchants and bankers, whose families in many cases were grossly ill-treated, while in the district the strong preyed upon the weak, and everywhere the auction purchasers were ousted by the former proprietors. Few persons of any note remained actively loyal. The prominent exceptions were the Raja of Bansi, who held fast to his allegiance under the greatest difficulties, and the Raja of Gopalpur, who defeated a force sent to demand revenue, but was ultimately compelled in October to seek refuge in Azamgarh. The Raja of Tamkuhi remained loyal, but was too remote to attract attention, while the Raja of Majhauli also protected Government servants and continued steadfast in spite of his failure to attend as a member of the committee. Subsequently he was exposed to great danger by the arrival of Har Kishan Singh, the brother of the famous Kunwar Singh, who with 500 men entered the district and advanced close to Salempur, but he was saved by the approach of the Saran column under Colonel Rowcroft.

Military operations.

The rule of Muhammad Hasan was not destined to endure for long. The second Nepalese army under Jang Bahadur reached Bettiah on the 22nd of December, and there it was joined by Brigadier MacGregor. At the same time a mixed force of Gurkhas, artillery, Bengal police and the Naval Brigade under Captain Sotheby, was organised by Colonel Rowcroft in western Bihar and collected in an entrenched camp at Mairwa, about 50 miles from Chapra. On the 26th of December he marched to attack a considerable body of rebels encamped at Sobhanpur on the Little Gandak and defeated them in a brilliant little action.

pursuing them with vigour to Majhauli. Thence after punishing several rebellious villages he marched to Barhalganj to await further instructions. In the meantime MacGregor and the Gurkhas had crossed the Great Gandak after a skirmish at Pipra, and thence proceeded towards Gorakhpur, reaching that place on the 11th of January, the only resistance being experienced at Pipraich, from which the rebels were expelled without difficulty. The recapture of Gorakhpur caused the insurgents to fly across the Rapti, while Muhammad Hasan escaped with such speed that on the same day he crossed the Ghagra at Tanda in the Fyzabad district. The rebels had made hardly any attempt to defend the city, breaking at the first attack and leaving behind them seven guns and some 200 killed and wounded, while many more were drowned in the Rapti. MacGregor then ordered Rowcroft to ascend the Ghagra in boats, while he himself left Gorakhpur with the main column on the 14th of February, effecting a junction with Rowcroft at Berari on the Ghagra in the Basti district. When the column entered Oudh Rowcroft was left behind in charge of Gorakhpur. Leaving Sotheby and his sailors on the river, he proceeded to headquarters and on the 20th of February he defeated a force of rebels near the town. He then marched westwards to Amorha in the Basti district, where for a long time he held a large rebel army in check, though he himself was practically blockaded there till June. The present district, however, witnessed no more fighting and nothing further occurred after the return of Jang Bahadur and his Gurkhas, who passed through Gorakhpur on their way to Bettiah, encumbered with an immense train of carts for the carriage of his sick and the abundant plunder gained in Oudh. With the reoccupation of the city civil administration was established, and the work was carried on quickly under the guidance of Sir Charles Wingfield, appointed commissioner of Gorakhpur.

Rewards and punishments.

The restoration of order coincided with the distribution of punishments and rewards. As mentioned in a preceding chapter, the Satasi and Barhiapar estates were confiscated, and a similar fate attended the properties of the Raja of Chillupar, the Musalman Raja of Shahpur in pargana Dhuriapar, the Babus of Tighra, Pandepar, Dumri and elsewhere, and Raja Randula

Son of Nichlaul, the last representative of the Butwal family, who by his rebellion forfeited the allowance granted in 1845 in compensation for his *taluqdari* rights in pargana Tilpur. The principal recipients of rewards were the Raja of Gopalpur, who obtained part of the Shahpur and other estates; the Mian Sahib of Gorakhpur, who remained conspicuously loyal in spite of grievous treatment at the hands of the rebels, protecting the Europeans and guarding much of their property in the *Imambara*; and Har Sahai, the *nazir* of the collector's court, who sheltered Mr. Bird and enabled him to escape, subsequently giving much valuable information to the British authorities, in return for which he was imprisoned and cruelly tortured by Muhammad Hasan. No actual reward was given to the Raja of Majhauli, but Government undertook to be responsible for his heavy debts, and the ancient estate was saved by the intervention of the Court of Wards.

Subsequent history.

The effects of the rebellion soon passed away, and subsequent years have witnessed no disturbance of the peace beyond the brief ebullition caused by the so-called *gaurakhshini* movement in 1893. Other events of importance have been noted elsewhere. The chief include the cession of the Tarai to Nepal in recognition of the assistance rendered during the Mutiny; the formation of the Basti district on the 6th of May 1865; the constitution of the Kasia and Deoria subdivisions; the revisions of the settlement, and the happily brief calamities of famine and scarcity which from time to time have visited the district. Generally Gorakhpur has achieved remarkable progress during the past half-century, and it may be confidently predicted that the district, whether it retains its present cumbrous shape or be split up into more conveniently administered portions, will exhibit even greater prosperity and a higher state of development in the near future.

GAZETTEER

OF

GORAKHPUR.

DIRECTORY.

GAZETTEER

OF

GORAKHPUR.

DIRECTORY.

CONTENTS.

AMWA KHAS, *Pargana* SIDHUA JOBNA, *Tahsil* PADRAUNA.

This immense village lies in 26° 50′ N. and 84° 14′ E. in tappa Rampur Dhab, that is to say in the *kachhar* of the Great Gandak, at a distance of some 68 miles east from Gorakhpur and about 16 miles from Padrauna, the nearest road being that from the latter place to Tiwaripatti. It has no claim to mention besides its great area and the consequent number of inhabitants, for it consists merely of an aggregation of scattered hamlets, in these respects resembling the adjacent village of Amwa Bairia on the other side of the Champaran boundary. The population numbered 5,158 souls in 1853, and by 1865 had risen to 5,510, subsequently increasing to 6,150 in 1872, to 8,785 in 1881 and to 8,872 ten years later, while in 1901 it amounted to 8,918, of whom 1,363 were Musalmans, Brahmans being the prevailing Hindu caste. The area is 5,366 acres and the revenue demand is Rs. 5,575. An upper primary school is maintained in the village and a market is held here twice a week. In former days the Gandak flowed close to the village, but it has receded eastwards; its old course being marked by a *sota*, while the low alluvium between Amwa and the river is subject to annual inundations.

BAIKUNTHPUR, *Pargana* SALEMPUR-MAJHAULI, *Tahsil* DEORIA.

A village of tappa Kachwar, situated in 26° 27′ N. and 83° 54′ E. on the right bank of the Little Gandak, about two miles north from the Nunkhar railway station, eight miles south-east from Deoria, and some 40 miles from Gorakhpur. The place is of no great size, the population at the last census being 1,063; the area is 426 acres and the revenue demand is Rs. 380, while the proprietors are Bisen Rajputs connected with the house of Majhauli. Baikunthpur possesses a post-office, an upper primary school, and a bazar, in which markets are held twice a week. Its chief claim to mention, however, lies in the fact that it is the scene of the largest fair in the district. The assemblage takes place during the month of Aghan on the occasion of the Dhanusjag festival, and on the principal day there is a dramatic representation of the contest for the hand of Sita, the breaking of the bow being accomplished by Ram Chandra, the successful suitor, on a large masonry platform, amid the applause of the spectators, who number some 50,000 souls. The gathering affords an opportunity for a great deal of traffic in cloth, metal vessels and the like. The fair has been in existence for about 80 years, and the presiding spirit is the Pauhari Ji of Paikauli, who is now erecting a fine Thakurdwara in the village.

BANSGAON, *Pargana* UNAULA, *Tahsil* BANSGAON.

The capital of the Bansgaon tahsil stands in 26° 33′ N. and 83° 21′ E., at a distance of 14 miles south from Gorakhpur. It is connected with the latter by a direct route, which leaves the Azamgarh road at Mahabir Chhapra, seven miles south from the headquarters station; but as this traverses the valley of the Ami, it is useless during the rains, and it then proves necessary to proceed to Kauriram and thence to Bansgaon by the cross-road to Rudrapur.

The place is built on rising ground overlooking the Ami valley, which terminates in the wooded ridge that marks the line of the metalled road just before the commencement of the Tucker *bandh.* Originally, it is said, Bansgaon was held by Chauhans, but they were ejected by the Sarnets, who still commemorate their conquest by assembling in Kuar to offer sacrifice at the old shrine of Debi. Though possessing a large population, Bansgaon is merely a village or rather a collection of villages, for there are really several *mauzas* with a common site, including Bansgaon, Shahpur Kabra, Baraban, Dunkhar, Majhgawan, Marwatia, Bhiti Dandi and Baidauli; but the average inhabitant is quite content to name them all Bansgaon, severally and collectively. The population was 3,340 in 1872, but had risen to 5,873 in 1881 and to 6,438 ten years later, though by the last census in 1901 the total had fallen to 5,034, of whom 267 were Musalmans. This figure does not include the inhabitants of Baraban, Dunkhar and Majhgawan, which together contained 710 souls. Despite this considerable number, the place has never been brought under the operations of Act XX of 1856.

The old tahsil buildings in Baraban were abandoned in 1905 and are now used for a dispensary, started in 1907; but they are built of mud and are in poor repair, so that it is hoped soon to provide new and more appropriate accommodation for the dispensary. The new tahsil, together with the munsif's court and residence and the sub-registrar's office, stand a few hundred yards to the south; they are excellent modern structures of masonry and add much to the appearance of the place. A little distance to the east is an inspection bungalow, with a court room for the use of touring officers, erected in 1905. Besides these, Bansgaon contains a police station, a post-office and the largest middle school in the district. Attached to the last, which occupies the site of the old distillery, is a training school for teachers and a very extensive boarding house. Markets are held twice a week in the bazar, but the trade is small. The area of the component villages is 668 acres, assessed to a revenue of Rs. 556.

BANSGAON *Tahsil.*

This tahsil forms the south-western subdivision of the district, comprising the country between the Basti boundary on the west and the Rapti on the east, which separates it from the tahsils of Gorakhpur, Hata and Deoria. To the north lie the Hasanpur Maghar and Bhauapar parganas of tahsil Gorakhpur, while to the south the Ghagra constitutes the dividing line between this district and Azamgarh. Within its limits are the three whole parganas of Unaula, Dhuriapar and Chillupar, as well as a portion of Bhauapar, consisting in all of 37 tappas, lists of which will be found in the several pargana articles. The total area is 357,867 acres or 559·1 square miles, but this is liable to change from time to time owing to fluvial action on the part of the great rivers. Occasionally these changes are very extensive. In 1904 a tract of 42,878 acres or 67 square miles was transferred to Azamgarh as the result of a marked northerly movement, which had taken place some twenty years or more previously, in the main channel of the Ghagra, the resumption of an ancient bed leaving 122 villages of pargana Dhuriapar on the south bank of the river. Altogether there are 165 alluvial *mahals*, all subject to the usual quinquennial revision, with the exception of five held on conditional long-term settlements.

The whole of this tract is a fertile plain, sloping gently in a south-easterly direction, with few undulations to break the monotony of its level surface. Besides the Rapti and Ghagra, there are three internal drainage channels of importance in the shape of the Ami on the northern border, discharging into the Rapti through the Amiar Tal; the Taraina in the centre, forming the Bhenri Tal in pargana Chillupar and thence sending its surplus waters into the Rapti; and the Kuwana in the south-west, which now unites with the Ghagra near Shahpur. There are several other lakes and *jhils* besides those already mentioned, and a large part of the area must be reckoned precarious owing to the damage done by inundations in years of heavy rainfall. Moderate floods in the *kachhar* of the Rapti are matters of almost annual occurrence, while in seasons of excessive and continuous precipitation the Ghagra proves very destructive, and even the Kuwana sometimes destroys the crops along its banks. The bulk of the tahsil, however, lies in the *bangar* or upland tract, and only the eastern edge along the Rapti and the south-west corner, mainly in tappa Belghat, consist of *kachhar* or new alluvium. In former days the northern part was covered with forest, as the name of tappa Bankata indicates; it had not entirely disappeared by 1840, but at the present time not a vestige remains.

The predominating soil is *doras* or loam, which at the last survey occupied 66·3 per cent. of the assessable area, *kachhar* coming next with 15·22; but owing to the subsequent transfer of a large alluvial strip to Azamgarh, the present proportion of the former soil is appreciably higher. For the rest, 13·02 per cent. consisted of *matiar* or clay, which alternates with loam throughout the tahsil, and 5·46 of *balua* or light sandy soil, which is most common on the banks of the Kuwana and in the Bhauapar and Chillupar parganas.

Though no early statements of area are available, it is well known that the country was in a deplorably backward state at the beginning of the 19th century, and that recovery was less rapid in the first forty years than in many other parts of the district. By 1860 the cultivated area was 224,593 acres, and this had risen at the settlement of 1884-89 to 264,979. The present average is somewhat less by reason of the decrease in the total area, but it amounts to 255,537 acres or 71 per cent. of the whole tahsil. As much as 51,391 acres is shown as barren, but most of this is either covered with water or else occupied by roads, village sites and the like, while of the 12,283 acres classified as actually unculturable the greater part lies on the banks of the Ghagra in the Dhuriapar and Chillupar parganas, where much land has been rendered useless by the deposits of sand brought down by that river when in flood. In all parts of the tahsil groves are abundant, and cover 13,227 acres or 3·7 per cent. of the entire area, a higher proportion than in any other subdivision. Many of these groves are really magnificent, and local tradition assigns their origin to the Banjaras, who planted trees to give shade to their encampments during the eighteenth century, though the majority are without doubt of more recent date. The remaining area includes 9,295 acres of current fallow, 16,501 of old fallow and 11,316 of unbroken waste. The last is seldom of any value as arable land, consisting for the most part of the tract covered with bush and tamarisk jungle along the Ghagra, and the patches of scrub and *dhak* jungle on the banks of the Taraina; open grass wastes are almost unknown, owing to the closeness of the cultivation. The tahsil is well provided with means of irrigation, and the average area watered is 116,581 acres or 45·7 per cent. of the land under the plough. Tanks, wells and other sources are in each case responsible for about one-third of this area, but it may be noted that some two-thirds of the well irrigation is to be found in pargana Dhuriapar, where good spring wells can be constructed in certain parts.

Owing to the nature of the soils and the general situation of the tract, the *rabi* harvest is the more important, averaging 197,233 acres as against 181,209 sown for the *kharif* during the five years ending with 1906-07. In the succeeding year the *rabi* was abnormally small on account of drought.* The double-cropped area is not remarkably large, averaging 61,030 acres or less than

* Appendix, table VI.

one-fourth of the net cultivation. In the spring harvest the cereals, wheat barley and the mixture called *gujai*, take up about three-fifths of the area sown, and are evenly distributed throughout the tahsil, though the Unaula pargana, which adjoins the great wheat-growing tract of Hasanpur Maghar, produces more wheat and less barley than the others. Peas are a very favourite crop, especially in Dhuriapar, while gram, either alone or mixed with barley, is extensively grown in every part. Oil-seeds are of little importance, but mention may be made of *masur*, which covers a considerable area in Chillupar, and of poppy, which is fairly common all over the tahsil, the balance being made up by vegetables, garden crops and tobacco. In the *kharif* rice takes the leading place, covering nearly two-thirds of the area sown, and five-sixths of this is under early rice, the conditions being unsuitable for the transplanted variety, which is found only in Unaula and parts of Dhuriapar. Next in order comes *kodon*, and then *arhar*, sown either by itself or in combination with *kodon*, *bajra* and other crops. Of less note are maize and *mandua*, though both are frequently grown in Dhuriapar, while sugarcane is less common than in any other part of the district; nearly all the cane grown is intended for eating, and though a little *gur* is made and consumed locally, there is not a single sugar factory in the tahsil.

In 1907-08 the total area included in holdings was 265,652 acres, and of this no less than 43·62 per cent. was cultivated by proprietors. The figure is much higher than in any other tahsil and shows a considerable increase since the last settlement, the reason lying in the unusually large and constantly increasing number of small farming landowners. Occupancy tenants hold 26·72 per cent., the proportion being higher in Unaula and Bhauapar than elsewhere, and tenants-at-will cultivate 26·75, while ·54 per cent. is in the hands of ex-proprietors and the remainder is rent-free, principally in the form of *goraits' jagirs*. Practically all the land is cash-rented, the present recorded occupancy rate being Rs. 3·53 and that of tenants-at-will Rs. 3·32 per acre, though the actual rents are probably much higher. Even the recorded figures show a marked increase since the settlement, and then it was ascertained that there had been a rise of 39·3 per cent. since 1865. The area sublet is 33,828 acres, or 12·43 per cent. of the holdings, and the *shikmi* rental averages Rs. 3·91.

The revenue demand for each pargana of the tahsil at successive settlements is shown in the appendix, as well as the present amount and its incidence.* A striking feature of the revenue administration of this tahsil is the unusual number of *malguzars* and the multitude of small amounts which are paid in separately. The former in 1907 numbered 90,730, and the demand on a single person's share was sometimes as low as one anna. The work of collection is consequently a matter of enormous difficulty: a state of affairs which results from the minute subdivision of the village lands and the disintegrating effects of unceasing partitions. There are 1,970 villages in the tahsil, at present divided into 3,059 *mahals*, of which 386 are *zamindari* and 2,673 are held by *pattidari* communities, the number of *mahals* having very greatly increased since the settlement. Under-proprietors are much more common than elsewhere in the district, and at settlement there were 1,082 *birtias* and 9,904 *arazidars*, the latter holding 17,767 acres.

The tract contains no large estates, with the exception of the 145 villages owned by the Pindaris, to whom reference has been made in Chapter III. The estate pays a revenue of Rs. 7,105 and is entirely in the hands of *birtias*. The Rani of Gopalpur owns 40 villages with a demand of Rs. 6,150: the heir to the Dhuriapar estate owns 15 villages paying a revenue of Rs. 1,311; and 67 villages, assessed at Rs. 9,800, belong to the Raja of Unaula. Of the Tiwaris of Rajgarh Sat Narayan Prasad owns 64 villages with a revenue demand of Rs. 6,771, now managed by the Court of Wards; and Babu Sant Kumar holds 63 villages, assessed at Rs. 6,589. Other landowners include Babu Bhagwati Prasad, the banker of Gorakhpur, who pays Rs. 3,089 on an estate of 50 villages, and Maulvi Subhan-ullah, also of Gorakhpur, whose 18 villages are assessed at Rs. 4,954.

The population of the tahsil numbered 348,086 persons in 1865, and, though it fell to 345,401 in 1872, it rose rapidly to 422,858 in 1881 and to 451,606 ten years later. At the census of 1901 the subdivision was found to have shared in the general

*Appendix, tables IX and X.

decline, the number of inhabitants being 438,364, of whom 222,335 were females. Since that date a tract with a population of 13,389 has been transferred to Azamgarh, and the density now averages about 758 to the square mile. Classified according to religions, there were 411,408 Hindus, 26,887 Musalmans, 43 Aryas, 15 Christians, six Jains and five Sikhs. In view of its past history, it is but natural that the Musalman element should be far less numerous, both absolutely and relatively, than in any other part of the district. Of the various Hindu castes the strongest are Chamars with 68,950 representatives, closely followed by Ahirs with 65,950. Next come Rajputs with 31,071, the principal clans being the Sarnets, Kausiks, Palwars, Bais, Bisens, Panwars and Surajbansis. After the Rajputs follow Brahmans with 29,491, Koeris with 21,428, Banias with 13,937, Kewats with 12,576, Telis with 12,485 and Kurmis with 12,109, no other caste having more than 10,000 members. Among the Musalmans only Sheikhs and Pathans occur in numbers exceeding 5,000.

The tahsil is almost wholly agricultural, and more than 76 per cent. of the people are directly or indirectly dependent on the tillage of the soil. There are no manufactures and no industries of any importance, and the trade is practically confined to grain. Out of 2,071 *mauzas* and 4,454 inhabited sites very few are of any size. The chief town is Barhalganj, which is still in a flourishing condition thanks to its situation on the great southern road and the river; but Gola and Gajpur, which could once boast a large trade, have sunk into insignificance. Dhakwa, Sikriganj and Shahpur are also small riverside marts, from which most of the business has departed, while Bansgaon itself and Sangrampur are merely overgrown agricultural villages.

Means of communication are but fair. There is no railway within the tahsil, but the north is within reach of the Sahjanwa and Gorakhpur stations, while that of Barhaj is fairly accessible to pargana Chillupar, and Barhalganj is only separated from Dohri-ghat by the Ghagra. Through Barhalganj the provincial road from Benares runs northwards past Gagaha, Kauriram and Belipar to Gorakhpur. The west of the tahsil is served by an unmetalled road from Gorakhpur, passing through Rudrapur to Sikriganj on the Kuwana, whence it turns to the south-east through Urwa Bazar, Gola and Barhalganj to Barhaj, where it crosses the Rapti by a ferry. From Rudrapur two cross-roads traverse the centre of the tahsil, one leading to Bansgaon, Kauriram and Gajpur, and the other southwards to Gopalpur near Gola, with a branch from Jaswantpur to Urwa Bazar and Shahpur. Other roads connect Gola with Kauriram, Bansgaon with Malhanpar and Gajpur with Gagaha. There are inspection bungalows at Kauriram, Gola and the bridge over the Taraina, and military encamping grounds at Belipar, Gagaha and Barhalganj. In addition to the Ghagra and Rapti, which are always navigable even for large boats and are still extensively utilised, the Kuwana is practicable for light craft at all seasons of the year; but the Ami is navigable only during the rains, and is very seldom used.

The tahsil is administered as a subdivision in the charge of a full-powered officer on the district staff, but the work is generally found too heavy for a single deputy collector, and usually a portion of it, together with a part of the work of the Sadr tahsil, is made over to a second officer. The headquarters of the tahsildar are at Bansgaon, where the munsif and the sub-registrar are also stationed. For police purposes the area is divided into five circles, with stations at Bansgaon, Barhalganj, Gola, Belghat and Rudrapur. The subdivision has remained unchanged since its first constitution in 1840, when the offices and courts were erected at Bansgaon, save for the transfer of pargana Chillupar from the old Salempur-Majhauli tahsil, which was effected very shortly afterwards.

BANSGAWAN, *Pargana* SIDHUA JOBNA, *Tahsil* PADRAUNA.

This large but otherwise unimportant village belongs to tappa Rampur Rogha and stands in 26° 48′ N. and 84° 11′ E., about a mile east of the road from Padrauna to Tiwaripatti, some 14 miles from the tahsil headquarters and 64 miles from Gorakhpur. Like the neighbouring village of Amwa, it covers a large area, amounting in all to 4,591 acres, and contains numerous hamlets. The population rose from 3,069 in 1872 to 4,548 in 1881 and to 5,128 ten years later; while in 1901 the total was 5,009, including 709 Musalmans. Bansgawan is the home of an ancient family of Rajput Babus, who are among the oldest residents of the pargana. They own the village, which is assessed at Rs. 4,081, and have a large house or *kot* here; but the present representative, Babu Dalip Narayan Singh, now lives at Kundwa in tappa Mainpur, a few miles east of Kasia. The village is the scene of a small market twice a week and possesses an aided school.

BARHAJ, *Pargana* SALEMPUR-MAJHAULI, *Tahsil* DEORIA.

The large and important town of Barhaj stands in 26° 16′ N. and 83° 43′ E. on the left bank of the Rapti, a short distance above its confluence with the Ghagra. In former days, it is said, this confluence was four miles to the west, but it has steadily progressed eastwards, although as late as 1873 it was still nearly two miles to the west of the town, opposite the contiguous village of Gaura. Barhaj forms a part of tappa Raipur, while Gaura lies in Kaparwar, the former being 41 miles south-east from Gorakhpur by the unmetalled road leading through Barhi and Rudarpur. It is the terminus both of a metalled road from Kasia and Deoria, and of a branch line of railway from Salempur; while through the town passes the unmetalled road from Chapra and Lar to Barhalganj. In the past Barhaj derived its importance from its position on the river, but now the bulk of the traffic to and from the town is carried by rail, though numbers of boats are still engaged in the transport of grain, timber and other articles, and the vessels of the India General Steam Navigation Company make this a regular port of call.

The name is traditionally derived from a Brahman named Barahan or Barhaji, who is said to have turned Musalman and to have been buried here, his supposed tomb being an object of veneration to this day. The town appears to have grown up with the foundation of a fort by a Rajput, presumably a Bisen, called Kunwar Dhir Sahi, but the place was destroyed by the Musalmans, though ruins of the old *kot* are still traceable. The present Barhaj is of modern growth and owes its existence to the action of the Raja of Majhauli in the eighteenth century: but it was not till 1830 or thereabouts that the first sugar factory was started and a commencement made of the great industry from which the town derives its wealth. There are now 49 refineries in Barhaj and Gaura which together rank with Rampur Karkhana as the foremost sugar-producing centres of the district; and the place has a great advantage over Rampur in that both rail and river routes are open to its merchandise without any previous cartage by road. The rapid rise of Barhaj is illustrated by the increase in the population from 5,080 in 1865 and 4,970 in 1872 to 11,715 in 1881, though subsequent enumerations have witnessed a slight decline, the total being 11,421 in 1891, while at the last census it was 10,054, of whom 1,659 were Musalmans.

Gaura has always been but a suburb of Barhaj and is now definitely included in the town. It is a place of little interest, consisting mainly of mud houses, and its population has exhibited changes similar to those of Barhaj. The total rose from 1849 in1891 1872 to 8,485 in 1881, but afterwards dr
while ten years later it was 7965 ncluding 545 Musalmans. The place was seprately administered under Act XX of 1856 from 1867 till 1908, when it was amalgamated with Barhaj to form a single notified area under Act I of 1900. The *mauza* of Gaura is 1,020 acres in extent, and is assessed to a revenue of Rs. 1,500.

Barhaj is a squalid and somewhat dirty place, though great improvements have recently been effected. It consists of a large collection of houses on either side of a long metalled street leading down to the river and the wharves, crossing the small Rakba *nala* by a bridge. The chief business centres are known as Farehata, Nimakhata, Dalhata and Naya Bazar, and the principal traders are a colony of Marwari Jains, Banias, Kalwars and Musalman Iraqis. The eastern portion is inhabited mainly by Mallahs, but their numbers have declined with the decay of the river-borne traffic. Markets are held weekly, and a considerable fair takes place on the *puranmashi* of Kartik. The town possesses a police station, a post-office, a dispensary, a middle vernacular school, a small school for girls and a cattle-pound. There is an inspection bungalow, and opposite the railway station is a good house belonging to the Raja of Majhauli, who is the owner of the place. The *mauza* of Barhaj is small, being only 274 acres in extent, with a revenue demand of Rs. 245; but the Raja derives a large sum from cesses and market dues. For this reason the Raja was held responsible for the watch and ward of the town, and also for the sanitary arrangements, Act XX of 1856 never having been put into force. The affairs of the notified area are now managed by a nominated committee consisting of the subdivisional officer as president, the tahsildar of Deoria as secretary and three ordinary members. The Raja contributes a sum of Rs. 6,200, and the new house and conservancy taxes will raise the income to Rs. 11,000 or thereabouts. Already much has been done to improve the sanitary condition of the town, and a number of street lamps have been erected.

BARHALGANJ, *Pargana* CHILLUPAR, *Tahsil* BANSGAON.

The town of Barhalganj stands in 26° 17′ N. and 83° 30′ E. the bank of the Ghagra and on either side of the provincial road from Gorakhpur to Azamgarh, opposite Dohri-ghat, to which access is gained by trains of a ferry, at a distance of 36 miles from the district headquarters. Through the town runs the unmetalled road from Gorakhpur and Sikriganj to Barhaj Lar and Chapra.

The eastern portion of the town is called Chillupar, from the fact that it lies on the far side of a small *nala* named the Chillu; and all the rest is known as Barhalganj, though, properly speaking, it consists of Qasba Barhal, Gola or the grain market, and Lalganj, named after the Lal Sahib, a brother of the rebel Bisen Raja of Chillupar or Narharpur, a village about a mile to the east. Up to the Mutiny the Raja was the owner of Barhalganj, but on the confiscation of his property the place was taken under direct management. Some of the land was bestowed on the loyal Raja of Gopalpur, but the latter was soon obliged to sell it in order to pay his debts, and the present owners are the Mahant of Paikauli and Maulvi Subhan-ullah of Gorakhpur. The remainder, 146 *bighas* in extent, has been retained as *nazul* property, and the income therefrom is credited to the town fund. Under the Narharpur Rajas the bazar dues amounted to Rs. 2,400 annually, but these were remitted on the change of ownership, and in their place a house tax was imposed, while from 1875 Barhalganj has been administered under Act XX of 1856. In 1908 the town contained 1,436 houses, of which 467 were assessed, and the average income from the house tax for the past three years has been Rs. 1,200, giving an incidence of Rs. 2-9-1 per assessed house and Re. 0-3-8 per head of population. The total receipts for the past year, including a considerable initial balance, were Rs. 2,702 and the expenditure Rs. 2,095, devoted mainly to the upkeep of the town police, the maintenance of a conservancy staff and minor improvements. The revenue *mauza* is 491 acres in extent and is assessed at Rs. 298; while Chillupar covers 287 acres and pays a revenue of Rs. 562.

The population of Barhalganj was 5,058 in 1853, but subsequently declined, being only 4,449 in 1872; and, though it rose to 5,779 in 1881, it again dropped during the next ten years to 5,682, while in 1901 it was 5,181, of whom 1,379 were Musalmans. This figure does not include the population of Chillupar, which was 786 at the last census. the decline is due mainly to the diversion of trade caused by the railway, and now the volume of traffic is but small, though the place will doubtless maintain its importance to some extent, owing to its position on the main road to the south. Markets are held here twice a week, and several noteworthy fairs take place during the year, such as the bathing fairs in Kartik, Chait and Asarh, and the festival of Ghazi Mian held on the first Sunday in Jeth. The town stands on a high *kankar* ridge, which renders the natural drainage good and at the same time removes all danger of erosion from the Ghagra. Along the main road stands the chief bazar, consisting of a street lined with brick-built shops and a fine market place flanked with stone drains. Barhalganj contains a police station, a dispensary, a post-office, a cattle pound, an opium bungalow, a middle vernacular school and a school for girls. A little to the north of the site is a military encamping ground by the side of the main road. Among the numerous temples in the place the most important include that of Jalesarnath Mahadeo, an ancient and celebrated building; the Thakurdwara of Charanpaduka, under the management of the Mahant of Paikauli; that of Jagmohan Das on the northern outskirts named after its founder, one of the leading merchants of the town; and a new temple erected by the Mahant of Paikauli.

BARHI, *Pargana* HAVELI, *Tahsil* GORAKHPUR.

An unimportant village of tappa Rajdhani, situated in 26°37′ N. and 83°29′ E. on the unmetalled road through the *kachhar* from Gorakhpur to Rudarpur and Barhaj, about 13 miles south-east from the district headquarters. Standing on low ground close to the Rapti, it is subject to inundations from the river, which has cut away the road for some distance immediately to the north of the village. In consequence of this the police station, though still known by the name of Barhi, has been moved to Gauri, a village standing about two miles to the north-east on the left bank of the Gurra, where the road is joined by that from Adda Motiram. The Gurra here is connected with the Rapti by means of a broad watercourse called the Semraona *nala*, up which the flood water of the Rapti passes. Close to the *thana* is a cattle-pound, while Barhi itself contains a post-office and an aided school. The village is the scene of a weekly market, and at the last census contained 1,423 inhabitants, principally Ahirs. The reason for the original establishment of a police station at this place was the prevalence of highway robbery on the roads in the vicinity on the part of the numerous outlaws who infested the neighbouring forests ; but crime of this description has practically disappeared with the clearance of the jungle.

About two miles east from Barhi, in the villages of Rajdhani, Tongri and Upadhauli, are the remains of a great city or fortress said to be the home of the Maurya dynasty.* This city appears to have extended from the Rapti to the Pharend, a distance of about four miles from east to west, and to have been about a mile in breadth. From Dihghat on the Rapti to the bank of the Gurra are several brick-strewn mounds, and on the east of the latter river is a very large mound called the Upadhaulia Dih, about a mile in length and some 1,600 feet in width, with the remains of two large brick stupas. Another mound occurs in Rajdhani to the north-east of Upadhaulia, and further on in the same direction, near the Pharend, are the traces of an extensive brick enclosure, about 1,900 by 1,300 feet. The site has never been explored, and all attempts at identification necessarily rest on pure conjecture.

* C. A. S. R., XVIII, 31, and XXII, 7.

BELGHAT, *Pargana* DHURIAPAR, *Tahsil* BANSGAON.

Belghat gives its name to the westernmost tappa of the pargana, and stands in 26°26′ N. and 83°10′ E. on the unmetalled road from Shahpur to the Basti border and the Kamharia ferry over the Ghagra, at a distance of some 26 miles from Gorakhpur, and six miles from Sikriganj on the Kuwana. Owing to the necessity of crossing the latter river, the place is difficult of access, especially in the rains. As its name implies, it formerly stood on the bank of the Ghagra, but the river now flows some three miles to the south, and Belghat has become a purely agricultural village of little importance. It contains a police station, a post-office, a cattle-pound and an upper primary school. The population of the village was 1,500 at the last census, and the principal residents are a family of Kausik Rajpath connected with the house of Gopalpur and non represented by Babu Rudra Prasad Sahi who owns this village and others in the neighbourhood. The area of the *mauza* is 982 acres and the revenue demand is Rs. 607.

BELIPAR, *Pargana* BHAUAPAR, *Tahsil* BANSGAON.

A small village of tappa Kuswasi, situated in 26° 35′ N. and 83° 25′ E., on the metalled road from Gorakhpur to Azamgarh at a distance of 12 miles south from the former. The village is built on the high ground overlooking the broad valley of the Ami, and lies opposite to Bansgaon, which is on the south side of this depression. The ridge terminates a short distance south of the village in the great embankment known as the Tucker *bandh*, which has been described elsewhere. Belipar formerly contained a police outpost, and still possesses a cattle-pound, an upper primary school and a military encamping ground. The population in 1901 numbered 958 souls, and the area of the *mauza* is 313 acres, assessed to a revenue of Rs. 410.

BHAGALPUR, *Pargana* SALEMPUR-MAJHAULI, *Tahsil* DEORIA.

A large village of tappa Ballia, standing in 26° 10′ N. and 83° 52′ E. on the high left bank of the Ghagra, at a distance of 52 miles south-east from Gorakhpur and a mile above the Turtipar railway bridge. It is approached either from Turtipar station or else by a road running northwards to Musela, while another leads north-east to Salempur. Owing to its position on the river, the place was once a market of some importance, but the diversion of the traffic to the railways has caused the bazar to sink into insignificance. The village had at the last census a population of 1,887 persons, the principal inhabitants being Brahmans; the area is 586 acres and the revenue demand is Rs. 930. There is a branch post-office here, as well as an upper primary school and a cattle-pound.

The name is said to be a corruption of Bhargiwapur or the village of the Bhargiwa Brahmans, who certainly have been settled here a very long period. It is obvious that Bhagalpur is a place of great antiquity, for traces of old buildings are visible for a considerable distance on either side of the river.* The principal monument is a pillar of rough grey sandstone, with a mutilated inscription of the tenth century, about half a mile to the east of the village site. The column is round on a square base and is about 17 feet in height, while the circular capital is surmounted by a plain cone. The date on the inscription is lost, but the pillar appears to have been erected by a Raja of the solar race of Ajodhya.

BHAUAPAR, *Pargana* BHAUAPAR, *Tahsil* GORAKHPUR.

The village, which gives its name to the pargana of Bhauapar, is a place of some size, situated in 26° 40′ N. and 83° 22′ E., between the metalled road to Azamgarh and the Rapti, north of the Nandaur Tal, at a distance of five miles south from Gorakhpur. It contained at the last census a population of 3,531 souls, and for a long time was the only town in the pargana, deriving its importance from the large fort, the remains of which are still visible on the high ground overlooking the Rapti. This was the residence of the Satasi Rajas prior to the foundation of Gorakhpur, and in old days the fort and the village stood in the midst of dense jungle. During the famine of 1769 it is said that the inhabitants were compelled to fly on account of the depredations of the famished tigers, and even in the beginning of the last century wild animals were responsible for seven or eight deaths annually and carried off some 250 cattle on an average

* C. A. S. R. I. 85: XVI. 130: XXII.: 60: and J. A. S. B.. VII. 34.

from the vicinity. Bhauapar is now an agricultural village of little importance, but possesses a small market, as well as a post-office and an upper primary school. It has a total area of 344 acres and is assessed at Rs. 362. The name of the revenue *mauza* is Tatha Jot.

BHAUAPAR *Pargana.*

The pargana of Bhauapar is a long and narrow strip of country extending along the right bank of the Rapti from the borders of Hasanpur Maghar on the north-west to the boundary of Chillupar on the south-east. On the west and south-west it marches with Unaula and Dhuriapar, while beyond the Rapti lie Haveli and Silhat. Though about 30 miles in length, the mean breadth is not more than seven miles, the total area bei‑ 87,787 acres or 137·1 square miles. The northern portion, comprising the tappas of Havely and Ret, belongs to the Sadr or Gorakhpur tahsil, and is 38,916 acres or 60·8 square miles in extent; and the southern five tappas of Kuswasi, Pachisi, Gurmhi, Kotha Rampur and Gagaha are included in tahsil Bansgaon, this tract having an area of 48,871 acres or 76·3 square miles.

Bhauapar itself lies in the northern half, which contains 158 *mauzas* and 207 inhabited sites, but no place of any size or importance. In the southern half there are 274 *mauzas* and 432 separate sites, including the considerable villages of Gajpur, Gangaha, Kotha, Belipar and Kauriram. The population of the entire pargana was 86,663 in 1853, when it was the most densely populated tract in the whole district. The two northern tappas contained 39,123 inhabitants in 1865, and though this fell to 33,852 in 1872, subsequent enumerations have shown a marked increase, the total being 46,758 in 1881 and 47,127 ten years later, while in 1901 it was 52,931, giving an average density of 870 to the square mile. The population of the Bansgaon tappas was 50,225 in 1865, dropping to 48,674 in 1872, but afterwards rising to 59,240 in 1881 and 63,174 in 1891, though at the last census there was a slight decline, the total being 62,447, which gives a mean density of 819 to the square mile.

Local tradition states that the tract was formerly held by Tharus and then by the Domkatars, the latter being overthrown by Chandra Sen, the Sarnet, who established himself at Domingarh. His eldest son became Raja of Satasi and appears to have extended his sway over the lands on both sides of the Rapti. The earliest seat of the family seems to have been at Bhauapar, where the remains of a large stronghold are still visible on the banks of the Rapti. When Fidai Khan seized Gorakhpur on behalf of Akbar in 1570, the Raja was ejected and took up his abode at Gajpur, where the family remained for fifty years till the reoccupation of Gorakhpur. Nothing further of note occurred in the history of the pargana till the fall of Satasi, in consequence of the Raja's rebellion in 1857. His descendants still reside at Gajpur in an unpretentious house of modern construction.

BHAUAPAR *Pargana, Tahsil* MAHARAJGANJ.

This is the northernmost pargna of the district, and consists of a somewhat narrow strip of country bounded on the north and west by Nepal, the dividing line on the west being the Ghunghi river. To the south lies Haveli, and to the east and south-east Tilpur, separated from Binayakpur by the river Piyas. Formerly the pargana was of much greater extent, both on the north and west; but the strip of country between the present northern border and the foot of the hills was given to Nepal after the Mutiny, as well as a considerable block beyond the Ghunghi. In 1865 the remainder of the western portion was detached and assigned to the Basti district. The present area is 92,892 acres or 145·1 square miles, and comprises the three tappas of Mirchwar, Sirsia and Nagwan.

There is no town or any large village in the pargana, which contains 132 *mauzas* and 361 inhabited sites. The population rose from 12,695 in 1853 to 19,205 in 1865, and has since increased rapidly to 21,722 in 1872, to 39,145 in 1881 and to 50,970 ten years later, while in 1901 it was 53,645, the density having risen in fifty years from 87 to 369 persons to the square mile.

The history of Binayakpur, like that of Tilpur, may be said to commence with the foundation of the Butwal principality in the fourteenth century. It was a separate pargana in the days of Akbar, though probably in a very undeveloped state. The tract suffered greatly from the troubles of the eighteenth century, and the war with Nepal completed its desolation. At the same time, however, the population was strengthened by the influx of refugees from Butwal and the Tarai, and soon afterwards under the direction of Captain Stoneham, who was appointed to improve the cultivation in this and the neighbouring parts of Haveli, embankments were built for irrigation, drainage works were undertaken and the land parcelled out among the settlers. Thanks to his efforts and the system of forest grants, almost the whole of the pargana has been reclaimed, and at the present day the proportion of barren waste is smaller than in any other part of the district. The pargana derives its name from a village called Binayakpur, now situated in Nepalese territory.

BIRAICHA, *Pargana* HAVELI, *Tahsil* MAHARAJGANJ.

This small village gives Its name to a tappa in the east of the pargana, and is situated in 27° 1′ N. and 83° 44′ E., between the Little Gandak and the road from Captainganj to Nichlaul, a short distance south-east from the Ghughli station on the railway to Bagaha, and some 34 miles north-east from Gorakhpur. The village, which has an area of 669 acres and is assessed at Rs. 622, contained at the last census a population of only 833 persons, principally Kewats. It deserves mention, however, as possessing a police station, a post-office, a cattle-pound and a lower primary school.

BISHUNPURA, *Pargana* SIDHUA JOBNA, *Tahsil* PADRAUNA.

A village of tappa Pirthipur, situated in 26° 47′ N. and 84° 10′ E., on the road from Padrauna to Tiwaripatti at a distance of some 62 miles east from Gorakhpur and about 14 miles south-east from the tahsil headquarters. The place adjoins the large village of Bansgawan, already mentioned, and is noticeable only as possessing a police station, a branch post-office and a cattle-pound, while a small market is held here twice a week. The population at the last census numbered 1,118 persons, residing in several scattered hamlets; the total area is 896 acres and the revenue demand is Rs. 845.

BRIDGMANGANJ, *Pargana* HAVELI, *Tahsil* MAHARAJGANJ.

Bridgmanganj, formerly known as Sahibganj, is named after Mr. J. H. Bridgman, the first grantee of the Lehra estate, and lies in 27° 11′ N. and 83° 12′ E., at a distance of nearly 40 miles north-west from Gorakhpur, and three miles west of Mr. Holdsworth's house at Lehra. It is connected with the roads from Gorakhpur to Uska and Lotan, while close to the bazar on the south is a station on the railway to Uska and Tulsipur. The construction of the line has attracted much of the trade with Nepal, which formerly accumulated at Dhani, some six miles to the south. The place is now a thriving market, and the bazar contains a good number of brick-built houses. The population numbered 1,727 persons in 1901 and has since increased to a considerable extent. Bridgmanganj contains a branch post-office, a lower primary school and an aided Sanskrit *pathshala*, while at Bela Haraiya, about a mile to the west, is a dispensary maintained by the district board.

CAPTAINGANJ, *Pargana* HAVELI, *Tahsil* HATA.

The small town of Captainganj lies in tappa Parwarpar, in 26° 55′ N. and 83° 43′ E., on the unmetalled road from Gorakhpur to Padrauna and on the branch line of railway to Bagaha, at a distance of some 28 miles north-east from the district headquarters and about 12 miles north from Hata. From Captainganj a road runs westwards through Partawal and Campierganj to Karmaini-ghat on the Rapti, a branch leaving this at the third mile and running northwards to Siswa and Nichlaul, while another road goes north-east from the town to Naurangia in the Padrauna tahsil. The origin of the name is unknown, but it appears to have arisen from the establishment of a police post here in the early days of British rule. The population numbered 3,647 persons in 1872, and by the last census it had risen to 3,946, and is likely to increase further with the advent of the railway and the consequent expansion of trade. In former days a certain amount of traffic was carried along the Little Gandak, which flows close to the town on the east, but this has almost disappeared since the opening of the railway in 1907, while a further diversion of trade may be expected on the completion of the proposed line from Captainganj to Padrauna and Thawe in Saran. The place contains a branch post-office, a cattle-pound, an upper primary school and a military encamping ground between the Padrauna road and the Gandak. The village lands are 3,077 acres in extent and are assessed at Rs. 1,635; they were confiscated after the Mutiny for the rebellion of their former owners, and the bazar, with an area of nine *bighas*, is still retained as Government property; it has been paved and drained, the cost being defrayed from the rents, which amount to Rs. 285 annually.

CHAURI CHAURA, *Pargana* HAVELI, *Tahsil* GORAKHPUR. Chauri Chaura stands in 26° 38′ N. and 83° 35′ E., on the road from Gorakhpur to Deoria and on the main line of railway station being some 15 miles south-west from the district head-quarters. From the station a branch road leads northwards to Dumri and Pipraich. The village belongs to tappa Keotali and is 311 acres in area, the revenue demand being Rs. 306. The population numbered 900 at the last census, including many Kalwars, and is on the increase. This is due to the railway, which has made Chauri Chaura into a local commercial centre of some importance. The Sikh owners of Dumri, who are the *zamindars* of the village have built a fine bazar near the station, and have recently erected modern machinery worked by steam power for the manufacture of sugar and for pressing oil; while several other sugar factories are worked on native lines by the Kalwars. Chauri Chaura is the centre for the hide trade of the district, and receives consignments from all parts for despatch to Calcutta and Cawnpore. Adjoining Chauri Chaura on the north is the bazar of Mundera, another large market and a vigorous rival, possessing several sugar factories and a considerable trade in grain; it is owned by the Rajputs of Bishunpura. Both places have, however, suffered from the construction of the Bagaha branch of the railway, which has intercepted most of the Nepal trade formerly brought hither from Siswa. Chauri Chaura is also noteworthy as possessing a police station, a post-office, an aided school and a cattle-pound.

CHILLUPAR, *vide* BARHALGANJ.

CHILLUPAR *Pargana*, *Tahsil* BANSGAON.

This is the smallest pargana in the district, and consists of a wedge-shaped block of country in the south-east corner of the Bansgaon tahsil, extending eastwards between the Rapti and Ghagra from the Dhuriapar boundary to the junction of the two rivers. It just touches pargana Bhauapar in the north-west corner, while the Ghagra separates it from the Azamgarh district, and beyond the Rapti lie Silhat and Salempur. The area is liable to change on account of the vagaries of the Ghagra, the average for the last five years being 65,944 acres or 103·03 square miles.

The pargana, which is made up of the five tappas of Majhaulia, Semra, Sikandarpur, Haveli and Qasba, contains 213 *mauzas* and 445 inhabited sites, but the only places of any hote a parhlhanj and Semra. The population numbered 56,551 in 185 , but thismay fallen to 51.202 by 1865, while in 1872 it was only 48,919. It then rose to 70,2‹2 in 1881 but ten years later a decline was again observed, the total being 64,324, while in 1901 it had risen once more to 68,630, the density averaging 666 to the square mile. It was the only part of the tahsil which exhibited any increase since 1891.

According to tradition the aboriginal Bhar inhabitants were ousted by the Kausiks during the fourteenth century under Dhur Chand, the founder of the Dhuriapar house, which for two centuries retained possession of Chillupar. Towards the end of the sixteenth century the quarrel between the rival claimants to the rule of Dhuriapar enabled Bernath Singh of Semra, a kinsman of the Bisen Raja of Majhauli, to seize the country and establish himself as Raja at Narharpur. This conquest in all probability resulted in the formation of the pargana, as the tract had originally been an integral part of Dhuriapar. It was certainly a separate *mahal* in the days of Akbar, with its capital at Chillupar, where was a brick fort, though no vestige of such a building can now be traced. The Bisens continued in possession till the cession, but in the early days of British rule they lost much of their estates, and the rebellion of the Raja in 1857 led to his execution, the extinction of the title and the forfeiture of his remaining property.

DEORIA, *Pargana* SALEMPUR-MAJHAULI, *Tahsil* DEORIA.

The town which gives its name to the tahsil and subdivision lies in 26° 30′ N. and 83° 47′ E. in tappa Deoria, on the metalled road from Kasia to Barhaj, and close to the main line of railway and the unmetalled road from Gorakhpur to Chapra, at a distance of 33 miles from the district headquarters. Unmetalled roads lead to Rudarpur on the south-west and to Hata on the north.

There are several villages of the same name in the neighbourhood, such as Deoria Khas to the west, Deoria Ramnath to the south-west and Bans Deoria to the south : but the present town has grown up in the village of Bharauli, which contains the railway station and the tahsil buildings. The latter stood originally in Mahua Dih, a village of pargana Silhat, where traces of the old treasury are still visible. The population was only 1,069 in 1872, but had risen by 1891 to 2,364, and though at the last census it had dropped to 2,151, there has been a considerable increase in subsequent years, especially since the constitution of the Deoria subdivision in 1905. For some years too the trade of the place has extended, largely owing to the heavy incidence of municipal taxation at Gorakhpur, and now Deoria is the centre of the wholesale trade in cloth and cotton stuffs on this section of the Bengal and North-Western Railway, while the business done by the grain dealers is already large and constantly tends to develop further. It has more than once been suggested that Deoria should be made the headquarters of a new district to be formed out of the eastern half of Gorakhpur, but the site lies low and is subject to extensive and prolonged floods in wet years.

In addition to the tahsil buildings, Deoria contains the court-house and lock-up of the subdivisional officer, the munsif's court, a registration office, a police station, a combined post and telegraph office, a dispensary, an inspection bungalow, an Anglo-vernacular school, an upper primary school, a school for girls and a cattle-pound. The residence of the subdivisional officer is poor and badly situated, and it is proposed to build a new bungalow for his use, to convert the existing house into an inspection bungalow and by means of suitable additions to make the present inspection bungalow into a residence for the subordinate deputy collector stationed here. The dispensary also is to be improved and quarters have recently been erected for the hospital assistant. The metalled road passes through the Bharauli bazar, and is flanked by the shops of wealthy Marwari merchants, who have built a *dharamsala* in the town and a fine tank beyond the level-crossing on the Kasia road.

Deoria was brought under the operations of Act XX of 1856 in 1892, but in 1907 it was made a notified area under Act I of 1900, the town including the small villages of Bharauli, Bans Deoria, Garulpur and Basewala, with a combined population of 3,553 souls. Its affairs are managed by a committee of five members, including the subdivisional officer as president and the tahsildar as secretary. During the first year of its existence the income, derived chiefly from house and conservancy taxes, amounted to Rs. 1,637, inclusive of a balance of Rs. 85 from the funds of the Act XX town; while the expenditure on conservancy, lighting, improvements and other objects was Rs. 1,469. Street lamps have been provided, a new vegetable market has been built to relieve the congestion in the old bazar and a new road has been made outside the town, along which many houses have already sprung up.

The name Deoria is commonly applied to places which contain a temple, and in this case appears to be derived from a ruined shrine of Shiva to the north, on a mound near the Karna river. In the adjacent village of Bamhni to the north-east, on the Kasia road, are extensive ruins, including the foundations of two ancient temples, in which sculptured fragments have been discovered, while to the west of these is an old masonry tank about forty yards square. On the Gorakhpur road, just beyond the Karna, are the remains of a mud fort, the summit being crowned by a Musalman tomb, said to be that of a *shahid* or martyr, though the name of the occupant is unknown.

DEORIA *Tahsil.*

This tahsil occupies the south-eastern corner of the district and comprises a fairly compact tract of a roughly rectangular shape, bounded on the south by the Ghagra, which separates it from Azamgarh and Ballia, and on the east by the Saran district of Bengal. The latter also forms the northern boundary in conjunction with the parganas of Sidhua Jobna and Shahjahanpur, while on the west the tahsil marches with Silhat, separated for the greater part of the distance by the river Karna, and with pargana Chillupar of the Bansgaon tahsil, lying beyond the Rapti. The tahsil is conterminous with the pargana of Salempur Majhauli, and contains the 23 tappas of Samogar, Nai, Raipura, Bairauna, Surauli, Deoria, Gobrain, Kachwar, Sathiaon, Khukhundu, Purainan, Mail, Ballia, Dondh, Salempur, Barsipar, Ghati, Bhatni, Haveli, Sohanpur, Gautaman, Baliwan and Kaparwar. The total area is 372,277 acres or 581·6 square miles, but is liable to vary from time to time on account of fluvial action on the part of the Rapti and Ghagra. There are, however, only 19 alluvial *mahals* in the whole tahsil, all of these being subject to the usual quinquennial revision.

The greater part of the area belongs to the upland *bangar* and is a stretch of extremely fertile and highly tilled soil, the level surface being broken only by occasional ridges of sand and the few river valleys. Of the latter the chief is that of the Little Gandak, which traverses the eastern portion of the tahsil from north to south, receiving the Khanua on its left bank near Bhatpar station. In the extreme south-east are the Siahi and Jharai, the latter for some miles forming the district boundary; but there are no streams of any note in the western half, between the Little Gandak, the Karna and the Rapti. Small *jhils* and *dahars* or deserted river beds occur in numbers throughout the tract, but there are no lakes of any size or importance. Along the Rapti and Ghagra is a somewhat narrow strip of *kachhar* or new alluvium, which is liable to damage from floods; while in the extreme north-east corner is a compact block of *bhat*, resembling that of Padrauna. Altogether *kachhar* embraced 2·91 per cent. of the area assessed at the last settlement, and *bhat* 12·03; but the prevalent soil of the tahsil is *doras* or loam, amounting to 58·9 per cent. The balance consists of *matiar* or clay with 15·3, and of the light sandy soil called *balua*, which is more common in this than in any other part of the district and makes up 10·86 per cent.

The tract has long attained a very high standard of development, and in consequence agriculture is far more advanced than in the other tahsils. As early as 1853 the area under tillage was 228,738 acres, rising to 257,272 in 1860. By 1889 it had risen to 289,117, and subsequent years have witnessed but a small further increase, the average for the five years ending with 1907-08 being 291,590 acres or 78·3 per cent. of the entire tahsil, while on occasions this figure has been largely exceeded. There is not much room for any great expansion of cultivation, and the growing pressure on the soil is illustrated by the rapid and extensive increase in the double-cropped area, which now averages 86,695 acres or 29·4 per cent. of the land under the plough, this being twice as much as that recorded in 1889. The barren area is 36,174 acres, but this includes 19,022 under water and 12,045 permanently taken up by railways, roads, sites and the like, while the remainder consists principally of sterile sand along the banks of the Ghagra. The extent of so-called culturable land is 44,513 acres, but from this should be dedicated 9,335 of new fallow, left untilled under the ordinary system of rotation, and 12,669 of groves, which are here abundant and occupy 3·4 per cent. of the total area. The balance consists of old fallow and unbroken waste, but though the amount is rather large for so closely cultivated a tract, most of it possesses little value as arable land. Forests have long disappeared, and even at the last settlement there was very little grass jungle, the bulk of the waste comprising sandy stretches covered with tamarisk on the banks of the Ghagra. Irrigation is much more generally practised in this tahsil than in other parts of the district, and the average area watered is remarkably large, amounting to 147,231 acres or 50·5 per cent. of the cultivation. It is true that Hata shows a very similar proportion, but this tahsil possesses a much larger area of *bhat* soil in which artificial irrigation is not required. Nearly three-fourths of the irrigation is derived from wells, which in most cases are spring-fed and on that account far superior to the percolation wells used in other parts of the district.

The two main harvests are practically equal in extent, the *kharif* as a rule showing a slight preponderance with an average of 189,394 acres as compared with 184,428 sown for the *rabi.*

The most important crop in the former season is rice, which occupies 28 per cent. of the area; and though this figure is smaller than that of any other tahsil, rather more than half of the rice is of the late or transplanted variety. In the predominance of the more valuable species Deoria resembles Binayakpur, though the conditions of the two tracts are very dissimilar, since here the relatively small amount of early rice grown is due to the preference shown for other crops. Chief among these are *arhar* and *kodon*, grown both alone and in combination, while there is a large area under maize, which thrives particularly well in the *bhat* tract. Sugarcane is a valuable and popular crop, covering 9·3 per cent. of the *kharif* area, and the small millets *tangan*, *sanwan*, *kakun* and *mandua* are very widely grown. Similarly garden crops are of more importance than in any other tahsil, including yams and vegetables as well as the pepper, ginger and betel for which this tract is celebrated. The autumn pulses are comparatively rare, and the only remaining crop deserving mention is hemp. In the spring harvest more than half the area is taken up by cereals, especially in the form of *gujai*, since very little unmixed wheat is produced and even barley by itself occupies but two-fifths of the area under the mixed crop. Next come peas, which alone and in combination cover more than one-fourth of the *rabi* area; gram, both by itself and mixed with barley; and garden crops, including potatoes and tobacco. Oilseeds are comparatively rare, and apart from the vetches and *boro* rice no other crop calls for mention except poppy, which is more extensively grown here than in any other part of the district and takes up 2·7 per cent. of the spring harvest.

The total area included in holdings in 1907-08 was 310,410 acres, and of this 34·95 per cent. was cultivated by proprietors, the proportion being higher than in any other tahsil except Bansgaon. Occupancy tenants held 35·7 and tenants-at-will 26·76, the former class outnumbering the latter in this tahsil and Hata alone; while ·64 per cent. was cultivated by ex-proprietors and the remainder, chiefly in the form of *jagirs* held by *goraits*, was rent-free. Rents are as usual paid almost exclusively in cash. The rental at the last settlement averaged Rs. 2·87 per acre, representing an increase of 30·19 per cent. since 1865; but of late years it has risen considerably, and though the recorded figures are much below the reality occupancy tenants in 1907-08 paid Rs. 3·76 and tenants-at-will Rs. 3·92, the incidence in either case being the heaviest in the district. The rate for sub-tenants, who cultivated 63,058 acres or 20·3 per cent. of the holdings, averaged Rs. 4·15 per acre, which is again a remarkably high figure. The revenue demand, as assessed at each successive settlement, as well as the present amount and its incidence, will be found in the appendix.*

The tahsil contains 1,454 *mauzas* or villages and these are divided into 2,744 *mahals,* of which 260 are *zamindari,* 2,481 *pattidari* and three *bhaiyachara.* There is a large number of under-proprietors, the settlement returns showing 743 *birtias* and 3,296 *arazidars.* The only large estate is that of the Majhauli Raja, who owns 94 villages with a revenue demand of Rs. 39,235. Other *zamindars* of importance include the Pandes of Barkagaon, who have 27 villages assessed at Rs. 5,244, and the Bhuinhars of Saraya, who pay Rs. 5,036 on a property of 41 villages.

The population of the tahsil numbered 321,425 souls at the first census of 1853, and by 1865 the total had risen to 343,925, though in 1872 it dropped to 318,648. It then rose again with astonishing rapidity, reaching 481,145 in 1881, while ten years later it was 517,793; but the following decade witnessed a decline, and in 1901 the tahsil contained 493,822 inhabitants, of whom 252,160 were females, the average density being 849 to the square mile. This total consisted of 453,731 Hindus, 40,006 Musalmans, 39 Sikhs, 22 Aryas, 16 Christians and 8 Jains. Among the various Hindu castes Ahirs take the lead with 56,900 representatives, closely followed by Chamars with 54,901. Next in order come Brahmans with 42,173, Koeris with 40,276, Kurmis with 26,099, Rajputs with 21,192 and Banias with 20,533, while other castes occurring in numbers exceeding 10,000 apiece are Kewats, Telis, Gonds, Kumhars and Mallahs. Of the Musalman population 8,748 were Julahas and 5,998 Dhunias, the rest being chiefly Sheikhs and Pathans.

* Appendix, tables IX and X.

About 65 per cent. of the inhabitants derive their support from cultivation, and if this is a somewhat low proportion, it is due to the fact that the tahsil contains several towns of moderate size and also boasts of a considerable trade. The manufacture of sugar, especially at Barhaj, is of great importance, while at Deoria there is a flourishing business in cloth and grain, and mention has been made elsewhere of the soap industry of Lar. In addition to the country cloth made at various places, a kind of coarse woollen blanket is woven from sheep's wool at Deoria, though the sale is purely local. There are altogether 1,455 *mauzas* and 2,990 inhabited sites. The chief towns are Barhaj-Gaura, Salempur-Majhauli, Lar, Paina and Deoria itself, while Kaparwar, Paikauli, Pariapur, Khampar, Khukhundu and Sohanpur possess large populations, though purely agricultural in character.

Means of communication are, on the whole, good. The main line of the Bengal and North-Western Railway traverses the tahsil from north-west to south-east, with stations at Deoria, Nunkhar, Bhatni, Bhatpar and Bankata. From Bhatni a line runs due south through the Salempur, Lar Road and Turtipar stations to the bridge over the Ghagra, whence it continues to Benares; and a second branch leads from Salempur to Barhaj, with an intermediate station at Sathraon. There are two metalled roads, one of which runs from Barhaj to Deoria and thence past Rampur Karkhana to Kasia, while the other leads from Salempur to Majhauli and Bhatpar station. The main unmetalled road is that from Gorakhpur to Chapra, passing through Deoria, Musela, Salempur and Lar. At the last mentioned place it is joined by that from Gorakhpur, Sikriganj, Barhalganj and Barhaj running parallel to the Ghagra. Cross roads connect Musela and Salempur with Bhagalpur near Turtipar, and other roads include those from Deoria and Barhaj to Rudarpur, and from Bhatpar station to Khampar and the Saran border. In addition, the Ghagra is an important waterway, while the Little Gandak is still to a certain extent used as a navigable channel. Inspection bungalows are to be found at Deoria and Nandapar, and military encamping grounds at Deoria, Khukhundu and Salempur.

The tahsil is united with Hata to form a subdivision in the charge of a full-powered officer resident at Deoria, which is also the headquarters of the tahsildar, munsif and sub-registrar. For police purposes there are stations at Deoria, Barhaj, Salempur, Khukhundu and Khampar. When first constituted in 1804 the tahsil embraced the parganas of Salempur-Majhauli and Chillupar, but the latter was detached in 1840, since which time no further change has occurred beyond the removal of the headquarters from Salempur to Deoria in 1853.

The history of the Salempur-Majhauli pargana is practically that of the Bisens, though we know from the many existing remains that the country was a centre of Buddhist civilization in the earliest times. This is proved by the pillars at Bhagalpur and Kahaon, the temples at Sohnag, Khukhundu and Bharauli, the forts at Bhagalpur, Surauli and Nai, and the ruins at Sahia Ranighat, Pariapur, Bairaunan, Khonda and Bamhai. It would appear that an established route from the south to Kasia and the northern shrines lay through Bhagalpur, Kahaon and Khukhundu, which were regular halting-places for pilgrims. After the Buddhists came the Bhars, who in turn gave way to the Bisens, whose chronicles have been recorded in the general account of the district. The Rajas of Majhauli were more successful in keeping their borders intact than other chieftains, with the result that in 1801 the country was the only part of the district which presented a flourishing appearance. The Mutiny did little to arrest the steady advance of agricultural prosperity, and in subsequent years the only noticeable feature has been the commercial expansion of the tahsil.

DHAKWA BAZAR, *Pargana* DHURIAPAR, *Tahsil* BANSGAON.

A considerable village of tappa Bhadar, standing in 26° 32′ N. and 83° 12′ E., on the north or left bank of the Kuwana, about a mile west of the unmetalled road from Gorakhpur to Sikriganj and 19 miles south-west from the district headquarters. In former days the place was an important grain market and a collecting centre for the large traffic on the Kuwana, but it has greatly declined since the construction of the railway, the export trade having been diverted to Sahjanwa. A certain amount of business, however, is still transacted here, while cloth, brass vessels and spices are sold in the bazar, the chief market days being Sunday and Wednesday in each week. The market belongs to Rani Manik Raj Kuari, the present representative of the Barhiapar family, who derives a small annual income therefrom. The village itself is small, being but 260 acres in extent and paying a revenue of Rs. 150. The bazar at the last census contained a population of 1,298 persons, and within its limits are a post-office, a lower primary school, two temples and a mosque.

DHANI, *Pargana* HAVELI, *Tahsil* MAHARÁJGANJ.

An important market town of tappa Rigauli, standing in 27° 7′ N. and 83° 10′ E. at a distance of nine miles from Rigauli, six from Bridgmanganj and 33 from Gorakhpur. The market is actually situated in Kanapar, an adjoining village to the south on the bank of the Dhamela, but is almost invariably known as Dhani Bazar. Formerly the place was the collecting centre for the trade of western Maharajganj and the adjacent parts of Nepal, occupying a position analogous to that of Nichlaul in the east of the tahsil, and from it large quantities of grain were being continually despatched by river. But just as Nichlaul has been eclipsed by Siswa Bazar, so Dhani has succumbed to Bridgmanganj. Though its importance has thus declined, it is still a flourishing bazar, and is always full of traders except during the rains, when the swollen state of the river renders navigation difficult and dangerous. At other times the stream flows quietly some 30 feet below the level of its banks. The Rajput and Brahman *zamindars* derive handsome profits from the bazar and also from the high rents paid on the fertile lands in the vicinity. The population fluctuates with the season, but is always large, and rose from 4,886 in 1872 to 6,271 at the last census. The chief market day is Monday in each week. The place possesses a middle vernacular school, a post-office and a cattle-pound.

DHURIAPAR, *Pargana* DHURIAPAR, *Tahsil* BANSGAON.

The place which gives its name to the Dhuriapar pargana is an insignificant village standing in 26° 25′ N. and 83° 15′ E., on the north or left bank of the Kuwana, where the river is crossed by the unmetalled road from Shahpur to Urwa Bazar, about 29 miles from the district headquarters. It is said to have been founded by Dhur Chand, the first of the Kausiks to settle in these parts, and for a long time was the seat of the Dhuriapar Rajas, the ruins of whose immense fort is still to be seen on the river bank. The village itself is very small, having an area of 89 acres, assessed at Rs. 104, and at the last census it contained a population of only 617 persons.

DHURIAPAR *Pargana, Tahsil* BANSGAON.

This is the largest pargana in the tahsil, occupying the centre and south-west of the subdivision. It is bounded on the south by the Ghagra, separating it from the Azamgarh district, on the west by the Basti district, on the north by Unaula and on the east by Bhauapar and Chillupar. It comprises no fewer than 24 tappas, known as Pali, Tiar, Gaur, Dandi, Narre, Kohra, Athaisi, Majuri, Khutahan, Barhaj, Chandpur, Shahpur, Bhadar, Parsi, Usri, Thati, Nakuri, Haveli, Bankat, Ratanpur, Belghat, Kurmaut, Bamhnauli and Chaurar. The present area is 173,555 acres or 271·1 square miles, but this is apt to vary from time to time owing to the fluvial action of the Ghagra.

The population of the pargana numbered 204,070 persons in 1853, but this fell to 180,180 in 1865 and to 177,692 in 1872, though it then rose to 214,405 in 1881 and to 230,767 ten years later. In 1901, however, a heavy decline was observed, the total being 203,971, and at the present time the figure is even lower, since in 1904 a tract of 67 square miles on the south bank of the Ghagra, containing a population of 13,389 persons, was transferred to the Azamgarh district, so that the present average density is 703 to the square mile. There are 1,183 *mauzas* and 2,735 inhabited sites; but most of the villages are very small, the only exceptions of note being Gola, Shahpur, Sikriganj and Dhakwa.

The history of the pargana may be said to begin with the invasion of the Kausiks under Dhur Chand, who drove out the Bhars and established himself on the north bank of the river. His successors increased their estates till the principality included

40 tappas, and their prosperity ceased only when the unfortunate quarrel for the succession arose between Pirthi Chand and Todar Chand during the 16th century. A long period of warfare ensued during which Chillupar and ten other tappas were lost before a settlement was made between the two parties, whereby the country was divided between the two estates of Barhiapar and Gopalpur. The weakness of the Kausiks rendered them helpless before the Banjaras and the revenue officials of the Oudh Government, and it was not till 1840 that the pargana recovered its old prosperity. The Barhiapar estate was confiscated after the Mutiny, but the descendants of the last Raja still reside at Bhadar and own 15 villages. The Raja of Gopalpur remained loyal and received a considerable grant of land in reward, 40 villages being still in possession of Dulhin Harpal Kuari.

DUMRI, *Pargana* HAVELI, *Tahsil* GORAKHPUR.

A large village of *tappa* Keotali, standing in 26° 43′ N. and 83° 36′ E., on the east side of the road from Chaura station to Pipraich and two miles south of the road from Gorakhpur to Kasia, at a distance of 15 miles east from the district headquarters. It contained at the last census a population of 2,139 persons, mainly Chamars, but it is noticeable chiefly as giving its name to an estate of 59 villages bestowed on Sardar Surat Singh for his services during the Mutiny. The village contains a large middle vernacular school, supported by the estate with the assistance of a grant from the district board. There is also a cattle-pound, a small market, and a dispensary which is guaranteed by the estate. The area of the village is 1,709 acres, and the revenue demand is Rs. 2,165.

GAJPUR, *Pargana* BHAUAPAR, *Tahsil* BANSGAON.

Gajpur is a small town in tappa Kotha Rampur, situated on the right bank of the Rapti in 26° 29′ N. and 83° 29′ E., at a distance of 21 miles from Gorakhpur and ten miles from the tahsil headquarters. It is approached by two unmetalled roads leading from Kauriram and Gagaha on the main road from Gorakhpur to Azamgarh, while a third road leads from the town to the river bank and a ferry, whence a track across the *kachhar* goes to

Rudarpur. It was formerly a place of call for boats on their voyage up and down the Rapti, but of late years the partial disappearance of the river traffic has led to the decline of Gajpur, which has lost all its commercial importance. The place from early days belonged to the Satasi family and was one of their strongholds. Near the river is a large house occupied by the widow of the Lal Sahib, son of the last Raja; it was built by Rani Sohas Kuari, grandmother of the Lal Sahib. The population of Gajpur was 3,290 in 1872 and rose in 1881 to 4,302, though ten years later it had fallen to 4,284, while at the last census the number of inhabitants was 3,702, of whom 669 were Musalmans. The decline of the place led in 1906 to the withdrawal of Act XX of 1856, which had been in force since 1867. The town contains a cattle-pound and an upper primary school, while a market is held here weekly. The *mauza* of Gajpur is 541 acres in extent and is assessed at Rs. 702, the owner being the so-called Rani of Satasi.

GAURA, *vide* BARHAJ.

GOLA, *Pargana* DHURIAPAR, *Tahsil* BANSGAON.

The town of Gola, also known as Madaria and Gola Gopalpur or the grain market of Gopalpur, stands in tappa Barhaj on the bank of the Ghagra, in 26° 20′ N. and 83° 22′ E., at a distance of 33 miles south from Gorakhpur. It is connected with the latter both by the road running through Sikriganj to Barhalganj, and also by an unmetalled road from Kauriram on the main road to Azamgarh. In former days Gola stood on the bank of the Kuwana, but in 1872 the stream diminished owing to the diversion of its waters into the Ghagra, with the result that the trade of the place suffered heavily. Subsequently the Kuwana again increased in volume and the prosperity of Gola revived; while eventually the Ghagra itself adopted a more northerly course by uniting with the Kuwana at Shahpur and thus flowing immediately beneath the town. But the advent of the railway both to Barhaj and to Dohri-ghat on the opposite bank of the Ghagra has dealt a far more fatal blow to the commercial importance of Gola than all the vagaries of the river; and as the trade routes have shifted to places on the line of the railway, most of the traders have left the town for Munderwa and elsewhere.

The population numbered 5,751 persons in 1853, but subsequently declined, though by 1872 a recovery was noticeable, the total then being 5,147. It rose further to 7,193 in 1881, but ten years later it dropped to 6,089, while in 1901 it was only 4,944, of whom 645 were Musalmans. The place consists of a narrow street lined with shops running parallel to the Ghagra, with narrow lanes leading from it between the densely packed houses to the river bank. The houses are for the most part built of mud, but there are some large masonry buildings near the river, and more than one temple built by local merchants in the days of Gola's prosperity. The town is divided into five *muhallas*, known as Bhikhiganj, Ruihata, Baramthan, Daldahi and Anjaiganj. Gola possesses a police station, a post-office, an inspection bungalow, a cattle-pound, a middle vernacular school and a small school for girls. The place was founded by one of the Gopalpur Rajas and still belongs to that family, the present representative receiving some Rs. 5,000 yearly in rents and bazar dues; while the town lands are 499 acres in extent and are assessed at Rs. 289.

Gola has been administered under Act XX of 1856 since 1871, but it is doubtful whether this measure will long remain in force owing to the decline of the place. In 1907-08 the town contained 1,373 houses, of which 481 were assessed, the house tax amounting to Rs. 1,203, at an average incidence of Rs. 2-0-8 per assessed house and Re. 0-3-11 per head of population. The actual income for the year was only Rs. 1,099, owing to the large arrears of collections, while the expenditure was Rs. 1,097, devoted principally to the upkeep of the local police and the maintenance of a conservancy staff.

GOPALPUR, *Pargana* DHURIAPAR, *Tahsil* BANSGAON.

A fair-sized village of tappa Chandpar, situated in 26° 22′ N. and 83° 20′ E., on the unmetalled road from Gorakhpur and Sikriganj to Barhalganj, some three miles north-west from Gola and 30 miles from Gorakhpur. Close to the village the road is joined by a cross-road running direct from Rudrapur.

Gopalpur has long figured in the history of the Kausiks of this pargana, and since the division of the estate, finally accomplished about the middle of the first half of the 18th century, it has been the headquarters of one branch of the family. The present representative is Dulhin Harpal Kuari, the widow of the late Raja's nephew, Lal Harihar Prasad Chand. She is generally known as the Rani of Gopalpur, and lives in a large house in the village, to the west of which is an extensive mound of bricks, apparently the remnants of an older fort built by the Kausiks after their invasion. The village at the last census contained 1,118 inhabitants, principally Rajputs; it has an area of 388 acres and is assessed at Rs. 340. The place is noteworthy only for its historical associations, and possesses nothing more interesting than an upper primary school.

GORAKHPUR, *Pargana* HAVELI, *Tahsil* GORAKHPUR.

The city of Gorakhpur, which gives its name to a tahsil, a district and a division, stands in 26° 45′ N. and 83° 22′ E., at a height of about 335 feet above the level of the sea, and at a distance of 506 miles by rail from Calcutta, 162 miles by road from Allahabad, 131 from Benares, and 85 from Fyzabad. It is built on the north or left bank of the Rapti, just below the junction of that river with the Rohin. The latter, called the Ajwania *nala* after it has passed under the railway bridge at Domingarh, forms the western boundary of the municipality, while the Rapti touches the fringe of it at Birdghat, thence turning off to take a more southerly course. To the east the Ramgarh Tal bounds the old cantonment, now administered as a separate notified area, on its southern edge, while the north-western corner of the town looks out over the level plain north of Domingarh, which during the rains is transformed into a huge sheet of water called the Domingarh and Karmaini Tals. Through the northern half of the town runs the main line of the Bengal and North-Western Railway, with its principal station in the notified area to the east, and another at Domingarh to the west. From the former a branch line runs northwards to Uska and Tulsipur, while a second has recently been constructed to Captainganj and Bagaha. The provincial road to Basti and

Fyzabad leaves the town on the west at Birdghat, where is a temporary bridge over the Rapti, and that to Azamgarh runs south to a similar crossing near Bhauapar. Several other roads radiate from Gorakhpur in all directions, as may be seen by a reference to the map, and most of them are metalled for a short distance beyond the municipal boundary.

The city is by far the largest in the part of the United Provinces to the north of the Ghagra, and its population has increased, though not to a very great extent, during the past sixty years. From 45,265 in 1847 it rose to 54,529 in 1853, but owing to the Mutiny and other causes it then declined, the total being but 50,853 in 1865. It was 51,117 in 1872, and subsequent enumerations have witnessed a constant advance, from 59,908 in 1881 to 63,620 ten years later, while in 1901 it was 64,148, of whom 31,550 were females. This figure includes the small population of 771 persons resident in the notified area. Of the whole number 41,451 were Hindus, 21,829 Musalmans, and 868 of other religions, for the most part Christians and Aryas. The proportion of Musalmans is thus 34 per cent. of the whole, a far higher figure than is to be found in any of the rural parts of the district, though this perhaps is only natural, since the place owes its importance in great measure to the fact that it long formed the chief Muhammadan garrison town on the north of the Ghagra.

The earliest settlers appear to have chosen a site considerably to the north of the present town, probably for the reason that in former days the Rapti flowed more to the north and east, traversing the existing site and passing through the Ramgarh Tal. Evidence of this has repeatedly been furnished by the discovery of driftwood and pieces of boats in excavating wells; and it would therefore seem that the original settlers selected the place as being protected on two sides by the Rapti and Rohin, while in the rear it was effectually closed in by the dense forests to the north and east. Tradition first centres round the name of Man Sen, variously described as a Rathor Rajput and a Tharu, who is said to have made the Mansarowar tank, while the Kauladah is ascribed to his wife Kaulavati. The legendary date of this prince belongs to the tenth century, and his power lasted till the advent of the Domkatars, who built the great fort of

Domingarh on an island, still traceable in the rains, at the junction of the Rohin and the Rapti. They in turn were overthrown by the Sarnets, who acquired a vast stretch of country, the portion round Gorakhpur falling to the lot of the Rajas of Satasi. About 1400 a quarrel arose in the family and certain members left the old stronghold on the banks of the Ramgarh Tal, settling probably in the place now called Purana Gorakhpur, near the shrine of Gorakh. The latter became famous owing to the reputation of Machhendra Nath, an ascetic better known as Gorakh Nath, in whose honour the new settlement received its present name. The place seems to have grown rapidly, and by the days of Akbar had become a large town, possessing a mint and a Musalman garrison which had been established after the expedition of Fidai Khan. In 1610, however, the Sarnets under Raja Basant Singh expelled the Muhammadan troops, and a new stronghold was built in the modern Basantpur *muhalla*, which seems to show that the Rapti must have retreated to a more southerly bed before this date. After a domination of seventy years the Hindu Rajas were once again driven out from the city they had founded, for in 1680 Qazi Khalil-ur-Rahman ejected Raja Rudar Singh, re-established a garrison and repaired the fort. The latter was seen by Tieffenthaler in the eighteenth century and was described by the Jesuit as a square building with a bastion at each angle and two intermediate bastions on each curtain. The same writer records that he crossed the Rapti on a bridge of boats, a hundred paces in length, the arrangement which is maintained to this day. Soon after came prince Muazzam, his primary object being to enjoy the sport for which the adjacent forests were famous, and in his honour the name of the city was changed to Muazzamabad, a title which it continued to bear in official documents till the cession of the district to the Company in 1801. From the days of Khalil-ur-Rahman to the advent of British rule a Musalman force held Gorakhpur, first on behalf of the imperial power and later as a part of Oudh, though at times the garrison displayed a spirit of mutinous independence.

When Mr. Routledge, the first collector, came to establish his headquarters at Gorakhpur, he is said to have pitched his camp on the site of the present racquet court, and the story goes that he kept his tents surrounded by a cordon of elephants as a protection against the tigers which infested the neighbouring forests, though a variant account states that a circle of bonfires had to be lighted in order to keep off the wild elephants. The original civil station was in the Captainganj *muhalla*, but during the hot weather all officers of Government, both civil and military, used to repair to the old fort for the sake of the coolness afforded by its thick walls. It appears that Gorakhpur became a military station in 1810, when some of the Company's troops were brought hither from Fyzabad with the object of keeping in check the raiders on the Nepalese frontier, and it was at this time that the cantonment was laid out on the east of the town. The execution of this measure seems to have aroused considerable opposition on the part of the inhabitants, and Buchanan quaintly remarks that "the natives will not in general consent to cut any tree that has been planted: and it required a very odious exertion of power to clear so much ground as was sufficient to form a parade and a kind of breathing-hole for the European officers of Government." Not long after this the civil officials moved from the west part of the town and took up their residence near the cantonment on the east. The place acquired some importance as the headquarters of a column during the first Nepalese campaign of 1815, and in the same year Sir Roger Martin, the officiating collector, laid out a racecourse, now a thing of the past, which was bisected by the road to Bhauapar. During the Mutiny, despite the occupation of the town and civil station by the rebels under Muhammad Hasan, little damage of an enduring nature appears to have been done, though many of the houses in the cantonment were set on fire; for the self-styled *nazim*, imagining his position to be secure, endeavoured as far as possible to prevent the destruction of property for his own advantage. It is for this reason that the civil station contains so large a number of substantial old houses dating from a period long antecedent to the Mutiny. The only subsequent events of any note have been the creation in 1891 of a civil division with headquarters at Gorakhpur, the abolition in 1886 of the cantonment, the growth of the railway settlement, and other movements indicative of peaceful progress, to which reference has already been made in the preceding pages of this volume.

The gradual shifting of the city from the earliest inhabited sites in the north towards the more recently formed land in the south has had a marked effect on the general aspect of the place. The town now consists of an aggregation of inhabited sites, several of the *muhallas* being in reality distinct villages, separated from the rest by considerable intervening spaces of cultivated land, though they all are included within municipal limits. Many *muhallas* too, even in the heart of the town, are built in a straggling and haphazard fashion, suggesting casual additions made to supply a fresh need. Everywhere the extent of cultivated ground interspersed among densely populated quarters is very noticeable, and it is only within living memory that the most southerly part of the town has been extensively inhabited. The result is that while in point of population Gorakhpur is not remarkably large, it occupies a space more than three miles in length from north to south, and an equal or even greater distance in breadth from east to west. The groves of fruit trees and the market gardens form a striking feature of the place, especially in the north, as also do the immense numbers of palm trees, which abound in every quarter of the city.

Excluding the notified area and the villages contained therein, the town contains 63 *muhallas*, of which 39 belong to the southern portion. A list of these is appended, and from this it will be evident that the majority of the names are of Musalman origin and are generally called after some distinguished personage or the dominant caste of the inhabitants.

1. **Madhopur.**
2. **Kalyanpur.**
3. **Tiwaripur.**
4. **Qazipur Kalan.**
5. **Ghosipur.**
6. **Ilahi Bagh.**
7. **Narsinghpur.**
8. **Daud Chak.**
9. **Purana Gorakhpur.**
10. **Humayunpur.**
11. **Mohanlalpur.**
12. **Piprapur.**
13. **Bakhtiarpur.**
14. **Bulaqipur.**
15. **Bind Tola.**
16. **Jafra Bazar.**
17. **Andhiari Bagh.**
18. **Alinagar.**
19. **Rudarpur.**
20. **Diwan Bazar.**
21. **Dilazakpur.**
22. **Hasanpur.**
23. **Captainganj.**
24. **Jateipur.**

25. Purdilpur.
26. Golghar.
27. Nizampur.
28. Ghazi Rauza.
29. Nasirabad.
30. Ghasi Katra.
31. Bu Bazar.
32. Bakhshipur.
33. Muftipur.
34. Khunipur.
35. Ismailpur.
36. Qazipur Khurd.
37. Bhua Shahid.
38. Sheikhpur.
39. Diwan Daya Ram.
40. Rakabganj.
41. Askarganj.
42. Nakkhas.
43. Sahibganj.
44. Mirzapur.
45. Khokharpur.
46. Rahmatnagar.
47. Shah Maruf.
48. Dhammal.
49. Halseyganj.
50. Paharpur.
51. Urdu Bazar.
52. Khurrampur.
53. Raiganj.
54. Jagannathpur.
55. Alahdadpur.
56. Bankati Chak.
57. Hata Bettiah.
58. Mian Bazar.
59. Chainpur.
60. Basantpur.
61. Turkomanpur.
62. Hansupur.
63. Birdghat.

The northern and southern portions of the city are divided by large patches of open land and market gardens, through which runs a considerable watercourse, now converted into a drain, to the Ilahi Bagh sluice-gates on the banks of the Ajwania *nala* from the Sumer Sagar, a broad but shallow pond in the north-east of the municipal area. The northern half is traversed from east to west by the main line of the railway, practically the whole distance from Gorakhpur station to Domingarh lying within municipal limits. To the north of the railway are the isolated *muhallas* of Madhopur, Humayunpur and Purana Gorakhpur, the last containing the Mansarowar and Kauladah tanks and the famous temple of Gorakhnath. This shrine stands to the north of the former tank, and is surrounded by mango groves; it is of undoubted antiquity, but presents no architectural features of note, having recently been rebuilt in a more substantial manner than before. The institution is in a very flourishing condition, and is still the resort of numerous pilgrims and worshippers, whose offerings bring in a considerable income to the Kanphata Jogis in attendance at the temple. The most important *muhallas* to the south of the railway in this part of the town are Alinagar and Dilazakpur. Speaking generally, this half of Gorakhpur represents the residential as opposed to the commercial quarter in the south, and Alinagar contains the houses of nearly all the wealthy business men and *mahajans*, while further to the west may be found several belonging to the leading landowners and gentry of the place. Consequently there are but few public buildings in this direction, and indeed none deserves mention save perhaps the Kirat Chand *dharmsala* in Jateipur, which has been erected within recent years, chiefly for the convenience of travellers by rail.

The principal *muhallas* in the south of the town are Mian Bazar, Urdu Bazar, Sahibganj and Basantpur. The last lies in the south-west extremity, bordering the river, and contains the site of the old jail which stood on the spot formerly occupied by the fort of Raja Basant Singh. It is at present a rather unsightly open space; and it is to be hoped that some use may be found for it before long. To the south of this site is the old masonry *sarai* built by Mr. Chester, a former collector of Gorakhpur, on the rising ground above the river bed. It is a large enclosure with a turreted wall and a fine entrance gateway, while within are numerous trees and a mosque. To the north of the jail site is the Bagladah tank, in old days an unsightly pit, but greatly improved during the famine of 1874, when the sides were given a regular slope and a municipal garden was laid out round the edge. Similar improvements were carried out by means of famine labour in 1878 in the case of the Kawwadah, another large tank to the east of the Bagladah. Between these two tanks runs the main road of the Sahibganj *muhalla*, so named after Mr. Routledge, the first collector of the district; and to the north of the Bagladah are the old police lines, which have recently been made over to the Salvation Army to be used as a Dom settlement with the object of attempting the reclamation of the Magahiyas. To the east of Basantpur is Halseyganj, a market with a tiled roof occupying a small triangular space at the junction of several important streets. It is on this account one of the most central and best frequented markets in the town, and brings in a sum of more than Rs. 1,300 annually in the shape of rents and dues. The bazar is municipal property, and is named after Mr. Halsey, who was once an assistant magistrate of Gorakhpur, and who afterwards did so much to improve the city of Cawnpore by constructing the great market of Collectorganj. The Urdu Bazar to the north-east of Halseyganj is the chief business centre of the town, though it consists of a street with houses on either side. Adjoining it is the Khudai or Jami Masjid, built by Qazi Khalil-ur-Rahman towards the end of the seventeenth century to commemorate the visit and, it is said, at the instance of Prince Muazzam, afterwards known as Bahadur Shah. Though plainly built and of somewhat heavy and inartistic design, it is still the principal place of Musalman worship in Gorakhpur. Further east again, on the boundary of the municipality, is the *muhalla* of Mian Bazar, called after the late Mian Sahib, who built a considerable market close to the Imambara of Raushan Ali, the first Mian Sahib of Gorakhpur. The latter is a fine building in the usual style, erected at the end of the eighteenth century, and hard by are the house and garden of the present incumbent. On the eastern side of this *muhalla*, adjoining the notified area, stand the dispensary and Dufferin hospital, as well as the post-office and the Campier Hall. The last is a handsome structure in oriental style built from a fund of Rs. 10,000 left by Mr. J. B. Campier to be used for the erection of a hall to commemorate his father, the original holder of several jungle grants in the north of the district. This fund was supplemented by a gift of Rs. 15,000 presented by the Raja of Padrauna, and the largest chamber in the building is in consequence known as the Padrauna room. The remainder of the cost was met from a public subscription among the leading residents of the town. In front of the hall stands a bronze statue of her late Majesty Queen Victoria, recently crowned with a white marble canopy. Since its completion in 1900 the hall has been used as an office for the municipal board, which has its meetings here, and also serves as a court-house for the bench of honorary magistrates, while it is utilised for public meetings when occasion arises. To the west of Mian Bazar, in the Nakkhas *muhalla*, is the Kotwali or central police station, and to the north-west are the Jubilee High School and the Gorakhpur Bank. To the south of the Campier Hall are the telegraph office and the magistrate's lock-up, while south again of these is the large *dharmsala* built in 1837 by Mr. Reade, the Commissioner of Gorakhpur. It is surrounded by a castellated wall with a tower over the entrance gate, and is under the management of the district board. Mention should also be made of the Government normal school, situated in the south of the town in the compound which formerly belonged to Mr. Bridgman, the grantee of the Lehra estate.

The notified area to the east of the municipality contains the civil station, the old cantonment and several villages to the south and east. The magistrate's office, the police office, the treasury, the fine new record room and the tahsil buildings form a compact group on an open space opposite the Campier Hall. Immediately to the south is the English church, which stands in a corner of the large compound belonging to the Church Missionary Society. The latter also contains, in addition to the two houses of the missionaries, a small Christian colony. Further east, beyond the dak bungalow, is a substantial new building in red brick, containing the commissioner's court and office; while adjoining it are the courts of the sessions and subordinate judges and the bar library. To the north of this were the infantry lines of former days, in the trees to the east of the club house; to the east of these is the parade ground; but the sole remaining relic of the old military station, save for a few outhouses, is the hospital, now used as the mess of the Gorakhpur squadron of the United Provinces Horse. In the north-east of the notified area stands the Gurkha *dharmsala*, built for the benefit of pensioners and other visitors from Nepal. South of this is the old Gurkha recruiting depôt, at present serving as temporary police lines; for owing to the rapidly growing importance of Gorakhpur as a recruiting centre, a new depôt is to be constructed beyond the bridge over the arm of the Ramgarh Tal on the road to Kasia. In the eastern extremity of the notified area is the racecourse, and south of this is the Hoey Park, laid out by Mr. Hoey for the use of the residents of the town and the civil station and opened by Sir Charles Crosthwaite in 1894. The cost was met from public subscriptions, and for its maintenance there is an endowment held in trust by the collector.

To the north of the notified area is the railway station, standing in a large plot of land, which extends on either side of the line, belonging to the railway company. The size and importance of the settlement have greatly increased since the selection of Gorakhpur as the headquarters of the Bengal and North-Western Railway, the place being the residence of the agent and all the principal officers of the company, while on the north side of the line are numerous quarters for the subordinate officials and a railway institute, as well as extensive engine sheds and workshops of all kinds. Beyond the railway settlement lie the new district jail and some recently erected bungalows, which it is now proposed to include within the limits of the notified area.

Some account has already been given in Chapter IV of the municipality of Gorakhpur and of the administration of the notified area, as well as of the schools and educational institutions of the town. Further mention may, however, be made of the question of sanitation and drainage, which has constantly presented a very serious problem. The reason is that a large part of the site on which the town is built lies below the high flood level of the Rapti, and but for embankments along the western boundary and the sluice gates at the Ilahi Bagh at the mouth of the watercourse in the northern half, all the southern portion of the town would be swept by a flood whenever the river rose to its normal high level in the rains. Considerable improvements both as regards drainage and in the matter of sanitation have been effected in the past, but a complete solution of the difficulty has not yet been attained, and after heavy rain the water may be seen standing in pools everywhere instead of draining away. It has recently been proposed to bring the Ramgarh Tal into use by conducting the surface drainage of the town along a broad drain from the Sumersagar tank through the notified area. Such a scheme was not practicable in former days, when the Ramgarh Tal itself was liable to be filled with the spill water from the Rapti; but since the construction of the embankment running southwards along the left bank of the river and the consequent closure of the channel leading from it into the lake, it is hoped that the level of the water in the latter will be permanently reduced. Under existing circumstances Gorakhpur has an indifferent reputation for healthiness, both the climate and the situation being favourable to malaria and sickness, though a marked improvement has resulted from the efforts of the municipal authorities in the matter of conservancy and sanitation.

Apart from the industries which are to be found in any large city, there are no special products or manufactures for which Gorakhpur is celebrated. It is true that the place has obtained a name for the manufacture of tobacco and for embroidery on leather, but these are relatively unimportant on account of the small outturn. The carpentry of the town enjoys a local reputation, and a certain number of *palkis* are still made in the Raiganj *mahalla*; but most of the skilled workmen have been absorbed by the railway shops, where there is constant employment for coach-builders and other artizans. Nor is Gorakhpur a commercial centre of the first importance. There is of course a considerable trade for the supply of local needs, and the town contains a number of large shops dealing in all kinds of goods, especially imports from Europe; but none of the larger Indian banks has thought it worth while to open a branch here, though the Gorakhpur and Kayasth banks are fairly prosperous concerns, doing a good deal of local business.

GORAKHPUR *Tahsil.*

The Gorakhpur or Sadr tahsil occupies the central portion of the western half of the district, and is a tract of fairly regular shape, bounded on the north by Maharajganj, on the west by the Basti district, on the east by Hata, and on the south by Bansgaon, the last being separated from this tahsil for a considerable distance by the Ami and Rapti rivers. The subdivision includes parts of three parganas, Haveli, Bhauapar and Hasanpur Maghar, most of the last now belonging to the Basti district. Within its limits are 21 tappas, lists of which will be found in the various pargana articles. The total area is 417,071 acres or 651·6 square miles, but this figure is apt to vary to some extent owing to changes in the course of the Rapti: there is a large number of alluvial *mahals*, of which several are situated on the borders of the tahsil. Of the total 143 are subject to the ordinary quinquennial revision, while four are held on conditional and three on unconditional settlements for the full term.

The entire tract is a fertile plain, and the few variations in its surface owe their origin to fluvial action, such as the high ground along the edge of the Rapti *kachhar* and the sandy ridges which appear in a few places, the most prominent being one to the south of Chaura and that on the road between Maniram and Peppeganj. The Rapti, flowing from the north-west to the south-east corner with a very tortuous course, divides the tahsil into two tracts of unequal size. Its only affluent of importance on the right bank is the Ami, which for some distance forms the boundary between Hasanpur Maghar and the Basti district, subsequently crossing that pargana in an easterly direction and then following the southern borders of Bhauapar. North of the Rapti the chief rivers are the Rohin and its tributary the Chillua, the Tura, the Gurra, and the Pharend, which flow southwards from pargana Haveli, while the Majhna for many miles forms the eastern border. The whole tract abounds in lakes and *jhils,* of which the largest and best known is the Ramgarh Tal. Other considerable sheets of water are the Jamuar, Likhia, Komar, Chillua and Maheshra Tals, which are of a permanent character while in the rains the inundation of the lowlands to the north of Domingarh creates two enormous lakes in the Domingarh and Karmaini Tals, which in ordinary seasons last for several months. There is still a little forest left in the tahsil, although the area is small in comparison with that recorded as late as 1860, when all the northern portion was unreclaimed and more than 100,000 acres of forest were in existence. At the last settlement the total had dropped to 27,442 acres, mainly Government reserves included in the Ramgarh and Tilkonia forests to the east of Gorakhpur. Adjoining this is a small area of private forest at Kusmahi belonging to the Mian Sahib.

The bulk of the tahsil is included in the *bangar* or uplands, though a very considerable strip on either side of the Rapti falls within the *kachhar* tract, the whole of this being liable to inundation in years of heavy rainfall. A certain amount of *kachhar* is also to be found along the Rohin, and altogether it constitutes 21·8 per cent. of the cultivated area, the proportion rising to 56·05 in pargana Bhauapar. Elsewhere the prevailing soil is *doras* or loam, occupying 78·2 per cent. of the area, though dropping to 42·05 in Bhauapar. The other varieties are unimportant, *matiar* or clay representing 5·82, and *balua* or light sandy soil 3·74 per cent.

In 1865 the cultivated area of the tahsil was 191,327 acres, and this rose to 293,822 at the last settlement; while during the five years ending with 1907-08 the average was 306,561 acres or 73·5 per cent. of the whole, this figure on occasions being largely exceeded. The barren area is extremely small, for though 39,669 acres come under this head, 23,386 are covered with water and 14,312 are permanently occupied by railways, roads, sites and the like. The culturable area of 70,841 acres includes 11,914 acres of current fallow and 9,874 of groves, the latter amounting to 2·3 per cent. of the whole tahsil. The proportion rises to 4·02 per cent. in Hasanpur Maghar and is well below the general average in Haveli; there are some magnificent groves immediately to the north of Gorakhpur, but elsewhere their comparative absence is due to the forests and to the fact that much of the land has been but recently reclaimed. The balance comprises 20,579 acres of old fallow, often of an indifferent description, and 28,474 of unbroken waste, either forest or else grass lands along the Rohin, Tura, Pharend, and other rivers. Irrigation extends on an average to 116,231 acres or 36·6 per cent. of the net area under tillage. The proportion rises to nearly one-half in Hasanpur Maghar, where the tanks and natural sources are very widely utilised. Elsewhere wells are more commonly employed, especially to the east of the Rapti; but throughout the *kachhar* area very little irrigation is practised or required.

The tahsil differs from many parts of the district in that the *rabi* harvest is the more extensive, averaging 219,164 acres as compared with 181,900 sown for the *kharif*. These figures are those for the period from 1902-03 to 1906-07, for the following year was quite abnormal on account of drought.* The double-cropped area is large, averaging 92,527 acres or 30·2 per cent. of the net cultivation, while in Bhauapur it attains the remarkable proportion of 87·6 per cent., owing mainly to the precarious nature of the *kharif* in the lowlands. Of the spring crops cereals occupy 57 per cent. of the land sown, the tahsil being the centre of the wheat-growing tract and containing nearly one-third of the entire wheat area in the district. This is notably the case in Hasanpur Maghar, where wheat constitutes one-fourth of the *rabi* harvest and is of particu-

* Appendix, table VI.

larly good quality; elsewhere barley and the mixture called *gujai* are more prevalent. Next come peas, either alone or mixed with barley, and then gram, which by itself or in combination is produced in large quantities everywhere. Oilseeds are practically confined to pargana Haveli, but *masur* is a popular crop in Hasanpur Maghar, while potatoes and garden crops are found chiefly in the neighbourhood of the city. Poppy is grown to a limited extent throughout the tahsil, though in this respect Gorakhpur cannot compare with other subdivisions and tobacco is almost unknown. In the *kharif* rice constitutes about 60 per cent. of the harvest, and only one-seventh of this is transplanted, while in Bhauapar *jarhan* is seldom to be seen. Nearly 20 per cent. is under *kodon*, which is most extensively grown in the latter pargana, but is common everywhere, as also is maize. The area under sugarcane is not large, in spite of the factories at Chauri Chaura and Pipraich, while *arhar* is less widely grown than in the southern tahsils, and only attains popularity to the south of the Rapti. A good deal of *kakun* and other small millets is raised in Haveli and Bhauapar, and in the former *til* is produced in noticeable quantities; but the autumn pulses take an unimportant place and the only other produce worth mention is *juar* and the garden crops grown in the vicinity of the city.

The total area included in holdings in 1907-08 was 320,669 acres, and of this 23·41 per cent. was the *sir* or *khudkasht* of proprietors, the proportion having slightly risen since the last settlement. Occupancy tenants held 34·11, tenants-at-will 40·8, and exproprietors ·33, the remaining 1·35 per cent. being rent-free, mainly in the shape of *jagirs* given to village watchmen. Rents are almost universally paid in cash, but there is a certain amount of grain-rented rice land in Hasanpur Maghar. The rate paid by occupancy tenants, who are very strong in Bhauapar and Hasanpur Maghar, averages Rs. 3·59 per acre as compared with Rs. 3·49 paid by tenants-at-will and Rs. 3·7 in the case of sub-tenants, who cultivate 29,973 acres or 9·4 per cent. of the holdings, a relatively low proportion. The recorded rents do not represent the actual condition of affairs, and it is certain that there has been a substantial rise since the settlement, when the general average was Rs. 2·95 or 19·39 per cent. more than that of 1865. The revenue demand at successive settlements and the present incidence in each pargana will be found in the appendix.*

The tahsil contains 1,336 villages, and these are divided into 2,467 *mahals*. Of the latter 582 are *zamindari* and 1,885 *pattidari*. The number of *birtias* was very small at the settlement, amounting to 82 in all; but there were 10,467 *arazidars* distributed over 808 *arazis*. Large estates are rare, the most important being that of Dumri, which comprises 59 villages with a revenue demand of Rs. 15,429. Saiyid Wilayat Ali Shah Sabzposh holds 37 villages assessed at Rs. 9,883; the Mian Sahib of Gorakhpur has 15 villages free of revenue and 17 others assessed at Rs. 5,067; the Sainthwars of Pali own 34 villages paying a revenue of Rs. 11,197, and the Dubes of Barhampur hold 29 villages paying Rs. 12,719. As might be expected, there are several wealthy landowners who reside in the city of Gorakhpur. The Kayasths, Rai Kishan Kishor Chand and Babu Kishan Mohan Lal, own 21 and 22 villages respectively, while of the Agarwalas Babu Bhagwati Prasad owns 23, Babu Girdhari Das 29, and Babu Parsotam Das 31 villages.

The population of the tahsil rose from 330,875 in 1872 to 416,293 in 1881 and to 477,588 ten years later. It then continued to increase, but with less rapidity, and in 1901 the number of inhabitants was 496,011, including 246,130 females, with an average density of 761 persons to the square mile, a remarkably high figure considering the still large extent of forest. The total consisted of 447,956 Hindus, 46,328 Musalmans, 1,356 Christains, 204 Aryas, 91 Jains, 44 Sikhs, 19 Buddhists, 8 Jews, and 5 Parsis. The principal Hindu castes were Chamars with 57,791 representatives, Ahirs with 53,149, Brahmans with 46,380, Kewats with 37,795, Kurmis and Sainthwars with 30,432, Koeris with 22 589 and Rajputs with 19,834, drawn principally from the Sarnet, Kausik, Panwar, Bisen, Dikhit and Surajbansi clans. Other castes found in numbers exceeding ten thousand are Telis, Kahars, Banias, Kumhars, Mallahs and Lunias. Among the Musalmans the foremost place is taken by the Julahas with a total of 12,447, and of the rest Sheikhs alone had more than 5,000 members.

* Appendix, tables IX and X.

Exactly 64 per cent. of the people depend directly or indirectly on cultivation, this proportion being somewhat lower than elsewhere owing to the large town population. Beyond the trades of the ordinary village craftsmen, there are few industries of importance, the chief being the manufacture of tobacco at Gorakhpur, of sugar at Chaura, Pipraich and elsewhere, and of oil at Chaura. The trade of the tahsil consists largely in grain, especially wheat, of which Sahjanwa is a great exporting centre. Other exports include sugar, oil and tobacco, while Chaura is the chief mart in the district for the collection and distribution of hides. The tahsil contains 1,337 *mauzas*, but the only place of any size is Gorakhpur itself. Pipraich is a small but thriving town, but apart from this the places with large populations are mere agricultural villages, those containing more than 2,500 inhabitants being Bhauapar, Pali, and Barhampur.

It is but natural that in the neighbourhood of the headquarters town communications should be better than in any other part of the district. Through the centre of the tahsil runs the main line of the Bengal and North-Western Railway, with stations at Chaura, Kusmahi near Adda Motiram, Gorakhpur, Domingarh, Jagatbela and Sahjanwa. From Gorakhpur the Uska and Tulsipur branch leads northwards through Maniram station, while that of Peppeganj is close to the tahsil boundary; and the new branch to Bagaha goes in a north-easterly direction through Pipraich. Metalled roads again are numerous, the tract in this respect affording a strong contrast to the rest of the district. From Gorakhpur the provincial road to Basti runs westwards over the bridge of boats at Birdghat, giving off a branch at Sahjanwa, unmetalled beyond the station of that name and leading to Bakhira and Bansi in the Basti district. A second provincial road goes south to Barhalganj and Azamgarh, crossing the Rapti by a pontoon bridge near Bhauapar. Of the local roads that to Kasia on the east is metalled as far as Jagdispur and in time the whole will be so treated, while those to Captainganj and to Nichlaul on the north-east are also metalled for some distance. Unmetalled roads run from Gorakhpur to Deoria on the south-east, to Rudrapur and Sikriganj on the south-west, and to Maniram, Bridgmanganj and Lotan on the north, while a fourth, of a fair-weather nature only, traverses the *kachhar* and leads to Rudarpur and Barhaj, with a cross-road from Barhi to Kusmahi station and Pipraich. There are inspection houses at Sahjanwa, Bargadahi, and Gorakhpur, the last also possessing a dak-bungalow, and military encamping grounds at Sahjanwa, Gorakhpur, Jagdispur and Pipraich. In addition to the roads, the Rapti is still a highway of some importance, but the Rohin, though navigable, is seldom put to any use.

The tahsil is administered as a subdivision in charge of a full-powered officer on the district staff, resident at headquarters; but the work is generally so heavy that it is divided between two joint or deputy magistrates. Gorakhpur too is the seat of the tahsildar, a munsif and a sub-registrar. For police purposes there are stations at Gorakhpur, Sahjanwa, Chaura, Barhi, and Pipraich, the circles of which comprise the entire area. As originally constituted in 1804, the tahsil formed an immense tract, embracing all Haveli and the parganas of Silhat, Maghar and Rasulpur Ghaus. The two last were detached in 1810, though Unaula and Bhauapar were added in exchange, and continued to form a part of the tahsil till the formation of Bansgaon in 1840. Five years later the constitution of the Mausurganj tahsil involved the loss of northern Haveli, though part was given back when the headquarters of that subdivision were moved in 1860 to Maharajganj. When the Basti district was made a separate unit in 1865, one-third of Maghar was given to this tahsil, and finally on the formation of the new Hata tahsil in 1872 Silhat and a further portion of Haveli were detached, so that the subdivision at length attained its present shape, the northern part of Bhauapar having been added to Gorakhpur some years previously.

HASANPUR MAGHAR *Pargana, Tahsil* GORAKHPUR.

This pargana comprises but a portion of the old Hasanpur Maghar, since on the constitution of the Basti district in 1865 twenty of the component tappas were transferred from Gorakhpur, leaving only the nine tappas of Bharsand, Bhadesri, Gahasand, Khajuri, Uttar Haveli, Aurangabad, Pachauri, Satgawan and Suras, with an area of 74,071 acres or 115·7 square miles. It lies in the west of the Gorakhpur tahsil, marching on the north and west with Basti, on the south with Unaula, and on the east with Haveli and Bhauapar.

The tract contains 333 villages and 513 inhabited sites, but there is hardly a place of any size, the most important perhaps being Sahjanwa, whose position on the metalled road and railway has attracted much traffic, especially in wheat. The population of the pargana rose from 65,810 in 1872 to 79,342 in 1881 and to 89,165 ten years later, but then a decline set in, the total in 1901 being 86,706, which gives an average density of 749 to the square mile.

Maghar was from early days the seat of one branch of the Sarnet clan, till the removal of the headquarters to Bansi in the Basti district, apparently as the result of pressure exercised by the Musalmans. In Akbar's day the town of Maghar was held by an imperial garrison, and in all probability the power of the Sarnets in this quarter was checked, while it certainly disappeared with the foundation of Khalilabad, though the northern tappas in this district were under the control of the Babus of Bakhira. This tract, however, appears to have been very backward when it first passed under British control. In Buchanan's day the *kachhar* lands were tolerably well cultivated, but the higher levels were clothed with forest and very sparsely inhabited. It was not long before the forest wholly disappeared, for progress under a peaceful and stable administration was very rapid, and the tract is now one of the most closely and successfully cultivated parts of the district.

HATA, *Pargana* SHAHJAHANPUR, *Tahsil* HATA.

The headquarters of the Hata tahsil are located in a large village of tappa Bachhauli, standing in 26°44′ N. and 83°45′ E., at a distance of 23½ miles east from Gorakhpur on the road to Kasia. An unmetalled road leads hence to Pipraich on the north-west, and another goes south to Deoria ; while from Dhara, four miles west of the village, a third road leads to Gauri Bazar station and Rudarpur. At the last census the place contained 1,762 inhabitants, while the area of the *mauza* is 640 acres, assessed at Rs. 820. The tahsil buildings are comparatively modern, dating from 1872, and form a well-built and compact block. In addition the place contains a registration office, a police station, a post-office, a cattle-pound and an upper primary school. Within recent years a spacious *dharmsala* and an *idgah* have been built by public subscription. Markets are held here twice a week, but the trade of the place is unimportant and purely local.

HATA *Tahsil.*

This tahsil occupies the central portion of the district, and is a long and somewhat narrow tract running north and south, and widening in the centre. It is bounded on the east by Padrauna, on the north and west by pargana Haveli in the Maharajganj and Gorakhpur tahsils, on the south-west by the Rapti, separating it from the Bhauapar and Chillupar parganas of Bansgaon, and on the south-east by pargana Salempur Majhauli. Within its limits lie the two parganas of Silhat and Shahjahanpur, as well as a portion of Haveli in the north, the whole comprising 32 tappas, a list of which will be found in the articles on the several component parganas. The total area is 365,714 or 571·4 square miles, and is subject to but little alteration from fluvial action, since the tahsil is only bordered for a short distance by the Rapti. There are altogether 25 alluvial *mahals,* in every case held on short term settlement under the ordinary rules.

The tract is a very fertile plain with a gently undulating surface, marked in places by low sandy ridges. Practically the whole of the area belongs to the upland *bangar*, though the eastern edge, especially in pargana Shahjahanpur, projects into the *bhat* zone, while in the extreme south lies a small strip of *kachhar*. In addition to the Rapti there are several rivers which traverse the tahsil. In the east the Little Gandak separates pargana Haveli from Padrauna and then passes through the middle of Shahjahanpur before entering the Deoria tahsil. It receives several tributaries, of which the chief are the Maun, passing through Haveli and then forming the southern boundary of that pargana as far as its junction with the larger stream; and the Duranchi, which flows along the borders of Shahjahanpur and Silhat, joining the Gandak in tahsil Deoria. In the west the Majhna constitutes the boundary between the Silhat and Haveli parganas for a considerable distance, and then strikes through the former pargana to join the Rapti, receiving on its right bank the Katna and on its left the Karna, which for several miles forms the dividing line between Silhat and Salempur-Majhauli. There are no lakes of any importance, though a large number of ponds and *jhils* are to be found scattered throughout the country. The forests of former days have almost entirely disappeared, but their reclamation is of comparatively recent date; since in 1860 more than 30,000 acres remained in Silhat alone.

Throughout the tract the prevailing soil is *doras* or loam, covering 69·04 per cent. of the assessable area at the last settlement; it is evenly distributed, for in every pargana more than half the land is of this description, though in Silhat the percentage rises to 78. The stiff clay called *matiar* amounted to 17·33, chiefly in pargana Haveli, and the sandy *balua* to 3·27 per cent., principally in Silhat, while 9·72 per cent. consisted of *bhat,* practically all of the *chaur* variety, and almost wholly confined to Shahjahanpur, where it comprises nearly one-third of the cultivated area. The extent of *kachhar* soil is inappreciable; it is found only in Silhat, and even there amounts to no more than ·14 per cent.

Owing to the recent constitution of the tahsil, it is impossible to ascertain the cultivated area of early days. It is clear, however, that an immense increase has been effected, during the past half-century, since in 1853 the land under tillage in Silhat and Shahjahanpur was only 128,343 acres, whereas by 1865 the figure had risen to 160,893, the total for the whole tahsil being 222,821 acres. At the last settlement it amounted to 279,595, while since that time there has been a further increase, the average for the five years ending with 1907-08 being 296,490 acres or no less than 81·06 per cent. of the entire tahsil. The barren area is exceptionally small, for of 26,061 acres thus classified 12,309 are covered with water and 11,860 are occupied by railways, roads, village sites and the like, leaving only 1,892 acres of actually unculturable waste. Similarly from the 43,190 acres of so-called culturable land must be deducted 8,248 under groves, which take up 2·2 per cent. of the whole tahsil, and 9,760 of current fallow. The balance consists of old fallow and unbroken waste, principally in the form of scattered patches of grove land and small areas of scrub jungle along the Majhna and other rivers, especially in pargana Silhat.

The irrigated area is remarkably large, averaging 141,076 acres or 47·6 per cent. of the cultivation. In the southern half the conditions resemble those found in Deoria, where good wells are common, while everywhere the area watered from wells greatly exceeds that supplied from tanks and other sources. The predominance of well irrigation is peculiarly marked in the south of Silhat, whereas in Haveli greater reliance is placed on tanks.

Of the two harvests the *kharif* is much the most important in that it covers a larger area, averaging 217,179 acres as against 180,106 sown for the *rabi* harvest. These figures are calculated on the returns from 1902-03 to 1906-07, since the conditions of the following year were quite abnormal, the *rabi* area being greatly reduced through drought.* Double-cropping is extensively practised, the average area under this head being 100,924 acres or more than one-third of the net cultivation. The chief autumn staple is rice, occupying two-thirds of the area sown. It includes a very considerable amount of late rice, the acreage under this crop being surpassed only in Maharajganj and Padrauna, but the early variety is sown over an area almost four times as great. The crop predominates in the north, the area under rice in Haveli being generally equal to that of all Silhat. Next comes *arhar*, often in combination with *kodon*, while the latter also is extensively grown by itself. There is a noticeable amount of maize produced in the southern parts, particularly the *bhat* lands of Shahjahanpur. Of more importance is sugarcane, which is grown everywhere and flourishes exceedingly in the *bhat* tract, this crop covering on an average 10·7 per cent. of the whole *kharif* area. For the rest, *mandua* is grown all over the tahsil, and the small millets such as *kakun*, *tangan* and *sanwan* are frequently to be seen in the south. Nearly half the *rabi* harvest consists of cereals, especially barley and the mixture known as *gujai*, the latter prevailing in Shahjahanpur and barley in Silhat, while wheat by itself is less widely grown. Next in order come peas, forming more than one-fourth of the harvests throughout the tahsil, followed by gram, whether sown alone or with barley. In the east there is a large area under *masur*, and oilseeds are to be found everywhere, though particularly in the rice lands of Haveli.

*Appendix, table VI.

The cultivation of poppy has never made much headway and is confined to pargana Silhat, while no other crop is of sufficient importance to deserve mention.

In 1907-08 the total area included in holdings was 311,439 acres, and of this amount 21·68 per cent. was owners' cultivation, the proportion being much higher in pargana Silhat than elsewhere. Occupancy tenants held 40·71, tenants-at-will 35·73, and exproprietors ·55 per cent., while of the rent-free remainder about three-fourths were comprised in the *jagirs* of *goraits*. Rents are paid almost exclusively in cash and the average rate for occupancy holdings is Rs. 3·49 and for tenants-at-will Rs. 3·19 per acre, though in either case the recorded figures are considerably below the actual rents paid. At all events there has been a marked rise since the settlement, when the attested rental averaged Rs. 2·56 per acre, the latter representing an enhancement of 24·65 per cent. on the rates of 1865. The recorded rent paid by *shikmis* or sub-tenants, who cultivate 51,495 acres or 16·5 per cent of the holdings area, averages Rs. 3·74, and this too is probably far short of the mark. In the appendix will be found tables showing the revenue as assessed at successive settlements, as well as the present demand and its incidence.*

The tahsil contains 994 villages, at present divided into 2,096 *mahals*, of which 628 are *zamindari*, 1,458 *pattidari*, and 10 *bhaiyachara*. At the settlement 167 *birtias* were recorded, while there were 469 *arazis* distributed among 2,895 persons. There are few large estates in the tahsil. The Maharani of Bettiah owns a considerable property assessed at nearly Rs. 10,000, and Babu Raghunath Prasad Singh pays almost the same amount. Babu Bhagwati Prasad of Gorakhpur holds 42 villages, with a demand of about Rs. 8,000, and other proprietors of note are the Bhuinhars of Gadrampur and the Babus of Paikauli.

It is not possible to ascertain the total population of the tahsil before the census of 1872, when the number of inhabitants was 287,230. It then rose rapidly to 371,284 in 1881 and to 430,069 ten years later; but in 1901 a slight decline was observed, the total being 428,846, including 215,152 females, with an average density of 751 persons to the square mile. Of the whole

* Appendix, tables IX and X.

number 392,730 were Hindus, 36,087 Musalmans, 18 Sikhs and two Christians. The principal Hindu castes were Chamars with 49,478 representatives, Brahmans with 48,864, Ahirs with 48,528, and Rajputs with 33,944, drawn mainly from the Panwar, Bais, Bandhalgoti, Bisen, Surajbansi and Sombansi clans. Next in order come Kurmis and Sainthwars with 30,112, Koeris with 16,338 and Kewats with 12,411, while Bhars, Lunias and Kahars also occur in numbers exceeding ten thousand. Of the Musalmans by far the most numerous are Sheikhs with 12,059, the only others of any importance being Julahas, Dhunias and Pathans.

The great majority of the people are directly or indirectly engaged in agriculture, which is the occupation of more than 72 per cent. of the whole. The only industry of any note is the manufacture of sugar, which is extensively carried on at Rampur Karkhana and elsewhere. Within the limits of the tahsil are 994 *mauzas* containing 3,085 inhabited sites, but very few are of any size. Rudarpur and Rampur alone can be described as towns, though possibly Captainganj may be included in the same category. Madanpur, Padri and Patharhat have large populations, but are mere agricultural villages.

Means of communication are fair, except in the *kachhar*, where during the rains the roads are impassable to wheeled traffic, so that the town of Rudarpur is practically isolated. The main line of the Bengal and North-Western Railway passes through the centre of the tahsil, but only the station of Gauri Bazar is situated within its limits, though those of Deoria and Chauri Chaura are easy of access. Through the north runs the new line from Gorakhpur to Bagaha, with stations at Badarwar and Captainganj. The only metalled road is that from Deoria to Kasia, with a short branch to the town of Rampur, traversing the Shahjahanpur pargana. The chief unmetalled roads are those from Gorakhpur to Captainganj on the north-east, with branches to Nichlaul and Hata taking off at Pipraich; to Hata and Kasia on the east; and to Deoria on the south-east, following the line of railway. A fourth runs from Gorakhpur through the *kachhar* to Rudarpur and Barhaj, joined at the former place by those from Hata and Deoria; and a similar cross-road connects Deoria with Hata.

The Rapti is of little use to this tahsil as a line of communication, but the Little Gandak is navigable during the rains as far as Ragarganj and bears a small traffic on its stream. There are no bungalows or inspection houses in the tahsil, but military encamping-grounds are to be found at Bhagnath on the Kasia road, at Captainganj and at Gauri Bazar.

For administrative purposes the area is included in the Deoria subdivision, and is in the charge of a full-powered deputy collector stationed at Deoria. There are police stations at Hata, Rudarpur, Mansurganj and Tarkulwa, the circles of which comprise the entire area with the exception of a few villages belonging to the circle of Ramkola in the Padrauna tahsil, while a small portion of the latter tahsil is included in the Tarkulwa circle. As an administrative unit the tahsil has a very brief history, since it did not come into existence till 1872, when pargana Silhat was detached from Deoria and Shahjahanpur from Padrauna to form a new subdivision in conjunction with six tappas of Haveli.

HAVELI *Pargana.*

The immense pargana of Haveli, the largest in this or any other district of the United Provinces, occupies the central and north-western portions of the district. It is a tract of irregular shape, stretching from the Nepal border to a point within 15 miles of the Ghagra, the maximum length from north to south being about 60 miles, while the greatest breadth is some 40 miles from east to west. The northern boundary is formed by Nepal and the parganas of Binayakpur and Tilpur. On the west and south-west it marches in succession with the Basti district, Hasanpur Maghar and Bhauapar, the Rapti constituting the dividing line for nearly two-thirds of the distance; while to the south-east and east lie Silhat, Shahjahanpur and Sidhua Jobna, the last separated by the river Majhna. The total area is no less than 917,303 acres or 1,433·29 square miles, and within its limits are 2,024 *mauzas* and 5,535 inhabited sites.

For administrative purposes the pargana has been split up between the three tahsils of Gorakhpur, Maharajganj and Hata, ten whole tappas being assigned to the first, twelve to the second, and six to the third. The whole pargana contained 412,400 inhabitants in 1853 and has since exhibited a remarkable increase, the total rising to 493,745 in 1865 to 541,846 in 1872, to 617,593 in 1881 and in the following decade to no less than 809,097. Nor did the pargana suffer any diminution, as was observed in other parts of the district, in the ensuing ten years, for in 1901 there was actually a slight increase, the total then being 810,059, which gives an average density of 565 persons to the square mile.

The portion included in the Sadr or Gorakhpur tahsil comprises two-thirds of that subdivision and consists of a broad belt of land extending eastwards from the Rapti. Its area is 303,597 acres or 474·3 square miles, and it is made up of the tappas of Haveli, Qasba, Pachwara, Marachhi Chandaur, Khutahan, Gaura, Patra, Keotali, Rajdhani and Rasulpur. There are 846 *mauzas* and 2,210 inhabited sites. The population rose from 231,213 in 1872 to 290,193 in 1881 and to 341,296 in 1891, while at the last census it was 356,374, with a mean density of 751, a higher rate than in any other part of the pargana.

The six tappas of Parkhauri, Bharsand, Parwarpar, Agaya, Dedupar and Bindwar in the east of the pargana belong to the Hata tahsil, of which they form the northernmost portion, bounded on the south by Silhat and Shahjahanpur, with the Little Gandak and the Padrauna tahsil to the east. This block has an area of 101,665 acres or 158·8 square miles, and includes 229 *mauzas* and 558 inhabited sites. The population was 69,821 in 1872, rising to 78,182 in 1881 and to 100,274 ten years later, though in 1901 the total fell to 95,991, being at the rate of 604 to the square mile.

The northern half of the pargana belongs to tahsil Maharajganj, and stretches from the Little Gandak on the east to the Basti district on the west. It has an area of 512,041 acres or 800 square miles, and contains the twelve tappas of Lehra, Katahra, Mathkopa, Sikra, Sumbhakhor, Rigauli, Bhari Baisi, Banki, Unti, Andhia, Biraicha, and Lakhman. There are altogether 949 *mauzas* and 2,767 inhabited sites, but very few places of any size, this being the most backward part of Haveli. The population rose from 240,812 in 1872 to 249,218 in 1881 and to 367,527 in 1891; but ten years later a marked decline was observed, the total being 358,294 or 495 to the square mile.

The pargana seems to have been held in early days by the Tharus and other aboriginal tribes. There is a vague tradition of one Man Sen, variously described as a Rathor or a Tharu, who was overthrown in the tenth century by the Domkatars. These people had their chief stronghold at Domingarh near Gorakhpur, and in turn succumbed to Chandra Sen and the Sarnets. From one of Chandra Sen's sons sprang the Rajas of Satasi, who for a long period held all the south of the pargana, as well as other territory to the south and east, while the rest was mainly forest save for a small area in the north included in the principality of Butwal. With the expulsion of the Sarnets from Gorakhpur in 1570 the pargana appears to have received its present name of Haveli, which properly denotes the suburbs of a headquarter's town, though in this case it is somewhat of a misnomer, since portions of the pargana are nearly fifty miles from Gorakhpur, while the town itself lies on the extreme south-western limits of the tract. It seems, however, that in Akbar's day the cultivated area was very small and that all the rest was forest, practically left out of account for administrative purposes. The Rajas of Satasi subsequently recovered Gorakhpur for a short period, but were again ejected in 1680 by Qazi Khalil-ur-Rahman, and from that date to the cession the place was the seat of a Musalman governor. In the eighteenth century the country suffered much from maladministration and the incursions of the Banjaras from the north, with the result that the forest spread in all directions, for even as late as 1835 there was a continuous belt of jungle from Gorakhpur to Deoria. Under British rule the tract made rapid progress, and cultivation advanced apace, especially in the south, while great results attended the experiment of forest grants in the north. At the present time most of the area has been reclaimed, apart from the reserved forests, and the pargana is agriculturally one of the richest parts of the district.

KAHAON, *Pargana* SALEMPUR MAJHAULI, *Tahsil* DEORIA.

Kahaon, a small village of tappa Mail, is one of the many ancient sites in the district, and deserves mention only on archæological grounds. It stands in 26°16′N. and 83°52′E.

at the junction of the roads from Musela to Bhagalpur and from Salempur to Paina, about five miles from Salempur station and 53 miles by road from Gorakhpur. The village forms part of the Majhauli estate and has an area of 606 acres, assessed at Rs. 1,000 : the population at the last census numbered 523 persons.

The place is best approached from the Sathraon station on the line from Salempur to Barhaj. The village is built on a great mound of no great height, but about 1,200 feet long and 400 feet broad, covered with remains of ancient bricks.* Only a part of this is occupied by houses, and on the site are some fine old wells constructed with very large bricks taken from the ruins. The chief object of interest is a coarse grey sandstone column, resembling that at Bhagalpur, but more elaborately wrought. It is 24½ feet in height above the ground and is surmounted by a metal spike, which seems to show that it was once crowned by a lion or some similar termination. The shaft is square at he base, then octagonal, then sixteen-sided, and finally circular, while the capital is bell-shaped below and square above, each side having a small niche containing Jain figures. On the western side of the square base is a naked figure of the Jain *tirthankara* Paras Ram, and on the pillar is an inscription recording the dedication of five Jain images by one Madra in the year 141 of the Gupta Sambat. To the north of this pillar, on the highest part of the mound, are traces of the brick walls of two temples, one of which probably contained the five images referred to in the inscription; and it would seem that many other temples and shrines must have been crowded round the pillar, in order to account for the great size of the mound. Close to the pillar too are three ancient *gars* or tanks called Purena, Karhahi and Jhakarahi. Near the edge of the first is a ruined temple with a broken image of Buddha, originally seven feet in height; while to the east of the village is another large tank called the Akaskamini, a name also applied to this temple. The place appears to be called Kakubha on the pillar, and the present name is seemingly a corruption of Kakubhagrama or Kakubhawan.

---

* C. A. S. R., I. p. 91; XVI, p. 129.

KASIA, *Pargana* SIDHUA JOBNA, *Tahsil* PADRAUNA.

The headquarters of the Kasia subdivision are located in a considerable village of Tappa Mainpur, standing in 26° 45′N. and 83°55′E. at a distance of 34 miles east from Gorakhpur, 21 miles north-east from Deoria, and 12 miles south south-west from Padrauna. An unmetalled road, to be metalled in the near future, leads from Gorakhpur through Kasia to Babhnauli and Pipra-ghat, crossing at Kasia at Padrauna to Deoria and Barhaj, the latter being metalled from Kasia southwards. A third roads runs in a south-easterly direction to Qazipur and Chapra. The village at the last census contained 1,723 inhabitants, as compared with 918 in 1872; it has an area of 450 acres and is assessed at Rs. 551. In addition to the resident joint magistrate's bungalow, court-house and office, the place contains a police station, a post and telegraph office, an inspection bungalow, a middle vernacular school, a cattle-pound, and a dispensary recently erected by the Raja of Salemgarh. The small jail was closed in 1906, and is now used as a lock-up, and the *patwari* school was abolished in 1908 on the opening of the new school at Gorakhpur. There is a military encamping-ground at the junction of the two main roads, and in the village a market is held twice a week.

In the village of Bishunpur to the west of Kasia, between the Gorakhpur road and the Ramabhar Tal, lies the most important group of ancient monuments hitherto discovered in this district. For the account of these I am indebted to Mr. V. A. Smith, and also to Dr. J. Ph. Vogel, who has supplied me with a note on his recent discoveries.* Cunningham's identification of the place with Kusinagara was generally accepted till challenged by Mr. Vincent Smith, who places Kusinagara beyond the Great Gandak. In the recent excavations a large number of clay seals were found bearing the inscription of the "Convent of the Great Decease," which would appear to supply the missing evidence; but it has been urged that such seals probably were attached to letters from elsewhere, though as yet no other site has yielded seals from the same place. A single seal was discovered

* *Vide* also J. R. A. S., 1907, pp. 365, 993; and 1902, p. 139.

with the inscription "of the Community of Friars at the Convent of Vishnudvipa," so that possibly this may represent the name of the old town, though such evidence is necessarily far from conclusive.

The remains comprise six groups, the first of which consists of an isolated brick stupa, some fifty feet in height and overgrown with trees, on the western edge of the Ramabhar Tal, bearing the name of Devisthan or Ramabhar Bhawani. The second is a small mound of ruins to the south-west of this stupa and a short distance to the north-east of the village of Anrudhwa. The third is the Matha Kunwar-ka-kot, about a mile west of the Ramabhar stupa, comprising a temple with a colossal recumbent image of the dying Buddha, a large stupa, several monasteries and other buildings. The fourth is a colossal statue of the seated Buddha, called Matha Kunwar, about 400 yards south-west from the *kot*; while the fifth consists of the remains of an enclosing wall and the last of a number of small earthen mounds and burrows, locally called *Bhimawat*, to the north and east of the *kot*. The first of these was opened some time ago by Mr. Lumsden, a former district officer, but it did not yield any relics and the structure was irretrievably damaged. The second has never been excavated or explored. All discussions as to the identity of the site centre round the third group.

This takes its present name from the colossal seated statue, which is made of the dark blue stone of Gaya and represents Buddha seated under the *bodhi* tree, attended by celestial beings. The whole is 10¾ feet high and 4⅔ wide, the figure itself being 5 feet 4½ inches in height. It is split into two pieces from top to bottom and is otherwise injured, an inscription on the base being much defaced, though a few letters remain to show that it is not later in date than the 11th or 12th century. The meaning of the name is unknown, for Cunningham's interpretation of "the dead prince" unfortunately cannot be maintained. The *kot* itself has been subjected to extensive exploration. When first discovered, it presented the appearance of a mound in which the top of a brick stupa was visible; and in 1861-62 Cunningham identified it with the site of the *sal* grove of Kusinagara, the capital of the Malla country, in which the Buddha attained Nirvana.

He considered the Ramabhar stupa to be that which marked the place where the remains were cremated, and he placed the city itself on the site of the modern Anrudhwa.* Subsequently, in 1876-77, Mr. A. C. L. Carleylle carried out some excavations in the *kot*, the results of which seemed to confirm the theory. His chief discovery was that of a brick temple adjoining the stupa, in which was an image of the dying Buddha, some 20 feet in length, corresponding exactly to that described by Huien Tsang as existing at Kusinagara in the seventh century. It bears a votive inscription recording its erection by an abbot named Haribala in the fifth century. In 1896 Mr. V. A. Smith, at the request of Sir Antony MacDonnell, visited Kasia in order to compare the remains with those described by the Chinese pilgrim; and his conclusion that Cunningham was wrong was based chiefly on the impossibility of reconciling the account given by Huien Tsang of the ruins as he saw them in 635, or thereabouts, with the position of those hitherto brought to light. He argues that if the remains near Kasia are those which adjoined Kusinagara, then the village of Anrudhwa must correspond with the fortified town of Kusinagara; a river must have flowed between that village and the Matha Kunwar-ka-kot; traces should be visible of a group of monuments north of the town as well as of another to the north-west; and there should be a stupa at the north-east angle of the city gate. He urged that none of these conditions is satisfied at Kasia, while further the great stupa called Matha Kunwar can never have been more than 85 feet high, whereas that seen by Huien Tsang was still about 200 feet high in its then ruinous condition. Nevertheless the last word has not yet been said on the subject, and it still remains to be proved that Kusinagara exists elsewhere. It is at least reasonable to demand that the identification may be allowed to stand till a more satisfactory site is discovered. The site of Sarnath, for example, is indisputably that of the Deer Park of the pilgrims, although it is extremely difficult to harmonize their accounts with existing conditions; while the wonderful intuition of General Cunningham has recently been vindicated by the discoveries in 1908 at Set Mahet.†

* C. A. S. R., I, pp. 76—85; XVIII, p. 55; XXII, p. 16. | † J. R. A. S., 1908, p. 971.

The destructive argument, moreover, is not stated with perfect fairness. If it be granted that the ancient site of the small fortified city of Kusinagara is identical with that of the modern Anrudhwa, then it is not unreasonable to suggest that the Ramabhar stupa is that mentioned as standing at the north-east angle of the walls, while in that case the remains at Matha Kunwar-ka-kot, which certainly bear a most striking resemblance to the *vihara* of Huien Tsang, lie to the north-west of the city as required. The argument as to the river is of little importance, for in this part of the country changes are frequent and easy, so that it may well be the case that the Ramabhar Tal, itself fed during the rains by an old channel called the Khanua, was once a river bed, in which event fluvial action may have brought about the complete disappearance of the old town and of the other minor monuments referred to by Huien Tsang. With regard to the height of the stupa Mr. Smith himself notes that from its composition it shows unmistakable signs of being a rebuilt structure; and from our knowledge of other Buddhist shrines, some of which are as late as the twelfth century at least, it is not too much to argue that the present building is different from that seen by the Chinese pilgrim. One must keep in view the fact that he wrote more than 1,200 years ago, and that this, like all other Buddhist sites in this region, has suffered terribly from neglect and the ravages both of nature and of the foes of the Buddhist faith.

Fresh excavations were carried out in 1904-05 and the two following years under the superintendence of Dr. Vogel. It was found that the stupa and temple of the dying Buddha form the nucleus of an extensive group of Buddhist buildings, comprising several large monasteries, a few small shrines and a great number of brick stupas of various sizes. These buildings belong to widely different periods, and those of later date have been raised on the ruins of earlier monuments. It also became evident that the history of this sacred site does not start from the erection of the Nirvana image, for the evidence of coins and other inscribed objects proves that several of the buildings date back to the Kushana and early Gupta epochs. In the 5th or 6th century a portion of the buildings was destroyed in a conflagration, possibly due to an invasion by the Huns. The matter of the clay seals has already been mentioned. These seemed to confirm Cunningham's theory, and there can be little doubt that "the congregation of Buddhist friars residing in the community of the Great Decease" refers to that which stood in the sacred *sal* grove of Kusinagara. The proof of identification is strong but not decisive. The seal of Vishnudvipa may afford a clue, since Vethadvipa, another form of the name, was one of the eight places in which a portion of the relics was preserved under a stupa. This seal, however, is as yet but a unique specimen, whereas the others were found in large numbers. It would certainly appear that they were used for affixing to packages or letters, and the fact that most of them were unearthed in a broken condition in what appears to have been a mere rubbish heap undoubtedly lends force to the contention that they came from another great and probably superior monastery. If on the other hand these clay tablets are not really seals of this nature, their presence in large quantities would occur most naturally in the place of their origin.

Dr. Vogel's excavations are far from complete as yet and, though the work was interrupted in 1908, much still remains to be done. It is incontestable that the site was one of unusual importance, from the nature and extent of the surrounding buildings laid bare by the excavations, while it seems clear that neither of the extreme views held by Cunningham and Carleylle on the one hand and by Smith on the other can, in the light of all the evidence now available, be reasonably maintained as a certainty. The place is to this day the object of veneration on the part of Buddhists, who come hither in large numbers every year from Burma and elsewhere. The colossal recumbent statue has recently been covered from head to foot with gold leaf by devout pilgrims to the shrine, for whose accommodation a small *sarai* has been erected close to the temple.

KAURIRAM, *Pargana* BHAUAPAR, *Tahsil* BANSGAON.

This small village of tappa Pachisi stands in 26°32′N. and 83°25′E., on the unmetalled road from Gorakhpur to Azamgarh, at a distance of 16½ miles from the former and five miles east from Bansgaon. It marks the southern extremity of the Tucker *bandh* over the valley of the Ami, and from it unmetalled roads radiate to Bansgaon and Rudrapur on the north-west, to Gola on the south and to Gajpur on the south-east. The population of the village at the last census was only 166, while the area is 244 acres and the revenue Rs. 235. The place is noticeable, however, as possessing a police outpost, a post-office, an inspection bungalow, and a weighing house belonging to the Opium department.

KHAMPAR, *Pargana* SALEMPUR MAJHAULI, *Tahsil* DEORIA.

A village of tappa Haveli, situated in 26°21′N. and 84°4′E., on the east side of the unmetalled road leading from Bhatpar station through the adjoining district of Saran to Tamkuhi in tahsil Padrauna at a distance of eight miles from Majhauli and 61 miles by road from Gorakhpur. The population at the last census numbered 2,334 persons, while the village has an area of 1,479 acres and is assessed at Rs. 2,680. It possesses a post-office and a cattle-pound, as well as a bazar in which markets are held twice a week. The police station known as Khampar is actually situated in Ghati, a village some four miles to the north-west on the other side of the Khanua, but it is now proposed to remove this *thana* to Khampar itself.

KHUKHUNDU, *Pargana* SALEMPUR MAJHAULI, *Tahsil* DEORIA.

The village of Khukhundu gives its name to a tappa, and stands in 26°24′N. and 83°51′E., about a mile to the east of the road from Gorakhpur to Salempur and Chapra, and two miles south-west from Nunkhar station, at a distance of some eight miles from Deoria and 44 miles south-east from the district head-quarters. It is a place of considerable size, having at the last census a population of 2,475 souls, while the area of the village is 1,000 acres, assessed at Rs. 1,200. It gives its name to a police station and an encamping ground, situated on the road-side near Musela, and also contains a cattle-pound and a lower primary school.

The interest of Khukhundu, however, is mainly archæological, for the ancient site to the south of the village was considered by General Cunningham as one of the most promising fields for excavation in the north of India; and, though little has so far been accomplished in the way of exploration, the place has been brought under the protection of the Ancient Monuments Preservation Act.* The old name is said by some to have been Kishkindapura, and Cunningham believed it to be the large village mentioned by Huien Tsang as lying 30 miles south-west from Kasia on the route from that place to Benares. In this unnamed village dwelt a rich Brahman who devoted his wealth to the decoration of a Buddhist monastery. The remains consist of a few large tanks and about thirty low mounds covered with broken bricks and jungle, scattered about the fields and altogether occupying a square mile of ground. The larger mounds are square in form, and obviously mark the sites of Jain and Hindu temples, whose destruction seems to have been accomplished by the roots of the lofty trees growing on their summits. The largest of these mounds is 120 feet square and about 18 feet high. Some have been ransacked by persons in search of building materials, but the objects, even now visible on the tops of the mounds, are of considerable interest. There are statues of Vishnu in blue stone, with representations of the deity in five incarnations; statues of Shiva, Parbati and Ganesh; statues of several Jain hierarchs, and many other fragments of moulded bricks, sculptured stone, walls and the like. On a long low mound to the south-west Cunningham discovered the remains of an octagonal building which he believed to be a Buddhist stupa.

The village contains a small Jain temple of modern origin, which is often visited by Agarwal Saraogis from Gorakhpur and Patna, and contains a large and ancient image in blue stone of Bishambharnath, the first *tirthankara*, though it is generally supposed to represent Parasnath, the 23rd hierarch: it is of the conventional type, with a bull on the pedestal and a triple umbrella above the statue.

KOTHIBHAR, *Pargana* TILPUR, *Tahsil* MAHARAJGANJ.

A small village of tappa Purani Karhi, standing in 27°8′ N. and 83°46′E., on the unmetalled road from Captainganj to

* C. A. S. R., I. pp. 85-91; XVI. p. 127; XVIII. p. 41.

Nichlaul, about a mile south of Siswa Bazar and 42 miles north-east from Gorakhpur. It deserves mention solely as possessing a police station, a post-office and a cattle-pound, but it is otherwise quite insignificant, having at the last census a population of only 551 persons. The area of the *mauza* is 464 acres and the revenue assessment Rs. 327. There was formerly a market here, but this has dropped out of existence with the recent rise of Siswa Bazar.

LAR, *Pargana* SALEMPUR MAJHAULI, *Tahsil* DEORIA.

A considerable town of tappa Ballia, standing in 26°12′N. and 83°59′E., at the junction of the road from Gorakhpur and Deoria to Chapra with that from Sikriganj, Barhalganj and Barhaj, at a distance of 58 miles from Gorakhpur, 24 from the tahsil headquarters and four miles east from the Bhatni-Benares line of railway, on which there is a station known as Lar Road.

The place has no history, and the only ancient building is a Hindu temple said to have been founded by Vasishta. This saint is said to have had a cow which was carried off by a tiger and was traced by the trail of foam (*lar*) which dropped from her mouth, though the tradition seems merely to have been invented in order to afford a derivation for the name. The population numbered 4,382 souls in 1872, and has since increased rapidly, rising to 7,403 in 1881 and to 7,572 in 1891, though at the last census a slight decline was observed, the total being 7,305, of whom 3,024 were Musalmans. The latter are unusually strong, and possess two or three mosques, as well as an *imambara* which is the best modern Muhammadan building in the district. They are chiefly Iraqis by caste and include a number of wealthy traders, who are persons of great enterprise, carrying on an extensive export trade in grain, spices, hemp and sugar with Patna and Calcutta, while in return they import cloth for the Nepal market. In Nepal too they conduct a large and valuable business in hides, sent from Lar to Cawnpore and Calcutta; while their connection with the north is further exemplified by the trade in soap, of which there are three factories in Lar and one in the adjoining village of Ramnagar to the north. Mention of this industry, which is in a very flourishing condition, has already been made in Chapter II.

Lar possesses a post-office and a middle vernacular school, to which a training class for teachers is attached. The *mauza* is 2,589 acres in extent and pays a revenue of Rs. 3,800, while the inhabited portion has since 1871 been administered under Act XX of 1856. The present number of houses in the town is 1,505, and in 1907-08 there were 605 assessed to taxation, the house-tax yielding Rs. 965, with an average incidence of Re. 1-7-7 per assessed house and Re. 0-2-1 per head of population, these rates being the lowest obtaining in any town of the district. The total income of the year was Rs. 1,171, while the expenditure of Rs. 1,022 was devoted chiefly to the upkeep of the town police, the maintenance of a conservancy staff and minor local improvements.

LEHRA, *Pargana* HAVELI, *Tahsil* MAHARAJGANJ.

Lehra is a small village giving its name to a tappa in the north-west of the pargana, and stands in 27°10′N. and 83°20′E., some five miles north-east from Pharenda station on an unmetalled road joining that from Bridgmanganj to Nichlaul. It is best known as giving its name to the great Lehra estate, originally acquired as a forest grant in 1833 by Mr. J. H. Bridgman. The headquarters of the estate and the residence of Mr. Holdsworth, known as Park House, stand about a mile and a half north-west along a metalled road from the Lehra station on the railway. The house is a handsome and spacious building standing in extensive grounds, laid out after the fashion of an English park. The place suffered considerable damage during the Mutiny at the hands of the rebels: but this was subsequently repaired, and the house is now very much as it was when originally constructed.

MAHARAJGANJ, *Pargana* HAVELI, *Tahsil* MAHARAJGANJ.

The headquarters of the northern tahsil are located in a considerable village of tappa Sonari, standing in 27°8′N. and 83°34′E., at a distance of 36 miles from Gorakhpur, with which it is connected by a branch from the unmetalled road to Nichlaul, taking off at Shikarpur. The latter place is now being connected by means of another unmetalled road with the Ghughli station on the new line to Bagaha; but hitherto the nearest railway station has been Pharenda on the Uska branch, from which a road runs through Maharajganj to Senduria on the Nichlaul route. The place was selected as the headquarters in 1860, and contains the tahsil, a considerable masonry building constructed at a cost of over Rs. 30,000, a police station, a dispensary, an inspection bungalow, a post-office, a cattle-pound and a newly erected *dharamsala.* Formerly a middle vernacular school existed here, but this was reduced to the upper primary standard owing to the poor attendance, although its restoration to the middle class has been recently suggested. The population of the village numbered 1,738 persons in 1901, while the area is 1,122 acres and the revenue demand Rs. 960. The tahsil buildings are close to the right bank of the Balia river, and are surrounded on all sides by rice fields. The excessive dampness of the climate, coupled with the proximity of the forest, renders it very unhealthy, especially during the rains, so that on this score it is quite as unpopular a station as Padrauna.

MAHARAJGANJ *Tahsil.*

This tahsil, the largest in the district, is a compact and roughly quadrangular tract, lying between the Nepal border on the north and north-west and the Gorakhpur and Hata tahsils on the south, while on the east the Little Gandak separates it from Padrauna and for a few miles the Great Gandak in the north-eastern corner constitutes the dividing line between this district and Champaran. On the west again the boundary is generally formed by natural features, the Ghunghi marking the borders of Nepal and Basti for a long distance, and further south, the Rapti performs a similar function for a part of its course. The subdivision comprises the parganas of Tilpur and Binayakpur, as well as a large portion of Haveli. The total area is 792,773 acres or 1,238·7 square miles, and is seldom liable to change, though fluvial action on the part of the Rapti and Great Gandak is a disturbing factor. There are 84 alluvial *mahals,* many of which lie on the banks of the Rapti: 34 are subject to the ordinary rules of quinquennial revision, 21 are held conditionally and 25 unconditionally on long-term settlements, and the remaining four are situated in unexpired jungle grants.

In several respects the tahsil differs markedly from the rest of the district. The northern portion belongs to the Tarai and in its climatic and agricultural characteristics presents many peculiar features, being the least developed part of the district, with considerable room for expansion both of tillage and of population. The chief drawback is the unhealthiness of the tract, for the climate is so feverish and enervating that the Tharu alone seems able to withstand its effects. Moreover cultivation is necessarily of a precarious nature, for an early cessation of the rains will result in almost total loss of the transplanted rice, the chief and almost the only product, on which the prosperity of the Tarai entirely depends. South of this belt, which is about ten miles in width, the conditions approximate more closely to those prevailing in the rest of the district, though the distinguishing feature is the large extent of forest, for, with the exception of a relatively small area in the Gorakhpur tahsil, practically the whole of the forests are situated in this subdivision. These forests form three distinct blocks, that on the west comprising two separate areas round Lehra and Campierganj, and that on the east including the Domakhand range, while the central and largest block lies round Sonari, along the Rohin and Piyas rivers. At the last settlement the forests covered 106,684 acres, and since that time very slight reductions have been made. Bordering on the forests are extensive stretches of open grass jungle which have not been reclaimed, being more valuable as pastures than as arable land. The bulk of the area is included in the ordinary upland *bangar*; but in the south-west corner there is a small stretch of *kachhar* along the Rapti, and in the extreme east, principally in pargana Tilpur, is a belt of *bhat.*

Thus parts of the tahsil fall within all the four main tracts into which the district is divided topographically. The change from one zone into another is effected gradually, and the Tarai blends slowly into the ordinary upland. In the former there are numerous streams which carry down the drainage from Nepal, such as the Ghunghi, Danda, Rohin, Baghela, Madrahi, Mohan, Piyas, Chandan and the Little Gandak,

In the *bangar* the chief drainage lines are the Rohin and Little Gandak, which intercept all the other streams, save those which discharge their waters directly into the Rapti or the Dhamela. Lakes, in most cases formed by abandoned channels of rivers, and *jhils* are very common, though none is of such importance as to deserve separate mention.

With such a diversity of natural features there is naturally a great variety in the soils. Generally, however, *doras* or loam is the most common type, especially in pargana Haveli, and altogether occupies 65·01 per cent. of the assessable area, though the proportion drops to 58·26 in Tilpur and to 43·63 in Binayakpur, as against 70·33 in Haveli. The stiff clay called *matiar* is more widely distributed in this tahsil than in other parts, amounting to 27·45 per cent., while it rises to 55·07 in Binayakpur, though in Tilpur it covers no more than 18·4 per cent. of the area. The latter pargana contains almost all the *bhat*, which is of the *chour* and *chauriar* varieties; for while *bhat* occupies 22·86 per cent. of Tilpur the proportion for the whole tahsil is only 5·55. For the rest, ·74 per cent. consists of sandy *balua*, which is exceedingly rare, and 1·25 of *kachhar* or new alluvium, confined to the north-east and south-west extremities.

The cultivated area in 1865 amounted to 280,441 acres and subsequently exhibited a very remarkable increase, the total at the last settlement being 434,967, while since that time a further expansion has occurred, for during the five years ending with 1907-08 the average was 489,104 acres, or 61·7 per cent. of the entire tahsil. The barren area is 45,298 acres, but of this 23,801 are covered with water and 18,890 are occupied by railways, roads, buildings and the like, leaving but a very small amount of sterile land. There is necessarily an unusual extent of unreclaimed waste, owing to the presence of the forests and grass jungle. In all 258,371 acres are returned as culturable; but from this must be deducted 34,135 acres of current fallow and the small area of 9,518 acres under groves, which are scarce everywhere and are almost unknown in Binayakpur. The remainder includes 58,240 acres of old fallow, which is more valuable than most of the land so described in other parts, since cultivation is still of a fluctuating nature and much is yet available for tillage, even if the forests be left intact. Irrigation is very little practised in the two northern parganas, where it extends to no more than 5·3 per cent. of the net cultivation, while for the whole tahsil the proportion is less than one-fifth. Wells, tanks, and other sources are utilised to an approximately equal extent, and the system of rude canals for the rice fields of the Tarai has been described elsewhere. The only canal irrigation deserving the name is to be found on the Lehra estate, but this affects no more than 200 acres or thereabouts.

The *kharif* is by far the more important harvest, averaging 419,617 acres as against 221,459 sown with *rabi* crops, a considerable tract depending almost entirely on the *kharif* produce.* Double-cropping is extensively practised and extends to one-third of the net cultivation, this high proportion arising from the custom of sowing linseed broadcast on the wet rice stubbles. Rice, it need hardly be said, is the great autumn staple, covering 86·1 per cent. of the area sown for this harvest. While *jarhan* or transplanted rice is more extensively produced than in any other part of the district, the area is little more than a third of that devoted to the early variety. Only in Binayakpur, where the heavy clay soil is particularly well suited to its growth, is *jarhan* preponderant, covering five-eighths of the rice area in that pargana. The only other *kharif* crops of any importance are *arhar* and *kodon* in pargana Haveli, maize in the *bhat* soil of Tilpur, and sugarcane which, though it cannot compare in area with that of the southern and eastern tahsils, shows a decided tendency to expand; and it is probable that with the improvement in cultivation Maharajganj will in time rival other parts of the district in this respect. Mention may also be made of *mandua, juar* grown for fodder and the oilseed called *til*, which is practically confined to this tahsil and has the advantage of being left untouched by wild animals, a pest to which the greater part of the area is constantly subjected. The *rabi* harvest is extensive only in pargana Haveli, which produces three times the quantity raised in the other two parganas. Wheat and barley are grown to an almost equal extent, but the mixture of the two is far more popular. Altogether cereals cover 43 per cent. of

* Appendix, table VI.

the area sown, while next come gram, both by itself and in combination with barley, peas and linseed, the amount of which is about half the total for the district. Other crops include *masur*, potatoes, the small vetches such as *kesari* and *boro* rice: poppy is almost unknown, though occasionally to be seen in pargana Haveli.

In spite of the recent expansion of tillage the tahsil is still far more backward than any other part of the district. In 1907-08 the total area included in holdings was 531,879 acres and of this no less than 58·76 per cent. was held by tenants-at-will, occupancy tenants being in possession of only 18·92 per cent., a far lower figure than in any other tahsil. Proprietors cultivated 21·16 per cent. as *sir* or *khudkasht* and the proportion has increased since the settlement; while ·21 was held by ex-proprietary tenants and ·95 per cent. was rent-free, almost exclusively in the form of *jagirs* assigned to *goraits*. Rents are paid in cash save on a very small area. The present rates are far lower than in the other tahsils, averaging Rs. 2·58 per acre for occupancy holdings and Rs. 2·47 for tenants-at-will, while even *shikmis* or sub-tenants, whose cultivation is confined mainly to the best land, pay no more than Rs. 3·37. It is highly probable, however, that these recorded figures are much below the actual rentals: but even so there has been a substantial rise since the settlement, when the average all-round rate was only Re. 1·89, and this again showed an enhancement of 24·9 per cent. on the recorded rates of 1865, when the average was Re. 1·53 per acre. There is, of course, a great difference between the rents of the various parganas, Haveli paying a fairly high amount as compared with that of Tilpur and Binayakpur, where the recorded occupancy rates are only Re. 1·96 and Re. 1·59 respectively. The revenue demand as assessed at successive settlements, as well as the present figure and its incidence, will be found in the appendix.*

The tahsil contains 1,402 villages and these are divided into 2,085 *mahals*, of which 642 are *zamindari* and 1,443 *pattidari*. Though the number of *mahals* has much increased of late their proportion to the total number of villages is lower than usual,

* Appendix, tables IX and X.

owing to the fact that the jungle grants often form large *mahals* containing in some instances many *mauzas.* Under-proprietary rights are relatively uncommon, for at the settlement there were but 126 *birtias* and 354 *arazi* plots distributed among 1,161 persons. The chief estate in the pargana is Lehra, which comprises 45 villages and is assessed at Rs. 14,581. The Tiwaris of Balua hold 37 villages, paying a revenue of Rs. 8,957; the Mahant of Harpur pays Rs. 7,318 for 36 villages; Babu Tikori Singh has 19 villages; Saiyid Wilayat Ali Shah Sabzposh has 16, and Pandit Harbans Prasad Tiwari of Rampur owns 15 villages. Mention may also be made of Babu Mahadeo Kishan Tiwari of Partawal, who holds six large villages with a revenue demand of Rs. 3,143.

The population of the tahsil numbered 319,555 in 1872 and has since increased with great rapidity, the total rising to 365,702 in 1881 and to 511,450 ten years later. A slight decline then set in, for in 1901 the number of inhabitants was 504,325 of whom 250,914 were females, the average density being 407 to the square mile. Classified by religions there were 444,322 Hindus, 59,941 Musalmans, 40 Christians, 12 Aryas and 10 Sikhs. The prevailing Hindu castes were Chamars, 68,662; Ahirs, 54,917; Brahmans, 44,435; Kewats, 33,839; Kurmis, 21,518, excluding Sainthwars, of whom there were more than 5,000; Koeris, 21,164; and Rajputs, 13,388, drawn mainly from the Bisen, Surajbansi and Panwar clans. Other castes with over 10,000 representatives are Kahars, Kumhars, Telis, Dhobis, Pasis and Banias, the last being almost exclusively Kandus and Kasaundhans. Mention may also be made of the Tharus who, though numbering but 1,229 persons, hold 14 per cent. of the cultivated area in Binayakpur. The Musalman community consists mainly of Pathans, 13,938; Julahas, 12,804; and Sheikhs, 10,918; for of the others Dhunias or Behnas alone occur in any strength.

Besides agriculture, on which over 76 per cent. of the people depend directly or indirectly, there is no other occupation of any importance save that of breeding and herding cattle. The hide business is mainly in the hands of large contractors residing elsewhere, though some smaller men may be found on the Nepal border. The forests afford employment to a considerable number of persons, but there are no industries or manufactures of any note. The tahsil contains 1,425 *mauzas* and 3,706 inhabited sites, but is destitute of any large town. The chief places are Siswa Bazar, a rising mart which has almost completely supplanted Nichlaul in the east and the combined villages of Dhani and Kanapar in the west. Maharajganj itself is quite unimportant, and Sanaura, though containing a population of more than 3,000, is a mere agricultural village of no interest; while no other place possesses as many as 2,000 inhabitants.

Apart from the railways, means of communication are very defective. The branch line from Gorakhpur to Uska, Tulsipur and Gonda traverses the south-west corner of the tahsil, with stations at Peppeganj, Rawatganj, Campierganj, Pharenda, Lehra and Bridgmanganj. The Bagaha branch of the same railway traverses the extreme east of the tahsil, running due north through the stations of Ghughli and Siswa Bazar, while a short distance beyond the latter it runs eastwards into Padrauna. There are no metalled roads with the exception of the short length connecting the Lehra station with Mr. Holdsworth's house and Bridgmanganj. The principal unmetalled roads comprise on the one hand that from Gorakhpur to Bridgmanganj and thence to Lotan in the Basti district, and that from Gorakhpur through Shikarpur and Senduria to Nichlaul, where it bifurcates, one branch leading to Thuthibari and the other to Bahwar, both on the Nepal frontier. Connecting these main arteries are three cross roads of some importance. The first runs from Bridgmanganj to Nichlaul, with a branch from Bagapar to Senduria and Siswa Bazar, whence a road leads to Padrauna and so to Chapra. The second goes from Pharenda to Maharajganj, whence branches lead to Senduria and Shikarpur, the latter being in process of extension to Ghughli station; and the third passes through the south of the tahsil, from Rigauli to Campierganj, Partawal and Captainganj. Two other roads lead southwards from Nichlaul, one by Harpur and Partawal to Pipraich, and the second by Siswa Bazar and Biraicha to Captainganj. In the north-west roads are almost unknown, save for those maintained by the Forest department, but the defect is being remedied to some extent by the construction of a road from Bridgmanganj to Nautanwan in pargana Binayakpur. There is an inspection bungalow belonging to the district board at Maharajganj, and numerous rest-houses kept up by the Forest department, of which a list has been given elsewhere.

The tahsil forms a subdivision in the charge of a full-powered officer on the district staff stationed at headquarters. The tahsildar and his subordinates, as well as the sub-registrar, reside at Maharajganj. The area comprises the entire police circles of Maharajganj, Semra, Rigauli, Panera, Nichlaul, Thuthibari and Paisia, while those of Kothibhar and Biraicha extend into Padrauna. A few villages of pargana Haveli belong to the Ramkola circle of the Padrauna tahsil. In the early days of British rule all the north of the district consisted of forest and waste, while the Tarai was under the virtual control of the Nepalese. After the conclusion of the war with Nepal in 1818 Tilpur and Binayakpur, then considerably larger than at present, were formed into a frontier tahsil, and in 1845 the headquarters were fixed at Mansurganj, a large part of Haveli being added to the subdivision. This arrangement proved unsatisfactory owing to the great distance of the place from the northern parganas, and a move was made to Maharajganj in 1860, while about the same time the area was reduced by the transfer to Nepal of a belt of Tarai between the existing boundary and the foot of the outer hills.

MAJHAULI, *vide* SALEMPUR-MAJHAULI.

MANSURGANJ, *pargana* HAVELI, *tahsil* HATA.

The village of Mansurganj is said to derive its name from Abul Mansur Khan, better known as Safdar Jang, the second Nawab Wazir of Oudh, and possibly was founded during the expedition against the recalcitrant Raja of Tilpur. It rose to temporary prominence when selected in 1845 as the headquarters of the northern tahsil of the district, but it had long been found too far south for administrative convenience when it was supplanted in 1860 by Maharajganj. It stands in tappa Parkhauri on the northern border of the present Hata tahsil, in 26°55′N. and 83°35′E., at a distance of some 18 miles north-east from Gorakhpur by the road from Pipraich to Partawal, Harpur and Nichlaul. Though of small size, having at the last census a population of 849, it possesses a police station, a post-office, a cattle-pound and an upper primary school, while a market is held here every Monday. The area of the village is 615 acres and the revenue demand is Rs. 658.

NICHLAUL, *Pargana* TILPUR, *Tahsil* MAHARAJGANJ.

The small market town of Nichlaul belongs to tappa Khas, and from this fact, coupled with the existence in the vicinity of the remains of a considerable fort, which may very possibly be that referred to in the *Ain-i-Akbari*, it is reasonable to suppose that the place represents the original Tilpur. It was also the residence of the Rajas of Tilpur during the brief period of their existence, while subsequently the ejected Rajas of Butwal made it their headquarters till the loss of their title and pension consequent on the rebellion of the last incumbent in 1857. Though it appears to have long been the principal place in the pargana, it is now a mere village, the population at the last census being but 1,564. Nichlaul stands in 27°18′N. and 83°44′E., some 51 miles from Gorakhpur and 16 from Maharajganj, at the junction of several roads. The chief of these lead to Gorakhpur and to Captainganj, the former being connected by a branch from Senduria with Maharajganj and Pharenda. Between these a third road runs due south to Harpur, Partawal, Mansurganj and Pipraich, while a fourth goes south-west to Bagapar and Bridgmanganj. On the north two roads lead to Thuthibari and Bahwar on the Nepal frontier, the place being a great centre for the trade with Nepal. From its position it must retain some commercial importance, and many Bania dealers still reside here; but the recent advent of the railway has altered the conditions, since the traffic now merely goes through Nichlaul to the rising mart of Siswa Bazar. The place contains a police station, a post-office and a cattle-pound, while markets are held here every Thursday. The area of the *mauza* is 1,624 acres and the revenue demand is Rs. 700.

PADRAUNA. *Pargana* SIDHUA JOBNA, *Tahsil* PADRAUNA.

The place which gives its name to the eastern tahsil of the district is a town formed by the aggregation of five separate villages.

It stands in 26°54′N. and 83°59′E., on the road from Captainganj to Bansi-ghat and Bettiah, at a distance of twelve miles north-north-east by road from Kasia and 49 miles from Gorakhpur. Other unmetalled roads lead from Padrauna to Naurangia and Siswa Bazar on the north, to Tiwaripatti and Tamkuhi on the south-east, and to Samur and Chapra on the south. Close to the town on the north flows the Banri, which becomes a running stream only in the rains. It probably represents an ancient course of the Gandak, a theory which was strengthened by the discovery in 1878 of a large boat during the excavation of a tank. The place is very unhealthy, malaria and goitre being unusually prevalent, and has an unenviable reputation.

The site is evidently of great antiquity, and General Cunningham identified it with the Pawa of the Buddhist pilgrims.* To the south of the town is a large mound covered with broken bricks, about 220 feet broad from east to west, 120 feet long and 14 feet high. It is supposed to mark the site of a Buddhist monastery, which perhaps contained one of the principal relic stupas, since the people of Pawa obtained one-eighth of the relics after Buddha's cremation. To the north of this is an old and ruinous Jain temple containing fragments of sculptures, close to which a new temple has recently been erected. The place is said to have been devastated by the Musalmans; but nothing is known of such an event, though some four miles to the east there stands the shrine of one Burhan Shahid, a name which occurs among the companions of Saiyid Salar Masaud. In the fifteenth century Padrauna is believed to have come under the sway of the Rajput adventurer Madan Singh, who gave the place to his family priest, Rasu; but the rise of the present town is due to the establishment of the Padrauna principality by the Kurmis, who have been settled here for at least two centuries. In the early days of British rule the Rais of Padrauna lost much of their estate and fortune, but the loss was restored by Rai Isri Partab Rai, who bought the large grant of Padrauna Jangal on the death of Mr. Sym, the original purchaser. The present representative of the family holds the title of Raja and is one of the largest landowners in the district, residing in a fine house near the town.

* C. A. S. R., I, 74; XVI, 118.

There are three main divisions of the town, comprising Padrauna proper, Sahibganj to the north along the Bansi-ghat road, and Chhaoni on the Kasia road, more than a mile to the south. Sahibganj belongs to tappa Bargaon Chaura, whereas the others are in Pakri Gangrani; it derives its name from its foundation by Mr. Finch, an indigo planter who had a bungalow at Shahpur, some four miles to the east, which is now owned and occasionally occupied by the Raja. Padrauna proper adjoins Sahibganj on the east, and the two together form the main bazar, containing a number of shops. The place has a fair trade, but the only notable manufacture is that of metal vessels in brass, copper and *phul:* the last has earned for the place a certain reputation, but the metal is too expensive for the general public. The place contains a police station, a post and telegraph office and a cattle-pound; while near the Raja's house is a new dispensary, recently erected at his expense and named the Victoria Memorial Hospital. In the north of the town is a tank filled with water from the Banri, and by this are two temples known as Shamdham and Ramdham, standing in a sacred grove of trees brought by Rai Isri Partab from Muttra.

Between Padrauna and Chhaoni are the encamping-ground and a fine middle vernacular school, built by the Raja but managed by the district board. The tahsil stands in Chhaoni, which derives its name from the fact that it was once a cantonment for the troops of the Nawab Wazir. The buildings are old, cramped and inferior, but have recently been improved by the addition of a new record-room and quarters for the tahsildar and naib-tahsildar. In the same quarter is the office of the sub-registrar.

The combined population of the town rose from 5,092 in 1872 to 8,939 in 1881, but has since declined, dropping to 7,240 in 1891, while at the last census it was 7,031, of whom 2,111 were Musalmans: that of Padrauna proper was 4,541. The three sites have been administered as a single town under Act XX of 1856 since 1871. They contained 1,421 houses in 1908, of which 350 were assessed, the income from the house-tax being Rs. 1,450, so that the average incidence of taxation was Rs. 4-2-3 per assessed house and Re. 0-3-3 per head of population. The total receipts for 1907-08 were Rs. 1,752 and the expenditure Rs. 1,460, devoted mainly to the upkeep of the town police, the maintenance of a conservancy staff and to minor improvements.

Three miles from Padrauna, on the road to Tiwaripatti, stands the insignificant village of Sidhua, from which apparently the pargana of Sidhua Jobna in part derives its name.

PADRAUNA *Tahsil.*

This tahsil comprises the eastern portion of the district and is a tract of irregular shape, bearing a rough resemblance to a triangle with its base resting on the Saran district of Bengal to the south. To the west lie the tahsils of Maharajganj and Hata, the boundary in the case of the former being the Little Gandak. To the north and east is the Champaran district of Bengal, separated for some distance in the north and south-east by the Great Gandak, while elsewhere the boundary consists as a rule of an old channel of that river. The tahsil is conterminous with the Sidhua Jobna pargana, and comprises the 22 tappas of Batsara, Naugawan, Papaur, Dandupur, Bansi Chirgora, Bargaon Chaura, Sandi, Pakri Gangrani, Parwarpar, Mainpur, Bhalwa, Rampur Rogha, Rampur Dhab, Pirthipur, Dhuria Bijaipur, Sapahi Kuchia, Jhankaul, Khan, Malsil Saraini, Bhatahi Badraon, Haveli and Bank Jogni. The total area is 593,983 acres or 928·09 square miles, but this is liable to vary somewhat, since the eastern boundary is subject to fluvial action on the part of the Great Gandak. There are 63 alluvial *mahals* along its banks, ten of which are settled quinquennially under the ordinary rules, 25 are held on unconditional long-term agreements, and 28 are situated in unexpired jungle grants.

As a whole the tract is a fertile plain with a gentle slope in a south-easterly direction, the level surface being diversified only by the river valleys and a few sandy ridges, one of which, between Kasia and Padrauna, rises to a height of 386 feet above the sea and is the greatest natural eminence in the district. In addition to the Great and Little Gandak there are several other streams. In the north the Banri takes its rise, flowing past Padrauna and then joining the Bansi, an old channel of the Gandak, which falls into that river near Tiwaripatti; while the

Jharai, rising on the eastern border, takes a southerly course and flows past Tamkuhi into Saran. In the west the chief stream is the Khanua, which flows to the west of Kasia and thence into Bengal, subsequently entering pargana Salempur Majhauli and joining the Little Gandak. It is fed by several minor streams such as the Ghaghi and Sonda, to which reference has already been made in Chapter I. A noteworthy peculiarity of the lesser rivers in this tahsil is that they generally flow along ridges and spill into each other. Thus the Little Gandak takes the overflow from the Great Gandak and itself discharges its surplus water into the Khanua, of which it practically forms its source. So too the Bansi and Jharai, as well as others, derive most of their volume from the spill water of the Great Gandak. Throughout the tract small lakes and *jhils* are to be found, but there are no great sheets of water excepting perhaps the Ramabhar Tal near Kasia. Though formerly a large area was covered with forest the whole of this has long disappeared, mainly as the result of the system of jungle grants introduced in the first half of the last century. There are, however, many extensive tracts of bush and scrub jungle in the north, and in places along the Gandak wide stretches of grassy waste are to be found. The area of cultivation in the valley of that river, known locally as the *dhab*, is small, for this part of the tahsil is always liable to damage from the sudden and violent floods to which the stream is periodically subject.

The prevailing and characteristic soil is *bhat*, which occupied 73·71 per cent. of the area assessed at the last settlement. Mention has already been made in Chapter II of the three subdivisions of this soil, the *bhat* proper or *chaur* occupying 59·47, the heavier *chauriar* or *chaunr* of the west 10·9, and the low *dhusi* on the eastern border 3·34 per cent. The remainder is either *bangar* or *kachhar*, the latter amounting to 2·8 per cent. in all and confined to small patches in the extreme north and south-east corner. The *bangar* comprises two wedge-shaped tracts running up into the *bhat* from the Saran border, with their respective points near Kasia and Padrauna. In this the prevailing soil is *doras* or loam, constituting 16·3 per cent., while *matiar* or clay makes up 6·6 and the sandy *balua* only

·66 per cent., the last being less common than in any other part of the district. The peculiar nature of the *bhat*, combined with the high water level, rarely more than ten feet below the surface and the dampness of the climate, renders the tahsil very unhealthy. The people as a rule are of poor physique, and the water of the *bhat* tract is said to be responsible for the unusual prevalauce of goitre, while for the same reason the number of deaf-mutes is remarkably large.

The cultivated area in 1853 was 266,786 acres, and has since exhibited a remarkable increase, rising to 347,968 in 1865 and to 411,960 at the last settlement. Subsequent progress has been less rapid, as there is now but little culturable land of any value left untilled. During the past five years the average was 430,894 acres or 72·5 per cent. of the whole, and on occasions this has been largely exceeded. The barren area averages 43,437 acres, but of this 18,586 are covered with water, while 19,292 are occupied by railways, roads, village sites and the like, leaving no more than 5,559 acres actually unfit for tillage, such land being generally barren sand on the banks of the Great Gandak. The so-called culturable area is 119,652 acres including 25,500 acres of current fallow and 11,151 acres under groves, the latter being equivalent to 1·8 per cent. of the total area—a decidedly low proportion. This leaves 56,994 acres of old fallow and 26,007 acres of culturable waste, in either case of very little value, since the bulk of such land is situated in the precarious tract along the Great Gandak and includes the *khair* jungles, in the north of the tahsil, and the expanses of waste covered with grass or scrub along the Little Gandak and elsewhere. Double-cropping is very extensively practised, the average area so treated being 173,290 acres or 40 per cent. of the net cultivation. The amount of irrigated land, on the other hand, is extremely small, averaging only 52,887 acres or just over 12 per cent. of the area under tillage. The *bhat* is so retentive of moisture as to render irrigation unnecessary or actually harmful: even sugarcane is habitually grown without artificial watering, and the only crops regularly irrigated are poppy and garden produce, which are mainly confined to the neighbourhood of the village sites. For this reason it is but natural to find that wells supply a greater area than the other sources of irrigation taken together.

Of the two main harvests the *kharif* is by far the more important, averaging 371,688 acres as against 236,585 sown for the *rabi.** The chief staple is rice, which occupies over 45 per cent. of the area under autumn crops. A little more than half of this consists of late rice, one variety of which seems almost peculiar to this district, though it is also produced in the Saran district. It is called *sengar* or *chenawe*, and is grown in *jhils* or ponds where the depth of water is too great in the rains for the ordinary varieties, for this *chenawe* is said always to keep pace with the most rapid rise of the water level and is cut from boats in November, if the floods have not subsided by this time. Another peculiar variety is an early rice sown before the rains break, especially in the *bhat* lands. Next in order comes maize, the tahsil producing more than half the total amount grown in the district, since the crop thrives particularly well in the higher *bhat* tracts to the south and east. An almost equal area is under *kodon*, while small millets, such as *mandua*, *tangan*, *sanwan* and *kakun*, are fairly common. The autumn pulses, however, are but little grown and even *arhar*, whether alone or as a mixed crop, is remarkable for its rarity. Sugarcane is a very valuable and important product, occupying on an average nearly 40,000 acres, which is a much higher figure than in any other tahsil. Indigo is now confined to the vicinity of the Babhnauli concern and its outworks, and still averages about 7,000 acres, while the only remaining crops worthy of notice are hemp and garden produce. In the *rabi* harvest wheat and barley, either sown alone or in the mixture known as *gujai*, take up more than 55 per cent. of the total area. Next come peas and *masur*, the latter being remarkably popular in this tahsil, where it usually takes the place of gram. Oilseeds are less common in Padrauna than in most parts of the district, with the exception of the castor-oil plant which is widely grown: but there is a very large area under garden crops consisting mainly in vegetables, for poppy has never made much headway and tobacco is almost unknown, though the tahsil is celebrated for its turmeric, capsicums,

* Appendix, table VI.

coriander, pepper and other condiments. A considerable area is taken up by miscellaneous crops, such as the vetches known as *kesari* and *lathri*, oats, mainly grown near the indigo factories, and *boro* or hot-weather rice.

Owing to the extensive areas held by large proprietors it is but natural to find a smaller extent of owner's cultivation than in any other tahsil. In 1907-08 the total area included in holdings was 465,860 acres, and of this no more than 16·21 per cent. was *sir* or *khudkasht*. The occupancy area has declined of late but is still considerable, amounting to 36·01 per cent., while 45·89 is held by tenants-at-will, ·36 by ex-proprietors and 1·53 per cent., principally the *jagirs* of *goraits*, is rent-free. Save for a small extent of precarious land rents are paid in cash and average Rs. 3·34 per acre for occupancy tenants and Rs. 3·09 for others, the former being usually in possession of the best soils. Sub-tenants cultivate 58,115 acres or 12·5 per cent. of the holdings, and pay an average rate of Rs. 4·11. Though the rents are relatively high for this district it is probable that concealment is extensively practised; but at all events there has been a very considerable rise since the settlement, when the corrected rent-rate for the whole area was only Rs. 2·56, even this representing an increase of 36·94 per cent. since 1865. The revenue demand at each succeeding settlement, together with the present amount and its incidence, will be found in the appendix.*

The tahsil contains 1,364 villages and these are divided into 2,135 *mahals*, of which 465 are *zamindari*, 1,467 *pattidari*, in most cases of the imperfect variety, and 203 are *bhaiyachara*, a tenure which in this district is practically confined to this tahsil. Under-proprietary rights are very numerous. At the settlement 235 *birtias* were recorded, in addition to 7,926 *arazidars* distributed among 1,925 *arazi* plots. The largest proprietors are the Rajas of Padrauna and Tamkuhi, of whom the former owns 364 villages, all in this tahsil, assessed at Rs. 86,365, while the latter holds 211 villages in Padrauna with a revenue demand of Rs. 80,433. The Raja of Salemgarh holds 63 villages, paying Rs. 22,001, and Babu Dalip Narayan Singh of Kundwa is the owner of 43 villages assessed at Rs. 19,559. Besides these the

* Appendix, tables IX and X.

Babus of Madhopur have a fine estate aggregating 105 villages, with a total assessment of Rs. 19,559, and Babu Thakur Rai, the Bhuinhar proprietor of Lachhmipur, has 30 villages paying Rs. 4,460 as revenue.

The population of pargana Sidhua Jobna was 383,535 in 1853, rising to 405,843 in 1865 and to 417,641 in 1872, while in 1881 it was 559,838 and ten years later it was 605,551. As in most other parts of the district a decline then set in, with the result that in 1901 the number of inhabitants was 595,706, of whom 299,914 were females, the average density being 641 to the square mile. Classified by religions there were 507,918 Hindus, 87,770 Musalmans, 14 Christians and four Buddhists. Of the various Hindu castes Ahirs take the first place with 62,762, followed by Chamars with 53,120, Brahmans with 51,493, Koeris with 30,488, Kurmis with 24,991 and Rajputs with 20,489. The last belong to many different clans, the strongest being Bisens, Chandels, Panwars, Sikarwars, Jadubansis and Bais. Next follow Banias with 17,697, principally Kandus, Kasaundhans, Gahois and Rauniars. Other castes with more than 10,000 members apiece are Lunias, Telis, Gonds, Sainthwars, who should properly be included with Kurmis, Lohars, Pasis and Barhais, while twelve other castes occur with more than 5,000 representatives. Among the Musalmans, who are far stronger here than in any other part of the district, the Julahas come first with 31,388, and of the rest Sheikhs alone are found in any strength, though Pathans, Behnas, Faqirs, Gaddis and Hajjams number from three to five thousand in each case.

The tahsil is essentially agricultural, and more than 81 per cent. of the population were found to be engaged directly or indirectly in cultivation. The manufactures, in addition to sugar and indigo, comprise the brass and metal-ware of Padrauna, a little hemp-matting and a coarse cloth called *kokti* woven from cotton grown locally. While the tahsil contains 1,365 *mauzas* and 4,838 inhabited sites, the only town deserving the name is Padrauna itself. There are many places with large populations, such as Amwa Khas and Bansgawan ; but these are mere collections of scattered hamlets, while other villages of the same nature are Kusmaha, Madar, Pipra-ghat,

Kundwa, Dhonipatti, Rampur Barhan and Kalan Bharpurwa, each of these having more than 3,000 inhabitants. Others with a population exceeding 2,500 are Semra Haveli, Taria Sujan, Tikwa Tar and Barwa Ratanpur, though none is of any importance.

Means of communication are still backward. Through the extreme north of the tahsil runs the recently constructed branch railway from Gorakhpur to Bagaha, with stations at Khada and Chhittauni, the latter being a flag station in the village of Bulahwa. For the remainder the nearest accessible points on the railway are Captainganj on the west and Deoria in the south; but a great improvement will result with the completion of the projected line from Captainganj through Ramkola, Padrauna and Tiwaripatti to Thawe in the Saran district The only metalled road is a small portion of that from Kasia to Deoria, while many of the unmetalled roads are serviceable for cart traffic only in dry weather. It is proposed to metal the road from Gorakhpur to Kasia, but this will affect merely a small tract. At Kasia this road bifurcates, one branch running through Sapaha and Babhnauli to Pipra-ghat on the Great Gandak, while the other leads south-east through Qazipur to Chapra. Another important road is that from Captainganj to Padrauna and Bansi-ghat, while from Padrauna roads run northwards to Siswa Bazar, crossing that from Captainganj to Bagaha; southwards to Kasia and south-eastwards to join the Chapra road on the Saran border, while a fourth leads to Tiwaripatti and Tamkuhi, thence continuing to join the Chapra road at the same point. Besides these a number of roads are maintained by the Tamkuhi estate and the Babhnauli concern for their own purposes, but are open to the public. Throughout its course the Great Gandak is navigable for large vessels, though in places progress is difficult or even dangerous. During the rains too the Little Gandak is practicable as far as Ragarganj, and a small volume of traffic is still to be seen on this stream. There are military encamping-grounds within the tahsil at Ramkola, Padrauna, Kasia, Qazipur and Tamkuhi. An inspection house is maintained at Kasia, an opium bungalow at Patherwa near Qazipur, and a canal bungalow belonging to the Public Works department of

Bengal at Siswa, the headworks of the Saran canal, in the extreme south-east corner; while a new inspection house is to be built at Padrauna.

The tahsil forms a subdivision in charge of a joint or assistant magistrate stationed throughout the year at Kasia. At the present time there are three honorary magistrates with third class powers, the Raja of Padrauna exercising jurisdiction in the police circle of that name, Babu Dalip Narayan Singh of Kundwa for the Kasia and Qazipur circles, and the Raja of Salemgarh for Taria Sujan and Bishanpura. The tahsildar has his headquarters at Padrauna, where the sub-registrar also resides. For police purposes there are six stations within the subdivision, at Kasia, Padrauna, Ramkola, Bishunpura, Qazipur and Taria Sujan. Their circles do not, however, comprise the whole area, for parts belong to those of Kothibhar, Biraicha and Tarkulwa. When first constituted in 1804 the tahsil embraced the parganas of Sidhua Jobna and Shahjahanpur, the latter remaining an integral part of the subdivision till the constitution of the new tahsil of Hata in 1871.

In the earliest times this region was undoubtedly a centre of Buddhist worship and civilization, as is abundantly proved by the remains at Kasia and at Padrauna. If, as is highly probable, the Kasia ruins are to be identified with those visited by the Chinese pilgrims in the fifth and seventh century, this tract contained one of the most venerated places of pilgrimage known to the Buddhist faith. With the decline of that religion the country seems to have relapsed into jungle, and even in the days of Huien Tsang it was covered with forest and infested by wild beasts and robbers. The name of the pargana is traditionally derived from the *siddhe*, or holy men, who came hither from the south to find in the forests a suitable retreat for the purposes of devotion and contemplation, while there exists a village named Sidhua in tappa Bargaon Chaura in which the shrine of Sidhua Baba is still held in veneration, the people asserting that the pargana takes its name from him. Possibly there was actually an ascetic named Sidhua Jobna, though more probably the name may be considered as a combination, since the Haveli tappa, which ought to contain the capital, lies in the extreme south-east corner.

The later history of the pargana is little less speculative. During the fifteenth century it would appear that the country was seized by one Madan Singh, who perhaps held Saran and Champaran. He was, it is said, a feudatory of the Pathan rulers of Bengal, but not even the name of his clan is known. When Akbar finally conquered Bengal, the descendants of Madan Singh were ejected by the Bisens of Majhauli, who appear to have held sway over the whole country, though it is doubtful whether Sidhua Jobna was actually incorporated in Dewapara, the old name of Salempur Majhauli, or it belonged to the *sarkar* of Saran. More probably the latter was the case, for it seems that the pargana was not added to Gorakhpur till 1730 or thereabouts. Not long after its acquisition the Bisen Raja made a grant of land in the vicinity of Padrauna to Bhopal Rai, the Kurmi ancestor of the Raja of Padrauna. This family did not, however, rise to prominence till the middle of the 18th century, when the Banjaras had commenced their aggressive policy in the north. The Bisens then abandoned their possessions in those parts, with the result that the smaller *zamindars* were compelled in self-defence to place themselves under the protection of the Rais of Padrauna, who thus became lords of a vast estate. About the same time too Raja Fateh Sahi established himself in tappa Bank Jogni and laid the foundations of the Tamkuhi *raj*. At the cession these two great *taluqas* comprised the greater part of the area, and until 1865 they were assessed to revenue separately from the rest of the pargana.

PAIKAULI, *Pargana* SALEMPUR-MAJHAULI, *Tahsil* DEORIA.

A large village of tappa Surauli, standing in 26° 26′ N. and 83° 44′ E., some two miles to the east of the road from Deoria to Rudarpur and seven miles south-west from the tahsil headquarters. The place contained in 1901 a population of 2,049 persons, principally Chaubaria Rajputs, who are the owners of the village. They are descendants of colonists from Saran, who were settled here by the Raja of Majhauli to garrison the large fort in the adjoining village of Surauli and to guard the marches of the principality. The area of the village is 1,444 acres and the revenue demand is Rs. 2,300. Markets are held here weekly, and an aided school has recently been opened.

In Paikauli is a large Thakurdwara, close to which are a tank and a celebrated *math* or monastery of Vaishnava Bairagis, founded about 80 years ago. There are branch establishments at Ajodhya, Barhalganj and Baikunthpur, while the Mahant, who is generally known as the Pauhari Ji and is greatly respected, spends his time in travelling from place to place in this and the adjoining districts, presiding over several fairs, notably those at Barhalganj, Baikunthpur and Sohnag in this district, at Sarkarpur in Saran and the Dadri fair at Ballia. From before the Mutiny till 1879 the Mahant was Siya Ram Das, and he was succeeded by Ajodhya Prasad Tiwari of Mahuain in the Azamgarh district. The latter retired in 1904, settling at Ajodhya, and his place was taken by Mani Ram Das of Gaunah in tappa Nagwan Tilkar of pargana Silhat. The monastery is supported by the offerings of worshippers, and the present Mahant has departed from the rule of his predecessors by accepting gifts of landed property.

PAINA, *Pargana* SALEMPUR-MAJHAULI, *Tahsil* DEORIA.

This remarkably large village belongs to tappa Raipur and stands on the north bank of the Ghagra, in 26°15′N. and 83° 47′E., between the river and the unmetalled road from Lar to Barhaj and Barhalganj, at a distance of four miles east from Barhaj and 44 miles from the district headquarters. The name Paina means an ox-goad, and the story goes that a devotee came here and was granted a stick's length of land; he lived for many years on this narrow space, and after his death a shrine was erected, round which a village sprang up. The place was formerly owned by Bisens, who still form the principal inhabitants together with Ahirs and Mallahs; but during the Mutiny they plundered and obstructed a Government bullock train, with the result that Mr. Bird visited the spot with a local levy and occupied the village, which was afterwards confiscated and bestowed on the Raja of Majhauli. The Bisens of Paina are held in low esteem by the neighbouring Rajputs, for the reason, it is said, that some of their women were carried off by the punitive force. The village possesses a school but nothing else of importance, deserving notice only for its size: the area being 5,281 acres, though the cultivated land is very limited and the revenue demand is no more than Rs. 836. The population rose from 5,331 in 1872 to 6,642 in 1881, but has since declined, being 5,423 in 1891, while ten years later it was 5,029 of whom 393 were Musalmans.

PAISIA, *Pargana* BINAYAKPUR, *Tahsil* MAHARAJGANJ.

An insignificant village of tappa Mirchwar, lying in 27° 20′N. and 83°23′E. on the banks of the Ghunghi, the overflow from which forms a large marsh known as the Ainjar Tal. It is some 40 miles due north from Gorakhpur, but is very difficult of access, being far from any recognised road, while in the rains all the surrounding country is under water. The place had a population of 434 at the last census, but is important only as giving its name to a police station, though this is actually situated in Naikot, an adjacent village to the south. The latter also contains a post-office, a cattle-pound and a lower primary school, while in Paisia a market is held weekly. The accessibility of the place will be much improved by the construction of the projected road from Bridgmanganj to Nautanwau, which will give direct communication between the *thana* and the railway.

PANERA, *Pargana* HAVELI, *Tahsil* MAHARAJGANJ.

The small village of Panera belongs to tappa Banki, and stands in 26°59′N. and 83°28′E., on the north side of the unmetalled road from Captainganj to Campierganj and Karmaini-ghat, at a distance of 16 miles from Captainganj and 24 miles north from Gorakhpur. It is noticeable as possessing a police station, as well as a cattle-pound and a branch post-office, while a small market is held weekly. The village stands on the edge of the forest, and is owned and cultivated by Ahirs; the area is 1,225 acres, but only a small portion of this is cultivated, and the revenue demand is Rs. 430. The population at the last census numbered 954 persons.

PIPRAICH, *Pargana* Haveli, *Tahsil* Gorakhpur.

This small town belongs to tappa Patra, and stands in 26° 49′N. and 83°32′E., at a distance of some 13 miles north-east from Gorakhpur on the road to Captainganj. Branch roads run hence to Barhi on the south, to Hata on the east and to Nichlaul on the north, while the importance of the place is likely to increase with the construction of the branch line from Gorakhpur to Captainganj and Bagaha, on which there is a station close to the Hata road. For a long time the market has been of some celebrity as a centre of the sugar industry for this part of the pargana; there are now 16 refineries, and a fair local trade is carried on in grain, cloth and metal vessels. In the adjacent village of Sidhawa on the north-east is another bazar, which has long been in competition with Pipraich. The town contains a police station, a post-office, a cattle-pound and an upper primary school, while by the side of the main road is a good encamping-ground. The *mauza* of Pipraich is 656 acres in extent and forms part of the revenue-free property of the Mian Sahib of Gorakhpur.

The population of the town numbered 2,208 persons in 1872, and thus rose to 2,932 in 1881 and to 3,538 ten years later, while in 1901 it was 3,265, including 393 Musalmans. The place has been administered under Act XX of 1856 since 1871, and in 1908 contained 759 houses, of which 244 were assessed; the income from the house-tax for that and the two preceding years averaged Rs. 700, which gives an incidence of Rs. 2-13-11 per assessed house and Re. 0-3-5 per head of population. The average expenditure for the same period was Rs. 570, devoted mainly to the upkeep of the local police, the maintenance of a conservancy staff and to minor improvements.

QAZIPUR, *Pargana* Sidhua Jobna, *Tahsil* Padrauna.

An insignificant village of tappa Jhankaul in the south of the pargana, situated in 26°41′N. and 84°4′E., at a distance of 47 miles east from Gorakhpur and 16 miles south-south-east from Padrauna, at the crossing of the roads from Rampur to Tamkuhi and from Kasia to Chapra. It deserves mention as possessing a police station, sometimes known as Fazilnagar or Fazla, from the name of an adjoining village. Close to the station is a post-office and a cattle-pound, while markets are held twice a week near the junction of the roads. The population at the last census amounted to no more than 328 persons, while the area of the village is only 199 acres with a revenue demand of Rs. 234.

RAMKOLA, *Pargana* SIDHUA JOBNA, *Tahsil* PADRAUNA.

This large agricultural village of tappa Papaur lies in 26° 54′ N. and 83° 50′ E., on the left bank of the Banri, which is here crossed by the road from Captainganj to Padrauna, at a distance of ten miles west from the latter and 33 miles from Gorakhpur. The population at the last census numbered 2,324 persons, the majority being Chamars, though the principal inhabitants are the Rajput owners of the village, which has an area of 756 acres and is assessed at Rs. 1,641. By the roadside stand a police station, a cattle-pound and a post-office, while adjoining the *thana* is an encamping-ground. In the village itself are an upper primary school and a small bazar where markets are held weekly.

RAMPUR KARKHANA, *Pargana* SHAHJAHANPUR, *Tahsil* HATA.

Rampur Khanpur or Rampur Karkhana, as it is more usually called, is a rising town of tappa Patna, standing in 26° 34′N. and 83°49′E., at a distance of five miles from Deoria, near the metalled road from that place to Kasia, and 38 miles from Gorakhpur. A short metalled branch connects the town with the main road, which thus affords access to the railway station of Deoria. The population numbered 2,308 persons in 1872, and has since increased to 4,056 in 1881 and 4,443 ten years later, while in 1901 it was 4,696, of whom 754 were Musalmans. The growth and the importance of the place are due to the sugar industry, of which it is one of the main centres in the district, for at the present time there are no less than 50 factories in the town and the trade is in a thriving condition. Rampur possesses a branch post-office and a lower primary school, while well-attended markets are held twice a week. The area of the town lands is 442 acres, and the revenue demand is Rs. 468.

In 1874 the town was brought under the operations of Act XX of 1856. It now contains 836 houses, of which 189 were assessed to taxation in 1908. The income from the house-tax and Rs. 1,149, which gave an incidence of Rs. 6-1-3 per assessed house and Re. 0-2-10 per head of population. The former is a remarkably high figure, and is due to the special character of the place, the principal assessees being a small number of well-to-do persons. The total income for the year was Rs. 1,327 and the expenditure Rs. 1,204, devoted to the maintenance of watch and ward, the upkeep of the conservancy staff and local improvements.

RIGAULI, *Pargana* HAVELI, *Tahsil* MAHARAJGANJ.

A village in the tappa of the same name, standing in 27° 1′N. and 83°13′E., at a distance of some 20 miles north-west from Gorakhpur and three miles west of the Campierganj railway station. The place is built on the banks of the Dhamela, close to its junction with the Rapti and almost opposite the ferry of Karmaini-ghat, on which three roads converge from Gorakhpur, Captainganj and Bridgmanganj. As this ferry is one of the most important crossings on the Rapti the place was long ago selected as the site of a police station, which is still in existence. Rigauli also contains a post-office, a cattle-pound and an upper primary school: a market of some local importance is held here once a week. The area of the village is 583 acres and the revenue Rs. 590, while the population at the last census numbered 1,232 persons, including many Julahas and a colony of Manihars, who carry on the manufacture of glass bangles.

RUDARPUR, *Pargana* SILHAT, *Tahsil* HATA.

Rudarpur is a town of considerable size standing in tappa Nagwan Tikar, in 26°26′N. and 83°37′E., on the unmetalled road from Gorakhpur to Barhaj, at a distance of 27 miles from the former. This road is here joined by two others, leading from Deoria on the north-east and from Dhara near Hata on the north. Close to the town on the west flows the Majhna or Bathua river, joined a short distance to the south by the Karna. The former is navigable during the rains for small boats, but is little used, for though possessing a large population Rudarpur is not a place of any commercial importance, and lies at some distance from the main trade routes of the district. The inhabitants are for the most part low caste Hindus, who keep great numbers of cattle, and round about the town are considerable open spaces used for grazing purposes. The population was 7,565 in 1865, but dropped to 6,538 in 1872, and though it afterwards rose to 9,843 in 1881, it again fell to 9,190 ten years later, while at the last census the place contained 8,860 inhabitants, of whom 911 were Musalmans. The town possesses a police station, a post-office, a dispensary, a cattle-pound and an upper primary school. The principal place of business is the Gola bazar or the grain market on the banks of the Majhna, and here markets are held twice a week.

The town lands have an area of 1,334 acres and are assessed at Rs. 2,092. The inhabited portion has been administered under Act XX of 1856 since 1867. In 1908 it contained 1,554 houses, of which 441 were assessed, the income from the house-tax being Rs. 1,250, which gives an incidence of Rs. 2-13-4 per assessed house and Re. 0-2-3 per head of population. The total income for the year was Rs. 1,412, while the expenditure was Rs. 1,253, devoted mainly to police and conservancy. The town itself occupies a fairly raised and well drained site, but during the rains a good deal of water accumulates in the neighbourhood, and the place has long had a bad reputation for dirtiness. During the monsoon the flooded state of the country renders the roads almost impassable, and it is largely on this account that commerce has shown so little development.

The chief interest of Rudarpur lies in its history and archæological remains.* The place has been tentatively identified with the Hansakshetra mentioned by the Chinese pilgrims, while local tradition states that in the beginning of the sixth century a Rajput named Vasishta Singh came hither from Ajodhya and founded a stronghold called New Kashi, which was afterwards seized by the Bhars. Subsequently the place was taken by the Sarnets of Satasi, and the town derived its present name from Raja Rudar Singh, who built a fort on the old site. The chief antiquity of the place is the great Hindu stronghold of Sahankot

* C. A. S. R. XVIII, 41, and XXII, 9.

or Nathnagar, some three-quarters of a mile to the north of the town. In outline it is an irregular quadrangle, the sides varying in length from 2,000 to 2,500 feet, while to the south is an outer and lower enclosure, measuring 2,500 feet from north to south and 3,700 from east to west, and now for the most part under cultivation. The fort itself is surrounded by immense ramparts varying in height from 15 to 25 feet; but they have been greatly damaged by the removal of brick and stone for building purposes, and the place, which contains numerous mounds of ruins, is now protected under the Ancient Monuments Preservation Act. Near the eastern side of the fort is an old temple of Dudhnath, surrounded by eight modern shrines; but it contains little of interest beyond a colossal statue of Vishnu and a small image of the last Jain *tirthankara*, though the temple probably marks the site of a much older building. The neighbourhood is full of mounds and ruins, but it has never been systematically explored. There can be no doubt that an ancient city once existed on this spot, since the ruins cover an area about two miles long and nearly two miles wide from east to west.

From the days of Raja Rudar Singh till the Mutiny Rudarpur was the headquarter of the Satasi family. The extensive palace of the last Raja adjoined the Sahankot, but is now in ruins. His property was confiscated and the title expired, but his daughter-in-law was generally known as the Rani of Satasi till her death in Benares in 1879. She held a small estate, which had been mortgaged to her father by the Raja, but even this has passed out of the family, the greater part having been bequeathed for religious and charitable purposes.

RUDRAPUR, *Pargana* UNAULA, *Tahsil* BANSGAON.

This small village, usually spelled Rudrapur for the sake of distinction, is situated in the Haveli tappa of Unaula, in 26°39′N. and 83°15′E., on the unmetalled road from Gorakhpur to Sikriganj, at a distance of eleven miles south-west from the district headquarters. The road is here joined by two others, one leading from Kauriram and Bansgaon, and the other from Gola and Gopalpur. The place contained 674 inhabitants at the last census, while the area of the *mauza* is but 328 acres and the revenue demand Rs. 304. It is noteworthy solely as possessing a police station, close to which are a cattle-pound and a post-office, but has no other claim to attention.

SAHJANWA, *Pargana* HASANPUR MAGHAR, *Tahsil* GORAKHPUR.

Sahjanwa itself is a small village of tappa Gahasand, situated in 26°45′N. and 83°13′E., at a distance of ten miles west from Gorakhpur. It is quite unimportant, being a purely agricultural place with a population of 782 at the last census, with an area of 238 acres and a revenue of Rs. 351. But Sahjanwa gives its name to a police station, a pound and an inspection bungalow standing in the adjoining village of Pipra, on the metalled road from Gorakhpur to Basti. Near the *thana* is a large grove and a military encamping-ground, and from the latter a short metalled road runs northwards to the Sahjanwa railway station on the main line from Gorakhpur to Basti and Gonda. The station stands in the village of Luchui, which contains a post-office and is the scene of a weekly market of some importance, since it serves as a depôt for the grain trade of a considerable tract of wheat-growing country.

SALEMPUR-MAJHAULI, *Pargana* SALEMPUR-MAJHAULI, *Tahsil* DEORIA.

The two contiguous towns of Majhauli and Salempur belong to tappa Haveli, and stand respectively on the east or left and the right or west bank of the Little Gandak at a distance of some 53 miles south-east from Gorakhpur and 19 miles from the tahsil headquarters. Majhauli is situated in 26°18′N. and 83°58′E., while Salempur is about a mile to the west, close to the road from Gorakhpur to Chapra. The two are connected by a metalled road, which leads to Bhatpar station on the main line, the southern continuation of this road from Salempur to Bhagalpur on the Ghagra being unmetalled. Close to Salempur is a station on the railway from Bhatni to Benares, and from it a branch goes westwards to Barhaj.

The foundation of Majhauli is traditionally ascribed to Mayur, the ancestor of the Bisens, whose first residence is said to have been at Kundilpur, two miles to the south-east. His descendants have since resided here, and the Raja now lives in a large brick castle of recent construction, overlooking the river. With regard to Salempur the popular accounts vary. One story states that a grant of land was given to Sheikh Salim Chishti, the famous saint of Fatehpur Sikri, by Akbar's officer Fidai Khan during his expedition into this district, and that the town which sprang up on this grant was called Salempur in his honour. More probable is the tradition that the place was selected as a residence by the pervert Raja Bodh Mal, who assumed the name of Islam or Salim Khan, though his date is somewhat uncertain. His tomb is a poor structure of brick standing on the river bank between the two towns, and its appearance suggests that it belongs to the eighteenth century.

At the present time Salempur and Majhauli practically form a single town, the former being the Musalman and the latter the Hindu quarter. The combined population rose from 4,850 in 1872 to 5,599 in 1881 and to 6,659 ten years later; but by 1901 the total had fallen to 6,051, of whom 1,252 were Musalmans. Salempur is a very small *mauza*, with an area of 128 acres and a revenue demand of Rs. 140; while Majhauli is 2,606 acres in extent and is assessed at Rs. 3,800. The place is of little commercial importance and has declined of late, the markets held twice a week being of purely local significance. The combined towns were administered under Act XX of 1856 from 1875 till 1906, when the measure was withdrawn. In the early days of British rule Salempur was the headquarters of a tahsil and a munsif held his court here; and it has recently been proposed to re-establish the tahsil in this town, as being more central than Deoria. Salempur at present contains a police station, a post-office, a cattle-pound, two mosques, one of which was built in 1654, a lower primary school and an aided school for girls. Majhauli possesses a combined post and telegraph office, a middle vernacular school, an aided school for girls and three temples.

SALEMPUR-MAJHAULI *Pargana* : *vide* DEORIA *Tahsil.*

SANGRAMPUR, *Pargana* UNAULA, *Tahsil* BANSGAON.

This small but compact town stands in tappa Haveli on the north side of the unmetalled road from Rudrapur to Bansgaon and Kauriram, in 26°38′N. and 83°18′E., at a distance of about six miles north-west from the tahsil headquarters and fourteen miles from Gorakhpur. The place is also known as Unwal, and as it has always been the headquarters of the Sarnet Rajas of Unaula, it is quite possible that it originally gave its name to the pargana, of which it has long been the principal town, although there is a small village actually called Unaula or Anaula, to which reference will be made later. Apart from the Raja's house—a large brick structure in the *qasba*—Sangrampur possesses nothing of interest save a lower primary school. The town was for some years administered under Act XX of 1856; but the measure was withdrawn long ago, since the place has no trade and is really nothing more than a large agricultural village. It has an area of 1,545 acres and is owned by the Raja, who pays a revenue of Rs. 1,085. The population was 2,735 in 1872 and has since increased, for at the last census the town contained as many as 4,095 inhabitants.

SEMRA, *Pargana* HAVELI, *Tahsil* MAHARAJGANJ.

The village of Semra lies in the east of tappa Lehra, in 27° 10′N. and 83′°23′E., between the road from Bridgmanganj to Nichlaul on the north and that from Pharenda to Maharajganj on the south, at a distance of six miles north-east from Pharenda station and some 36 miles from Gorakhpur. The place contains a police station, a post-office and a cattle-pound, but the village itself is quite unimportant. It lies close to the forest along the Rohin, and is inhabited mainly by Ahirs. The total area of the village is 648 acres, assessed at Rs. 620 and the population at the last census amounted to 706 persons.

SHAHJAHANPUR, *Pargana* SHAHJAHANPUR, *Tahsil* HATA.

The village of Shahjahanpur is situated in tappa Nagwan, on the right or west bank of the Little Gandak, in 26°40′N. and 83°52′E., about six miles south-west from Kasia and eight miles south-east from Hata, the metalled road from Kasia to Deoria being some three miles to the east. The name is said to be derived from the Emperor Shahjahan, but nothing is known of its history, and it is difficult to understand how so obscure a village came to be selected as the capital of a pargana, unless the choice was due to its position on the banks of a navigable river. The population at the last census numbered only 466 persons, while the area of the village is 514 acres, assessed at Rs. 489.

SHAHJAHANPUR *Pargana, Tahsil* HATA.

This pargana comprises a small and compact block of country in the east of the tahsil, lying between Silhat on the west and Sidhua Jobna on the east, while to the north is Haveli and to the south Salempur-Majhauli. It comprises the nine tappas of Majhwa, Tarkulwa, Bhainsa Dabar, Patna, Bhitni, Bichhauli, Chakdeia, Nagwan and Pariapar, the total area being 87,572 acres or 136·83 square miles.

The pargana contains 258 villages and 594 inhabited sites. The chief town is Rampur Karkhana in the extreme south, while other places worthy of note are Hata, Tarkulwa and Hetimpur. The total population was 72,233 in 1853, and this rose to 78,507 in 1865, to 81,562 in 1872 and to 95,911 in 1881, while ten years later it was 113,361. During the next decade it remained stationary, the number of inhabitants at the census of 1901 being 113,331, which gave an average density of 828 persons to the square mile.

Very little is known of the history of this tract. According to tradition it was held by the Bhars and, at the beginning of the 15th century, was seized by a Rajput adventurer named Madan Singh, who appears to have gained possession of all Sidhua Jobna and to have been a tributary of the Pathan Sultans of Bengal. On the overthrow of the latter by Akbar the original Rajput holders were ejected by the Bisens of Majhauli, by whom the country was included in Dewapara, the old name of Salempur. It seems to have been formed into a separate fiscal division at the end of the 17th century.

SIDHUA JOBNA *Pargana, vide* PADRAUNA *Tahsil.*

SILHAT, *Pargana* SILHAT, *Tahsil* HATA.

Silhat gives its name to a pargana which was formed towards the end of the 17th century, but the reason for its selection is unknown, since it is a very insignificant place, less than four miles from the old and important town of Rudarpur. It belongs to tappa Nagwan Tikar, and lies in 26°27′N., and 83° 34′E., on the left bank of the Katna, due west from Rudarpur. The village had at the last census a population of 575 persons, principally Sainthwars: the area is 557 acres and the revenue Rs. 588. Being situated in the *kachhar* it is at all times difficult of access, and during the rains is practically isolated.

SILHAT *Pargana, Tahsil* HATA.

Silhat is the central and southern pargana of the tahsil, and comprises a long and somewhat narrow stretch of country, bounded on the west and north by pargana Haveli, on the east by Shahjahanpur, on the south-east by Salempur and on the south-west by the river Rapti, beyond which lie Chillupar and Bhauapar. The western boundary is formed for most of its length by the Majhna, while the Duranchi separates this pargana from Shahjahanpur and the Karna for a considerable distance constitutes the dividing line between Silhat and Salempur. The tract comprises the 17 tappas of Banchara, Singhpur, Cheoraha, Kataura, Bakhra, Binayak, Chariaon, Paharpur, Adrakpur, Donth, Barnai, Gaura, Dhatura, Sirjam, Indupur, Nagwan Tikar and Madanpur. The total area is 176,503 acres or 275·7 square miles.

The pargana contains 507 *mauzas* and 1,933 inhabited sites, but the only town within its limits is Rudarpur, the rest being mere agricultural villages of varying size. The population rose from 102,445 in 1853 to 141,735 in 1865, and though it then fell to 135,847 in 1872, each subsequent enumeration has shown a marked increase, the total being 197,191 in 1881 and 216,484, in 1891, while ten years later it was 219,524, giving an average density of 796 to the square mile.

Of the early history very little is known, though it is certain that Rudarpur was the centre of an ancient civilisation for a long period. This is said to have been due to colonisation from Ajodhya, and to have disappeared beneath the waves of Bhar and Tharu invasions. Subsequently on the establishment of the Rajput principalities, the country became an object of contention between the rival houses of Majhauli and Satasi, the former proving victorious after a century of warfare. Their conquest, however, does not appear to have been of a permanent nature, for when the Musalmans occupied Gorakhpur the Raja of Satasi took up his residence at Rudarpur without opposition on the part of the Bisens; the town remaining the headquarters of the estate till its extinction after the Mutiny. Originally the pargana was included in Haveli, and its separation did not take place till Rudar Singh came hither from Gorakhpur in the days of Aurangzeb. The tract suffered terribly under the rule of the Nawab Wazirs, and in 1801 was found to be in a most disturbed and backward condition. Matters did not mend for several years, but when confidence was once re-established rapid progress was achieved, and the pargana is now one of the best developed and most carefully cultivated portions of the district.

SISWA BAZAR, *Pargana* TILPUR, *Tahsil* MAHARAJGANJ.

The town of Siswa Bazar stands in tappa Purani Karhi, in 27°9′N. and 83°46′E., on the road from Captainganj to Nichlaul, at a distance of 43 miles north-east from Gorakhpur and about eleven miles due west from the tahsil headquarters. To the south of the village the road is crossed by the railway from Gorakhpur to Bagaha, on which there is a station to the east of the main site, and the construction of the line has greatly enhanced the importance of the place. The rice trade from Nepal used formerly to go by road from Nichlaul to Gorakhpur and Chauri Chaura, but is now brought to the railway at Siswa, a distance of but twelve miles from Nichlaul, so that the town has thus become the principal market in the east of the tahsil. Several local Marwaris have attained considerable wealth, and grain dealers from other districts have opened agencies here, while many new *golas* are being built. It is possible that a rival market may be formed at Khada, the next station on the railway, under the patronage of the Raja of Padrauna; but even if this scheme be carried into effect it is probable that both bazars will have a prosperous future owing to the rapid increase in the volume of trade.

The population numbered 1,732 persons in 1872 and has since increased steadily, rising to 2,538 in 1881 and to 2,735 ten years later, while in 1901 the town contained 2,901 inhabitants, of whom 494 were Musalmans. The area of the *mauza* is 942 acres and the revenue Rs. 663. The inhabited portion has been administered under Act XX of 1856 since 1871. There are at present 1,150 houses, of which 147 were assessed to taxation in 1908, the average income from the house-tax for that and the two preceding years being Rs. 300, which gives an incidence of Rs. 2-0-8 per assessed house and Re. 0-1-8 per head of population. The total income for 1907-08 was Rs. 368 and the expenditure Rs. 323, the principal objects being the upkeep of the local police and the maintenance of a conservancy staff.

SOHNAG, *Pargana* SALEMPUR-MAJHAULI, *Tahsil* DEORIA.

A diminutive village of tappa Mail, situated in 26°15′N. and 83°55′E., at a distance of three miles south-west from Salempur and a mile west of the unmetalled road from that town to Bhagalpur. The area of the village is but 41 acres, while the population at the last census amounted to no more than 50 souls. The place is nevertheless of considerable importance on archæological grounds, containing an ancient tank about 18 acres in extent and a large mass of ruins and sculptures, dating apparently from the later Buddhist period. To the west of the tank and along its entire length rises a mound of large bricks, the extreme elevation of which is about 50 feet, while the breadth in its widest part is 100 feet. It seems never to have been excavated, but apparently the higher portion was a stupa, and the lower part, showing traces of a quadrangular building, a *vihara* or monastery. On the summit of the mound is a small ruined brick enclosure containing a modern Hindu temple dedicated to Parasram, and within the temple are four Buddhist sculptures, while outside are the remains of cloisters and a small temple of Shiva, locally known as Maharudranath. Other temples are to be seen in the vicinity, and in every case the images appear to be of Buddhist origin.*

Tradition relates that the place was originally called Nagpur, and that here Parasram remained during the period of his penance. The temples afterwards fell into ruin, but were restored

* J. R. A. S., 1900, p. 431.

by a king of Nepal named Sohan, who was on his way to Benares in order to seek a cure for his leprosy, but was miraculously healed by bathing in the tank. On his account the name was changed to Sohnag; but a variant story relates that Sohan was a Bisen, and it would seem that the Bisens of Majhauli claim to be connected in some way with the worship at the shrine. The place is still an object of veneration and a large fair, attended by some 30,000 persons, takes place in the month of Baisakh. The priests of the shrine are the Atiths of Karwania in tappa Ballia, but the place is practically in charge of a family of Bhats, who own two-thirds of the village, the tank and the ground on which the fair is held having passed into the hands of a family residing in the adjoining village of Tilauli. Close to this ancient site is a modern shrine belonging to a body of Ramanandis. This was founded by one Dharmi Das, who was succeeded by a noted ascetic named Jiwa Ramji. The latter disappeared on a pilgrimage, leaving behind him a *kundi* or stone cup which he announced would fall to pieces on the day of his death. The cup broke twelve years after his departure, but no one knows where he died. There have been six *mahants* since his time, but none of them have attained much celebrity. The shrine of Jiwa Ramji still contains the fragments of the cup, and is an object of popular veneration.

TAMKUHI, *Pargana* SIDHUA JOBNA, *Tahsil* PADRAUNA.

The village of Tamkuhi belongs to tappa Haveli and stands in 26°41′N., and 84°11′E., on the road connecting Tiwaripatti with Bihar Khurd, or Samur, on the road from Kasia to Chapra, at a distance of some 55 miles east from Gorakhpur and about 22 miles by road from Padrauna. A branch road runs westwards to Qazipur, crossing the Jharai some two miles west of the village. The population at the last census numbered 1,490, including a large community of Banias. The place possesses a post and telegraph office, an upper primary school and an encamping-ground; but it is chiefly noticeable as the headquarters of the Tamkuhi estate, containing the palace of the Raja and a bungalow for the residence of the special manager on behalf of the Court of Wards.

A road leads directly north from Tamkuhi for about three miles to Babhnauli on the road from Kasia to Pipra-ghat. This place is well-known as the headquarters of a large factory with outworks at Sapaha, Domath and Baikunthpur, now managed and partly owned by Mr. F. Mackinnon. Babhnauli is one of the oldest indigo factories in the district, and is still the centre of the industry ; the proprietor has a fine residence here, while the factory is well furnished with the various apparatus employed in the preparation of the dye.

TARIA SUJAN, *Pargana* SIDHUA JOBNA, *Tahsil* PADRAUNA.

A large but purely agricultural village of tappa Haveli, standing in 26° 39′N., and 84° 17′E., at a distance of six miles south-east from Tamkuhi and five miles west from the Great Gandak. Being off the road it is somewhat inaccessible but has long been the site of a police station, while it also possesses a post-office, a cattle-pound and an upper primary school. Markets of purely local importance are held here twice a week. The population at the last census numbered 2,616 persons, residing in a main site and numerous small hamlets. The village, which has an area of 2,161 acres and is assessed at Rs. 2,393, forms part of the Tamkuhi estate.

TARKULWA, *Pargana* SHAHJAHANPUR, *Tahsil* HATA.

This considerable village gives its name to a tappa, and stands in 26° 37′ N. and 83° 54′ E., on the west side of the metalled road from Deoria to Kasia, at a distance of twelve miles from the former, 40 miles east-south-east of Gorakhpur, and a mile east from the Little Gandak. The place is built on one of the sandy ridges which intersect the pargana, and for this reason is more healthy than the surrounding *bhat* country. It contained a population of 1,597 at the last census, and is the site of a police station, a post-office and a cattle-pound, while markets are held here twice a week. The area of the village is 823 acres and the revenue demand is Rs. 842.

TILPUR *Pargana, Tahsil* MAHARAJGANJ.

The pargana of Tilpur occupies the north-east portion of the Maharajganj tahsil, and comprises a large tract of country projecting southwards from the Nepal frontier. It marches on the west with Binayakpur, on the south with Haveli and on the east and south-east with Sidhua Jobna, the dividing line in this case being the Little Gandak, while on the north-east the Great Gandak for a few miles separates it from the Champaran district of Bengal. The pargana contains the seven tappas of Sonari, Sukrahar, Khas, Domakhand, Bharatkhand, Purani Karhi and Nai Karhi, the total area being 187,832 acres or 293·4 square miles.

There are within this area 344 *mauzas* and 578 inhabited sites, the principal places being Nichlaul in the north and Siswa Bazar in the south. The population of the pargana has always been somewhat sparse owing to the nature of the country and the still considerable amount of forest. The total in 1853 was 37,330 but by 1865 had risen to 46,426, the increase being well maintained at subsequent enumerations, since in 1872 there were 57,021 inhabitants, while the figure rose to 77,339 in 1881 and to 92,953 ten years later. It then continued stationary, the total in 1901 being 92,386, which gives an average density of 314 to the square mile.

The history of Tilpur practically begins with the establishment of the Chauhan principality of Butwal by Makund Singh in the fourteenth century. He and his descendants by degrees acquired all this pargana and Binayakpur, as well as other territory to the north; but in the course of time it would appear that a younger branch of the family set itself up in Tilpur as an independent state, since the pargana had come into existence by the days of Akbar, when we are told that there was a brick fort at Tilpur, probably that still traceable at Nichlaul. In the beginning of the eighteenth century Tilak Sen of Tilpur openly declared his independence of the lord of Butwal, and with the aid of his Banjara allies carried on a long warfare with his suzerain. This led to the devastation of the pargana and heavy arrears of revenue, with the result that the Nawab Wazir despatched an army to collect the dues from the Raja. Tilak Sen's son was defeated and then came to terms with the Raja of Butwal, who re-annexed the pargana; but the country was again laid waste in the war between Butwal and Satasi, which culminated in the defeat of the latter in 1788. Nor did the cession bring peace: for the Gurkhas soon after laid claim to all the domains of the Butwal Raja; and the troubles which then ensued from 1806 to the peace of Sigauli have already been described. After the Mutiny the area of the pargana was reduced by the cession of a strip of country in the north to Nepal, in consideration of the services rendered against the rebels. Among the latter was the Raja of Nichlaul, the descendant of the Butwal Raja, who had resided there for two generations. He was attainted and his estates were confiscated, the title being finally extinguished.

THUTHIBARI, *Pargana* TILPUR, *Tahsil* MAHARAJGANJ.

This village stands in the extreme north of the district, at the trijunction of Tilpur, Binayakpur and Nepal, being actually situated in 27° 25′ N. and 83° 42′ E., on the bank of the Piyas river in tappa Sukrahar of pargana Tilpur. It is some 60 miles from Gorakhpur by a road leading to Nichlaul and thence to Captainganj, and 25 miles from the tahsil headquarters. The place contained in 1901 a population of 1,860 persons, including a number of Bania traders. Markets are held here weekly, and a considerable traffic to and from Nepal passes through the village. The total area is 1,054 acres, but much of this is waste and the revenue demand is only Rs. 380. Thuthibari possesses a police station, a post-office and a cattle-pound: it is the usual exchanging place for prisoners sent to or received from Nepal, the corresponding village on the north side of the frontier being known as Aminiganj.

UNAULA, *Pargana* UNAULA, *Tahsil* BANSGAON.

The village of Unaula, frequently written Anaula, is supposed to be the place from which the pargana derives its name, though the matter is at least doubtful, since Unaula lies in tappa Mohsan, while Unwal, the alternative name for Sangrampur, is not only the chief village of the Haveli tappa, but has always been the residence of the Unaula Rajas. Unaula is situated in 26° 36′ N. and 83° 14′ E., a short distance to the west of the road from Gorakhpur and Rudrapur to Sikriganj, about seven miles north-west from Bansgaon and 13 miles south-west from the district headquarters. Whatever its history, the place is now wholly insignificant. It has an area of only 247 acres, assessed at Rs. 220, and the population at the last census was but 312.

UNAULA *Pargana, Tahsil* BANSGAON.

This small pargana comprises the northern portion of the Bansgaon tahsil and lies to the north of Dhuriapar. On the north-west it marches with Hasanpur Maghar and on the west with the Basti district, while to the north and east lies Bhauapar, the boundary for the greater part of the distance being formed by the river Ami. The total area is 70,205 acres or 109·7 square miles, and is made up of the three tappas of Haveli, Bankata and Mohsan.

The pargana has been included in the territory of the Sarnets since their rise to power in the days of Chandra Sen, and was the special domain of his youngest son, Randhir Singh, the founder of the Unaula house. His descendants remained in undisturbed possession, and the history of the family is uneventful to a degree, being unbroken by any occurrence of note. The Raja still retains most of his ancestral estate and lives in the family home at Unwal or Sangrampur. The pargana too has maintained its ancient form, and remained unaffected by its transfer to the British in 1801, the disturbances of the Mutiny and the formation of the Basti district in 1865.

It contains altogether 401 *mauzas* and 842 inhabited sites; the villages are generally of diminutive size, Sangrampur and Bansgaon being the only places of importance. The population of the pargana numbered 67,231 as early as 1853, and though this dropped to 66,449 in 1865 it had risen to 70,116 in 1872, and subsequently increased rapidly, reaching 78,941 in 1881 and 93,337 ten years later. The last census in 1901, however, witnessed a decline, the total being 89,927, which yet gives the high average of nearly 820 persons to the square mile.

Gazetteer of Gorakhpur.

APPENDIX.

GAZETTEER

OF

GORAKHPUR.

APPENDIX.

CONTENTS.

TABLE I.—*Population by Tahsils*, 1901.

Tahsil.	Total.			Hindus.			Musalmans.			Others.		
	Persons.	Males.	Females.	Persons.	Males.	Females.	Persons.	Males.	Females.	Persons.	Males.	Females.
1	2	3	4	5	6	7	8	9	10	11	12	13
Bansgaon	438,364	216,029	222,335	411,408	202,822	208,586	26,887	13,168	13,719	69	39	30
Maharajganj ...	504,325	253,411	250,914	444,322	223,218	221,104	59,941	30,154	29,787	62	39	23
Padrauna	595,706	295,792	299,914	507,918	251,948	255,970	87,770	43,832	43,938	18	12	6
Hata	428,846	213,694	215,152	392,739	195,525	197,214	36,087	18,153	17,934	20	16	4
Deoria	493,822	241,662	252,160	453,731	222,254	231,479	40,006	19,359	20,647	85	51	34
Gorakhpur... ...	496,011	249,881	246,130	447,956	225,600	222,356	46,328	23,372	22,956	1,727	909	818
Total ...	2,957,074	1,470,469	1,486,605	2,658,074	1,321,365	1,336,709	297,019	148,038	148,981	1,981	1,066	915

TABLE II.—*Population by Thanas*, 1901.

Name of Thana.	Total.			Hindus.			Musalmans.			Others.		
	Total.	Males.	Females.	Total.	Males.	Females.	Total.	Males.	Females.	Total.	Males.	Females.
1	2	3	4	5	6	7	8	9	10	11	12	13
Kotwali	237,131	120,277	116,854	203,138	103,052	100,086	32,283	16,329	15,954	1,710	896	814
Barhi	60,384	30,051	30,333	58,392	29,043	29,349	1,988	1,005	983	4	3	1
Chaura	63,530	31,802	31,728	60,750	30,374	30,376	2,770	1,421	1,349	10	7	3
Sahjanwa	62,988	31,587	31,401	59,721	29,913	29,808	3,264	1,671	1,593	3	3	...
Rudrapur	81,475	40,819	40,656	76,867	38,597	38,270	4,608	2,222	2,386	...	...	...
Bansgaon	131,647	65,195	66,452	124,176	61,493	62,683	7,450	3,686	3,764	21	16	5
Belghat	71,641	35,509	36,132	66,854	33,180	33,674	4,747	2,313	2,434	40	16	24
Gola	71,209	34,825	36,384	66,512	32,555	33,957	4,693	2,267	2,426	4	3	1
Barhalganj	106,110	51,512	54,598	99,163	48,117	51,046	6,943	3,391	3,552	4	4	...
Maharajganj	83,089	41,098	41,991	70,795	34,938	35,857	12,283	6,151	6,132	11	9	2
Semra	109,862	55,597	54,265	94,544	47,875	46,669	15,290	7,709	7,581	28	13	15
Rigauli	73,998	37,281	36,717	69,709	35,084	34,625	4,280	2,190	2,090	9	7	2
Panera	29,247	14,655	14,592	27,719	13,871	13,848	1,528	784	744	...	...	...
Biraicha	54,248	28,482	25,766	48,472	25,552	22,920	5,775	2,929	2,846	1	1	...
Paisia	51,756	26,524	25,232	45,679	23,399	22,280	6,073	3,122	2,951	4	3	1
Nichlaul	46,930	23,581	23,349	41,614	20,887	20,727	5,309	2,689	2,620	7	5	

Thuthibari	25,917	13,255	12,662	22,250	11,455	10,975	3,665	1,799	1,866	2	1	1
Kothibhar	102,040	50,538	51,502	89,474	44,310	45,164	12,566	6,228	6,338	...	...	...
Padrauna	100,747	49,034	51,713	85,054	41,118	43,936	15,693	7,916	7,777	...	...	...
Ramkola	56,763	28,060	28,703	50,134	24,793	25,341	6,629	3,267	3,362	...	...	...
Kasia	93,091	46,536	46,555	79,940	39,928	40,012	13,144	6,603	6,541	7	5	2
Qazipur	91,605	45,875	45,730	75,964	38,197	37,767	15,637	7,676	7,961	4	2	2
Bishunpura	50,007	24,545	25,462	43,581	21,354	22,227	6,424	3,189	3,235	2	2	...
Taria Sujan	78,470	38,242	40,228	66,114	32,113	34,001	12,352	6,127	6,225	4	2	2
Hata	128,278	64,434	63,844	117,568	59,055	58,513	10,697	5,370	5,327	13	9	4
Mansurganj	75,597	37,462	38,135	66,941	33,163	33,778	8,654	4,297	4,357	2	2	...
Pipraich	74,782	37,459	37,323	69,077	34,564	34,513	5,705	2,895	2,810	...	...	...
Tarkulwa	117,739	59,128	58,611	99,658	49,917	49,741	18,080	9,210	8,870	1	1	...
Rudarpur	133,530	65,340	68,190	126,320	61,826	64,494	7,210	3,514	3,696	...	...	...
Deoria	101,249	50,816	50,433	93,226	46,675	46,551	7,960	4,105	3,855	63	36	27
Musela	84,448	41,903	42,545	79,788	39,594	40,194	4,657	3,307	2,350	3	2	1
Barhaj	71,308	35,211	36,097	66,424	32,713	33,711	4,870	2,489	2,381	14	9	5
Salempur	114,649	54,817	59,832	100,626	48,410	52,216	14,021	6,405	7,616	2	2	...
Khampar	121,609	59,019	62,590	111,830	54,250	57,580	9,771	4,762	5,009	8	7	1
Total ...	2,957,074	1,470,469	1,486,605	2,658,074	1,321,365	1,336,709	297,019	148,038	148,981	1,981	1,066	915

TABLE III.—*Vital statistics.*

Year.	Births.				Deaths.			
	Total.	Males.	Fe-males.	Rate per 1,000.	Total.	Males.	Fe-males.	Rate per 1,000.
1	2	3	4	5	6	7	8	9
1891	90,596	47,003	43,593	30·26	90,469	47,516	42,953	30·22
1892	96,555	50,134	46,421	32·25	93,449	49,652	43,797	31·21
1893	108,864	56,004	52,360	36·19	59,697	31,487	28,210	19·94
1894	97,058	50,010	47,048	32·41	131,079	68,581	62,498	43·78
1895	78,303	40,728	37,575	26·15	75,689	40,388	35,301	25·28
1896	81,729	42,459	39,270	27·30	83,409	46,570	36,839	27·86
1897	71,230	36,942	34,288	23·79	107,540	60,714	46,826	35·92
1898	99,481	51,717	47,764	33·23	57,211	31,060	26,151	19·11
1899	141,111	72,457	68,654	47·13	74,883	40,202	34,681	25·01
1900	99,332	51,901	47,431	*33·18	67,319	36,805	30,514	22·48
1901	97,031	50,822	46,209	32·81	58,234	31,598	26,636	19·69
1902	118,344	61,624	56,720	40·02	71,952	38,566	33,386	24·33
1903	118,896	61,471	57,425	40·21	94,408	50,068	44,340	31·93
1904	120,618	62,843	57,775	40·79	77,581	40,558	37,023	26·23
1905	106,712	55,392	51,320	36·08	84,994	44,731	40,263	28·74
1906	90,751	47,890	42,861	30·88	93,259	49,763	43,496	31·73
1907	109,832	56,935	52,897	37·36	90,260	46,414	43,846	30·71
1908								
1909								
1910								
1911								
1912								
1913								
1914								
1915								
1916								
1917								

* The rates from 1891 to 1900 are calculated from the 1891 census.

TABLE IV.—*Deaths according to cause.*

Year	Total deaths from—					
	All causes.	Plague.	Cholera.	Small-pox.	Fever.	Bowel complaints.
1	2	3	4	5	6	7
1891	90,469	...	8,835	11,117	30,770	8,541
1892	93,449	...	11,178	1,868	42,826	8,121
1893	59,697	...	698	393	32,054	4,187
1894	131,079	...	26,081	254	62,144	13,707
1895	75,689	...	1,234	78	48,716	5,554
1896	83,409	...	7,328	470	50,910	5,018
1897	107,540	...	3,977	3,370	69,770	6,498
1898	57,211	...	52	590	37,824	1,787
1899	74,883	...	154	281	49,228	2,087
1900	67,319	...	3,590	90	43,238	2,894
1901	58,284	...	1,621	49	41,825	2,309
1902	71,952	3,677	2,567	162	48,691	2,026
1903	94,408	4,142	3,577	479	67,438	2,392
1904	77,581	7,884	382	198	56,898	1,245
1905	84,994	7,432	4,776	89	62,429	1,329
1906	93,259	4,780	15,132	581	62,880	1,176
1907	90,260	7,441	1,041	3,166	63,732	1,038
1908						
1909						
1910						
1911						
1912						
1913						
1914						
1915						
1916						
1917						

TABLE V.—*Statistics of cultivation and irrigation*, 1315 Fasli.

Pargana and tahsil.	Total area.	Waste.	Culturable.	Cultivated. Irrigated. Total.	Canals.	Wells.	Tanks	Other sources.	Dry.	Total.	Double-cropped.
1	2	3	4	5	6	7	8	9	10	11	12
	Acres.	Acres.	Acres.	Acres.	Acres.	Acres.	Acres.	Acres.	Acres.	Acres.	Acres.
Bhauapar	48,843	4,970	7,928	11,887	...	5,796	...	6,091	24,058	35,945	4,245
Unaula	70,204	5,299	10,194	26,456	...	18,197	...	8,259	28,255	54,711	7,753
Dhuriapar	171,308	23,405	31,683	53,318	...	40,828	...	12,490	62,902	116,220	15,043
Chillupar	65,714	13,929	12,032	9,575	...	5,327	...	4,248	30,178	39,753	6,550
Tahsil Bansgaon ...	356,069	47,603	61,837	101,236	...	70,148	...	31,0[illegible]8	145,393	246,629	33,591
Haveli	512,041	31,566	166,828	58,189	1,031	49,400	...	7,758	255,458	313,647	121,199
Binayakpur	92,900	4,146	32,123	3,566	...	98	...	3,468	53,065	56,631	17,905
Tilpur	187,832	8,769	89,823	4,913	..	1,931		2,982	84,327	89,240	35,473
Tahsil Maharajganj ...	792,773	44,481	288,774	66,668	1,031	51,429	...	14,208	392,850	459,518	174,577
Sidhua Jobna ...	593,965	44,025	118,864	52,742	...	49,135	...	3,607	378,334	431,076	153,217
Tahsil Padrauna ..	593,965	44,025	118,864	52,742	..	49,135	.	3,607	378,334	431,076	153,217
Silhat	176,505	11,567	19,446	73,328	..	59,488	...	13,840	72,164	145,492	29,731
Shahjahanpur ...	87,572	6,144	10,758	31,963	...	30,816	...	1,147	38,707	70,670	17,386
Haveli	101,664	8,112	11,633	34,229	...	26,802	...	7,427	47,630	81,859	24,069
Tahsil Hata ...	365,741	25,823	41,897	139,520	..	117,106	...	22,414	158,501	298,021	71,186
Salempur-Majhauli ...	372,374	36,416	45,809	137,067	...	131,658	...	5,409	153,082	290,149	54,276
Tahsil Deoria ...	372 374	36,416	45,809	137,067	...	131,658	...	5,409	153,082	290,149	54,276
Bhauapar	39,298	4,610	3,863	9,950	...	2,847	...	7,103	20,875	30,825	5,824
Haveli	303,584	27,923	59,031	81,180	...	61,692	...	19,488	135,451	216,631	36,566
Maghar	74.330	6,068	12,168	23,440	...	13,275	...	10,165	32,644	56,094	7,275
Tahsil Gorakhpur ...	417,212	38,600	75,062	114,570	...	77,814	...	36,756	188,980	303,550	49,665
Total District ...	2,898,134	236,948	632,243	611,803	1,031	497,290	...	113,482	1,417,140	2,028,943	535,512

TABLE VI.—*Area in acres under the principal crops, Tahsil Bansgaon.*

Year.	Rabi.								Kharif.					
	Total.	Wheat alone.	Barley alone.	Wheat and barley.	Peas.	Linseed.	Opium.	Gram alone and mixed.	Total.	Rice.	Maize.	Sugar-cane.	Kodon.	Arhar.
Fasli.														
1305 ...	168,518	18,163	25,264	57,561	17,375	7,665	2,965	26,247	144,169	52,635	9,826	3,396	28,334	27,025
1306 ...	200,103	19,919	22,846	60,862	33,026	9,619	3,076	35,746	139,034	68,494	7,940	3,422	22,189	21,647
1307 ...	218,235	21,537	25,240	60,056	43,691	10,993	3,313	39,081	131,623	81,028	5,465	2,869	18,458	5,556
1308 ...	177,632	20,735	30,084	54,718	31,123	8,729	2,920	24,384	148,165	75,560	6,695	3,542	19,548	21,406
1309 ...	174,883	19,929	23,496	57,158	29,739	4,332	3,278	31,131	153,468	86,487	9,925	4,152	19,842	11,419
1310 ...	179,788	20,997	19,594	61,020	30,364	6,672	3,102	30,993	151,807	77,036	10,154	4,057	20,593	17,701
1311 ...	209,729	22,437	23,875	71,010	35,311	9,214	3,247	37,808	145,309	75,291	9,572	3,592	20,731	16,921
1312 ...	197,652	24,238	16,857	67,443	40,351	9,878	2,890	30,959	135,107	79,697	7,259	2,435	21,732	10,029
1313 ...	208,676	21,217	24,207	64,641	41,727	5,768	3,070	42,672	133,422	87,817	6,055	2,729	17,435	6,082
1314 ...	190,319	19,507	25,151	59,266	32,548	5,367	2,942	40,292	140,402	93,581	5,659	3,696	20,612	928
1315 ...	137,340	15,011	28,520	52,260	16,499	517	4,082	15,958	144,562	84,595	5,661	5,289	27,958	1,155
1316 ...														
1317 ...														
1318 ...														
1319 ...														
1320 ...														
1321 ...														
1322 ...														
1323 ...														
1324 ...														
1325 ...														

TABLE VI—(continued).—*Area in acres under the principal crops, Tahsil Maharajganj.*

Year.	Rabi.								Kharif.					
	Total.	Wheat alone.	Barley alone.	Wheat and barley	Peas.	Linseed.	Opium.	Gram alone and mixed.	Total	Rice.	Maize	Sugar-cane.	Kodon.	Arhar.
Fasli.														
1305 ...	227,495	24,703	24,748	32,140	24,231	67,827	177	32,047	397,444	335,585	6,855	4,473	19,923	11,669
1306 ...	230,392	26,860	27,627	39,709	25,835	50,527	188	41,027	397,221	343,307	6,185	6,415	13,287	10,003
1307 ...	194,221	27,936	24,318	41,464	23,811	23,108	257	39,131	383,759	345,256	4,190	5,477	7,981	9,789
1308 ...	226,363	29,857	35,730	38,669	19,340	44,914	203	44,607	405,567	352,603	4,838	4,493	15,709	16,541
1309 ...	255,394	25,475	28,229	38,286	25,885	56,993	334	59,989	415,206	349,939	8,191	6,008	13,996	18,066
1310 ...	225,735	27,584	24,029	40,112	25,798	60,042	292	58,656	415,867	341,442	11,123	4,995	16,546	20,457
1311 ..	310,285	34,317	26,651	50,092	32,364	91,795	335	56,376	397,392	338,513	10,009	3,822	14,157	14,141
1312 ...	250,619	34,101	20,794	47,970	31,403	53,792	283	44,895	416,258	359,496	8,072	5,373	12,595	16,130
1313 ...	218,744	25,204	31,339	46,192	22,922	22,844	303	51,020	426,656	376,988	8,488	6,642	10,842	11,121
1314 ...	201,910	25,544	32,341	46,602	17,335	11,345	267	52,317	441,914	395,534	6,830	8,485	8,899	8,771
1315 ...	176,270	24,805	43,157	39,713	16,429	7,365	183	...	456,447	393,387	6,867	11,239	20,731	8,473
1316 ...														
1317 ...														
1318 ...														
1319 ..														
1320 ...														
1321 ...														
1322 ...														
1323 ..														
1324 ...														
1325 ...														

TABLE VI—(continued).—*Area in acres under the principal crops, Tahsil Padrauna.*

Year.	Rabi.								Kharif.					
	Total.	Wheat alone.	Barley alone.	Wheat and barley.	Peas.	Linseed.	Opium.	Gram alone and mixed.	Total.	Rice.	Maize.	Sugar-cane.	Kodon.	Arhar.
Fasli.														
1305 ...	214,492	25,167	56,754	40,855	27,151	30,776	3,952	4,277	366,608	130,398	65,472	25,633	82,786	2,223
1306 ...	226,651	31,966	55,704	47,679	37,248	18,405	4,149	4,508	351,920	142,225	65,380	30,571	58,850	776
1307 ...	233,937	34,559	52,413	49,569	41,216	19,210	4,080	5,057	329,583	143,537	58,375	30,606	50,869	944
1308 ...	200,071	30,640	53,019	43,252	26,277	18,988	3,728	3,568	357,579	162,815	58,569	31,483	58,345	1,197
1309 ...	231,935	35,279	61,542	48,593	30,092	19,314	4,312	7,279	365,270	154,809	60,298	30,448	62,414	726
1310 ...	237,823	32,453	51,195	46,433	33,296	35,871	4,140	5,789	375,112	149,412	63,932	30,566	71,045	1,010
1311 ...	254,912	43,401	40,560	50,324	42,423	33,729	4,527	6,890	363,425	151,670	63,224	30,660	76,059	987
1312 ...	229,701	43,973	28,412	48,241	41,685	23,465	3,207	5,437	370,577	163,738	61,485	36,872	55,031	1,257
1313 ...	225,491	33,637	39,069	53,136	29,100	3,978	2,833	9,729	369,401	168,811	62,046	39,461	53,762	374
1314 ...	234,999	33,406	42,211	54,407	28,137	18,347	2,376	14,076	379,836	187,075	60,048	42,899	45,074	271
1315 ...	189,003	22,126	49,627	43,473	23,066	9,993	1,863	5,776	394,181	182,311	53,062	48,606	60,835	908
1316 ...														
1317 ...														
1318 ...														
1319 ...														
1320 ...														
1321 ...														
1322 ...														
1323 ...														
1324 ...														
1325 ...														

TABLE VI—(continued).—*Area in acres under the principal crops, Tahsil Hata.*

Year.	Rabi.								Kharif.					
	Total.	Wheat alone.	Barley alone.	Wheat and barley.	Peas.	Linseed.	Opium.	Gram alone and mixed.	Total.	Rice.	Maize.	Sugarcane.	Kodon.	Arhar.
Fasli.	161,238	18,202	33,645	31,719	32,556	25,401	1,210	13,744	205,687	112,716	9,604	19,444	17,158	1,625
1305 ...	175,6·3	18,995	26,179	33,102	55,150	19,845	1,208	15,711	205,281	130,118	8,183	21,025	15,694	793
1306 ...	175,068	17,923	27,922	30,643	61,334	15,866	1,203	15,451	200,131	139,758	7,011	20,431	12,011	439
1307 ...	161,750	18,075	33,179	26,219	43,313	23,812	984	13,080	214,927	140,337	7,221	21,112	10,884	1,232
1308 ...	155,284	19,701	28,284	31,488	41,294	11,067	1,046	18,803	218,688	137,142	8,891	21,768	12,694	924
1309 ...	170,712	21,099	23,833	34,757	43,308	25,052	1,074	18,031	215,263	135,716	8,955	20,712	9,531	1,330
1310 ...	199,609	23,810	21,773	38,190	55,991	32,771	1,212	22,355	207,870	131,494	8,574	20,347	11,261	965
1311 ...	185,048	25,517	21,066	35,387	66,710	22,251	1,230	18,938	216,070	142,619	8,091	22,177	7,876	985
1312 ...	180,666	19,922	30,389	34,465	50,595	11,838	1,432	27,035	217,689	149,988	7,621	23,338	5,997	574
1313 ...	173,495	19,082	30,798	31,804	42,755	7,529	1,228	35,717	229,002	157,921	6,894	25,983	5,189	786
1314 ...	133,387	15,431	43,517	26,518	12,573	955	988	21,038	234,483	155,275	6,726	26,602	24,179	1,831
1315 ...														
1316 ...														
1317 ...														
1318 ...														
1319 ...														
1320 ...														
1321 ...														
1322 ...														
1323 ...														
1324 ...														
1325 ...														

Table VI—(continued).—*Area in acres under the principal crops, Tahsil Deoria.*

Year.	Rabi.								Kharif.					
	Total.	Wheat alone.	Barley alone.	Wheat and barley.	Peas.	Linseed.	Opium.	Gram alone and mixed.	Total.	Rice.	Maize.	Sugar-cane.	Kodon.	Arhar.
Fasli.														
1305 ...	158,667	3,772	34,391	61,805	30,852	9,475	5,466	8,969	185,106	59,083	20,713	12,767	13,371	182
1306 ...	191,955	4,574	28,801	68,206	60,139	9,142	5,391	10,753	186,773	69,091	18,711	14,644	16,617	44
1307 ...	202,376	3,807	30,926	65,806	69,530	9,335	5,453	11,933	173,691	76,319	16,673	15,226	24,454	21
1308 ...	150,601	3,547	28,423	64,105	30,647	9,299	5,148	6,889	189,369	67,888	18,127	17,093	10,010	197
1309 ...	158,682	3,855	28,706	65,616	37,471	3,501	5,241	10,483	192,106	66,018	20,044	16,754	14,771	27
1310 ...	155,951	4,110	24,309	69,602	34,874	6,101	5,158	7,935	190,954	64,095	20,787	15,409	8,705	117
1311 ...	188,694	4,227	22,163	81,358	48,402	11,928	5,631	11,052	181,154	60,849	20,082	13,748	11,670	203
1312 ...	192,286	4,611	15,904	81,194	58,319	12,000	5,220	10,506	189,605	69,902	20,002	15,803	14,818	80
1313 ...	197,330	3,155	27,454	72,058	58,216	5,228	5,517	19,038	186,321	75,338	18,872	17,023	16,366	17
1314 ...	187,878	3,194	28,858	65,845	51,697	3,919	4,987	24,276	198,938	81,578	18,519	20,616	16,815	40
1315 ...	137,340	1,862	44,684	45,443	25,160	517	12,481	15,958	203,174	70,195	16,193	21,625	60,339	630
1316 ...														
1317 ...														
1318 ...														
1319 ...														
1320 ...														
1321 ...														
1322 ...														
1323 ...														
1324 ...														
1325 ...														

TABLE VI—(concluded).—*Area in acres under the principal crops, Tahsil Gorakhpur.*

Year.	Rabi.								Kharif.					
	Total.	Wheat alone.	Barley alone.	Wheat and barley.	Peas.	Linseed.	Opium.	Gram alone and mixed.	Total.	Rice.	Maize.	Sugar-cane.	Kodon.	Arhar.
Fasli.														
1305 ...	175,198	30,158	30,304	38,250	20,522	14,178	1,474	32,899	173,500	71,930	16,066	4,116	36,970	18,206
1306 ...	203,855	31,708	28,040	41,386	36,761	12,741	1,592	42,796	163,673	82,586	12,823	4,450	29,315	13,254
1307 ...	218,715	33,355	27,548	42,622	43,733	16,366	1,494	45,122	149,954	93,359	6,464	3,745	21,597	9,422
1308 ...	189,583	36,097	28,983	38,026	29,423	15,186	1,532	34,242	170,574	101,254	9,921	3,925	30,287	9,895
1309 ...	182,000	32,227	22,702	39,498	29,483	8,858	1,971	40,457	190,561	101,565	14,904	4,098	35,054	9,535
1310 ...	194,026	33,117	22,350	45,986	29,567	17,081	1,848	37,664	187,386	108,176	17,017	4,217	35,614	17,194
1311 ...	230,842	32,530	26,392	56,749	38,657	19,589	2,040	48,624	174,235	104,156	14,179	3,663	34,878	8,546
1312 ...	221,508	37,824	34,041	51,605	40,265	17,542	1,762	42,245	178,290	101,121	14,020	3,882	35,228	8,049
1313 ...	228,893	31,782	32,438	46,984	40,042	10,675	3,137	58,509	179,793	109,862	12,505	4,403	28,952	7,953
1314 ...	220,549	29,259	33,743	46,019	32,622	5,889	1,851	65,065	189,799	112,562	11,238	6,211	28,954	13,140
1315 ...	147,259	23,498	37,389	38,773	15,066	755	1,522	27,029	201,826	111,821	10,844	8,694	45,411	728
1316 ...														
1317 ...														
1318 ...														
1319 ...														
1320 ...														
1321 ...														
1322 ...														
1323 ...														
1324 ...														
1325 ...														

TABLE VII.—*Criminal Justice.*

Year.	Number of persons convicted or bound over in respect of—												Cases under—	
	Offences against public tranquillity (Chapter VIII).	Offences affecting life.	Grievous hurt.	Rape.	Cattle-theft.	Criminal force and assault.	Theft.	Robbery and dakaiti.	Receiving stolen property.	Criminal trespass.	Bad livelihood.	Keeping the peace.	Opium Act.	Excise Act.
1	2	3	4	5	6	7	8	9	10	11	12	13	14	15
1898 ...	113	64	50	4	132	53	479	86	105	272	313	34	21	78
1899 ...	162	41	42	1	141	52	690	64	161	380	187	31	10	74
1900 ...	237	42	31	1	193	51	1,040	37	262	518	192	65	14	44
1901 ...	195	50	33	1	108	37	733	39	118	426	176	69	12	73
1902 ...	114	34	31	1	80	43	480	24	120	317	204	52	12	81
1903 ...	77	35	36	2	24	33	366	38	60	316	171	65	8	42
1904 ...	111	20	18	2	22	23	304	17	118	188	259	41	7	36
1905 ...	63	13	33	3	49	7	434	18	164	288	241	48	6	28
1906 ...	90	14	23	1	65	21	635	15	192	386	231	30	10	26
1907 ...	129	16	18	2	85	12	543	34	241	405	213	46	15	28
1908 ...														
1909 ...														
1910 ...														
1911 ...														
1912 ...														
1913 ...														
1914 ...														
1915 ...														
1916 ...														
1917 ...														

TABLE VIII.—*Cognizable crime.*

Year.	Number of cases investigated by police—			Number of persons—		
	Suo motu.	By orders of Magistrate.	Sent up for trial.	Tried.	Acquitted or discharged.	Convicted.
1	2	3	4	5	6	7
1891	6,001	26	3,150	4,206	951	3,255
1892	3,938	26	2,180	3,203	654	2,549
1893	3,775	256	2,415	3,333	783	2,550
1894	3,954	231	2,676	3,676	795	2,881
1895	4,043	182	2,699	3,771	826	2,945
1896	4,739	135	3,086	4,334	1,200	3,134
1897	5,377	43	3,660	5,197	1,117	4,080
1898	3,121	182	1,961	2,814	940	1,874
1899	3,512	33	2,004	2,666	699	1,967
1900	4,948	196	2,991	3,907	888	3,019
1901	3,794	163	2,370	3,019	749	2,270
1902	3,008	229	1,769	2,310	616	1,994
1903	2,404	289	1,348	2,571	1,080	1,491
1904	2,298	326	1,408	2,634	1,100	1,534
1905	2,647	...	1,534	2,014	482	1,532
1906	3,300	...	2,054	2,600	449	2,151
1907	4,095	...	2,032	2,569	434	2,135
1908						
1909						
1910						
1911						
1912						
1913						
1914						
1915						
1916						
1917						

NOTE.—Columns 2 and 3 should show cases instituted during the year.

TABLE IX.—*Revenue demand at successive settlements.*

Pargana and tahsil.	Year of settlement.						
	1803.	1806.	1809.	1813.	1840.	1860.	1889.
	Rs.	Rs.	Rs.	Rs.	Rs.	Rs.	Rs.
Haveli	9,192	6,974	8,985	15,222	85,161	1,41,267	2,50,725
Bhauapar	3,619	3,634	4,825	6,220	17,287	24,942	43,106
Maghar	8,691	7,273	9,517	11,292	36,859	61,659	86,717
Tahsil Gorakhpur	21,502	17,881	23,327	32,734	1,39,307	2,27,868	3,80,548
Bhauapar	11,811	11,087	9,925	11,033	25,394	32,099	49,006
Unaula	11,698	10,648	9,452	12,368	30,498	43,200	72,119
Dhuriapar	44,907	41,948	37,743	40,358	87,223	1,12,391	1,71,328
Chillupar	12,283	12,145	14,204	14,543	30,586	40,449	62,365
Tahsil Bansgaon	80,699	75,828	71,414	78,302	1,73,701	2,28,139	3,54,818
Haveli	22,169	27,990	35,173	38,115	1,37,735	1,73,912	2,83,378
Binayakpur...	...	...	...	520	688	7,505	17,283
Tilpur	9,803	9,821	7,646	11,470	41,501	41,888	61,810
Tahsil Maharajganj	31,972	37,811	42,819	50,105	1,79,924	2,23,305	3,62,466
Sidhua Jobna	96,949	87,195	80,361	83,668	2,24,477	3,18,934	5,27,866
Tahsil Padrauna	96,949	87,195	80,361	83,668	2,24,477	3,18,934	5,27,866
Haveli	24,298	24,723	25,888	25,953	53,714	84,930	1,06,913
Shahjahanpur	15,734	10,645	11,242	12,406	39,445	77,070	96,797
Silhat	8,516	9,283	12,657	16,461	54,300	1,02,621	1,62,660
Tahsil Hata	48,548	44,651	49,787	54,820	1,47,459	2,64,621	3,64,470
Salempur	67,035	67,737	82,158	88,141	2,23,709	2,90,740	4,47,944
Tahsil Deoria	67,035	67,737	82,158	88,141	2,23,709	2,90,740	4,47,944
Total District ...	3,46,705	3,31,103	3,49,866	3,87,770	10,88,577	15,53,607	24,38,112*

* Net final demand

TABLE X.—*Present demand for revenue and cesses for the year* 1315 Fasli.

Pargana and tahsil.	Where included in *Ain-i-Akbari.*	Revenue.	Cesses.	Total.	Incidence per acre.	
					Cultivated.	Total.
1	2	3	4	5	5	7
		Rs.	Rs.	Rs.	Rs. a. p.	Rs. a. p.
Bhauapar	Bhuapara	50,509	5,162	55,671	1 8 9	1 2 3
Unaula	Anhaula	72,573	7,296	79,869	1 7 4	1 2 2
Dhuriapar	Dhuriapar	1,53,464	17,074	1,70,538	1 7 6	0 15 11
Chillupar	Chillupara	62,950	6,299	69,249	1 11 10	1 0 10
Tahsil Bansgaon ...	...	3,39,496	35,831	3,75,327	1 8 3	1 0 10
Haveli	Haveli, Gorakhpur ...	3,17,868	32,250	3,50,118	1 1 10	0 10 11
Binayakpur	Binayakpur	26,831	2,683	29,514	0 8 4	0 5 1
Tilpur	Tilpur	69,620	7,130	76,750	0 13 9	0 6 6
Tahsil Maharajganj ...	...	4,14,319	42,063	4,56,382	0 15 10	0 9 3
Sidhua Jobna	Dewapara	5,37,452	53,970	5,91,422	1 5 11	0 15 11
Tahsil Padrauna ...	...	5,37,452	53 970	5,91,422	1 5 11	0 15 11
Silhat	Haveli, Gorakhpur ...	1,80,803	18,265	1,99,068	1 5 10	1 2 1
Shahjahanpur	Dewapara	96,028	9,602	1,05,630	1 7 10	1 3 3
Haveli	Haveli, Gorakhpur ...	1,05,888	10,893	1,16,781	1 6 10	1 2 4
Tahsil Hata ...	...	3,82,719	38,760	4,21,479	1 6 7	1 2 5
Salempur-Majhauli	Dewapara	4,47,580	44,886	4,92,468	1 11 2	1 5 2
Tahsil Deoria ...	...	4,47,580	44,886	4,92,466	1 11 2	1 5 2
Bhauapar	Bhuapara	43,889	4,526	48,415	1 9 2	1 3 8
Haveli	Haveli, Gorakhpur ...	2,70,821	28,297	2,99,118	1 6 1	0 15 9
Maghar	Maghar-Ratanpur ...	86,976	8,696	95,672	1 11 2	1 4 7
Tahsil Gorakhpur ...	...	4,01,686	41,519	4,43,205	1 7 4	1 1 0
Total District ...	...	25,23,252	2,57,029	27,80,281	1 5 11	0 15 4

TABLE XI.—*Excise*

Year.	Receipts from foreign liquors.	Country spirit.		Receipts from *Tari* and *Sendhi*.	Drugs.			Opium.		Total receipts.	Total charges.	Incidence of receipts per 10,000 of population from—			Number of shops for sale of—		
		Receipts.	Consumption in gallons.		Total receipts.	Consumption in maunds of—		Total receipts.	Consumption.			Liquor including *Tari*.	Drugs.	Opium.	Country spirit.	Drugs.	Opium.
						Ganja.	*Charas.*										
1	2	3	4	5	6	7	8	9	10	11	12	13	14	15	16	17	18
	Rs.	Rs.	Rs.	Rs.	Rs.	Md. s.	Md. s.	Rs.	Md. s.	Rs.	Rs.	Rs.	Rs.	Rs.			
1890-91...	675	1,87,553	39,212	23,345	24,224	Not available...		11,243	27 22	2,47,051	2,414	707	81	38	320	348	11
1891-92...	515	1,71,458	36,050	22,708	23,846			12,341	28 28	2,30,872	2,991	650	80	41	323	248	11
1892-93...	1,043	1,90,452	41,680	23,165	25,573	88 1	5 36	13,829	34 27	2,54,068	3,014	717	86	46	319	257	11
1893-94...	909	2,06,515	40,360	21,289	23,000	42 35	6 8	11,669	31 1	2,63,382	2,315	764	77	39	322	257	46
1894-95...	797	2,14,876	38,150	20,963	29,000	37 21	12 0	13,105	33 12	2,78,756	2,426	783	97	44	310	257	46
1895-96...	989	1,94,660	32,238	21,443	29,000	30 32	9 16	11,586	33 17	2,57,680	1,375	711	97	39	324	261	46
1896-97...	821	1,42,795	29,644	19,703	27,567	51 33	6 37	12,016	35 19	2,02,913	2,259	537	92	40	307	271	46
1897-98...	867	1,70,133	38,809	21,119	31,651	48 18	7 32	12,704	37 19	2,36,497	1,676	629	106	42	311	261	46
1898-99...	870	2,20,058	48,083	22,085	31,087	54 21	12 18	13,848	41 27	2,87,939	1,697	808	109	44	314	261	46
1899-1900	947	2,47,348	43,863	29,677	54,271	40 26	19 6	13,708	41 2	3,45,964	3,418	921	110	46	331	261	46
1900-01...	867	2,32,856	39,253	35,047	40,501	31 24	18 39	13,800	37 30	3,23,315	3,463	909	137	46	335	261	46
1901-02...	843	2,29,179	40,354	29,537	36,365	38 34	17 31	14,275	38 0	3,10,284	2,854	879	123	48	337	261	46
1902-03...	867	2,74,420	44,819	37,052	40,023	50 26	15 15	15,085	40 38	3,67,511	3,125	1,059	136	51	337	261	46
1903-04...	1,039	3,27,964	45,743	34,836	41,045	24 10	15 25	16,055	41 34	4,20,948	3,547	1,233	139	54	337	261	46
1904-05...	1,449	3,55,657	46,874	28,532	43,177	31 37	19 2	15,789	43 11	4,44,714	3,382	1,307	146	54	337	261	46
1905-06...	1,326	3,50,649	33,643	41,346	39,199	22 1	6 27	15,614	41 6	4,48,242	3,153	1,342	134	53	337	261	46
1906-07...	1,207	2,56,154	47,046	39,121	40,453	15 38	7 0	20,368	52 39	3,57,502	3,117	1,012	138	70	186	261	46
1907-08...	1,383	2,65,932	30,974	38,695	41,911	14 36	5 21	15,704	39 0	3,63,625	4,029	1,044	143	54	171	260	46
1908-09...																	
1909-10...																	
1910-11...																	
1911-12...																	
1912-13...																	
1913-14...																	
1914-15...																	
1915-16...																	
1916-17...																	
1917-18...																	

TABLE XII.—*Stamps.*

Year.	Receipts from—			Total charges.
	Non-judicial.	Court-fee, including copies.	All sources.	
1	2	3	4	5
	Rs.	Rs.	Rs.	Rs.
1890-91	63,563	2,24,863	2,88,657	5,442
1891-92	64,303	2,48,034	3,13,067	4,219
1892-93	60,097	2,41,035	3,01,630	3,096
1893-94	60,976	2,42,176	3,03,825	3,983
1894-95	67,517	2,17,904	2,85,585	3,290
1895-96	65,283	2,13,224	2,78,755	4,007
1896-97	70,364	2,06,246	2,76,914	5,711
1897-98	74,936	2,07,277	2,83,647	5,837
1898-99	61,346	2,07,350	2,72,198	4,296
1899-1900	68,563	2,00,224	2,73,033	5,454
1900-01	76,968	2,25,403	3,06,181	4,713*
1901-02	74,270	2,35,880	3,13,989	8,686
1902-03	64,082	2,24,956	2,92,864	6,195
1903-04	62,364	2,25,050	2,91,278	7,166
1904-05	66,731	2,36,222	3,07,316	8,134
1905-06	71,741	2,12,614	2,88,135	6,379
1906-07	70,344	2,44,545	3,19,152	6,265
1907-08	82,240	2,79,027	3,66,184	8,780
1908-09				
1909-10				
1910-11				
1911-12				
1912-13				
1913-14				
1914-15				
1915-16				
1916-17				
1917-18				

* Discount only.

TABLE XIII.—*Income-tax.*

Year.	Total receipts.	Collected by companies.		Profits of companies.		Other sources, Part IV.				Total charges	Objections under Part IV.	
						Under Rs. 2,000.		Over Rs. 2,000.				
		Assessees.	Tax.	Assessees.	Tax.	Assessees.	Tax.	Assessees.	Tax.		Number filed.	Wholly or partly successful.
1	2	3	4	5	6	7	8	9	10	11	12	13
	Rs.		Rs.		Rs.		Rs.		Rs.	Rs.		
1890-91	1,09,739	356	8,678	1	27,726	Not available			...	1,357	Not available.	
1891-92	1,16,259	292	9,468	1	32,476	2,158	35,149	242	30,784	1,328	756	239
1892-93	1,25,598	282	10,499	1	42,471	2,086	34,180	243	30,272	1,255	842	286
1893-94	1,28,813	252	9,558	1	43,795	2,088	34,090	258	32,408	1,234	776	178
1894-95	1,34,739	253	10,542	1	42,975	2,095	34,866	286	37,180	2,914	1,023	306
1895-96	1,44,258	274	12,243	1	45,590	2,252	28,128	320	39,081	3,651	1,255	283
1896-97	1,42,158	282	12,402	1	45,812	2,173	36,623	352	38,509	499	1,470	467
1897-98	1,52,609	369	17,751	1	45,682	7,172	36,333	366	43,843	4,324	1,530	662
1898-99	1,52,335	412	18,891	2	47,516	2,113	36,701	337	40,023	354	1,002	394
1899-1900	1,63,972	444	20,586	2	54,065	2,106	36,197	376	43,414	227	1,293	294
1900-01	1,75,732	469	20,853	2	72,998	2,062	35,192	350	37,044	356	1,155	346
1901-02	1,71,075	432	20,503	2	68,198	2,040	35,713	359	37,187	169	1,271	300
1902-03	1,83,421	453	20,445	2	79,561	2,023	35,723	368	37,929	374	1,249	376
1903-04	1,61,763	213	16,683	2	79,975	770	21,613	351	35,663	482	592	191
1904-05	1,88,844	233	18,574	2	1,01,931	796	22,165	370	38,268	720	795	261
1905-06	2,04,458	258	20,298	3	1,15,156	800	22,370	373	38,099	471	622	155
1906-07	1,88,095	267	21,500	3	95,491	791	21,936	378	39,897	622	573	166
1907-08	2,15,700	295	24,291	3	1,11,288	812	23,218	430	46,878	401	738	232
1908-09												
1909-10												
1910-11												
1911-12												
1912-13												
1913-14												
1914-15												
1915-16												
1916-17												
1917-18												

TABLE XIV.—*Income-tax for City and Tahsils (Part IV only).*

Year.	Gorakhpur City. Under Rs. 2,000. Assessees.	Gorakhpur City. Under Rs. 2,000. Tax.	Gorakhpur City. Over Rs. 2,000. Assessees.	Gorakhpur City. Over Rs. 2,000. Tax.
1	2	3	4	5
		Rs.		Rs.
1890-91 ...	271	4,398	66	11,750
1891-92 ...	275	4,490	64	11,640
1892-93 ...	279	4,578	63	11,592
1893-94 ...	274	4,510	65	11,742
1894-95 ...	269	4,352	66	11,810
1895-96 ...	275	4,408	64	11,612
1896-97 ...	271	4,342	65	11,663
1897-98 ...	284	4,080	67	12,685
1898-99 ...	273	4,828	57	11,157
1899-1900 ...	281	5,210	65	11,712
1900-01 ...	263	4,900	62	8,293
1901-02 ...	237	3,975	58	7,553
1902-03 ...	227	2,722	58	7,495
1903-04 ...	83	2,238	55	7,344
1904-05 ...	90	2,282	63	8,251
1905-06 ...	81	2,139	63	8,370
1906-07 ...	86	2,166	64	7,783
1907-08 ...	85	2,153	63	8,234
1908-09 ...				
1909-10 ...				
1910-11 ...				
1911-12 ...				
1912-13 ...				
1913-14 ...				
1914-15 ...				
1915-16 ...				
1916-17 ...				
1917-18 ...				

Year.	Tahsil Bansgaon. Under Rs. 2,000. Assessees.	Tahsil Bansgaon. Under Rs. 2,000. Tax.	Tahsil Bansgaon. Over Rs. 2,000. Assessees.	Tahsil Bansgaon. Over Rs. 2,000. Tax.
1	2	3	4	5
		Rs.		Rs.
1893-94 ...	333	4,890	35	6,902
1894-95 ...	333	4,818	40	7,906
1895-96 ...	353	5,678	40	5,768
1896-97 ...	325	5,203	41	6,657
1897-98 ...	323	5,238	40	5,848
1898-99 ...	317	5,140	40	5,907
1899-1900 ...	325	5,103	41	6,028
1900-01 ...	335	5,117	39	5,883
1901-02 ...	286	5,[illegible]06	42	7,235
1902-03 ...	341	5,451	38	6,020
1903-04 ...	98	2,553	37	6,335
1904-05 ...	89	2,316	36	6,208
1905-06 ...	93	2,320	34	4,961
1906-07 ...	92	2,264	36	4,629
1907-08 ...	92	2,340	35	4,742
1908-09 ...				
1909-10 ...				
1910-11 ...				
1911-12 ...				
1912-13 ...				
1913-14 ...				
1914-15 ...				
1915-16 ...				
1916-17 ...				
1917-18 ...				

TABLE XIV—(continued).—*Income-tax for City and Tahsils (Part IV only).*

Year.	Tahsil Maharajganj.				Tahsil Padrauna.				Tahsil Hata.			
	Under Rs. 2,000.		Over Rs. 2,000.		Under Rs. 2,000.		Over Rs. 2,000.		Under Rs. 2,000.		Over Rs. 2,000.	
	Assessees.	Tax.	Assessees.	Tax.	Assessees.	Tax.	Assessees.	Tax.	Assessees.	Tax.	Assessees.	Tax.
1	2	3	4	5	1	2	3	4	1	2	3	4
		Rs.		Rs.		Rs.		Rs.		Rs.		Rs.
1890-91 ...	340	4,270	10	1,251	Not available ...				312	6,153	37	4,253
1891-92 ...	338	4,680	8	1,236					311	6,338	34	4,018
1892-93 ...	335	4,586	10	1,257					310	6,176	38	4,191
1893-94 ...	341	4,737	9	1,024					325	6,453	35	3,935
1894-95 ...	340	5,024	17	1,632					338	6,842	37	4,268
1895-96 ..	348	5,227	26	2,638	321	5,379	52	4,583	370	7,332	38	4,498
1896-97 ...	527	7,477	34	4,116	328	5,576	54	4,443	384	7,371	57	5,850
1897-98 ...	362	6,290	28	2,789	218	4,938	38	3,703	335	6,482	55	5,997
1898-99 ...	428	6,816	36	3,758	290	4,701	39	3,702	319	6,340	53	5,565
1899-1900 ...	359	5,954	30	2,588	338	5,524	56	4,850	302	5,879	62	5,933
1900-01 ...	337	5,247	32	2,323	333	5,511	57	4,935	296	5,684	55	5,345
1901-02 ...	337	5,201	31	2,169	325	5,923	56	4,758	287	5,792	55	5,405
1902-03 ...	365	5,560	34	2,420	339	6,211	63	6,076	294	6,093	57	5,596
1903-04 ...	98	2,662	36	2,526	153	4,025	60	5,720	151	4,587	61	5,786
1904-05 ...	110	3,033	37	2,452	164	4,218	58	6,019	156	4,826	71	6,861
1905-06 ...	108	3,034	37	2,524	164	4,292	59	5,726	153	4,645	72	6,220
1906-07 ...	103	2,986	36	2,592	154	4,017	61	7,739	164	4,909	72	6,784
1907-08 ...	93	2,635	37	2,597	163	4,290	59	6,824	162	5,294	94	9,658
1908-09 ...												
1909-10 ...												
1910-11 ...												
1911-12 ...												
1912-13 ...												
1913-14 ...												
1914-15 ...												
1915-16 ...												
1916-17 ...												
1917-18 ...												

TABLE XIV—(concluded).—*Income-tax for City and Tahsils (Part IV only).*

Year.	Tahsil Deoria. Under Rs. 2,000. Assessees.	Tahsil Deoria. Under Rs. 2,000. Tax.	Tahsil Deoria. Over Rs. 2,000. Assessees.	Tahsil Deoria. Over Rs. 2,000. Tax.	Year.	Tahsil Gorakhpur.* Under Rs. 2,000. Assessees.	Tahsil Gorakhpur.* Under Rs. 2,000. Tax.	Tahsil Gorakhpur.* Over Rs. 2,000. Assessees.	Tahsil Gorakhpur.* Over Rs. 2,000. Tax.
1	2	3	4	5	1	2	3	4	5
		Rs.		Rs.			Rs.		Rs.
1890-91 ...	295	5,409	80	8,948	1890-91 ...	174	2,690	17	1,462
1891-92 ...	332	6,663	40	4,755	1891-92 ...	173	2,630	18	1,482
1892-93 ...	380	6,094	48	4,663	1892-93 ...	176	2,644	16	1,290
1893-94 ...	358	6,591	53	5,407	1893-94 ...	175	2,632	16	1,248
1894-95 ...	370	6,860	68	7,347	1894-95 ...	177	2,746	18	1,500
1895-96 ...	388	8,589	90	8,340	1895-96 ...	176	2,807	18	1,510
1896-97 ...	398	7,136	113	10,000	1896-97 ...	176	2,777	18	1,616
1897-98 ...	379	6,693	107	10,603	1897-98 ...	206	3,169	19	1,632
1898-99 ...	359	6,979	101	10,704	1898-99 ...	214	3,314	21	1,550
1899-1900 ...	328	6,033	103	9,415	1899-1900 ...	217	3,284	23	2,017
1900-01 ...	295	5,409	89	8,947	1900-01 ...	209	3,335	20	1,565
1901-02 ...	313	5,563	107	10,156	1901-02 ...	204	3,933	14	962
1902-03 ...	268	5,165	101	9,054	1902-03 ...	188	4,488	19	1,252
1903-04 ...	105	3,338	86	7,645	1903-04 ...	81	2,154	16	1,216
1904-05 ...	102	3,259	85	7,801	1904-05 ...	79	2,112	20	1,416
1905-06 ...	110	3,508	87	8,475	1905-06 ...	91	2,432	22	1,824
1906-07 ...	112	3,410	90	8,881	1906-07 ...	80	2,184	19	1,488
1907-08 ...	130	4,103	127	13,606	1907-08 ...	87	2,403	15	1,217
1908-09 ...					1908-09 ...				
1909-10 ...					1909-10 ...				
1910-11 ...					1910-11 ...				
1911-12 ...					1911-12 ...				
1912-13 ...					1912-13 ...				
1913-14 ...					1913-14 ...				
1914-15 ...					1914-15 ...				
1915-16 ...					1915-16 ...				
1916-17 ...					1916-17 ...				
1917-18 ...					1917-18 ...				

* Excluding figures for City.

TABLE XV.—*District Board.*

Year.	Receipts.							Expenditure.										
	Education.	Medical.	Scientific, &c.	Miscellaneous.	Civil works.	Pounds.	Ferries.	Total expenditure.	Contributions to Provincial funds.	General administration.	Education.	Medical.	Scientific, &c.	Miscellaneous.	Civil works.	Pounds.	Debt.
1	2	3	4	5	6	7	8	9	10	11	12	13	14	15	16	17	18
	Rs.	Rs.	Rs.	Rs.	Rs.	Rs.	Rs.	Rs.	Rs.	Rs.	Rs.	Rs.	Rs.	Rs.	Rs.	Rs.	Rs.
1890-91 ..	1,435	4,352	...	1,532	...	10,077	...	97,828	...	1,380	33,347	14,368	...	1,774	46,959	...	...
1891-92 ...	1,552	4,050	...	1,432	...	11,815	...	1,04,981	...	1,414	32,579	15,965	...	1,855	53,168	...	...
1892-93 ..	1,604	6,721	...	1,113	2	7,747	...	99,839	...	1,723	38,147	15,180	...	1,840	47,949	...	...
1893-94 ...	1,718	4,266	...	1,179	...	7,381	...	1,05,594	...	1,946	32,969	16,361	...	1,781	52,537	...	...
1894-95 ...	1,575	4,932	...	1,253	14	8,183	...	1,17,642	...	1,885	32,741	18,686	...	1,865	62,465	...	...
1895-96 ..	1,724	5,056	...	1,302	662	9,366	...	97,672	...	1,797	32,376	18,024	...	230	45,245	...	...
1896-97 ...	1,340	4,868	...	1,117	808	9,121	...	1,07,625	...	1,815	35,815	18,553	...	373	51,069	...	...
1897-98 ...	1,862	5,692	...	2,961	3,865	7,152	...	2,14,227	99,523	1,690	35,469	18,451	120	...	58,974	...	...
1898-99 ...	3,270	5,778	...	2,961	2,878	7,495	...	1,84,505	59,022	2,672	36,388	18,977	181	...	65,750	...	1,515
1899-1900...	4,479	7,324	...	2,962	13,160	*16,506	...	2,10,100	53,000	3,016	42,870	19,786	258	86	84,183	6,436	1,515
1900-01 ...	4,328	6,164	...	2,961	3,895	16,352	†672	2,13,200	58,000	3,001	44,817	19,885	251	94	77,528	6,324	3,300
1901-02 ...	6,569	10,190	...	30	5,085	13,843	13,752	2,12,547	62,000	2,958	47,480	20,891	188	200	68,514	8,001	2,315
1902-03 ...	5,912	8,550	...	...	3,384	15,639	5,508	2,67,226	...	3,617	52,932	21,955	396	40	1,77,896	7,919	2,471
1903-04 ...	6,243	11,538	...	20	5,203	16,202	14,740	3,19,692	...	3,533	54,627	22,679	678	71	2,28,404	7,370	2,330
1904-05 ...	5,101	10,530	...	85	7,489	15,947	16,116	2,58,796	...	3,889	54,476	23,373	1,064	162	1,66,888	6,502	2,442
1905-06 ...	6,825	10,045	...	105	3,419	16,281	16,248	2,59,761	...	4,099	66,872	25,394	2,179	369	1,50,315	6,866	3,667
1906-07 ...	5,011	10,598	...	93	2,335	19,003	21,812	2,27,099	...	5,636	70,076	26,984	2,189	504	1,07,908	8,045	5,697
1907-08 ...	11,641	9,680	...	143	2,587	18,149	23,289	2,64,609	...	5,737	84,262	27,969	2,592	560	1,28,427	7,151	7,911
1908-09 ...																	
1909-10 ...																	
1910-11 ...																	
1911-12 ...																	
1912-13 ...																	
1913-14 ..																	
1914-15 ...																	
1915-16 ...																	
1916-17 ...																	
1917-18 ..																	

* Formerly net receipts only were shown. From this year receipts and also expenditure are given.

† From this year the gross receipts from ferries were for the first time credited to the District Board.

TABLE XVI.—*Municipality of Gorakhpur.*

Year.	Income.							Expenditure.									
	Octroi.	Tax on houses and lands.	Other taxes.	Rents.	Loans.	Other sources.	Total.	Administration and collection of taxes.	Public safety.	Water supply and drainage.		Conservancy.	Hospitals and dispensaries.	Public works.	Public instruction.	Other heads.	Total.
										Capital.	Maintenance.						
1	2	3	4	5	6	7	8	9	10	11	12	13	14	15	16	17	18
	Rs.	Rs.	Rs.	Rs.	Rs.	Rs.	Rs.	Rs.	Rs.	Rs.	Rs.	Rs.	Rs.	Rs.	Rs.	Rs.	Rs.
1890-91...	35,894	...	392	1,377	...	15,181	52,844	7,807	6,955		1,161	12,639	1,228	16,283	6,097	5,732	58,052
1891-92...	36,494	...	457	5,220	...	11,370	53,541	7,171	7,492	3,215	162	14,710	1,163	12,814	6,209	4,806	57,742
1892-93...	39,833	...	855	6,173	...	13,371	60,232	10,694	7,495	521	1,355	14,485	1,478	11,119	6,263	2,976	56,376
1893-94...	40,485	180	712	7,218	...	12,319	60,914	11,012	8,806	1,803	545	14,426	2,857	12,926	6,580	5,320	63,775
1894-95...	40,115	...	1,542	1,318	...	17,838	60,313	8,014	9,233	186	672	14,894	830	13,188	6,748	8,346	62,111
1895-96...	49,357	...	1,591	1,234	...	17,679	69,861	8,413	10,389	711	777	14,487	840	12,690	6,986	10,200	65,493
1896-97...	43,358	...	1,067	1,184	...	15,764	61,373	9,095	11,415	...	407	14,830	1,072	10,648	7,095	9,427	63,989
1897-98...	48,472	...	892	843	..	17,087	67,294	8,168	9,731	...	227	12,396	1,108	11,003	6,665	7,846	57,144
1898-99...	60,903	...	921	1,231	...	19,137	82,192	7,858	9,993	...	247	16,219	1,020	28,873	6,796	7,936	78,942
1899-1900	58,335	...	1,091	1,251	...	20,393	81,070	9,160	11,040	741	68	23,537	840	21,818	7,845	14,753	89,802
1900-01...	58,328	...	1,691	2,810	...	19,732	82,561	9,864	12,134	159	401	18,303	840	11,080	9,945	10,395	73,121
1901-02...	63,169	...	1,553	2,408	...	20,573	87,703	10,112	12,463	...	113	24,118	3,508	6,260	10,712	21,119	88,405
1902-03...	44,279	...	1,372	2,005	...	18,631	66,287	10,192	12,136	...	391	21,654	3,588	6,583	10,844	12,076	77,464
1903-04...	50,565	...	1,067	1,788	...	18,927	72,347	10,534	11,615	...	1,229	22,927	3,708	5,449	11,213	10,272	76,947
1904-05...	61,643	...	1,071	2,926	...	21,815	87,455	12,518	12,784	...	1,307	20,303	3,708	6,694	11,480	8,713	77,507
1905-06...	53,833	...	1,534	2,745	...	25,721	83,833	12,232	3,869	256	1,734	25,130	3,708	12,503	13,293	9,721	82,446
1906-07...	73,542	...	1,705	2,937	...	17,343	95,527	15,545	3,793	...	1,988	19,769	3,708	14,979	13,232	14,051	87,065
1907-08...	69,946	...	1,946	3,412	...	9,043	84,347	14,091	6,355	...	1,466	24,297	3,708	15,203	5,464	9,588	80,172
1908-09...																	
1909-10...																	
1910-11...																	
1911-12...																	
1912-13..																	
1913-14...																	
1914-15...																	
1915-16 ..																	
1916-17...																	
1917-18...																	

TABLE XVII.—*Distribution of Police*, 1908.

Thana.	Sub-Inspectors.	Head-constables.	Constables.	Town Police.	Rural Police.	Road Police.	Goraits.
1	2	3	4	5	6	7	8
Kotwali	4	14	130	...	89	2	472
Barhi	1	1	8	...	52	2	142
Chaura	1	1	12	...	37	2	183
Sahjanwa	1	1	9	...	75	4	204
Rudrapur	1	1	8	...	96	2	385
Bansgaon	2	2	15	...	101	6	549
Belghat	1	1	9	...	147	...	825
Gola	2	1	10	10	109	2	250
Barhalganj	2	1	10	9	86	2	337
Maharajganj ...	2	1	9	..	67	...	209
Semra	2	1	12	...	64	...	228
Rigauli	1	1	10	...	59	2	125
Panera	1	1	8	...	32	...	52
Biraicha	1	1	7	...	30	.	110
Paisia	1	1	8	...	32	...	114
Nichlaul	1	1	8	...	43	...	142
Thuthibari	1	1	7	...	13	...	59
Kothibhar	2	1	10	2	71	.	298
Padrauna	2	1	11	9	78	...	220
Ramkola	1	1	10	...	49	...	85
Kasia	2	1	11	...	68	2	218
Qazipur	1	1	10	...	78	...	237
Bishunpura ...	1	1	7	...	80	...	68
Taria Sujan ...	1	1	8	...	61	...	149
Hata	2	1	11	...	74	...	296
Mansurganj ...	1	1	8	...	39	...	171
Pipraich	1	1	10	5	68	...	235
Tarkulwa	2	1	10	8	84	4	264
Rudarpur	2	1	11	8	87	...	291
Deoria	2	1	12	6	71	2	267
Masela	2	1	10	...	87	..	308
Barhaj	1	1	9	26	41	2	134
Salempur	2	1	12	7	104	...	320
Khampur	2	1	13	...	107	...	315
Civil Reserve ...	9	...	70	...	...	...	.
Armed Police ...	2	24	167			...	...
Mounted Police ...	...	2	20	..	...	...	...
Total ...	63	74	710	90	2,329	34	7,662

TABLE XVIII.—*Education.*

Year.	Total.			Secondary education.			Primary education.		
	Schools and colleges.	Scholars.		Schools.	Scholars.		Schools.	Scholars.	
		Males.	Females.		Males.	Females.		Males.	Females
1	2	3	4	5	6	7	8	9	10
1896-97 ...	252	10,597	462	17	1,992	48	233	8,376	414
1897-98 ...	256	10,841	616	18	2,161	32	236	8,462	584
1898-99 ...	273	13,477	1,111	19	2,532	33	252	10,704	1,078
1899-1900...	358	21,732	997	21	3,075	157	334	18,388	840
1900-01 ...	320	21,847	1,153	22	3,467	145	295	18,166	963
1901-02 ...	330	22,317	1,185	20	3,284	163	307	18,865	917
1902-03 ...	329	20,340	609	17	2,777	88	311	17,537	611
1903-04 ...	325	17,032	525	17	2,554	70	307	14,449	455
1904-05 ...	331	19,796	640	19	3,053	97	301	16,707	543
1905-06 ...	437	26,079	677	19	3,086	107	417	22,960	570
1906-07 ...	516	29,158	743	18	3,330	...	500	25,828	743
1907-08 ...	527	33,509	826	19	3,775	27	510	29,834	799
1908-09 ...									
1909-10 ...									
1910-11 ...									
1911-12 ...									
1912-13 ...									
1913-14 ...									
1914-15 ...									
1915-16 ...									
1916-17 ...									
1917-18 ...									

List of Schools, 1908.

Tahsil.	Pargana.	Tappa.	School.	Class.	Average attendance.
Gorakhpur.	Haveli.	Qasba ... Gorakhpur.	St. Andrew's College.	Collegiate, C.M.S.,	324
			Jubilee High School.	High School ...	471
			Normal School,	Provincial Training School.	133
			Swinton Memorial.	Middle vernacular aided.	112
			Alinagar ...	Middle Anglo-vernacular, aided.	40
			Hansupur ...	Lower Primary, Municipal.	76
			Allahdadpur ...	Ditto ...	35
			Ahata Pande ...	Ditto ..	37
			Khunipur ...	Ditto ...	39
			Reti ...	Ditto ...	27
			Tiwaripur ...	Ditto ...	25
			Ilahi-bagh ...	Ditto ...	30
			Andhiari Bagh,	Ditto ..	47
			Captainganj ...	Ditto ...	39
			Ghasiketra ...	Ditto ...	28
			Mian Bazar ...	Ditto ...	41
			Ditto ...	Lower Primary, aided, Municipal.	23
			Purdilpur ...	Ditto ...	23
			Jafra Bazar ...	Ditto ...	24
			Bargadwa ...	Ditto ...	20
			Urdu Bazar ...	Upper Primary aided, Municipal.	54
			Alinagar ...	Ditto ...	53
			Chauk ...	Lower Primary, District Board.	27
			Mian Bazar ...	Lower Primary, Municipal, girls'.	27
			Ditto ...	Lower Primary aided, girls'.	54
			Alinagar ...	Ditto ...	56
			Khunipur ...	Ditto ...	74
			Allahdadpur ..	Ditto ...	69
			Basharatpur ...	Ditto ...	19
			Alinagar ...	Lower Primary, Private, girls'.	24
			Khunipur ...	Ditto ...	29
		Gaura ...	Doharia ...	Upper Primary ...	56
		Ditto ...	Majhgawan ...	Ditto ...	57
		Ditto ...	Mirpur ...	Lower Primary ...	32
		Rasulpur ...	Barampur ...	Upper Primary ...	83
		Ditto ...	Mithabel ...	Lower Primary ...	52
		Haveli ...	Raiganj ...	Ditto ..	21
		Do. ...	Bargaon ...	Ditto ...	41
		Do. ...	Mirzapur ...	Upper Primary, aided.	55
		Patra ...	Pipraich ...	Upper Primary ...	67

List of Schools 1908—(continued).

Tahsil.	Pargana.	Tappa.	School.	Class.	Average attendance.
Gorakhpur—(contd.).	Haveli—(concld.).	Patra ...	Pipraich ...	Lower Primary, girls'.	20
		Pachwara ...	Barhia Chak ...	Upper Primary ...	95
		Ditto ...	Rajabari ...	Lower Primary, aided.	27
		Ditto ...	Kaithaulia ...	Ditto ...	16
		Ditto ...	Piprahinian ...	Ditto ...	29
		Ditto ...	Sidborwa ...	Ditto ...	60
		Ditto ...	Kauria ...	Ditto ...	43
		Ditto ...	Rakhnakhor ...	Aided Pathshala.	30
		Keotali ...	Dumri ...	Middle vernacular.	106
		Ditto ...	Jagdispur ...	Upper Primary, aided.	33
		Ditto ...	Bela ...	Ditto	30
		Ditto ...	Rakba Raja ...	Lower Primary, aided.	39
		Ditto ...	Chauri Chaura ...	Ditto ...	34
		Khutahan ...	Phulwaria ...	Lower Primary ...	32
		Ditto ...	Gularia ...	Lower Primary, aided.	28
		Ditto ...	Jangal Saligram.	Ditto ...	29
		Marichhi Chandaur.	Sarahri ...	Ditto ...	47
		Ditto ...	Tikaria ...	Ditto ...	20
		Ditto ...	Rampur Gopalpur.	Upper Primary, aided.	39
		Rajdhani ...	Rajdhani ...	Ditto ...	25
		Ditto ...	Baksauri ...	Ditto ...	69
		Ditto ...	Koin Bazar ...	Ditto ...	37
		Ditto ...	Bishunpura ...	Upper Primary ...	118
		Ditto ...	Barhi ...	Lower Primary, aided.	52
		Ditto ...	Dihghat ...	Ditto ...	41
		Ditto ...	Thumbhi Bazar ...	Ditto ...	34
		Ditto ...	Jhangha ...	Ditto ...	33
	Bhauapar.	Haveli ...	Bhauapar ...	Upper Primary ...	90
		Do. ...	Hardia ...	Ditto ...	127
		Do. ...	Kakrakhor ...	Ditto ...	94
		Rafi ...	Bhagwanpur ...	Ditto ...	94
		Do. ...	Piprauli ...	Ditto ...	189
		Do. ...	Ditto ...	Lower Primary, aided, girls'.	20
		Do. ...	Khanampur ...	Lower Primary ...	48
		Do. ...	Bargahan ...	Ditto ...	26
		Do. ...	Nagwa ...	Ditto ...	37
		Do. ...	Bhiti Bhilaura ...	Upper Primary, aided.	37
		Do. ...	Barwal ...	Lower Primary, aided.	40
	Maghar.	Gahasand ...	Minwa ...	Middle vernacular.	203
		Ditto ...	Gahasand ...	Lower Primary, aided.	36
	Hasanpur Maghar.	Satgawan ...	Sargahna ...	Ditto ...	30
		Khajuri ...	Sonbarsa ...	Ditto ...	38

List of Schools, 1908—(continued).

Tahsil.	Pargana.	Tappa.	School.	Class.	Average attendance.
Gorakhpur—(concld.).	Hasanpur Maghar—(concld.).	Khajuri ...	Bankata ...	Lower Primary...	42
		Bharsand ...	Bharsand ...	Ditto ...	58
		Bhadesri ...	Harpur ...	Upper Primary...	188
		Aurangabad ..	Dumri Newas ...	Ditto ...	89
		Ditto ...	Charaon ...	Ditto ...	101
		Ditto ...	Newas ...	Lower Primary...	40
		Ditto ...	Naurang Patti ...	Lower Primary, aided.	42
		Ditto ...	Dumri ...	Lower Primary, girls'.	20
		Uttar Haveli ...	Rithuakhor ...	Upper Primary...	94
		Ditto ...	Pali ...	Ditto ...	124
		Ditto ...	Ghagsara ...	Lower Primary...	71
		Ditto ..	Banauli ...	Lower Primary, aided.	43
		Ditto ...	Bhimapar ..	Ditto ...	43
		Ditto ...	Sihapar ..	Ditto ...	38
		Ditto ...	Dukdaya ...	Ditto ...	31
		Ditto ...	Chandhari ...	Ditto ...	49
Bansgaon.	Bhauapar.	Pachisi ...	Dhanaura ...	Upper Primary...	112
		Kotha ...	Gajpur ...	Ditto ...	79
		Do. ...	Bhalwan ...	Ditto ...	81
		Do. ...	Kotha ...	Ditto ...	92
		Do. ...	Do. ...	Lower Primary, girls'.	28
		Do. ..	Basudiha ...	Lower Primary, aided.	38
		Ghagha ...	Ghagha ...	Upper Primary...	109
		Ditto ...	...	Lower Primary, girls'.	22
		Ditto ...	Rakhat ...	Upper Primary; aided.	43
		Ditto ...	Bilkaur ...	Lower Primary, aided.	35
		Kuswansi ...	Belipar ...	Upper Primary...	133
		Ditto ...	Kusmaul ...	Upper Primary, aided.	50
		Ditto ...	Charpau ...	Ditto ...	42
		Ditto ...	Malaon ...	Lower Primary, aided.	35
		Gurmhi ...	Malauli ...	Upper Primary...	79
		Ditto ...	Chawaria ...	Ditto ...	115
		Ditto ...	Sohgaura ...	Lower Primary, aided.	33
		Ditto ...	Haraya ...	Ditto ...	60
	Unaula.	Mahsan ...	Bansgaon ...	Middle vernacular,	159
		Ditto ...	Ditto ...	Lower Primary, girls'.	15
		Ditto ...	Barhni ...	Upper Primary ...	80
		Ditto ...	Baidauli ...	Ditto ...	71
		Ditto ...	Bhainsa ...	Ditto ...	71
		Ditto ...	Hariharpur ...	Upper Primary, aided.	41

List of Schools, 1908—(continued).

Tahsil.	Pargana.	Tappa.	School.	Class.	Average attendance.
Bansgaon—(*contd.*).	Unaula—(*concld.*).	Mahsan ...	Kator ...	Upper Primary, aided.	27
		Ditto ...	Pagar ...	Lower Primary, aided.	38
		Bankata ..	Ahmadpur ...	Upper Primary, aided.	40
		Ditto ...	Bankata ...	Lower Primary ...	46
		Ditto ...	Barigaon ...	Ditto ...	30
		Haveli ...	Bishunathpur ...	Upper Primary, aided.	75
		Do. ...	Ditto Pathshala.	Ditto ...	34
		Do ...	Katya Bazar ...	Ditto ...	65
		Do. ...	Baghi ...	Ditto ...	39
		Do. ...	Chitai ...	Ditto ...	49
		Do. ...	Basiakhor ...	Ditto ...	54
		Do. ...	Jhondia ...	Ditto ...	46
		Do. ...	Pipra Banwari ...	Ditto ...	42
		Do. ...	Khultamau ...	Ditto ...	58
		Do. ...	Unwal ...	Lower Primary ...	37
	Dhuriapar.	Barhuj ...	Gola ...	Middle vernacular,	99
		Ditto ...	Do. ...	Lower Primary, girls'.	18
		Ditto ...	Bhereh ...	Upper Primary ...	66
		Haveli ...	Dughera ...	Ditto ...	82
		Gaur ...	Keshwapar ...	Ditto ...	10
		Do. ...	Gaur ...	Upper Primary, aided.	70
		Do. ...	Narayanpur ...	Ditto ...	43
		Pali ...	Pali ...	Ditto ...	40
		Do. ...	Bhainsahi ...	Lower Primary ...	57
		Bhadar ...	Dhakwa Chak ...	Ditto ...	47
		Ditto ...	Barhiapar ...	Ditto ...	37
		Ratanpur ...	Sahdauli ...	Lower Primary, aided.	46
		Ditto ...	Tirirpur ...	Ditto ...	30
		Kurmaut ...	Barai Buzurg ...	Upper Primary ...	58
		Ditto ...	Purwa ...	Ditto ...	75
		Ditto ...	Araon Jagdispur,	Upper Primary, aided.	30
		Ditto ...	Naryajpar ...	Lower Primary, aided.	31
		Nakauri ...	Nakauri ...	Ditto ...	43
		Bankata ...	Murarpur ...	Ditto ...	44
		Ditto ...	Kurawal ...	Upper Primary, aided.	49
		Ditto ...	Bangaon ...	Ditto ...	43
		Kohra ...	Pakri ...	Ditto ...	46
		Tiar ...	Dubauli ...	Ditto ...	46
		Athaisi ...	Gaurapar ...	Ditto ...	43
		Ditto ...	Majhgawan ...	Upper Primary ...	94
		Usri ...	Mahui ...	Ditto ...	78
		Babhnauli ...	Malhanpar ...	Ditto ...	92

List of Schools, 1908—(continued).

Tahsil.	Pargana.	Tappa.	School.	Class.	Average attendance.
Bansgaon—(contd.).	Dhuriapar—(concld.).	Majuri ...	Hata ...	Upper Primary...	87
		Khutahan ...	Madaria ...	Ditto ...	80
		Ditto ...	Durmaha ...	Lower Primary...	35
		Ditto ...	Belsara ...	Lower Primary, aided	41
		Parsi ...	Sikriganj ...	Lower Primary...	40
		Do. ...	Ahrauli ...	Upper Primary, aided.	39
		Chandpar ...	Gopalpur ...	Upper Primary...	92
		Ditto ...	Didhia ...	Ditto ...	80
		Ditto ...	Kawadil ...	Upper Primary, aided.	45
		Ditto ...	Diwapar ...	Lower Primary, aided.	43
		Ditto ...	Harpur ...	Ditto ...	28
		Ditto ...	Patra ...	Ditto ...	33
		Ditto ...	Kakrahi ...	Ditto ...	45
		Ditto ...	Badela ...	Ditto ...	45
		Thati ...	Thati ...	Upper Primary ...	95
		Do. ...	Shukulpura ...	Upper Primary, aided.	55
		Chorar ...	Chitanua ...	Ditto ...	36
		Ditto ...	Dehra Tikar ...	Lower Primary, aided.	40
		Narhi ...	Chillua ...	Upper Primary...	59
		Ditto ...	Manon ...	Lower Primary...	26
		Ditto ...	Narhi Buzurg ...	Upper Primary, aided.	72
		Ditto ...	Rampur Bhagua...	Lower Primary, aided.	47
		Belghat ...	Belghat ...	Upper Primary...	67
		Ditto ...	Shahpur ...	Ditto ...	61
		Ditto ...	Ratanpura ...	Lower Primary...	20
		Ditto ...	Kuri ...	Upper Primary, aided.	36
		Ditto ...	Shankarpur ...	Lower Primary, aided.	33
		Ditto ...	Piparsandi ...	Ditto ...	32
		Ditto ...	Bhahia ...	Ditto ...	81
	Chilupar.	Haveli ...	Barhalganj ...	Middle vernacular,	100
		Ditto ...	Ditto ...	Lower Primary, girls'.	15
		Ditto ...	Tanda ...	Upper Primary...	111
		Ditto ...	Mohnapur ...	Upper Primary, aided.	52
		Ditto ...	Dhabauli ...	Lower Primary, aided.	33
		Ditto ...	Sidhawapar ...	Ditto ...	22
		Semra ...	Khut Bihar ...	Ditto ...	29
		Sikandarpur ...	Padhni ...	Ditto ...	22
		Ditto ...	Khairauti ...	Upper Primary, aided.	90

List of Schools, 1908—(continued).

Tahsil.	Pargana.	Tappa.	School.	Class.	Average attendance.
Bansgaon—(*concld.*).	Chillupar—(*concld.*).	Sikandarpur ...	Patna ...	Upper Primary, aided.	42
		Majhaulia ...	Ghewarpar ...	Ditto ...	85
		Ditto ...	Rayaun ...	Lower Primary, aided.	47
		Ditto ...	Bairiadih ...	Ditto ...	30
Maharajganj.	Haveli.	Katahra ...	Maharajganj ...	Upper Primary...	131
		Ditto ...	Pipra Qazi ...	Upper Primary, aided.	56
		Ditto ...	Nandabhar ...	Lower Primary, aided.	50
		Ditto ...	Dharampur ...	Ditto ...	42
		Ditto ...	Gaunaria ...	Ditto ...	41
		Ditto ...	Basantpur ...	Ditto ...	34
		Rigauli ...	Dhani ...	Middle vernacular.	159
		Ditto ...	Rigauli ...	Upper Primary...	101
		Ditto ...	Sonaura ...	Ditto ...	71
		Ditto ...	Balewa ...	Lower Primary, aided.	83
		Ditto ...	Bankata ...	Ditto ...	25
		Ditto ...	Badua ...	Ditto ...	28
		Audhaya ...	Puralmau ...	Ditto ...	37
		Sumbhakhor ...	Machhligaon ...	Ditto ...	39
		Ditto ...	Indarpur ...	Ditto ...	21
		Unti ...	Barahra ...	Ditto ...	39
		Do. ...	Mahrawa ...	Ditto ...	35
		Matkopa ...	Rampur ...	Upper Primary...	66
		Ditto ...	Harpur ...	Upper Primary, aided.	36
		Ditto ...	Belwa ...	Lower Primary, aided.	37
		Biraicha ...	Partawal ...	Lower Primary ...	43
		Ditto ...	Ditto ...	Lower Primary, aided.	20
		Ditto ...	Biraicha ...	Upper Primary, aided.	37
		Ditto ...	Banspar ...	Ditto ...	49
		Bhari Baisi ...	Sahibganj ...	Upper Primary...	126
		Ditto ...	Nanapar ...	Ditto ...	70
		Ditto ...	Suras ...	Upper Primary, aided.	28
		Ditto ...	Chomkha ...	Ditto ...	41
		Ditto ...	Netwar ...	Lower Primary, aided.	55
		Ditto ...	Bhaunrabari ...	Ditto ...	17
		Banki ...	Khotha Bazar ...	Lower Primary...	40
		Lehra ...	Pharenda ...	Upper Primary...	72
		Do. ...	Kasauli ...	Ditto ...	39
		Do. ...	Pakardiha ...	Lower Primary...	69
		Do. ...	Purandarpur ...	Ditto ...	51
		Do. ...	Bridgmanganj ...	Ditto ...	56
		Do. ...	Ditto ...	Upper Primary, aided.	33
		Do. ...	Lehra ...	Ditto ...	30

List of Schools, 1908—(continued).

Tahsil.	Pargana.	Tappa.	School.	Class.	Average attendance.
Maharajganj—(*concld.*).	Haveli—(*concld.*).	Lohra ...	Lalpur ...	Upper Primary, aided.	32
		Do. ...	Pipra ...	Ditto ...	38
		Do. ...	Pokhar Bhanda...	Ditto ...	40
		Do. ...	Mahadewa ...	Lower Primary, aided.	34
		Do. ...	Lajrua ...	Ditto ...	57
		Do. ...	Sahjanua ...	Ditto ...	40
		Do. ...	Karmahwa ...	Ditto ...	53
	Binayakpur.	Nagwar ...	Deoghati ...	Upper Primary, aided.	76
		Ditto ...	Bishunpura ...	Lower Primary, aided.	26
		Sirsia ...	Sirsia ...	Ditto ...	31
		Mirchwar ...	Nautanwa ...	Upper Primary, aided.	41
		Ditto ...	Paisia ...	Lower Primary, aided.	16
	Tilpur.	Sukrahar ...	Turkahia ...	Ditto ..	40
		Domakhand ...	Baithaulia ...	Ditto ...	20
		Bharatkhand ...	Pakri ..	Ditto ...	46
		Khas ...	Somri Chak ...	Ditto ...	48
		Do. ...	Mithaura ...	Lower Primary ...	36
		Nai Karhi ...	Karmahi ...	Ditto ...	50
		Ditto ...	Rampur ...	Ditto ...	33
		Purani Karhi ...	Siswa ...	Upper Primary, aided.	105
Padrauna.	Sidhua Jobna.	Batsara ...	Bhujauli ...	Ditto ...	34
		Ditto ...	Singhapatti ...	Ditto ...	34
		Ditto ...	Naurangia ...	Lower Primary aided.	22
		Ditto ...	Khada ...	Ditto ...	40
		Ditto ...	Lakhua Lakhui...	Ditto ...	35
		Ditto ...	Bhirhari ..	Ditto ...	30
		Naugawan ...	Barwa Ratanpur..	Ditto ...	21
		Ditto ...	Khajuri ...	Ditto ...	47
		Ditto ...	Baraipatti ...	Lower Primary...	26
		Papaur ...	Ramkola ...	Upper Primary...	100
		Ditto ...	Barwa Bazar ...	Upper Primary, aided.	51
		Ditto ...	Khunthi ...	Lower Primary, aided.	64
		Dandopur ...	Dandopur ...	Ditto ...	35
		Bansi Chirgora ...	Mansa Chhapra...	Ditto ...	23
		Bhalua ...	Sukhawan ...	Upper Primary...	82
		Ditto ...	Bhatrauli ...	Lower Primary...	27
		Ditto ..	Amwa ...	Upper Primary, aided.	56
		Khan ...	Jaura ...	Ditto ...	42
		Do. ...	Saria ...	Lower Primary...	51
		Jhankaul ...	Mahua ...	Upper Primary...	95
		Do. ...	Sohang ...	Upper Primary, aided.	30

List of Schools, 1908—(continued).

Tahsil.	Pargana.	Tappa.	School.	Class.	Average attendance.
Padrauna—(*concld.*).	Sidhua Jobna—(*concld.*).	Jhankaul ...	Basdila ...	Upper Primary, aided.	40
		Ditto ...	Fazilnagar ...	Lower Primary, aided.	33
		Sapahi Kuchia ...	Chandrauta ...	Ditto ...	54
		Bhatni Badraon...	Badraon ...	Lower Primary...	40
		Ditto ...	Jogia ...	Upper Primary, aided.	46
		Mahil Saraini ...	Sidhamai ...	Upper Primary...	89
		Ditto ...	Baghanch ...	Lower Primary, aided.	60
		Ditto ...	Pathardewa ...	Ditto	42
		Haveli ...	Salemgarh ...	Upper Primary...	92
		Ditto ...	Lachhmipur ...	Upper Primary, aided.	52
		Ditto ...	Patherwa ...	Ditto ...	49
		Ditto ...	Madhopur ...	Lower Primary, aided.	38
		Pakri Gangrani...	Padrauna ...	Middle vernacular,	120
		Ditto ...	Piprasi ...	Lower Primary, aided.	30
		Dhuria Bijaipur,	Tamkuhi ...	Upper Primary...	89
		Ditto ...	Tiwari Patti ...	Upper Primary, aided.	35
		Ditto ...	Guraulia ...	Ditto ...	42
		Ditto ...	Mathia Bhukari...	Lower Primary, aided.	38
		Bargaon Chaura.	Lachhmipur ...	Upper Primary, aided.	41
		Rampur Dhab ...	Barwa Patti ...	Lower Primary, aided.	35
		Bank Jogni ...	Sahibganj ...	Ditto ...	35
		Ditto ...	Perozha ...	Ditto ...	30
		Ditto ...	Johi ...	Ditto ...	15
		Ditto ...	Mathia Sri Ram ..	Ditto ...	47
		Sandi ...	Sandi ...	Ditto ...	33
		Do. ...	Sakhopar ...	Lower Primary...	32
		Mainpur ...	Kasia ...	Middle vernacular,	189
		Ditto ...	Malludih ...	Lower Primary, aided.	41
		Parwarpar ...	Parwarpar ...	Upper Primary...	59
		Ditto ...	Deoria ...	Lower Primary ..	48
		Ditto ...	Tikwatar ...	Ditto ...	45
		Ditto ...	Kusmaha ...	Ditto ...	33
		Ditto ...	Ahrauli ..	Lower Primary, aided.	20
Hata.	Silhat.	Nagwan Tikar ...	Rudarpur ...	Upper Primary...	124
		Ditto ...	Saraon ...	Upper Primary, aided.	45
		Ditto ...	Khurma ...	Ditto ...	45
		Ditto ...	Nagwan ...	Lower Primary, aided.	32
		Ditto ...	Bishunpura ...	Ditto ...	27
		Ditto ...	Nakail ...	Ditto ...	22

List of Schools, 1908—(continued).

Tahsil.	Pargana.	Tappa.	School.	Class.	Average attendance.
Hata—(*contd.*).	Silhat—(*contd.*).	Nagwan Tikar ...	Jagannathpur ...	Lower Primary, aided.	44
		Ditto ...	Dahrauli ...	Ditto ...	19
		Ditto ...	Pachdari ...	Ditto ...	42
		Dhatura ...	Barhia Buzurg ..	Ditto ...	48
		Ditto ...	Barari ...	Ditto ...	24
		Indupur ...	Patharhat ...	Upper Primary...	75
		Ditto ...	Sanda ...	Upper Primary, aided.	38
		Ditto ...	Lamkani ...	Ditto ...	44
		Ditto ...	Deogaon ...	Lower Primary, aided.	23
		Madanpur ...	Madanpur ...	Lower Primary...	44
		Kataura ...	Kataura ...	Ditto ...	28
		Sirjam ...	Sirjam ...	Upper Primary...	60
		Banchara ..	Padri ...	Ditto ...	63
		Donat ...	Baripar ...	Upper Primary, aided.	40
		Singhpur ...	Rampur ...	Ditto ...	51
		Ditto ...	Dhara ...	Upper Primary...	60
		Binayakpur ...	Raisri ...	Lower Primary...	52
		Chariaon ...	Khaira ...	Lower Primary, aided.	40
	Shahjahanpur.	Bachhauli ...	Hata ...	Upper Primary...	[illegible]5
		Ditto ...	Patni ...	Lower Primary, aided.	40
		Ditto ...	Majhawa ...	Ditto ..	53
		Ditto ...	Gannar Barwa ...	Ditto ...	46
		Nagwan ...	Ahrauli ...	Lower Primary...	29
		Ditto ...	Narayanpur ...	Ditto ...	71
		Ditto ...	Pipra Madan Gopal.	Lower Primary, aided.	35
		Ditto ...	Nautan ...	Ditto ...	38
		Ditto ...	Dwarka ...	Ditto ...	37
		Ditto ...	Dasaihi Deoria ...	Ditto ...	39
		Patna ...	Mundahra ...	Upper Primary...	88
		Do. ...	Rampur Karkhana,	Lower Primary...	45
		Do. ...	Sirsia Kalan ...	Ditto ...	48
		Bhainsadabar ...	Baghra ...	Lower Primary, aided.	45
		Dedupar ...	Bhainsahi ...	Ditto ...	42
		Bhatni ...	Pipra ...	Ditto ...	39
		Ditto ...	Hetimpur ...	Lower Primary...	41
		Pandiapar ...	Balkuan ...	Ditto ...	51
		Ditto ...	Dhamaur ...	Lower Primary, aided.	45
		Tarkulwa ...	Rampur Garh ...	Upper Primary...	70
	Haveli.	Parwarpur ...	Captainganj ...	Ditto ...	41
		Ditto ...	Barahra ...	Lower Primary, aided.	42
		Ditto ...	Mathauli ...	Ditto ...	40
		Ditto ...	Akatha ...	Ditto ...	49
		Bandwar ...	Dhaunan ...	Ditto ...	28
		Dedupar ...	Paikauli ...	Lower Primary...	36

List of Schools, 1908—(continued).

Tahsil.	Pargana.	Tappa.	School.	Class.	Average attendance.
Hata—(concld.).	Haveli—(concld.).	Parkhori ...	Kondar ...	Upper Primary, aided.	39
		Ditto ...	Bardiha ...	Lower Primary, aided	34
		Barsand ...	Sakhupur ...	Ditto ...	50
		Ditto ...	Badarwa ...	Lower Primary ...	53
		Ditto ...	Barahra ...	Lower Primary, aided, girls'.	37
Deoria.	Salempur-Majhauli.	Haveli ...	Majhauli ...	Middle vernacular,	125
		Ditto ...	Ditto ...	Lower Primary, girls'.	18
		Ditto ...	Bankata ...	Upper Primary ...	88
		Ditto ...	Bhatwa ...	Ditto ...	82
		Ditto ...	Bhiari Baghel ...	Ditto ...	101
		Ditto ...	Bhingari ...	Lower Primary...	46
		Ditto ...	Tikampur ...	Upper Primary, aided.	34
		Ditto ...	Bhatpar ...	Lower Primary, aided.	35
		Gautama ...	Pipra Baghel	Ditto ...	54
		Ditto ...	Ahrauli Baghel...	Lower Primary...	43
		Sohanpur ...	Sohanpur ...	Upper Primary...	146
		Ditto ...	Rampur ...	Upper Primary, aided.	55
		Balwan ...	Rohanian ...	Lower Primary, aided.	37
		Ghati ...	Motipur Bhual ...	Upper Primary, aided.	42
		Do. ...	Saria ...	Lower Primary, aided.	29
		Bhatni ...	Hatwa ...	Upper Primary ...	91
		Ditto ...	Piasi ...	Lower Primary...	48
		Ditto ...	Naunapar ...	Ditto ...	62
		Salempur ...	Tilauli ...	Upper Primary...	176
		Ditto ...	Bishunpura ...	Ditto ...	93
		Ditto ...	Salempur ...	Lower Primary...	45
		Barsipar ...	Domaulia ...	Upper Primary .	88
		Ditto ...	Chakarwa ...	Upper Primary, aided.	28
		Ditto ...	Dhanauti ...	Ditto ...	54
		Ditto ...	Pipra Deoraj ...	Ditto ...	29
		Kachwar ...	Rampur ...	Ditto ...	50
		Ditto ...	Baikunthpur .	Upper Primary...	114
		Ditto ..	Barzarpur ...	Lower Primary...	59
		Ditto ...	Nautan ...	Lower Primary, aided.	50
		Nai ...	Parsia ...	Ditto ...	27
		Do. ...	Thakur Deoria ...	Upper Primary, aided.	38
		Sarauli ...	Ahlwar Buzurg ..	Ditto ...	37
		Do. ...	Paikauli ...	Lower Primary, aided.	36
		Deoria ...	Deoria ...	Anglo-vernacular, aided.	166

List of Schools, 1908—(concluded).

Tahsil.	Pargana.	Tappa.	School.	Class.	Average attendance.
Deoria—(*concld.*).	Salempur-Majhauli—(*concld.*).	Deoria ...	Deoria ...	Upper Primary...	131
		Ditto ...	Do. ...	Lower Primary, aided, girls'.	20
		Samogar ...	Samogar ...	Lower Primary...	43
		Khakhundu ...	Khakhundu ...	Ditto ...	38
		Ditto ...	Padri ...	Upper Primary, aided.	56
		Kaparwar ...	Kaparwar ..	Upper Primary...	82
		Ditto ...	Mahawan ...	Upper Primary, aided.	30
		Ditto ...	Rajpur ...	Ditto ...	38
		Ditto ...	Karail Shukul ...	Lower Primary, aided.	33
		Raipura ...	Barhaj ...	Middle vernacular,	147
		Ditto ...	Ditto ...	Lower Primary, girls'.	18
		Ditto ...	Paianan ...	Upper Primary...	117
		Ditto ...	Sonari ...	Lower Primary...	54
		Ditto ...	Garer ...	Ditto ...	34
		Ditto ...	Bakuchi ...	Upper Primary, aided.	29
		Ditto ...	Bhaluani ..	Ditto ...	41
		Ditto ...	Mahoi ...	Lower Primary, aided.	36
		Ditto ...	Piprakot ...	Ditto ...	40
		Bairauna ...	Bairauna ...	Upper Primary...	48
		Ditto ...	Bardiha ...	Lower Primary ..	56
		Balia ...	Ditto ...	Middle vernacular,	71
		Do. ...	Kundauli ...	Upper Primary...	121
		Do. ...	Peri ...	Ditto ...	109
		Do. ...	Bhagalpur ...	Ditto ...	64
		Do. ...	Ramnagar ...	Lower Primary ...	50
		Do. ...	Nadauli ...	Lower Primary, aided.	50
		Do ...	Nima ...	Ditto ...	52

ROADS, 1908.	Length.	
	Miles	fur.
A.—PROVINCIAL.		
(i) Fyzabad, Basti and Gorakhpur road	15	6
(ii) Ghazipur, Dohri-ghat and Gorakhpur road	35	0
(iii) Cantonment roads	2	0·2
Total ...	52	6·2
B.—LOCAL.		
I.—First-class metalled roads.		
(i) Gorakhpur station roads	16	4
(ii) Ditto to Kasia [*vide* II-B (iii)]	11	0
(iii) Ditto to Nichlaul [*vide* II-B (i)]	13	2
(iv) Ditto to Captainganj [*vide* II-B (ii)] ...	1	7
(v) Metalled diversion at Chillua Tal	0	4·5
(vi) Bhatpar to Majhauli	5	0
(vii) Barhaj to Kasia	39	5
(viii) Link to Rampur Karkhana	0	7·8
Total ...	88	6·3
II(A).—Second-class unmetalled roads, bridged and drained throughout.		
(i) Gorakhpur to Lotan	38	0
(ii) Kasia to Padrauna	12	0
(iii) Gola to Kauriram	13	4
Total ...	63	4
II(B).—Second-class unmetalled roads, partially bridged and drained.		
(i) Gorakhpur to Nichlaul [*vide* I (iii)]	33	0
(ii) Ditto to Captainganj [*vide* I (iv)]	22	0
(iii) Ditto to Kasia and Samaur [*vide* I (ii)] ...	37	6·2
(iv) Ditto to Deoria and Chapra	52	3 5
(v) Ditto to Sikriganj, Barhaj and Lar	74	0
(vi) Gola to Rudarpur	20	0
(vii) Karmaini-ghat to Captainganj and Bansi-ghat ..	53	1·5
(viii) Pharenda station to Maharajganj and Senduria ...	25	0
(ix) Sikriganj to Shahpur	8	0
(x) Pipraich to Barhi [*vide* III (iii)]	5	0
(xi) Pipraich to Partawal	10	2
(xii) Hata to Pagra	3	3·5
(xiii) Hata to Rudarpur [*vide* III (v)]	6	0
(xiv) Kauriram to Gajpur and Ghagha	10	7·7
(xv) Debipur to Lachhmipur	0	1·4
(xvi) Gauri Bazar station road	0	1·8
(xvii) Samaur to Tiwari Patti and Padrauna [*vide* III (viii)] ...	2	0
(xviii) Padrauna to Nichlaul [*vide*]	6	0
(xix) Nichlaul to Tengri	2	0
(xx) Pharenda to Parsauni	10	5
(xxi) Sahjanwa to Bansi	9	5·4
Total ...	391	6

ROADS, 1908—(*concluded*).	Length.	
	Miles	fur.
III.—Third-class roads, banked and surfaced, partially bridged and drained.		
(i) Gorakhpur to Barhi	11	2·3
(ii) Ditto (Alinagar) to Basharatpur	2	4·4
(iii) Barhi to Pipraich [*vide* II-B (x)]	11	0
(iv) Pipraich to Pagra	11	1
(v) Hata to Rudarpur [*vide* II-B (xiii)]	15	0
(vi) Hata to Deoria	14	4·5
(vii) Deoria to Rudarpur	10	5·1
(viii) Samaur to Padrauna [*vide* II-B (xvii)]	25	0
(ix) Samaur to Padrauna direct	20	0
(x) Tiwari Patti to Qazipur	6	5
(xi) Kasia to Pipra-ghat	24	0·8
(xii) Rudarpur to Barhaj	14	0
(xiii) Bhagalpur to Musela...	14	2·3
(xiv) Bhagalpur to Bhingari	16	0
(xv) Nichlaul to Thuthibari	8	3
(xvi) Nichlaul to Khajuria	28	3·5
(xvii) Nichlaul to Partawal...	24	3·5
(xviii) Nichlaul to Bagapar and Uska	37	5
(xix) Bagapar to Bagaha	34	0
(xx) Bagapar to Maharajganj and Shikarpur	9	7
(xxi) Captainganj to Naurangia	15	0
(xxii) Captainganj to Sabia	19	1·4
(xxiii) Bansgaon to Rudrapur	10	0
(xxiv) Urwa Bazar to Jaswantpur	5	0
(xxv) Kauriram to Malhanpur	8	4
(xxvi) Shahpur to Belghat and Kamharia	8	5·4
(xxvii) Chaura station to Jadupur	14	0
(xxviii) Dumri to Keoladahar	4	3·6
(xxix) Dhani Bazar to Bela Haraya and Lotan	11	1
(xxx) Khirkia to Jatha	9	4
Total ...	444	2·8
IV.—Fourth-class roads, partially bridged and drained.		
(i) Peppeganj station to Jaswal	4	0
Total ...	4	0
GRAND TOTAL ...	1,045	1·3

FERRIES, 1908.

River.	Ferry.	Pargana.	Tahsil.	Management.	Income.
					Rs.
Rapti ...	Karmainj ...	Haveli ...	Maharajganj,	District Board,	
	Belaha ...	Do. ...	Ditto ...	Ditto ...	3,300
Dhamela.	Madra ...	Do. ...	Ditto ...	Ditto ...	
	Kahrauli ...	Do. ...	Ditto ...	Ditto ...	850
Rapti ...	Madarha ...	Do. ...	Gorakhpur ...	Ditto ...	260
	Belghat ...	Do. ...	Ditto ...	Ditto ...	405
	Tharauli ..	Do. ...	Ditto ...	Ditto ...	1,050
	Thatbar ...	Do. ...	Ditto ...	Ditto ...	
	Naudwa ...	Do. ...	Ditto ...	Ditto ...	950
	Sisai ...	Hasanpur Maghar,	Ditto ...	Ditto ...	1,200
	Kartahri ...	Ditto	Ditto ...	Ditto ...	
	Netwar ...	Ditto ..	Ditto ...	Ditto ...	880
	Bird-ghat ...	Bhauapar ...	Ditto ...	Provincial ...	...
	Bhauapar ...	Ditto ..	Ditto ...	Ditto ...	...
	Kaleswar ...	Ditto ...	Ditto ...	District Board,	310
	Chanda .	Ditto ...	Bansgaon ...	Ditto ...	400
	Rajpur Kaparwar	Salempur ...	Deoria ...	Ditto ..	550
Ghaghra.	Basai ...	Dhuriapar ...	Bansgaon ...	Ditto ...	500
	Belwa	Ditto ..	Ditto ...	Ditto ...	
	Kalyanpur ..	Ditto ...	Ditto ...	Ditto ..	2,000
	Shahpur Tapatia,	Ditto ...	Ditto ...	Ditto ...	
	Godiana ...	Ditto ...	Ditto ...	Ditto ..	1,850
	Gola Nainijor ...	Ditto ...	Ditto ...	Ditto ...	
	Dohri ...	Ditto .	Ditto ..	Provincial ...	
	Pohila Rampur .	Chillupar ...	Ditto ...	District Board,	510
	Madarha Gangipur.	Ditto ..	Ditto ...	Ditto ...	
	Turtipar ...	Salempur ...	Deoria ...	District Board, Ballia.	...
	Karimganj ...	Ditto ...	Ditto ..	Ditto ...	...
	Duha Behra ...	Ditto ...	Ditto ...	Ditto ...	...
Rohin...	Tirmohani ..	Binayakpur ...	Maharajganj,	District Board,	175
	Maniram ...	Haveli ...	Gorakhpur ...	Ditto ...	725
Little Gandak.	Captainganj ...	Ditto ...	Hata ...	Ditto ...	380
	Hetimpur ...	Shahjahanpur ...	Do. ...	Ditto ...	215
	Goria ..	Ditto ...	Do. ...	Ditto ...	25
	Ghutni ...	Salempur ...	Deoria ...	Private ...	...

POST-OFFICES, 1908.

Tahsil.	Pargana.	Locality.	Class of office.
Gorakhpur ...	Haveli ...	Gorakhpur ...	Head office.
	Do. ...	Ditto railway station,	Sub-office.
	Do. ...	Urdu Bazar ...	Ditto.
	Do. ...	Alinagar	Ditto.
	Do. ...	Jafra Bazar ...	Branch office.
	Do. ...	Raiganj	Ditto.
	Do. ...	Sahibganj	Ditto.
	Do. ...	Pipraich	Ditto.
	Do. ...	Chauri Chaura ...	Ditto.
	Do. ...	Kusmahi	Ditto.
	Do. ...	Barhi	Ditto.
	Maghar ...	Sahjanwa	Ditto.
	Bhauapar ...	Bhauapar	Ditto.
Bansgaon ...	Bhauapar ...	Ghagha	Sub-office.
	Ditto ...	Kauriram	Ditto.
	Unaula ...	Bansgaon	Ditto.
	Dhuriapar ...	Gola	Ditto.
	Ditto ...	Shahpur	Branch office.
	Ditto ...	Belghat	Ditto.
	Ditto ...	Dhakwa	Ditto.
	Ditto ...	Sukulpura	Ditto.
	Chillupar ...	Khajuri	Ditto.
	Ditto ...	Ajaipura	Ditto.
	Ditto ...	Barhalganj ...	Sub-office.
Maharajganj ...	Haveli ...	Maharajganj ...	Sub-office.
	Do. ...	Bridgmanganj ...	Ditto.
	Do. ...	Peppeganj	Branch office.
	Do. ...	Rigauli	Ditto.
	Do. ...	Campierganj ...	Ditto.
	Do. ...	Biraicha	Ditto.
	Do. ...	Panera	Ditto.
	Do. ...	Semra	Ditto.
	Do. ...	Pharenda	Ditto.
	Do. ...	Dhani	Ditto.
	Tilpur ...	Nichlaul	Ditto.
	Ditto ...	Kothibhar	Ditto.
	Binayakpur ...	Thuthibari... ...	Ditto.
	Ditto ...	Paina	Ditto.
Padrauna ...	Sidhua Jobna ...	Padrauna	Sub-office.
	Ditto ...	Kasia	Ditto.
	Ditto ...	Tamkuhi	Ditto.
	Ditto ...	Gazipur	Branch office.
	Ditto ...	Bishunpura ...	Ditto.
	Ditto ...	Taria Sujan ...	Ditto.
	Ditto ...	Ramkola	Ditto.
	Ditto ...	Kindarpatti ...	Ditto.
Hata ...	Haveli ...	Mansurganj ...	Sub-office.
	Ditto ...	Captainganj ...	Branch office.
	Shahjahanpur ...	Hata	Sub-office.
	Ditto ...	Rampur	Branch office.
	Ditto ...	Hatimpur	Ditto.

POST-OFFICES, 1908—*(concluded).*

Tahsil.	Pargana.	Locality.	Calss of office.
Hata—*(concld.).*	Shahjahanpur ...	Tarkulwa	Branch office.
	Silhat ...	Gauri Bazar ...	Ditto.
	Do. ...	Rudarpur	Sub-office.
Deoria ...	Salempur ...	Deoria	Sub-office.
	Ditto ...	Majhauli	Ditto.
	Ditto ...	Lar	Ditto.
	Ditto ...	Bhatpar	Ditto.
	Ditto ...	Barhaj	Ditto.
	Ditto ...	Bhagalpur	Branch office.
	Ditto ...	Bhatni	Ditto.
	Ditto ...	Bankata	Ditto.
	Ditto ...	Khampar	Ditto.
	Ditto ...	Tikampar	Ditto.
	Ditto ...	Nunkhar	Ditto.
	Ditto ...	Salempur	Ditto.
	Ditto ...	Baikunthpur ...	Ditto.
	Ditto ...	Garer	Ditto.
	Ditto ...	Tilia	Ditto.

MARKETS, 1908.

Tahsil.	Pargana.	Tappa.	Locality.	Market days.
Bansgaon.	Bhauapar.	Kuswansi ...	Kusmaul ...	Sunday.
		Ditto ...	Dharwarpar ...	Tuesday and Friday.
		Ditto ...	Bharwal ...	Saturday.
		Kotha ...	Bhalwan ...	Ditto
		Do ...	Kotha ...	Monday.
		Do. ...	Gajpur ...	Wednesday.
		Do. ...	Banspar ...	Sunday.
		Gurmhi ...	Gurmhi ...	Ditto
		Ditto ...	Pandepar ...	Thursday.
		Pachisi ...	Dhanaura ...	Tuesday.
		Ghagha ...	Ghagha, Hatwa ...	Ditto
		Ditto ...	Ghagha, Paspurwa	Sunday.
		Ditto ...	Gadhi	Thursday.
	Unaula.	Haveli ...	Chatai... ...	Thursday.
		Ditto ...	Katya	Tuesday.
		Ditto ...	Bishunpur ...	Friday.
		Ditto ...	Doharia ...	Monday.
		Ditto ...	Khutahan ...	Wednesday.
		Mahsan ...	Bhatauli ...	Ditto
		Ditto ...	Bansgaon ...	Monday and Friday.
		Ditto ...	Gajar Jagdis ...	Sunday and Wednesday.
		Ditto ...	Barahan ...	Friday.
		Ditto ..	Raghwadih ...	Sunday.
		Ditto ..	Unwal (Sangrampur),	Thursday.
		Ditto ...	Bhainsa ...	Saturday.
		Ditto ...	Barpurwa ...	Ditto
		Bankata ...	Ahmadpur ...	Ditto
		Ditto ...	Bankata ...	Thursday.
		Ditto ...	Muhammadpur ...	Tuesday.
	Dhuriapar.	Barhaj ..	Gola Bazar ...	Tuesday and Friday.
		Belghat ...	Shahpur ...	Thursday.
		Ditto ...	Kuri	Sunday and Thursday.
		Ditto ...	Nargara ...	Sunday and Wednesday.
		Ditto ...	Gaighat ...	Tuesday and Saturday.
		Ditto ...	Gaurganj ...	Monday.
		Ditto ...	Belghat ...	Friday.
		Babhnauli ...	Malhanpur ...	Ditto
		Athaisi ...	Karwal (Majhgawan),	Ditto
		Ditto ...	Rawatpar ...	Wednesday.
		Bankat ...	Murarpur ...	Ditto
		Khutahan ...	Anandgarh ...	Monday and Thursday,
		Narhi ...	Sihaijpar ...	Monday.
		Tiar ..	Sahudad ...	Wednesday.
		Do. ...	Janipur ...	Sunday.
		Majuri ...	Hata	Ditto
		Parsi ...	Sikriganj ...	Sunday and Wednesday.
		Bhadar ...	Dhakwa ...	Ditto.
		Usri ...	Asaunji ...	Thursday.
		Ratanpur ...	Baranagar ..	Ditto
		Kurmaut ...	Urwa	Saturday.
		Pali ...	Pali Khas ...	Ditto

MARKETS, 1908—(*continued*).

Tahsil.	Pargana.	Tappa.	Locality.	Market days.
Bansgaon—(*concld.*).	Chillupar—(*concld.*).	Haveli ...	Barhalganj ...	Saturday and Wednesday
		Ditto ...	Pharsand ...	Tuesday and Friday.
		Sikandarpur ...	Ramgarh ...	Ditto.
		Majhaulia ...	Aswandpar ...	Thursday.
Maharajganj.	Haveli.	Matkopa ...	Harpur ...	Thursday.
		Ditto ...	Rampur ...	Monday.
		Ditto ...	Pakri ...	Ditto.
		Ditto ...	Belwa ...	Friday.
		Bitaicha ...	Chaumukha ...	Ditto.
		Ditto ...	Partawal ...	Sunday and Thursday.
		Ditto ...	Bariha Buzurg ...	Wednesday.
		Ditto ...	Khanpur ...	Saturday.
		Unai ...	Barahra ...	Ditto.
		Do. ...	Semargarh ...	Wednesday.
		Sambhakhor ...	Bhaura Bari ...	Thursday.
		Ditto ...	Machhligaon ...	Tuesday and Saturday.
		Ditto ...	Chautarwa ...	Wednesday.
		Bhari Baisi ...	Narkatha ...	Ditto.
		Ditto ...	Mahuag ...	Sunday.
		Ditto ...	Aktahwa ...	Monday.
		Ditto ...	Sahibganj ...	Tuesday.
		Ditto ...	Peppeganj ...	Ditto.
		Ditto ...	Satgur ...	Thursday.
		Ditto ...	Gangi ...	Saturday.
		Ditto ...	Netwar ...	Sunday.
		Banki ...	Mundila ...	Monday.
		Do. ...	Kamari Buzurg ...	Wednesday.
		Do. ...	Panera ...	Friday.
		Do. ...	Dinguri ...	Ditto.
		Andhaya ...	Baijauli ...	Tuesday.
		Rigauli ...	Rigauli ...	Ditto
		Ditto ...	Dhani Bazar ...	Monday.
		Lehra ...	Bridgmanganj ...	Sunday.
		Do. ...	Mathuranagar ...	Wednesday.
		Do. ...	Lehra ...	Ditto.
		Do. ...	Pharenda station ...	Ditto.
		Do. ...	Mahua Adda ...	Ditto.
		Do. ...	Pipra ...	Monday and Friday.
		Do. ...	Tola Bargadwa ...	Tuesday.
		Do. ...	Bardand ...	Ditto.
		Do. ...	Paina ...	Ditto.
		Do. ...	Pipra Parsauni ...	Friday.
		Do. ...	Purandarpur ...	Thursday.
		Katahra ...	Rajwal ...	Ditto.
		Ditto ...	Maharajganj ...	Saturday.
		Ditto ...	Siswa ...	Tuesday and Saturday.
		Ditto ...	Khajuria ...	Wednesday.
		Ditto ...	Semra (Haidarganj),	Ditto.
		Ditto ...	Dhanewa ...	Tuesday.
		Ditto ...	Nadiwa ...	Sunday.
		Ditto ...	Baulia Babu ...	Ditto.
		Ditto ...	Dharampur ...	Ditto.

MARKETS, 1908—(*continued*).

Tahsil.	Pargana.	Tappa.	Locality.	Market days.
Maharajganj—(*concld*.).	Haveli—(*concld*.).	Katahra ...	Bagapar ...	Friday.
		Ditto ...	Bhagatar ...	Ditto
	Binayakpur.	Nagwan ...	Deoghati ...	Friday.
		Ditto ...	Sheotari ...	Thursday.
		Sukrahar ...	Turkahia ...	Wednesday.
		Ditto ...	Thuthibari ...	Monday.
		Sirsia ...	Khoria ...	Ditto
		Do. ...	Bhagwanpur ...	Sunday.
		Mirchwar ...	Nautanwa ...	Saturday.
		Ditto ...	Sonauli ...	Tuesday.
		Ditto ...	Naunia ...	Wednesday.
	Tilpur.	Purani Karhi ...	Siswa ...	Wednesday.
		Ditto ...	Sonbarsa ...	Monday and Friday.
		Domakhand ...	Bahwar ...	Ditto
		Ditto ...	Baithaulia ...	Ditto
		Ditto ...	Lachhmipur Khurd,	Sunday.
		Bharatkhand ...	Kaini ...	Monday.
		Khas ...	Nichlaul ...	Thursday.
		Do. ...	Garaura ...	Tuesday.
		Nai Karhi ..	Basdila ...	Ditto
Padrauna.	Sidhua Jobna.	Batsara ...	Bhujauli ...	Tuesday and Wednesday.
		Ditto ...	Kohargaddi ...	Sunday and Thursday.
		Ditto ...	Kotwa ...	Ditto.
		Ditto ...	Terhi ...	Sunday.
		Ditto ...	Maghi ...	Ditto
		Ditto ...	Ramnagar ...	Ditto
		Ditto ...	Nibua Raiganj ...	Friday.
		Ditto ...	Lakhua Lakhui ...	Ditto
		Ditto ...	Nisrauli ...	Ditto
		Ditto ...	Tin Bardaha ...	Tuesday.
		Ditto ...	Khada ...	Ditto
		Ditto ...	Bhainsaha ...	Wednesday.
		Ditto ...	Siswa Gopal ...	Saturday.
		Ditto ...	Mathia ...	Monday.
		Ditto ...	Bulahwa ...	Tuesday and Thursday.
		Naugawan ...	Barwa Ratanpur ...	Sunday and Thursday.
		Ditto ...	Morar ...	Ditto.
		Ditto ...	Khajuri ...	Tuesday and Saturday.
		Papaur ...	Dhuna Tikar ...	Ditto.
		Ditto ...	Mahua Dih ...	Friday.
		Ditto ...	Dingrapur ...	Ditto.
		Ditto ...	Sohrauli ...	Sunday.
		Ditto ...	Khutahi ...	Sunday and Wednesday.
		Ditto ...	Barwa ...	Monday and Wednesday.
		Ditto ...	Baghi ...	Monday.
		Dandopur ...	Ranwari ...	Sunday.
		Ditto ...	Patehra ...	Ditto.
		Ditto ...	Baghparna ...	Wednesday.

MARKETS, 1908—(*continued*).

Tahsil.	Pargana.	Tappa.	Locality.	Market days.
Padrauna—(*continued*).	Sidhua Jobna—(*continued*).	Dandopur ...	Misrauli (Bahadurganj).	Monday and Thursday.
		Bansi Chirgora...	Harpur ...	Ditto.
		Ditto ...	Dhaurahra ...	Ditto.
		Ditto ...	Pipra ...	Monday and Saturday.
		Ditto ...	Shambhu Chhapra ...	Sunday and Wednesday.
		Ditto ...	Jatha ...	Sunday and Thursday.
		Ditto ...	Barhia Chhapra ...	Tuesday and Friday.
		Ditto ...	Balkunria ...	Thursday.
		Ditto ...	Kothi Bazar ...	Monday and Friday.
		Bhalua ...	Langri Bazar ...	Ditto.
		Ditto ...	Karkhana Mahua ...	Sunday and Wednesday.
		Ditto ...	Kothi Sapaha ...	Tuesday and Saturday.
		Khan ...	Jaura ...	Ditto.
		Do. ...	Belwa ...	Ditto.
		Do. ...	Lachhmipur ...	Wednesday.
		Do. ...	Marchandia ...	Sunday and Thursday.
		Jhankaul ...	Fazilnagar ...	Ditto.
		Ditto ...	Sondra ...	Ditto.
		Ditto ...	Jhankaul ...	Monday and Friday.
		Ditto ...	Dhaurahra ...	Wednesday and Saturday.
		Ditto ...	Jakwa ...	Sunday and Wednesday.
		Ditto ...	Gangi Tikar ...	Ditto.
		Sapahi Kuchia ...	Karmaini ...	Ditto.
		Ditto ...	Doghra ...	Tuesday and Saturday.
		Bhatni Badraon...	Darjia ...	Monday and Friday.
		Ditto ...	Bishunpura ...	Ditto.
		Ditto ...	Bardiha Raja ...	Wednesday and Saturday
		Ditto ...	Duldiba ...	Tuesday and Saturday.
		Malsil Saraini ...	Baghauch ...	Ditto
		Ditto ...	Deoria ...	Sunday and Thursday.
		Ditto ...	Ramnagar ...	Ditto.
		Ditto ...	Pathardewa ...	Monday and Saturday.
		Ditto ...	Banjaria ...	Monday and Friday.
		Haveli ...	Taria Sujan ...	Ditto
		Ditto ...	Lachhmipur ...	Monday and Thursday.
		Ditto ...	Salemgarh ...	Ditto.
		Ditto ...	Bihar Khurd ...	Sunday and Wednesday.
		Ditto ...	Rajwatia ...	Ditto.
		Ditto ...	Dubanath ...	Ditto.
		Ditto ...	Dibni Banjarwa ...	Tuesday and Saturday.
		Ditto ...	Patherwa ...	Monday, Tuesday and Wednesday.
		Ditto ...	Basantpur ...	Ditto.
		Pakri Gangrani...	Padrauna ...	Tuesday and Saturday.
		Ditto ...	Piprasi ...	Friday.
		Ditto ...	Mathi ...	Ditto.
		Ditto ...	Horilapur ...	Monday and Thursday.
		Dhuria Bijaipur...	Tamkuhi ...	Ditto.
		Ditto ...	Bhataulia ...	Ditto.
		Ditto ...	Tiwari Patti ...	Sunday and Wednesday.
		Ditto ...	Mathia Bhukaria ...	Saturday.
		Ditto ...	Babhnauli ...	Friday.

MARKETS, 1908—*(continued)*.

Tahsil.	Pargana.	Tappa.	Locality.	Market days.
Padrauna—*(concld.)*.	Sidhua Jobna—*(concld.)*.	Pirthipur ...	Madhopur ...	Friday.
		Bargaon Chaura..	Kahraulia ...	Sunday and Wednesday.
		Ditto ...	Semaria ...	Ditto.
		Ditto ...	Dubauli ...	Ditto.
		Ditto ...	Lachhmipur ...	Thursday.
		Ditto ...	Semra ...	Monday and Friday.
		Ditto ...	Barwa Buzurg ...	Ditto.
		Ditto ...	Pachrukhia ...	Tuesday and Saturday.
		Rampur Dhab ...	Barwa patti ...	Ditto.
		Bank Jogni ...	Sahibganj ...	Ditto
		Ditto ...	Piparia ...	Monday and Friday.
		Ditto ...	Somahi Sondiha ...	Ditto.
		Ditto ...	Siswa ...	Monday and Thursday.
		Ditto ...	Rajpur Khas ...	Sunday and Wednesday.
		Ditto ...	Somahi Lochi ...	Tuesday and Friday.
		Rampur Rogha...	Baikunthpur ...	Tuesday.
		Ditto ...	Chirgora ...	Wednesday and Saturday.
		Ditto ...	Charangwa ...	Monday and Thursday.
		Sandi ...	Kasia ...	Sunday, Monday, Thursday and Friday.
		Do. ...	Sandi ...	Sunday and Wednesday.
		Do. ...	Domarbhar ...	Ditto.
		Do. ...	Sakhopar ...	Tuesday and Saturday.
		Mainpuri ...	Malludih ...	Ditto.
		Ditto ...	Narkatia ...	Friday.
		Ditto ...	Kundwa Dhanipatti,	Monday and Friday.
		Parwarpar ...	Deoria ...	Ditto.
		Ditto ...	Amwa ...	Ditto.
		Ditto ...	Urdaha ...	Sunday, Thursday and Friday.
		Ditto ...	Ragarganj ...	Wednesday and Saturday.
		Ditto ...	Tikwatar ...	Thursday and Saturday.
		Ditto ...	Parwarpar ...	Sunday.
		Ditto ...	Mahua Dih ...	Monday.
		Ditto ...	Satwarhi ...	Tuesday.
		Ditto ...	Barahra ...	Wednesday.
		Ditto ...	Rambar ...	Monday and Tuesday.
		Ditto ...	Ahrauli ...	Sunday and Wednesday.
Hata.	Silhat.	Nagwan Tikar ...	Narayanpur ...	Sunday.
		Ditto ...	Saraon ...	Ditto.
		Ditto ...	Awadhpur ...	Ditto.
		Ditto ...	Misraulia ...	Ditto.
		Ditto ...	Koil Garha ...	Ditto.
		Ditto ...	Rudarpur ...	Tuesday and Friday.
		Ditto ...	Nagwan ...	Monday.
		Ditto ...	Ikauna ...	Ditto.
		Ditto ...	Kanhauli ..	Ditto.
		Ditto ...	Chithi ...	Ditto.
		Ditto ...	Jogam ...	Ditto.
		Ditto ...	Lachhmipur ...	Wednesday.
		Ditto .	Usra ...	Thursday.
		Ditto ...	Belkaund ...	Ditto.

MARKETS, 1908—(continued).

Tahsil.	Pargana.	Tappa.	Locality.	Market days.
Hata—(continued).	Silhat—(concluded).	Nagwan Tikar ...	Lothni Bazar ...	Wednesday and Saturday.
		Ditto ...	Sakhui ...	Tuesday.
		Ditto ...	Jagannathpur ...	Friday.
		Ditto ...	Pachua ...	Thursday.
		Ditto ...	Bhali Chaur ...	Wednesday.
		Dhatura ...	Behli ...	Ditto.
		Ditto ...	Khoruram ...	Friday.
		Indupur ...	Indupur ...	Wednesday.
		Ditto ...	Patharhat ...	Monday.
		Ditto ...	Gauri Bazar ...	Saturday.
		Ditto ...	Gauri Khurd ...	Friday.
		Ditto ...	Atardiha ...	Tuesday.
		Narayanpur Chauraha.	Haria Basantpur...	Ditto.
		Ditto ...	Amari Jhanga ...	Monday.
		Ditto ...	Bikrampur ...	Thursday.
		Madanpur ...	Madanpur ...	Wednesday and Saturday.
		Adrakpur ...	Beltikra ...	Sunday.
		Katanra ...	Chorkhari ...	Ditto.
		Ditto ...	Sirsia ...	Tuesday.
		Sirjam ...	Barhia ...	Ditto.
		Ditto ...	Sirjam ...	Saturday.
		Ditto ...	Balua ...	Friday.
		Donat ...	Araipar ...	Wednesday.
		Bakhira ...	Bakhira ...	Ditto.
		Dhariaon ...	Chariaon ...	Tuesday.
		Ditto ...	Gulariha ...	Monday and Friday.
		Banchara ...	Bishunpur ...	Sunday.
		Ditto ...	Fadri ...	Saturday.
		Ditto ...	Misrauli ...	Ditto.
		Singhpur ...	Darha ...	Monday.
		Ditto ...	Rampur ...	Saturday.
		Ditto ...	Malaon ...	Wednesday.
	Shahjahanpur.	Bachhauli ...	Ahrauli ...	Wednesday.
		Ditto ...	Jhanga ...	Thursday.
		Ditto ...	Piprahi ...	Sunday.
		Ditto ...	Karmaha ...	Saturday.
		Ditto ...	Hata ...	Tuesday and Friday.
		Nagwan ...	Shampur ...	Thursday.
		Ditto ...	Dwarka ...	Ditto.
		Ditto ...	Bishunpur ...	Saturday.
		Ditto ...	Pipra Madan Gopal,	Ditto.
		Ditto ...	Kaithauli ...	Monday.
		Ditto ...	Shamipatti ...	Sunday and Wednesday.
		Ditto ...	Barwa Mir ...	Ditto.
		Ditto ...	Nautan Hatiagarh,	Saturday.
		Patna ...	Rampur Karkhana,	Monday and Thursday.
		Do. ...	Sirsia Kalan ...	Thursday.
		Do. ...	Pokarbhinda ...	Tuesday.
		Bhainsadabar ...	Baghra Mahreri ...	Ditto.
		Ditto ...	Bhainsadabar ...	Monday and Thursday.
		Bhatni ...	Pipra ...	Ditto.

MARKETS, 1908—(*continued*).

Tahsil.	Pargana.	Tappa.	Locality.	Market days.
Hata—(*concld.*).	Shahjahanpur—(*concld.*).	Bhatni ...	Hetimpur ...	Tuesday and Saturday.
		Chakdaia ...	Sikria ...	Friday.
		Pandiapar ...	Mahua ...	Monday and Friday.
		Ditto ...	Samogar ...	Tuesday.
		Ditto ...	Balkuan ...	Sunday.
		Tarkulwa ...	Tarkulwa ...	Wednesday and Saturday
		Ditto ...	Rampur Garh ...	Sunday and Thursday.
		Ditto ...	Sirsia Gaunthi ...	Ditto.
		Ditto ...	Mahua Patan ...	Monday and Thursday.
		Ditto ...	Sohas Chhapra ...	Monday and Wednesday.
		Ditto ...	Narayanpur ...	Sunday and Wednesday.
	Haveli.	Bandwar ...	Anantpur ...	Friday.
		Ditto ...	Balua ...	Wednesday.
		Ditto ...	Lehui ...	Ditto.
		Dedupar ...	Bhainsahi ...	Ditto.
		Ditto ...	Sonbarsa ...	Thursday.
		Ditto ...	Mangalpur ...	Sunday.
		Parkhori ...	Mansurganj ...	Monday.
		Ditto ...	Harpur ...	Friday.
		Barsand ...	Barsand ...	Ditto.
		Ditto ...	Badarwar ...	Wednesday and Saturday.
		Parwarpur ...	Captainganj ...	Tuesday.
		Ditto ...	Harpur ...	Sunday.
		Ditto ...	Mehra ...	Ditto.
		Ditto ...	Sukrauli ...	Saturday.
		Ditto ...	Narayanpur ...	Sunday and Thursday.
		Ditto ...	Mathauli ...	Tuesday and Friday.
Deoria.	Salempur-Majhauli.	Haveli ...	Rani Bazar ...	Ditto.
		Do. ...	Bhatpar ...	Ditto.
		Do. ...	Paroha ...	Ditto.
		Do. ...	Bherapakar ...	Ditto.
		Do. ...	Bahiari ...	Monday and Thursday.
		Do. ...	Khampar ...	Ditto.
		Do. ...	Barkagaon ...	Sunday and Wednesday.
		Do. ...	Babhnauli ...	Wednesday and Saturday.
		Do. ...	Tikampar ...	Tuesday and Saturday.
		Do. ...	Bhingari ...	Sunday.
		Gautama ...	Ahrauli Baghel ...	Ditto.
		Sohanpur ...	Naunar Pande ...	Ditto.
		Ditto ...	Sohanpar ...	Monday, Wednesday and Thursday.
		Ditto ...	Inguri Sarai ...	Tuesday and Friday.
		Ditto ...	Bhainsahi ...	Monday and Thursday
		Balwan ...	Balwan ...	Ditto.
		Ditto ...	Bagra ...	Wednesday and Saturday.
		Ditto ...	Bhawani Chhapra...	Ditto.
		Ditto ...	Sikatia ...	Saturday.
		Ditto ...	Parsia ...	Monday and Friday.
		Ditto ...	Katarwa ...	Tuesday and Friday.
		Ditto ...	Rampur ...	Sunday and Wednesday.
		Ghati ...	Lachhmipur ...	Ditto.

MARKETS, 1908—(*continued*).

Tahsil.	Pargana.	Tappa.	Locality.	Market days.
Deoria—(*contd.*).	Salempur-Majhauli—(*contd.*).	Ghati ...	Ghati ...	Wednesday and Saturday.
		Do. ...	Khairant ...	Tuesday.
		Do. ...	Motipur Bhual ...	Monday and Thursday.
		Bhatni ...	Hatwa ...	Monday and Friday.
		Salempur ...	Tilauli ...	Ditto.
		Ditto ...	Salempur ...	Sunday and Thursday.
		Ditto ...	Ichauna ...	Tuesday and Saturday.
		Bhraipar ...	Nunkhar ...	Wednesday and Saturday.
		Ditto ...	Padri Pande ...	Ditto.
		Ditto ...	Khurdar Khan ...	Sunday and Thursday.
		Paraina ...	Parsia Bhagauli ...	Ditto.
		Ditto ...	Balepur Kalan ...	Tuesday.
		Kachwar ...	Gaur ...	Wednesday and Saturday.
		Ditto ...	Rawatpar ...	Monday.
		Ditto ...	Banspar ...	Monday and Friday.
		Ditto ...	Mahua Patan ...	Sunday.
		Ditto ...	Sidhua ...	Ditto.
		Ditto ...	Dhuswa ...	Tuesday.
		Ditto ...	Baikunthpur ...	Sunday and Wednesday.
		Ditto ...	Mathia Khurd ...	Wednesday.
		Ditto ...	Majhua Dube ...	Thursday.
		Ditto ...	Bara Dih ...	Friday.
		Nai ...	Langra ...	Ditto.
		Do. ...	Karaundi ...	Thursday and Saturday.
		Do. ...	Pakri ...	Monday.
		Do. ...	Bardiha Dal ...	Thursday.
		Sarauli ...	Sarauli ...	Saturday.
		Ditto ...	Paikauli ...	Tuesday.
		Ditto ...	Bahorwa ...	Friday.
		Ditto ...	Pipra Chandrabhan,	Sunday.
		Ditto ...	Hata ...	Wednesday.
		Deoria ...	Bharauli Bazar ...	Daily.
		Samogar ...	Baraon ...	Sunday.
		Ditto ...	Mathia ...	Saturday.
		Kaparwar ...	Mahen Babu ...	Monday.
		Raipura ...	Sonari ...	Ditto.
		Ditto ...	Garer ...	Monday, Wednesday and Saturday.
		Ditto ...	Karohia ...	Tuesday.
		Ditto ...	Bhalauni ...	Tuesday and Thursday.
		Ditto ...	Karauna ...	Sunday and Thursday.
		Ditto ...	Barhaj ...	Wednesday.
		Ditto ...	Marahwa ...	Friday.
		Ditto ...	Nima Garhwa ...	Tuesday and Saturday.
		Ditto ...	Bijaipur ...	Sunday and Friday.
		Bhairauna ...	Bharauli ...	Thursday.
		Ditto ...	Domaria ...	Tuesday.
		Ditto ...	Pachauhan ...	Friday.
		Khakhundu ...	Khakhundu ...	Sunday and Thursday.
		Balia ...	Lar ...	Ditto.
		Do. ...	Kurauli ...	Tuesday and Saturday.
		Do. ...	Mahrauna ...	Ditto.
		Do. ...	Peri ...	Ditto.

MARKETS, 1908—(*continued*).

Tahsil.	Pargana.	Tappa.	Locality.	Market days.
Deoria—(*concld.*).	Salempur-Majhauli—(*concld.*).	Balia ...	Nema ...	Thursday.
		Do. ...	Bhagalpur ...	Wednesday and Saturday.
		Do. ...	Balia ...	Monday and Tuesday.
		Do. ...	Dharmer ...	Monday and Friday.
		Do. ...	Ekna Kalawat ...	Ditto.
		Do. ...	Aujana ...	Ditto.
		Mail ...	Paniha ...	Ditto.
		Do. ...	Mailkhas ...	Sunday and Thursday.
		Do. ...	Pipra ...	Sunday and Wednesday.
		Dond ...	Bardiha Dalpat ...	Tuesday.
		Do. ...	Rartha ...	Wednesday and Saturday.
Gorakhpur.	Bhauapar.	Haveli ...	Bhauapar ...	Saturday.
		Ditto ...	Siwai ...	Monday.
		Rait ...	Ekla ...	Thursday.
		Do. ...	Barahwan ...	Wednesday.
	Haveli.	Patra ...	Pipraich ...	Sunday.
		Do. ...	Kusmahi ...	Tuesday and Friday.
		Do. ...	Bhainsaha ...	Wednesday and Friday.
		Pachwara ...	Ragarganj ...	Saturday.
		Ditto ...	Jaswal ...	Wednesday.
		Ditto ...	Raghokhor ...	Ditto.
		Ditto ...	Chineotaha ...	Sunday and Wednesday.
		Ditto ...	Terhabir ...	Friday.
		Ditto ...	Fardahi ...	Ditto.
		Keotali ...	Mundahra ...	Wednesday and Saturday
		Ditto ...	Chaura ...	Monday and Friday.
		Ditto ...	Dumri ...	Saturday.
		Ditto ...	Jagdispur ...	Thursday.
		Ditto ...	Bhauapar ...	Sunday.
		Ditto ...	Hemdhapar ...	Tuesday.
		Gaura ...	Doharia ...	Ditto.
		Do. ...	Bhitni ...	Friday.
		Rasulpur ...	Barampur ...	Sunday.
		Ditto ...	Mithabel ...	Thursday.
		Ditto ...	Raghopatti ...	Ditto.
		Khutahan ...	Jhungia ...	Ditto.
		Ditto ...	Karmaha Buzurg ...	Ditto.
		Ditto ...	Dumri, I ...	Sunday.
		Ditto ...	Tura ...	Ditto.
		Ditto ...	Langri Gularia ...	Friday.
		Ditto ...	Dumri II ...	Saturday.
		Ditto ...	Phulwaria ...	Tuesday.
		Ditto ...	Sarai Gularia ...	Monday.
		Marachhi Chandaur.	Banspatti ...	Ditto.
		Ditto ...	Sarahri ...	Friday.
		Rajdhani ...	Jhangha ...	Ditto.
		Ditto ...	Jagdispur ...	Saturday.
		Ditto ...	Gauri ...	Ditto.
		Ditto ...	Dih-ghat ...	Sunday.
		Ditto ...	Barhi ...	Thursday.
		Ditto ...	Bishunpura ...	Monday.

MARKETS, 1908—(*concluded*).

Tahsil.	Pargana.	Tappa.	Locality.	Market days.
Gorakhpur—(*concld.*).	Haveli—(*concld.*).	Rajdhani ...	Thumbhi Bazar ...	Tuesday.
		Ditto ...	Kuni ...	Ditto.
		Haveli ...	Mirzapur ...	Wednesday.
		Do. ...	Tilkonia ...	Tuesday and Friday.
		Do ...	Belwar ...	Saturday.
		Do. ...	Raiganj ...	Friday.
		Do. ...	Sonwai ...	Sunday.
		Do. ...	Khorabar ...	Tuesday and Thursday.
	Hasanpur-Maghar.	Bharsand ...	Bhiti ...	Friday.
		Uttar Haveli ...	Ghaghsara ...	Ditto.
		Ditto ...	Niamatganj ...	Tuesday.
		Ditto ...	Baraipar ...	Monday.
		Ditto ...	Bhatwah ...	Sunday.
		Gahasand ...	Luchui ...	Tuesday.
		Ditto ...	Tenduari ...	Sunday.
		Ditto ...	Bhagaura ...	Thursday.
		Ditto ...	Minwa ...	Saturday.
		Aurangabad ...	Pipri ...	Ditto.
		Ditto ...	Math ...	Sunday.
		Ditto ...	Sonbarsa ...	Friday.
		Bhadesri ...	Harpur ...	Thursday.

FAIRS, 1908.

Tahsil.	Pargana.	Tappa.	Locality.	Name of fair.	Date.	Approximate attendance.
Bansgaon.	Unaula...	Mahsan ...	Bansgaon ...	Dasahra ...	Kuar Sudi 10th..	1,300
		Ditto ..	Ditto ...	Sheoratri ...	Phagun Badi 13th.	600
		Ditto ...	Ragho Dih...	Dasahra ...	Kuar Sudi 10th..	1,000
		Ditto ...	Karhal ...	Do. ..	Ditto ...	400
		Ditto ...	Pindra ...	Sheoratri ...	Phagun Badi 13th.	900
		Haveli ...	Satwabhar ...	Dasahra ...	Kuar Sudi 10th,	300
		Ditto ...	Baghi ...	Ditto ...	Ditto ...	600
		Ditto ...	Sarai Tiwari,	Ditto ...	Ditto ..	700
		Ditto ...	Tekuar ...	Ditto ..	Ditto ...	800
	Dhuriapar.	Ditto ..	Kurawai ...	Ditto ...	Ditto ..	3,000
		Barhaj ...	Gola ..	Puranmashi..	Kartik Sudi 15th,	2,000
		Belghat ...	Jhapitra ...	Ditto ...	Ditto ...	3,000
		Ditto ...	Belghat ...	Dhanusjag ...	Aghan Sudi 15th,	2,500
		Ditto ..	Ditto ..	Dasahra ...	Kuar Sudi 10th,	3,200
		Ditto ...	Chhitauni ...	Ditto ...	Ditto ...	3,000
		Ditto ...	Ditto ...	Dhanusjag...	Aghan Sudi 5th,	2,000
		Ditto ...	Indrapar ...	Sheoratri ...	Phagun Badi 13th.	1,500
		Narhi ...	Rajpur ...	Puranmashi..	Chait Sudi 15th,	600
		Khutahan ...	Khutahan ...	Dasahra ...	Kuar Sudi 15th,	5,000
	Chillupur.	Haveli ...	Barhalganj...	Ditto ...	Kuar Sudi 10th.	4,000
		Ditto ...	Ditto ...	Makar ...	Magh Badi Amawas.	2,000
		Ditto ...	Ditto ...	Rathjatra ...	Asarh Sudi 2nd,	3,000
		Ditto ...	Ditto ...	Saiyid Salar..	1st Sunday in Jeth.	1,000
		Ditto ...	Ditto ...	Puranmashi..	Kartik Sudi 15th	22,000
		Ditto ...	Bhenri Tal ...	Ramnaumi...	Chait Sudi 9th ...	4,000
Maharajganj.	Haveli...	Matkopa ...	Harpur ...	Sheoratri ...	Phagun Badi 13th.	500
		Ditto ...	Narayanpur..	Debi ..	Chait Sudi 9th ...	500
		Ditto ...	Harakhpur...	Ramlila ..	Kuar Sudi 10th,	600
		Rigauli ...	Dhani ...	Do. ..	Ditto ...	6,000
		Ditto ...	Do. ...	Sheoratri ..	Phagun Badi 13th.	5,000
		Lehra ...	Banarsia .	Do. ...	Ditto ...	200
		Do. ...	Jhawal ...	Do. ...	Ditto ...	200
		Do. ...	Mahadewa ...	Do. ...	Ditto ...	3,000
		Do. ...	Bishunpur ...	Ramnaumi ...	Chait Sudi 9th,	8,000
		Do. ...	Bridgmanganj.	Ramlila ...	Kuar Sudi 10th,	6,000
		Do. ...	Jogia Bari ...	Puranmashi,	Kartik Sudi 15th,	200
		Do. ...	Mangalpur ...	Do. ...	Ditto ...	200
		Lakhman ...	Lakhman ...	Sheoratri ..	Phagun Badi 13th.	500
		Katara ...	Katahra ...	Do. ...	Ditto .	1,000
		Ditto ...	Basahia ...	Tirmohani-ghat.	Kartik Sudi 15th,	6,000
		Ditto ..	Murila ...	Ramlila ...	Kuar Sudi 10th,	600

FAIRS, 1908—(*continued*).

Tahsil.	Pargana.	Tappa.	Locality.	Name of fairs.	Date.	Approximate attendance.
Maharajganj —(*concld.*).	Tilpur.	Domakhand...	Kaluahi ...	Bhauragha ..	Kartik Sudi 15th	500
		Ditto ...	Do. ...	Ditto ..	Magh Badi Amawas.	500
		Nai Karhi ...	Girma ...	Ramlila ...	Kuar Sudi 10th,	600
Padrauna.	Sidhua Jobna.	Batsara ...	Bhainsaha ...	Ramnaumi ...	Chait Sudi 9th...	250
		Papaur ...	Dharsamda .	Ditto ...	Ditto ...	1,600
		Ditto ...	Pachpera ...	Ramlila ...	Kuar Sudi 10th,	3,000
		Bansi Chirgora.	Kindarpatti,	Ramnaumi ...	Chait Sudi 9th,	500
		Jhankaul ...	Mahua Buzurg.	Ramlila ..	Kuar Sudi 10th,	500
		Ditto ...	Sathiaon ...	Ditto ...	Aghan Sudi 5th,	500
		Bhatni Badraon.	Badraon ...	Sheoratri ...	Phagun Badi 13th.	400
		Malsil Saraini.	Bishunpura,	Ditto ...	Ditto ...	400
		Haveli ...	Saria Buzurg	Ditto ...	Ditto ...	1,000
		Ditto ..	Salemgarh .	Ditto ...	Ditto ...	700
		Ditto ...	Hariharpur ..	Ramnaumi ...	Chait Sudi 9th,	500
		Pakri Gangrani.	Padrauna ...	Ramdham ..	Baisakh Sudi 3rd	4,000
		Ditto ...	Do. ...	Ghazi Mian..	1st Sunday in Jeth.	1,000
		Ditto ...	Do. ...	Dasahra ...	Kuar Sudi 10th,	3,000
		Dhuria Bijaipur.	Babhnauli ...	Ramnaumi...	Chait Sudi 9th...	500
		Pirthipur ...	Pharhibhar...	Ditto ...	Ditto ...	1,000
		Bargaon Chaura.	Singhapatti..	Bansi Ashnan	Kartik Sudi 15th,	25,000
		Ditto ..	Lachhmipur .	Dhanusjag...	Aghan Sudi 9th,	800
		Ditto ...	Khanwar Bakulahi.	Mela Kunwar	Chait Sudi 9th...	1,000
		Ditto ..	Shahpur ...	Budhan Shah	4th Shawwal ...	4,000
		Ditto ...	Kohrauha ...	Kuber Nath..	Baisakh Badi 13th.	8,000
		Sandi ..	Narsar ...	Karahia ...	Ditto	1,500
		Bank Jogni..	Sahibganj ...	Sheoratri ...	Phagun Badi 13th.	700
		Ditto ...	Bhagwanpur.	Ditto ...	Ditto	500
		Ditto ..	Pipraghat ...	Pipraghat ...	Kartik Sudi 15th,	5,000
		Ditto ...	Parsauni ...	Ashnan ..	Ditto	3,000
		Ditto ...	Jagdispur ...	Ramnaumi	Chait Sudi 9th...	400
		Rampur Rogha.	Dudhai ...	Dasahra ...	Kuar Sudi 15th,	1,000
		Muinpur ...	Kundwa Khanipatti.	Kalka Asthan	Chait Sudi 9th,	1,600
		Parwarpar...	Mahua Dih ...	Ramnaumi ...	Ditto ...	500
		Ditto ...	Puriani ...	Ditto ...	Ditto ..	1,800
Hata.	Silhat ...	Nagwan Tikar.	Rudarpur ...	Sheoratri ...	Phagun Badi 13th.	50,000
		Indupur ...	Indupur ...	Dasahra ...	Kuar Sudi 10th,	1,000

FAIRS, 1908—(*concluded*).

Tahsil.	Pargana.	Tappa.	Locality.	Name of fairs.	Date.	Approximate attendance.
Hata—(*concld.*).	Silhat—(*concld.*).	Narayanpur Chauraha.	Bikramp u r Bishunpur.	Ramnaumi ...	Chait Sudi 9th,	800
		Donat ...	Ararpur ...	Sheoratri ..	Phagun Badi, 13th.	3,500
		Banchara ...	Banchara .	Dasahra ...	Kuar Sudi 10th,	800
		Paharpur ...	Lachhmipur..	Ditto .	Ditto	400
		Singhpur ..	Darha ...	Ditto ...	Ditto ..	500
	Shahjahanpur.	Bichhauli ...	Karmaha ...	Ditto ...	Kuar Sudi 10th,	1,000
		Ditto ...	Ditto ...	Dhanusjag ...	Aghan Sudi 5th,	2,500
		Nagwan ...	Dwarka ...	Dasahra ...	Kuar Sudi 10th,	500
		Patna ...	Rampur Karkhana.	Ditto ...	Ditto ..	500
		Bhatni ...	Hetimpur ..	Ditto ...	Ditto ...	200
	Haveli ...	Dedupur ...	Mangalpur ...	Dhanusjag ...	Aghan Sudi 5th,	500
		Ditto ...	Hanskhor ..	Ditto ...	Ditto ...	500
		Ditto ...	Sahulia ...	Sheopargarh,	Baisakh Badi, 13th.	500
		Ditto ...	Dedupar	Ramnaumi ...	Chait Sudi 9th	500
		Parwarpar ...	Mathauli ...	Ditto ...	Ditto ..	300
		Ditto ...	Captainganj,	Dasahra ...	Kuar Sudi 10th,	3,000
		Ditto ..	Gajra ...	Krishnlila ...	Kuar Sudi 15th,	3,000
Deoria.	Salempur-Majhauli.	Kachwar ...	Baikunthpur,	Dhanusjag ...	Aghan Badi 5th,	40,000
		Sarauli ...	Paikauli .	Janamashtmi	Bhadon Badi 8th,	3,000
		Ditto ...	Ditto ..	Ramnaumi ...	Chait Sudi 9th,	5,000
		Mail ...	Sohnag ..	Parasramji ...	Baisakh Sudi 3rd.	5,000
Gorakhpur.	Bhanapar.	Haveli ...	Bhanapar ..	Sheoratri ...	Phagun Badi 13th.	2,000
		Rait ...	Kalesar ...	Ditto ...	Ditto ...	1,000
	Haveli ...	Patra ...	Tarkulha ..	Ramnaumi ...	Chait Sudi 9th,	20,000
		Pachwara ...	Raghokhor ..	Dasahra ...	Kuar Sudi 10th,	400
		Ditto ...	Bharohia ...	Sheoratri ...	Phagun Sudi, 13th.	2,000
		Khutahan ...	Zainpur ...	Ditto ...	Ditto ...	700
		Ditto ...	Bankatra ...	Dargah ...	3rd Shawwal ..	2,000
		Ditto ...	Phulwaria ...	Ramnaumi ...	Chait Sudi 9th ...	500
		Keotali ...	Dumri ...	Ditto	Ditto ...	1,000
		Qasba ...	Bahrampur ...	Saiyid Salar..	1st Sunday in Jeth	4,000
		Haveli ...	Jharkhandi ...	Sheoratri ...	Phagun Badi 13th.	400
	Hasanpur-Maghar,	Aurangabad,	Newas ..	Ditto ..	Ditto ...	500
	Ditto ...	Uttar Haveli,	Tilaura ...	Ditto ...	Ditto ...	700

GAZETTEER OF GORAKHPUR.

INDEX.

A.

B.

C.

D.

E.

F.

G.

L.

M.

T.

U.

V.

W.